WHAT GOD
HAS JOINED
TOGETHER

WHAT GOD HAS JOINED TOGETHER

The Annulment Crisis
in American Catholicism

ROBERT H. VASOLI

New York   Oxford
OXFORD UNIVERSITY PRESS
1998

Oxford University Press

Oxford   New York
Athens   Auckland   Bangkok   Bogotá   Bombay
Buenos Aires   Calcutta   Cape Town   Dar es Salaam
Delhi   Florence   Hong Kong   Istanbul   Karachi
Kuala Lumpur   Madras   Madrid   Melbourne
Mexico City   Nairobi   Paris   Singapore
Taipei   Tokyo   Toronto   Warsaw

and associated companies in
Berlin   Ibadan

Copyright © 1998 by Robert H. Vasoli

Published by Oxford University Press, Inc.
198 Madison Avenue, New York, New York 10016

Oxford is a registered trademark of Oxford University Press, Inc.

Library of Congress Cataloging-in-Publication Data
Vasoli, Robert H.
What God Has Joined Together:
the annulment crisis in American Catholicism / Robert H. Vasoli.
p. cm.   Includes bibliographical references and index.
ISBN 0–19–510764–0
1. Marriage—Annulment (Canon law)—Popular works.
2. Marriage—Annulment—United States—Popular works.   I. Title.
LAW   262.9'4–dc21   97—32843

2 4 6 8 9 7 5 3 1

Printed in the United States of America
on acid-free paper

To the children of divorce and annulment

Contents

Introduction

This study began as an expression of gratitude to Monsignor George A. Kelly, a holy and indefatigable priest, incredibly well informed about the inner workings of the Catholic Church. More than five decades removed from ordination, he is still going strong as a valued elder statesman and author. Above all, he lives the faith and, true to his Gaelic genes, pulls no punches defending it. Our paths crossed fortuitously, shortly after I became respondent in an annulment proceeding. Being notified that you are a litigant is not among life's more precious moments. Learned Hand, a legendary American jurist, once opined that he would fear a lawsuit more than illness and death. Hand was concerned with the law's vagaries, not his personal inability to deal with them. My reaction was an amalgam of shock, confusion, and helplessness. How and why the marriage failed was enigma enough without further perplexity created by a Church tribunal even considering the nullification of so patently valid a union. Like nearly all respondents, I was practically a *tabula rasa* in regard to the specifics of canon law and procedure. Yet I sensed that the validity of the marriage I had contracted more than fifteen years earlier was in mortal danger.

The official notice, prepared by a diocesan marriage tribunal six hundred miles distant, offered little enlightenment. The tribunal's chief official—the judicial vicar or *officialis*—had already assumed competence (jurisdiction) and declared the marriage "dead." No effort had been made to solicit my views on either determination. Two mimeographed forms accompanied the tribunal's letter, one asking for authorization to appoint a procurator-advocate, the other a brief questionnaire. The latter half of the prospective appointee's hyphenated title required no explanation. But as far as I knew, a procurator was some sort of administrative official in the days of early Rome. The nominee designated to serve as procurator-advocate was a priest but not a canon lawyer. According to the judicial vicar, the appointment would ensure protection of my rights. Delineation of those rights, however, was not expressly covered in the material sent by the tribunal.

The second form was a single-page questionnaire asking for several "preferences." (Later I would learn some of the preferences embodied important rights.) Did I wish to be interviewed by telephone or in person at the tribunal office? Did I "oppose the annulment process," did I want to be "informed of the final decision," and, astonishingly, as though it was already a fait accompli, did I "oppose the annulment"? The form allocated one-and-a-half lines for giving a reason for any opposition. At the respondent's option, a "statement of perception of the break-up of the marriage" could supplement the preferences. It was suggested that the statement deal with the childhood and home life of both parties, the dating process, how the decision to marry was reached, marital problems and when they began, attempts to resolve them, how the decision to divorce was reached, ability of the parties to communicate with one another, how the parties played their roles as spouses and parents, and whether either party had alcohol or drug problems.

The tone and substance of the tribunal materials were consistent with what little I had heard up to that time about annulment in the United States. I was not yet familiar with the hard data, but any reasonably perceptive Catholic could hardly fail to witness or hear about the sudden return to the sacraments of relatives, friends, and neighbors who had divorced and remarried. Books and articles on the annulment option began to appear in the Church-related press. Such signs pointed to a major change in the Church's approach to the permanence and indissolubility of marriage, evidenced by an unprecedented increase in annulments granted by American marriage tribunals.

Once surprise and befuddlement dissipate, the first sensible reaction to unexpected involvement in litigation is consulting with an attorney. In the Church's legal system that is more easily said than done. Canon lawyers are not nearly as numerous or as accessible as their secular counterparts. While not conveniently listed in the telephone book, the names and addresses of clerical canonists appear throughout *The Catholic Directory*. Upwards of 40 percent of the bishops hold degrees in canon law. Nearly all the other canon lawyers, including many retirees, serve on the diocesan tribunals. A very small number are engaged in teaching canon law. In some smaller dioceses the judicial vicar is the only canon lawyer. My own diocese had but three canon lawyers when I was casting about for assistance. Parties to annulment usually deal directly with auditors and notaries lacking degrees, not with full-fledged canon lawyers. In retrospect, the difficulty of securing a canonist of my choosing was fortuitous. As I would learn later, practically every canonist within a 150-mile radius was annulment-friendly.

Some trustworthy Notre Dame colleagues, better connected within the Church than I, were approached for advice on defending the validity of a marriage. But on that particular issue their expertise approximated my own. One of them, however, steered me to Monsignor Kelly. When contacted, he mentioned having guided several cases similar to mine to successful resolution. Before making a commitment, however, he wanted to see a brief narrative on the marriage. I sent him much the same marital history prepared for the tribunal. After giving it careful study, he generously agreed to lend a hand.

While fully cognizant of my lack of formal training in canon law when I became a respondent, even then I was not a complete novice in matters legal. Courses I taught throughout my professional life dealt extensively with criminal law and procedure and the law of corrections. For twenty years I offered a seminar in the sociology of law that often delved into comparative legal systems. My exploration of canon law began in earnest with the purchase of a copy of the English translation of the *Code of Canon Law*. I pored over Title VII, which covers marriage, and Part II, dealing with the contentious trial. (Among the first things to come to my attention was that the tribunal where the petition was presented and accepted had improperly assumed competence. Venue was subsequently changed to the tribunal in my own diocese.) I began a search of the literature, reading everything on annulment written in English that I could lay hands and eyes on. I also started to seek out, through word-of-mouth referrals, individuals who had experienced annulment, either as petitioners or respondents, and who were willing to talk about it. All this continued over a ten-year span, getting as much attention as other professional responsibilities would allow.

Compared to compilations of secular law, the body of Church statutory law is minuscule. A copy of the *Code of Canon Law*, shelved among the volumes of statutes for any state in America, would be barely discernible. Secular law is positive law, formulated by human effort alone. Some Church statutes are positive, but unlike secular law in the United States, canon law embodies or reflects divine and natural law. The compleat canon lawyer should be conversant with theology, philosophy, Church tradition, and her teaching authority (the Magisterium). But canon law is not worlds apart from secular law; the two types bear similarities as well as differences. To cite some examples, both attempt to control large swatches of human behavior, both specify rights and duties, both arrange courts hierarchically, both strive for procedural fairness, and both provide for appellate review.

Neither theologian nor canonist nor Church historian am I, yet as a lifelong Catholic, who as an undergraduate and graduate attended Catholic institutions, I have more than a nodding acquaintance with aspects of Catholicism built into Church law. Having taught marriage and the family at the outset of my career as a sociologist, I was particularly attuned to the Church's views on marriage. Enroute to an undergraduate degree, papal encyclicals, including those on marriage, were required reading. Down through the years I kept abreast of key Church pronouncements on marriage found in the documents of Vatican II, in papal instructions, and in commentaries appearing in other Church publications. It was not, therefore, intuition alone informing me that something was amiss when a tribunal in another state decided to adjudicate the authenticity of our marriage.

"Amiss" proved far too inadequate a term. Apparently something quite profound was occurring with respect to Church doctrine on the meaning of marriage and its permanence and indissolubility. If the Church had altered course on these vital issues, official pronouncements on the changes had somehow eluded me. The manner in which my case was processed attested to such changes. Two American tribunals found psychological reasons to rule the marriage invalid because of defective consent. Nearly five years later their decree of nullity was itself nullified by two panels of Sacred Roman Rota judges. Of hundreds of appellate court decisions I had read, few provided as comprehensive a reversal of a lower court action as this one.

While the case wended its way through the Church's judiciary, I continued to interview people with annulment experience and intensify my investigation of the American tribunal system. The research led to a hypothesis that my case, far from being an aberration, might be fairly representative of the thousands of defective consent annulments being decreed annually. Many other cases exhibited irregularities and errors, both substantive and procedural, some even worse than those occurring in mine. What was needed more than a review of case histories was a study of the system that produced them. With that flash of insight, what would have been an article burgeoned into a study of the American tribunal system.

My indebtedness extends well beyond Monsignor Kelly's Good Samaritanism. Dozens of nameless parties to annulments should not be ignored. Their candor was refreshing and surprising, but even more surprising was how little they still knew about canon law and procedure, particularly with respect to their rights and the grounds for nullity. Two early critics with undergraduate majors in English—Tracey Malesa and Bridgette Tompkins—kindly read portions of early drafts of the manuscript to test whether it would be intelligible to average readers. A similar favor was bestowed by Charles McCollester, long a copy editor for the University of Notre Dame's *American Midland Naturalist*. Apparently the same mysterious forces of Fate (or Providence) that brought Monsignor Kelly to my side led to a lengthy and rewarding tie with Monsignor Clarence J. Hettinger, a canon lawyer in the Diocese of Peoria with Rota-caliber mastery of canon law. That mastery was demonstrated time and again in response to countless queries raised during evening and weekend phone conferences. Whether or not he realizes it, he gave me the equivalent of several graduate courses in the finer points of Church law and doctrine on marriage. Of all the blessings to come the book's way, none surpassed Cynthia A. Read's superlative editing. Without fail, she would pose the right question, make the necessary deletion or addition, and come up with the right word, phrase, or syntax. Working with her was a rare and edifying privilege. She and the others merit thanks that are heartfelt and undying.

If any errors mar the book, my breast alone will receive the beating to go with the requisite mea culpas. It is my devout yet modest hope that what appears herein will contribute to conserving the integrity of the sacrament of marriage.

WHAT GOD HAS JOINED TOGETHER

❖ 1 ❖

Profaning Marriage

"Bless me father, for I have sinned. It's been three weeks since my last confession. I have a problem. My wife left me three years ago and I attend weekly parish meetings for divorced, separated, and widowed Catholics. Well, a very attractive woman in the group is hitting on me."

"What's that supposed to mean?"

"She's making sexual advances toward me. I'm tempted to go along with them, but I'm still a married man."

"Have you given any thought to an annulment?"

This colloquy, occurring in the summer of 1995, would have been unimaginable in the pre–Vatican II Church in the United States. The confessor would have told the penitent that the woman's overtures were an occasion of sin, instructed if not ordered him to avoid adulterous entanglements, specified the terms of his penance, and wondered whether the line outside the confessional was getting shorter. The confessor in this case was not newly ordained and thus still under the influence of the latest in pastoral counseling taught at the seminary. He was, in fact, a veteran priest, several years beyond his Golden Jubilee. His leap from carnal desire to annulment ignored or glossed over some highly relevant circumstances: the penitent was not divorced, had no desire to divorce, desperately wanted to reconcile with his spouse, and was still in a marriage that had lasted forty years. He departed the confessional confused, disappointed, angry, and no better equipped morally and spiritually to deal with the recovery group seductress.

A mere generation ago few American Catholics could identify another Catholic whose marriage had been annulled. Church annulments were rare, perhaps even more so than those granted by civil authorities. In the eyes of the faithful, annulments might be available only to the wealthy or those whose unions did not measure up to rigid tests of validity. Among Catholics whose marriages had failed, annulment was seldom regarded as a realistic option. The more viable choices were to bear one's cross with Christian resignation or, if divorced and already in a remarriage, to remain in the Church without access to the Eucharist or simply drop out.

In the early 1970s the incidence of annulment began a meteoric rise, increasing at a rate without precedence in Church history. In 1968 the entire American diocesan tribunal system granted fewer than four hundred "formal case" annulments—those requiring trial by a tribunal. Another one hundred or so decrees of nullity were granted administratively, without benefit of trial. Within ten years, hardly an eyeblink in two millennia of Church history, several diocesan tribunals[1] were each issuing more decrees of nullity annually than had been previously granted in any one year by the American Church as a whole. In 1979, for example, the Archdiocese of Chicago's tribunal granted approximately 1,100 annulments, roughly double the total granted by all American tribunals a decade before.[2]

Today there is hardly any adult American Catholic who cannot point to kin or acquaintances with one or more marriages annulled by Church authority. Exchange a random peace greeting during Mass with a stranger in the next pew and the odds are roughly one in fifty that you shake the hand or buss the cheek of a parishioner who has had at least one marriage voided by a diocesan tribunal. If the person greeted has never been party to an annulment proceeding, he or she will surely know several who were. Whether these probabilities persist in the years ahead cannot be foretold with certainty. But given the current propensity of Catholics to resort to divorce, together with the premises and policies driving America's tribunals, the number of Catholics with annulments will keep inching closer to the number with civil divorces. To arrest the trend would require a radical upheaval within the American tribunal system, to be achieved only by a near-draconian intervention by Rome.

Viewed cross-culturally, annulment data provide stunning comparisons. The Church in the United States, by a wide margin, has been annulling far more marriages than the rest of the Catholic world combined. In 1980 tribunals worldwide processed 89,065 cases judicially and administratively. Of that number 63,962 (72 percent) emanated from America's busy tribunals.[3] Back then, Vatican statistics published in English did not provide the number of annulments actually granted. Cases processed cannot be equated with decrees of nullity. But at the very least they show that American tribunals were hyperactive compared to tribunals in the rest of the Catholic world.

Beginning with the 1984 edition, the *Statistical Yearbook of the Church* provides data on annulments granted and denied per annum as well as on the number of cases processed. The change in reporting was concomitant with the introduction of the revised code of canon law on the first day of Advent in 1983.[4] Ordinarily introductory chapters spare readers the task of poring over tabular data. But a table, like a picture, sometimes can be worth a thousand

Table 1–1. Cases Closed by Nullity at First and Second Instance, 1984–1994

	United States		Rest of World	
Year	Ordinary process	Documentary process	Ordinary process	Documentary process
1984	36,461	14,777	10,197	2,306
1985	37,032	16,288	10,607	2,527
1986	40,117	17,564	13,682	2,421
1987	42,503	18,067	14,915	2,141
1988	41,325	19,258	14,511	2,587
1989	40,685	20,731	14,051	2,702
1990	41,123	21,701	14,709	2,534
1991	43,104	20,829	14,504	2,274
1992	40,676	18,354	15,544	5,065
1993	38,280	15,372	15,021	1,788
1994	38,868	15,595	14,433	2,727
TOTALS	440,174	198,536	152,174	29,072

Source: Statistical Yearbooks of the Church, 1984–1994.

words. Our pictorial summary of official nullity statistics for 1984–1994 (Table 1-1) shows with dramatic clarity the magnitude of the problem addressed by this study. It also documents how American tribunals are unrivaled in the issuance of decrees of nullity. Indeed, the disparity between America's annulment output and that of the rest of the world is so striking that the term *preeminence* understates America's primacy. About 6 percent of the world's Catholic population in the United States accounts for 78 percent of the annulments granted by the Church universal. Breaking the gross percentage into smaller components, we find that American tribunals were responsible for 74 percent of all decrees of nullity reached through *ordinary process* (i.e., after trial) and 85 percent of those reached through *documentary process* (i.e., usually administratively, without trial). The latter category consists predominantly of "lack of form" cases, which are virtually automatic decrees of nullity for baptized Catholics who marry outside the Church without proper dispensation. Churches in other English-speaking societies and in western Europe show strong tendencies to move in the same direction the American tribunal system has taken, but do not yet pose a major threat to America's status as the annulment colossus of the world.

America's disproportionately high contribution to the world annulment total has shown few signs of slackening since its initial upward surge. It is too early to tell whether the data for 1992–1994 foreshadow a long-or short-term trend. More annulments of both kinds were granted in 1994 than 1984. The United States has averaged just under 59,000 recorded annulments annually since 1984. Moreover, the official figures understate the extent to which divorce and remarriage has gained approval within the American Church. Although they are supposed to be exceedingly rare, there are probably thousands of extralegal "annulments" are given out in the United States.[5] Properly speaking, they are "internal forum" *solutions* rather than annulments, marriages voided de facto without benefit of processing by the "external forum" provided by a Church tribunal. But like "external forum" annulments, they allow recipients to return to the sacraments. It is not terribly farfetched to speculate that between 1980 and 1994 the American Church[6] annulled more marriages than did the entire Church since its founding. At all events, within a relatively brief time frame a sea change occurred in the American Church's approach to the permanence and indissolubility of Christian marriage. Small wonder, therefore, that Archbishop Vincenzo Fagiolo, head of the Pontifical Council for the Interpretation of Legislative Texts, was moved to refer to the volume of annulments in the United States as a "grave scandal."[7]

Explanations abound for America's quantum leap in the production of decrees of nullity. Demographic and sociocultural attributes of American society are often cited as almost inexorable determinants of the proliferation. Such claims contain kernels of truth. The divorce rate among American Catholics today approximates that of society at large. But to advance a causal linkage between these two variables is simplistic and misleading. In spite of what many canonists maintain, the size of the pool of those eligible for annulments does not necessarily vary directly with increases in the divorce rate, unless one assumes that marriages ending in divorce are usually canonically invalid.[8] Precisely such an assumption is frequently implied or taken for granted by American tribunalists. But in terms of social science methodology the assumption is tenuous and gratuitous. In terms of Church teaching and law, it is untenable, a doctrinal non sequitur. While figures are not available, the vast majority of marriages broken by divorce are in fact certainly valid. The rising frequency of divorce among Catholics increased the demand for nullity, but it is a fanciful and illogical leap to infer a corresponding increase in the size of the pool of deserving eligibles. High rates of separation and divorce also occur among Catholics in other societies, but with far less likelihood of eventual annulment. Finally, Catholics did divorce before Vatican II, but it is quite improbable that the percentage securing decrees of nullity was even close to the percentage that obtains today.

The heterogeneity of American society is conducive to mixed marriages, which are said to contribute to the heavy flow of annulments. The *CLSA's* annual statistical summaries provide data on the mixed-marriage cases processed by American tribunals, but the outcome of these cases, whether for or against nullity, is not specified, so really the data merely show that mixed-marriage cases are common. Evidently the reader is supposed to infer that mixed marriages are especially vulnerable to nullity. In fact, however, such marriages, are not ipso facto invalid and indeed can be just as valid canonically as Church marriages between two Catholics.

Heterogeneity may be a factor in documentary process cases subject to automatic nullity. Unquestionably "lack of form" cases have been on the increase in the United States. It is no secret that some Catholics, fearing marital failure and Church sanctions against remarriage, enter what are in effect trial marriages or marry outside the Church. Along with other documentary process cases (such as those involving the "Privilege of Faith," *ligamen* [previous marital ties], and unconsummated unions) "lack of form" cases account for about one third of the annulments granted by American tribunals. These kinds of annulments may actually derive more from failures of catechesis and lapses in faith than heterogeneity.

The sociocultural conditions invoked by the American canonical community to account for the flood tide of annulments might be termed secondary or diversionary variables. They have weak explanatory power at best when it comes to accounting for ordinary process declarations of nullity. Citing them may serve to deflect attention from, or temper, primary variables which are theological, canonical, psychological, and pastoral in nature. Developments in these areas have created a tribunal system committed to facilitating annulment. A salient premise that undergirds the system, one seldom stated for public consumption, is captured succinctly in an anonymous tribunalist's comment: "There is *no* marriage which, given a little time for investigation, we cannot declare invalid."[9] Many tribunals appear to do their utmost to live by what the anonymous tribunalist preached.

The system has produced among its theorists and practitioners a collective pronullity consciousness which embodies, among other qualities, righteousness, canonical cleverness, misdirected pastoralism, and arrogance. The reach of this mindset has few boundaries. It can transcend time and space, as evidenced by canonical excursions into history. Thus, one canonist writes that certain contemporary scholars claim that if only Clement VII had availed himself of jurisprudence extant in the sixteenth century, Henry VIII's marriage to Catherine of Aragon could have been annulled.[10] Unwittingly perhaps, the conjecture betrays the tendency of many modern canonists to impute to jurisprudence, even in speculative form, much the same authoritativeness as a pope might claim. It also reiterates, by implication, the contention that every marriage is vulnerable to nullity. A resourceful twentieth-century canonist, transported 450 years into the past, could have done what Cardinal Wolsey failed to do: find in Henry's marital consent and demeanor "personalist" and incapacitating deficiencies to serve as grounds for annulling his marriage to Catherine.

How Thomas More fits into this hypothetical back-to-the-future scenario is a question that puts imagination to test. It seems improbable that his grasp of sixteenth-century canonical jurisprudence was less sophisticated than that of today's canonists. Not for nothing is he the patron saint of lawyers. His opposition to the king's matrimonial adventurism betrayed no ignorance of Church law. If anything, he understood it only too well. An intellectual exercise more fascinating than projecting today's canonists into the past would be to resurrect Thomas More into the present. After comparing annulment in sixteenth-century England with annulment in post–Vatican II America, he might have become the first saint to achieve martyrdom by losing his mind instead of his head.

While documentary process annulments have contributed significantly to the skyrocketing annulment output, they are not the focus of this study. The increase in such annulments, unlike the ordinary process variety, did not flow from perceived changes in Church teaching, Church law, and the theology of marriage. We will concentrate on ordinary process decrees of nullity, those granted after trial by tribunal, because they account for most of the sharp rise in nullity decrees. Throughout, our attention will be directed to ordinary process nullity based on defective matrimonial consent, the ground for more than two thirds of annulments granted in the United States. They constitute the form of annulment that raises Rome's hackles and impel Vatican officials such as Archbishop Fagiolo to refer to the volume of American annulments as a "grave scandal." According to Vatican statistics, nearly all ordinary process decrees of nullity declared by the American tribunal system involve forms of defective (invalid) consent. Analysis of defective consent annulments, more than any other research strategy, shows how the United States became the annulment center of the Catholic world. It will also show that defective consent annulments are themselves often defective.

The first section of the study will survey salient doctrinal, canonical, and pastoral developments that provided the conceptual framework for increasing the number of annulments. The second will treat the psychologization of the annulment process, a trend necessitated by tribunal reliance on defective consent to annul. The third segment will deal with ancillary forces brought to bear by the tribunal system to implement and sustain the blueprint's design for permissive annulment. That portion of the study will examine administrative aspects of the tribunal system which work toward maximizing the production of decrees of nullity. Then will follow an analysis of the plight of respondents in annulment proceedings, along with discussions on the "right of defense" and appellate review.

Some prefatory comments are in order. The study is made from the perspective of a lay Catholic, a career sociologist whose areas of specialization are the sociology of deviant behavior, the sociology of law, criminal justice, and social psychology. To the best of my knowledge, it is the first study of the American tribunal system conducted by anyone trained in behavioral science. Sociology credentials notwithstanding, I readily concede that Catholicism has transcendental dimensions which are inherently nonempirical, but that does not preclude subjecting many facets of Catholicism to behavioral science analysis. The Church, however otherworldly, encompasses a host of sociocultural structures and procedures amenable to empirical scrutiny. When not dashing off best-selling novels, Andrew Greeley, working out of the National Opinion Research Center, has conducted extensive surveys of Catholic attitudes and behavior. Many others have engaged in similar research. The sociology of religion is a well established specialization within the discipline. Furthermore, behavioral scientists and legal scholars have conducted hundreds of studies of court systems and the administration of justice. The American diocesan marriage tribunals constitute a social as well as juridical system. Their policies, practices, and personnel are all amenable to behavioral science research. As it happens, currently the principal juridical mission of diocesan tribunals is the granting or denying of annulments. Their preoccupation with marriage cases and the attendant burgeoning of decrees of nullity are eminently fit subjects for sociological analysis.

To an overwhelming degree, scholarly treatment of annulment has occurred within a relatively closed circle. Canonists dialogue with other canonists, theologians trade nuances with fellow theologians, and canonists and theologians display their considerable erudition to each other. An outsider trained in sociology should be able to provide a fresh and useful perspective to understanding annulment in America. This seems to be particularly the case in light of efforts by canonists to use behavioral science in adjudicating defective consent cases. Without going into chapter and verse here, suffice it to say that their dalliance with the human sciences typically shows little sophistication and balance. Seldom does it progress beyond citation of marriage, divorce, and remarriage rates; truisms on the pluralistic character of American society; and vague allusions to social, cultural, and psychological determinants of human behavior.[11] When canonists refer to behavioral science, they usually have psychology in mind. The impression conveyed is that deliberations on the propriety of marital consent are guided by the findings of psychiatry and clinical (or abnormal) psychology. But the system's affinity with psychology turns out to be more catholic. Some tribunals do indeed retain a psychiatrist or psychologist for expert input in defective consent cases, while others settle for a marriage counselor or social worker. The ramifications this has for the annulment process will be analyzed in a subsequent chapter. The point here is that the tribunal system's consort with behavioral science generally gives psychology carte blanche and little more than a wink and a nod to such disciplines as sociology, economics, and anthropology.[12]

Behavioral science does not deal in absolutes. It gathers data from documents or develops its own through case studies and observation, and by canvassing respondents in samples drawn from larger populations. It collects and analyzes data for tendencies, correlations, and percentage differences, in the hope of testing theories or establishing relationships between specific variables. Impressive as this may sound, its findings are seldom definitive. Not even economics, reputedly the hardest behavioral science of all, traffics in certainty. The limitations of economic analysis are manifested in perennial discrepancies in annual estimates of the size of the federal budget deficit. Depending on their degree of commitment to aping the physical sciences, behavioral scientists are divided on whether they must be able to predict behavior, seek out its causes, or simply better understand it. Despite these limitations, behavioral science has much to contribute toward making the American tribunal system and its annulment practices more comprehensible.

What follows here falls within this general framework. It relies primarily on an examination of the annulment literature, canon law, Church statistics on nullity, discussions with many involved in annulment proceedings as tribunalists or parties, and personal experience. There is no way of knowing, with a high degree of confidence, how representative those interviewed are of a much larger universe of petitioners and respondents. I am persuaded that they are not untypical. Most interviewees relate similar experiences, and what they report frequently appears in the literature, especially in decisions handed down in Rome. The study, then, is an effort to identify and analyze trends and patterns that give the American tribunal system its defining characteristics. Generalizations about this or any other system, while based on the best available evidence, require built-in hedges. They do not necessarily apply with equal force to all tribunals and canonists or to every defective consent case. Extraordinarily strong consensus exists among American tribunalists on the pros and cons of annulment, but agreement does not occur at every juncture. It cannot be overemphasized that there are American tribunalists who struggle valiantly for honesty, restraint, and fidelity to Church teaching on the permanence and indissolubility of marriage. Regrettably, their efforts are smothered by the performance of the system as a whole. It also bears repeating that while this study is intended as a system analysis, it will focus primarily on one particular class of annulments—those granted on psychological grounds under the aegis of defective consent. This research strategy derives from two indisputable facts, one quantitative the other qualitative, that require no hedging: the American system turns out more decrees of nullity than any other in the world, and *defective consent* is the basis for approximately two thirds of the total number produced. It is also virtually coterminous with annulments granted by trial by tribunal. More than any other type, defective consent annulments exemplify the theological and canonical premises that have driven America's tribunal system for nearly three decades.

Theologians and canonists have contributed much to the Church's understanding of marriage, though certainly not always with the stamp of infallibility. They have also been a source of confusion, at odds with traditional Church teaching and papal pronouncements. In any event, whether viewed as an institution, a sacrament, or a special relationship, the phenomenon of marriage is not their private preserve. Few theologians and canonists marry, and even fewer go through the annulment process as petitioner or respondent. What follows is the handiwork of a lay Catholic and behavioral scientist who experienced marriage and annulment firsthand.

The book is written in the expectation that it will be received in some quarters as a mean-spirited polemic, an atavistic and perhaps nostalgic retreat to conditions the Church has supposedly outgrown. It might also be regarded as an untimely and unwelcome attack on the post-Conciliar pastoralism, compassion, and nonjudgmentalism so instrumental in Church renewal. The term *polemic* denotes disputation for its own sake. A polemicist has an ax to grind, an ax honed more with rhetoric than the facts and documentation that are the tools of empirical analysis. Throughout the study an effort is made to let the facts and sources speak for themselves. Since their ability to articulate is imperfect, some interpretative amplification is necessary. Whenever that sort of commentary and analysis is appropriate, I strive to keep it well within the bounds of the evidence. To the extent that it is possible, my motivation is impersonal and always directed toward truth, justice, and the integrity of the sacrament of marriage.

In the same year Vatican Council II ended, Daniel Patrick Moynihan, an assistant secretary in the Department of Labor, prepared a brief report on the state of the black family in the United States.[13] Moynihan documented the growing fragility of black families, particularly in urban areas. Long before the "feminization of poverty" became part of everyday speech, he envisioned the consequences of unstable families and female-based households. Though intended for limited circulation within the government bureaucracy, the report gained national notoriety. Moynihan was pilloried for allegedly impugning black family morality and dwelling on the untoward effects of broken homes and illegitimacy,[14] but he was far more prophetic than he and his critics realized. If anything, the black family's condition has worsened. Taking one leading indicator, since 1965 the percentage of black babies born out of wedlock has nearly tripled, going from 26 percent to 68 percent. This and other morbidity factors formerly most closely associated with urban blacks are now increasingly common among nonblack families. One of the most striking developments of the mid-1990s has been the emerging consensus that the American family is in woeful shape. The media provide daily reminders of its deterioration with accounts of single-parent families, the feminization of poverty, fatherless children, fathers who neglect child support, child and spouse abuse, and rancorous divorces. Remarkably, this new awareness transcends party, ethnic, and racial lines.

There is no single definitive explanation for breakdown of the family, but easy divorce is surely a leading cause. Despite the obviousness, very little has been done about it. Government and private agencies have set up hundreds of programs to deal with consequences of divorce, but the primary root cause has gone relatively untouched. The horse has long since fled, yet the barn door remains wide open. Only recently have marriage counselors, once inclined to see divorce as a simple and convenient answer to family problems, come to realize that the antidote might be worse than the disease. The experts are discovering what was long part of folk wisdom: seldom do the scars divorce inflicts on children go away. There appears to be more openness to the traditional belief that spouses in troubled marriages should strive to remain together for the sake of the children, a belief that had been superseded by enshrinement of self-fulfillment and sanguine assumptions on the ability of children to adapt to family rupture.[15]

Any libidinous, fecund couple can make a child, but families are formed by marriage. Demographically, even with allowance for out-of-wedlock births, families are chiefly responsible for replenishing population. Ecclesially, the family is the principal social unit in which the children of God perpetuate the people of God through the centuries. It is the instrument by which souls are created to give honor and glory to their Creator. Catholics are taught that the family may be considered the domestic Church. "[P]arents, by word and example, are the first heralds of the faith with regard to their children."[16] The family, in short, is the Church's as well as society's primary agent of socialization.

Tribunals tend to see defective consent annulment as appropriate pastoral and juridical redress for divorce. The causal linkage between these two instruments for ending marriage is commonly regarded as one-directional: annulment is a by-product of divorce. Rarely is it recognized that annulment can cause divorce. Its ready availability often provides inducement to terminate troubled marriages rather than work through the difficulties matrimony presents. The annulment literature contains occasional pieces on the emergence of an annulment mentality among America's Catholics. Left unsaid is the fact that annulment mentality and divorce mentality are kindred states of mind. Together they have the potential for posing a grave threat to the well-being, integrity, and permanence of the family, the "domestic church."

Crisis has been with the Church since its inception. Peter and Paul did not always see eye to eye. Arianism, the first major Christian heresy, plagued the Church for much of the fourth century. The Dominican order came into being early in the thirteenth century to combat Albigensianism, while the Society of Jesus was formed three centuries later to counter the Protestant Reformation. The list is easily expanded. Ultimately, every crisis faced by the Church, including the outpouring of annulments in the United States, is reducible in one way or another to the overarching issues of faith and authority. Granting their generic primacy, the state of marriage and the family is among more the momentous problems these issues subsume. Annulment, in turn, is a reliable weather vane for the condition of marriage and the family in the contemporary American Church. Its significance was eloquently underscored in Pius XII's address on October 3, 1941 to the Roman Rota:

> As regards declarations of the nullity of marriage, everyone knows that the Church is rather wary and disinclined to favor them. Indeed if the tranquillity, stability, and security of human intercourse in general demands that contracts be not lightly set aside this is still more true of a contract of such importance as marriage whose firmness and stability are necessary for the common welfare of human society as well as for the private good of the parties and the children and whose sacramental dignity forbids that it be lightly exposed to the danger of profanation.[17]

Although uttered more than a half century ago, Pius XII's words cannot be dismissed as Magisterial dead letter. They reappear verbatim, in John Paul II's 1981 address to the Rota.[18] He quoted them not only to reiterate age-old Church teaching, but also to demonstrate his awareness that the solemn pronouncements of a fairly recent predecessor were being flouted.

Profanation is a strong term, signifying irreverence, disrespect, desecration, or debasement of something sacred. All these marks of profanation are operative in the American tribunal system. Disinclination to annul has been transmuted into almost irresistible inclination. The chapters that follow will chronicle and analyze how tribunals in the United States are profaning Christian marriage.

❖ 2 ❖

Winds of Change

Although America's exponential leap in annulments happened suddenly, it did not develop out of nothingness. No single event or idea accounts for the seismic change in the production of decrees of nullity. Several factors were at work simultaneously, some with more impact than others. Cumulatively, however, their effect on traditional Church teaching on the permanance and indissolubility of marriage was devastating. In this chapter we shall examine some precursors to change that predate Vatican II and the impetus to change provided by the Council itself. This is not the place for an exhaustive history of the preConciliar theological and canonical ferment which set the stage for what has been visited upon Christian marriage in recent years. A few examples will suffice to show whither the winds of change were blowing.

The starting point for those wishing to alter the Church's position on the nature of marriage and indissolubility is the ambiguity associated with Matthew 19:9. Christ, put to test by the Pharisees, replies that "whoever divorces his wife (unless the marriage is unlawful) and marries another commits adultery." Among scriptural exegetes the precise meaning of the passage remains somewhat controversial to this day, but the official Church position is that it never constituted an invitation to put asunder what God Himself had joined together. Nevertheless, it is claimed that not even in the early Church was the doctrine of indissolubility universally accepted without reservation. Popishil, surveying commentaries on divorce and remarriage during the first five centuries of the Church's existence, maintains that several prominent Church figures recognized exceptions to indissolubility. There was special concern for innocent spouses, particularly husbands, who were abandoned by their marriage partners or were victims of a spouse's adultery.[1] Saint Cyril of Alexandria, for example, is credited with declaring that the bond of marriage is dissolved by adultery. But Popishil concedes that it cannot be determined whether Cyril condoned remarriage.[2] He also reviews canons emanating from several regional synods which addressed these issues. While the activities of the synods might relate to the problem of divorce and remarriage, they cannot be equated with the position of the Church universal. According to Popishil, a passage in Gratian's Decree has Pope Gregory II permitting divorce and remarriage when a wife, due to some unspecified ailment, is unable to satisfy her conjugal obligations.[3] Secondary sources, however, are not the stuff from which Church doctrine is definitively set forth.

A more thorough and scholarly treatment of indissolubility is found in the work of Mackin.[4] Still, he shares Popishil's aim to establish that indissolubility in the absolute sense was never the official position of the Church, and that under limited circumstances, divorce and remarriage were allowed. One such circumstance is provided by the Pauline privilege, based on 1 Corinthians 7:12–16:

> To the rest I say (not the Lord): if any brother has a wife who is an unbeliever, and she is willing to go on living with her, he should not divorce her; and if any woman has a husband who is an unbeliever, and he is willing to go on living with her, she should not divorce her husband. For the unbelieving husband is made holy through his wife, and the unbelieving wife is made holy through the brother. Otherwise your children would be unclean, whereas in fact they are holy. If the unbeliever separates, however, let him separate. The brother or sister is not bound in such cases; God has called you to peace. For how do you know, wife, whether you will save your husband; or how do you know, husband, whether you will save your wife?[5]

Several narrow conditions attach to exercise of the Pauline privilege. One of two spouses, both unbaptized ("unbelievers," in Saint Paul's terminology) before their marriage, is later baptized. The unbaptized partner separates or is unwilling to live harmoniously with the baptized spouse. The privilege does not apply if the baptized spouse unjustly separates or is responsible for the marital conflict. If the baptized spouse, having satisfied these terms, enters a new marriage, the previous marriage is thereby dissolved. Similar norms operate with respect to marriages dissolved in virtue of the "Privilege of Faith"—the Petrine Privilege. Here one of the spouses was baptized, the other unbaptized, when the marriage was contracted. If certain conditions are met, the pope has the power to dissolve the marriage "in favor of the faith." His power can thus be applied in cases where one spouse, subsequently baptized, has multiple spouses who are unbaptized. One marriage partner can be kept as a spouse and the others dismissed. Marriage with that one spouse serves to dissolve the other unions. The term "Privilege of Faith" is sometimes used to cover both of these situations.

Pauline and Petrine Privilege cases are dealt with by documentary process, that is, without trials. The former can be handled administratively by a diocesan First Instance tribunal, whereas privilege of faith cases are decided by the Holy

Father. For 1990, 172 of the 188 dioceses and archdioceses in the United States reported 600 Pauline Privilege and 512 privilege of faith annulments.[6] That same year, American tribunals granted 41,123 ordinary process and 21,701 documentary process decrees of nullity (Table 2-1). Even when allowance is made for tribunals not reporting, Pauline and Petrine Privilege annulments accounted for no more than one percent of all documentary process annulments and less than half of 1 percent of the total number of annulments granted in the United States. Accordingly, such cases will not be treated in any detail here, since the focus of this study is on the mass production of ordinary process cases.

Reminders of the Pauline and Petrine privileges scarcely qualify as breakthroughs in the contemporary theology of marriage. Both methods of nullification have been operative and discussed for centuries without leading to the volume of annulments we have today. Yet for revisionists such as Mackin and Popashil it is not enough to identify these privileges as cracks in the wall of indissolubility. Rather, they essay to translate them into defining principles that represent a historical, theological, and canonical basis for widening eligibility for nullity. In other words, the revisionists' objective goes far beyond clarifying the question of baptismal status as it relates to the validity of marriage. Without necessarily admitting it, they seek to place practically all marriages within the target area of nullity. Only in terms of precedent and principle can the Pauline and Petrine privileges be factored into the recent profusion of decrees of nullity. Only in those capacities can they be said to have anything to do with defective consent annulments.

Revisionist efforts to amend the norm of indissolubility do not depend solely on what this or that Church figure has written or said. Alleged new rules may be ingeniously insinuated into the silence of Church Fathers and popes. Mackin, for example, finds it significant that Paul VI did not use *Humanae Vitae* as a vehicle to pontificate on the indissolubility of marriage.[7] Because the issue is not broached, Mackin theorizes that Paul VI deliberately avoided closing the door on dissolubility.[8] Papal muteness on an issue, however, is a feeble basis for inferring that long-standing Church teaching on marriage is ripe for change. In fact, the encyclical does not address numerous Church issues on marriage. It says nothing about allowing priests to marry, recognizing marriages between homosexuals, access to the sacraments for the divorced and remarried, the legitimacy of children of annulment, and quite a few other marriage related issues. It is, after all, a comparatively brief encyclical.

Rare are the revisionists who do not solemnly pay lip service to indissolubility. Yet their own theological and canonical alchemy has made indissolubility practically synonymous with fragility. If the Pauline and Petrine privileges are construed as the camel's nose under the tent, revisionists may be credited with gaining entree for the hind quarters as well. But rendering indissolubility soluble, as will be shown, required considerably more than tenuous flights into early Church history and theological ventriloquy that puts words into the mouths of popes.

The Omnipotent "Spirit"

Dissident views on indissolubility remained largely academic until the end of Vatican II. No doubt they stimulated debate and, in retrospect, functioned as warnings of what was to come. But in themselves their effect on the volume of annulments was minimal. In identifying the influences responsible for the ground swell of American annulments, it is difficult not to confer primacy on the potent, amorphous, and ubiquitous "spirit of Vatican II." The official theme of the Council was undeniably pastoral. While some Council Fathers sought modifications in certain doctrinal areas, Vatican II left the body of Church doctrine unchanged. But doctrine has pastoral and administrative implications, and Church history is replete with disparities between word and deed. Doctrinal absolutes have at one time or another been relativized, treated as mere ideals, or targets of dissent, and regarded as being expressions of long-defunct cultural forces. At the very least, the "spirit" of the Council was perceived as a leading agent of change and "reform." It has functioned as a multipurpose deus ex machina, a broad and nebulous rationale for the Church's need to strike out in new directions. As regards annulment, it gave new life to old murmurings, offering theologians and canonists apparent license to soften what the Council Fathers really said about indissolubility.

Seeds of change broadcast before and during the Council swiftly germinated and took root in the United States. Given America's reputation as one of the world's most dynamic societies, that was not surprising. What did surprise was the celerity with which the "spirit" permeated the whole of Church life—the liturgy, the hierarchy, chanceries, religious orders, colleges and universities, seminaries, and, not least, the diocesan marriage tribunals. Those in the pews, reputedly the best-educated Catholics in the world, would be the last to know why the changes were occurring and what the consequences would be for them and their Church. More by fiat and osmosis than formal catechesis, the "spirit" was inserted into their minds, hearts, and behavior.[9] The laity's reactions to what was happening tended to run along either of two gamuts, one ranging from enthusiastic approval to bewilderment, the other from sheepish acquiescence to overt hostility. Disagreement and dissatisfaction were routinely rebutted with pious assurances that the changes in question were part of a new order mandated by the Council Fathers. Rarely were documentary mandates from the Council distinguished from those ordained by its "spirit." There was some recognition that reform might engender some short-term malaise and alienation, but eventually submission and enthusiastic acceptance would carry the day. And while this occurred, a veritable iron curtain descended around Church teaching on such issues as divorce, personal sin, Satan, Purgatory, Hell, and artificial contraception.

There were, of course, other spirits at work in the American Church. The once-immigrant Church, ethnically varied but doctrinally unified, was rapidly becoming Americanized. Parochial or sectional tendencies has always been present within the Church. The Colossians did not present Paul with the same challenges as the Corinthians. A millennium and a half later, the Church made accommodations to the emergent nation-states, just as it had earlier adapted to preferences of emperors and kings. Catholicism would not be entirely the same throughout the world, or even in each section of a single country. Within limits, Rome tolerated subcultural variations, but always with the understanding that the core of the faith would transcend national and regional differences and remain fixed around the globe. Acculturation of the American Church brought with it agitation for democratization and for the redistribution of power, new thrusts that often emboldened dissent from even core beliefs.

PreConciliar critics of American Catholicism frequently characterized the average communicant as unduly passive. One catchy cliché summed up the laity's role: "pray, pay, and obey." That pithy portrayal was especially in vogue among those seeking to revitalize the Church by modifying its mode of governance. Talk of a Second Magisterium became more overt. So did proposals favoring the election of bishops and pastors by the laity. Conjecture and wishful thinking were metamorphosed into the coin of the realm. Ironically, the lay passivity long scorned by the reformers worked to their advantage. The laity, effectively socialized into an authoritarian system, sheepishly acquiesced to changes initiated by articulate progressives. While not always enthusiastic about many new departures, the laity—along with many religious—were generally inclined to take it for granted that the changes had been mandated by the Council Fathers. Some, of course, were. But others were more the progeny of the Council's mystique than its deliberations and official directives. Few laypersons were equipped to distinguish between what was authentically decreed and what emanated from the omnipresent "spirit" of the Council. Even when authority for novelty was sought in specific Conciliar documents, face meaning of the texts was often tinctured, or countermanded, by recourse to the "spirit."

The inevitability and beneficence of change are first principles for zealous reformers. Seldom do they acknowledge that change can have untoward as well as salutary effects. Champions of transitional developments rightly or wrongly credited to Vatican II usually lumped them together under the rubric of "renewal." From their perspective, the term was indeed felicitous. Whether or not a measure for revamping the Church was truly authorized by the Council, designating it as part of the renewal process provided at least nominal legitimacy. That had the effect of making such measures more palatable to Catholics disturbed or even disoriented by some of the changes occurring. Actually, much of the "renewal" shaded over into what might more properly be called "radical reform." It was radical in the sense that it reversed the traditional direction of reform. Historically Church reform consisted mainly of getting local churches to hew to Vatican standards. The new expectation, however, entailed making Rome bend to the will of its constituents, the People of God. Undeniably preConciliar Catholicism in the United States had its fair share of imperfections. But in terms of an array of objective criteria it was in much better shape than the Church in most other societies. Church attendance was high, vocations plentiful, dissent minimal, conversions to the faith frequent, and the educational system the envy of the rest of the Catholic world. Nonetheless, reformists were convinced that its condition was basically unhealthy, desperately in need of the strong medicine of sweeping change.[10]

None of this is meant to suggest that American Catholics were Amishlike in their encounters with modernity, foregoing automobiles for horses and buggies. In secular matters Catholics were as anxious as other minorities for fuller participation in the American dream. For decades Catholics formed one of the "safe" blocs in the liberal wing of the Democratic party. But a large constituency of the faithful drew a line when it came full-scale Americanization of their religion. When all was said and done, the Church was probably the principal spiritual, institutional, and psychological constant in their lives, a stable refuge in a society ever on the move. It could scarcely have been otherwise. Active membership in the Church required commitment to tradition dating back to the time of Christ, to the Magisterium, and to a body of unchanging dogmatic principles. But due in large measure to Vatican II and its diffusive "spirit," religion became both an agent of change and an institutional sphere in need of change. The Church, renewal disciples maintained, was engaged in a vital and long-overdue two-pronged enterprise—journeying back to its ancient roots while finally coming to terms with modern times. Explanations on precisely how the two epochs, separated by nearly two millennia, might be acceptably synthesized were not always lucid, convincing, or even forthcoming.

The "New Pastoralism"

While there is general agreement that the dominant theme of Vatican II was pastoral rather than doctrinal and legalistic, serious differences arise on whether pastoralism takes precedence over Church teaching and law, the order favored by what may be termed the "new pastoralism." In his January 28, 1994 Address to the Rota, John Paul II, drawing on *Veritatis Splendor*, touched on this issue as it relates to the granting of annulments. "[E]xploiting justice to serve personal interests or pastoral forms that, however sincere, are not based on truth, will result in creating social and ecclesial situations of distrust and suspicion, in which the faithful will be tempted to see merely a contest of competing interests and not a common effort to live in accordance with justice and right."[11] The "new pastoralism" implied that pre-Conciliar pastoralism was moribund, in need of a kick-start to get it moving in the right direction. Indeed, most tradition, unless rooted in the primitive Church, was automatically suspect. Together with doctrine and law, tradition suggested fetters and rigidity. In contrast, the "new pastoralism" and the free-floating "spirit of Vatican II" suggested freedom, flexibility, and growth. The old pastoralism, in short, had seen its day.

As their submission to acculturative forces gathered momentum, Catholics— other than recent Hispanic immigrants just beginning the process of Americanization—relinquished some of their prior religious identity. Poll after poll showed Catholics' attitudes, values, and behavior on a variety of moral and religious issues converging with, or being supplanted by, those of the dominant secular culture.[12] If the "spirit of Vatican II" provided generalized leverage for the American Church's drift from resolute orthodoxy, perhaps the most specific catalytic agent was *Humanae Vitae*. Numerous commentators have argued that the lukewarm-to-hostile reception given Paul VI's encyclical was a critical turning point in the relationship between American Catholics and the Magisterium. Although many deplored the estrangement, in some theological and canonical circles it was regarded as a singular blessing, a sign that Catholics in the United States had attained an overdue level of maturity. Weakening or even severing the old umbilical cord would afford opportunities for growth in a variety of directions more consistent with the perceived message of Vatican II and the American way of life. In the progressive lexicon of Church renewal, growth usually signifies unalloyed good. In medical terms, however, growth can be malignant as well as benign. Rome saw America's annulment explosion as baneful. But for many Americans—theologians, canon lawyers, bishops, priests, and lay persons—it was a healthy embodiment of the pastoral renewal prescribed by Vatican II.

The almost instant beatification of the Council's pastoral theme cultivated the absurd implication that the preConciliar Church wanted for solicitous impulses. The poor boxes still found at the rear of most churches testify otherwise, as do Catholic hospitals, orphanages, and other welfare agencies that predate the Council by generations. Incalculable solicitude occurred in the prayer life of the faithful. There was also compassion aplenty for the separated, divorced, and divorced and remarried. For anyone who cares to listen, older parish priests can spend hours reminiscing about counseling and consoling those who suffered unfortunate marriages. But while the older solicitude was predominantly spiritual, moral, and material in nature, the newer version is more consciously therapeutic, leaning heavily on healing powers attributed to contemporary psychology and on safety nets cast by the state. The old pastoralism assiduously conformed to Church teaching and law, while the new sought to free itself of ecclesial shackles.

Behavioral science and the "new pastoralism" were natural bedfellows. Most behavioral scientists believe human action is the product of genetic and environmental forces beyond the individual's control. That assumption was one of several that dovetailed neatly with the elements of the "spirit of Vatican II" ethos. Part of that ethos was anticipated by psychiatrist Karl Menninger when he titled one of his books *Whatever Became of Sin?*[13] Menninger wrote of personal sin, which many within the American Church were determined to deemphasize, or replace with social sin.[14] Perhaps the worst remaining personal sin was judgmentalism. Downgrading personal responsibility and sin made confession and penance obsolete. Penance is not only predicated on sin, it also connotes guilt and punishment, both regarded askance by modern psychology. A twentieth-century Judas, instead of hanging himself to quell his guilty conscience, would more likely use the thirty pieces of silver to engage the services of a therapist.

The psychological premises suffusing the "new pastoralism" influenced the American outlook on annulment. Denying annulments to those who experienced divorce was regarded as unpastoral, hard-hearted, and punitive. Denying access to the sacraments to those divorced and remarried went beyond ordinary punishment; it was cruel and unusual. That the threat of losing access to the Eucharist might motivate a couple to work through marital difficulties and avoid divorce seldom seemed worthy of discussion. Deterrence and sanctions, handmaidens of punishment, are alien to the "new pastoralism." Annulment came to be regarded as a pastoral necessity rather than simply a possible option for those kept from the sacraments by divorce and remarriage. American tribunals, as one distinguished canonist puts it, are "a resource for the salvation of souls."[15]

John Paul II has cautioned that "pastoral sanctions" is not an oxymoron. The sanctions built into Church law are part of its pastoral nature. We easily forget that "justice and law in the strict sense—and consequently general norms, proceedings, sanctions and other typical juridical expressions, should they become necessary—are required in the Church for the good of souls and are thus intrinsically pastoral."[16] Much the same idea was expressed earlier by a member of the Apostolic Signatura. "Not rarely one encounters a rather simplistic *pastoral* approach which in the end cannot ever be efficacious in the formation of true Christians. Such simplistic approaches attempt to tranquilize, or to 'tuck away' the disturbed consciences of those in an irregular matrimonial situation, rather than to form conscience in the light of the Gospel. . . . In such an attitude it seems that sometimes *love* for the couples in the broken marriage becomes stronger than [love] for the Lord and his law."[17] That the pope was moved to reaffirm views the Signatura had expressed several years earlier attests to the persistence of this premise of the "new pastoralism." As should be all too evident, the "new pastoralism" often propagates a painless form of Christianity which attempts to factor out the lessons of the Cross.

The proannulment mindset did not catch on throughout the Church. Its warmest reception occurred in western Europe and North America. The vanguard consisted mainly of a tightly knit group of theologians and canonists pursuing objectives that would necessitate jettisoning much of the Church's past. Few were so unrealistic as to call for complete abrogation of the Church's traditional teaching on the nature of marriage, its permanence and indissolubility, divorce and remarriage, and eligibility for annulment. Better to promote incremental change within a context of apparent legitimacy and fidelity to the Magisterium. Occasionally a radical voice would rise above the rest. Thus one prominent canonist, presiding judge of the Archdiocese of New York's marriage tribunal for seven years, authored a book whose fourfold purpose was

(1) to advocate the abolition of all Catholic Church marriage tribunals; (2) to vindicate the right of persons to divorce themselves if their marriages are irretrievably broken down and existentially dead; (3) to vindicate the right of

divorced Catholics and Catholics marrying divorced persons to marry publicly in the Church; (4) to vindicate the right of these Catholics to full membership in the Church and particularly their right to open participation in the Eucharist.[18]

The radical nature of the scheme leaps off the page. Options sternly prohibited for centuries—divorce, divorce and remarriage in the Church, full access to the sacraments for those divorced and remarried—are not simply permitted. They become a matter of right. Nothing is said about whether any Church official or body would decide if marriages are "irretrievably broken." Evidently the decision would be left to the spouses themselves. Kelleher's scheme was reprised recently by Kenneth Untener, Bishop of Saginaw, who reportedly observed, "I wonder if the church should get out of the marriage business. I question whether or not we belong in the business of arbitrating marriages. I'd much rather pray for people and wish them well."[19]

Kelleher's use of the phrase *irretrievably broken* may be more than mere coincidence. The phrase is prominent in the lexicon of no-fault divorce. But there is court involvement in no-fault divorce, precisely what Kelleher and and Untener wished to eliminate. Their proposals are more reminiscent of modes of dissolution found in primitive societies. Not terribly long ago a Plains Indians brave could divorce his squaw merely by putting her moccasins outside their tepee. Presumably this mode of marital dissolution was abandoned as the Indians came under the influence of the state and Christianity.

Most American canonists who wanted to change the rules of dissolution preferred flanking movements over the kind of frontal assault favored by Kelleher and Untener. The basic strategy was more subtle, usually paying fealty to traditional teaching while simultaneously doing almost everything imaginable to neuter it. The quest for loopholes was relentless. Changes that ensued were credited to the Council Fathers, developments in the Church's legal system, advances in the behavioral sciences, and tribunal efficiency. Despite their fascination with behavioral science, many theologians and canonists were blind to the psychological dynamics of their own thought processes. Unwittingly, they were indulging in projection, the psychological defense mechanism whereby one's own intentions and actions are ascribed to others.

The strategy of change was rooted in the contention that the Church, owing to Vatican II, had modified its age-old teaching on the essence of marriage. By doing so the Church ostensibly signaled its willingness to adapt to the realities of marriage in the twentieth century. In the practical order, this assumption cleared the way for more innovative, compassionate pastoral and canonical initiatives for dealing with divorce, divorce and remarriage, and those estranged from the Church by virtue of unsuccessful marriages. Terms such as *permanence* and *indissolubility* were retained to mollify traditionalists—and Rome—even as they were being emptied of their meaning. The traditional lexicon became more a reflection of idealistic catchwords and slogans than doctrinal imperatives, thus facilitating lowering barriers against granting annulments on the wholesale. Verbally and conceptually, the revisionists positioned themselves to have their cake and eat it. Aware that what was being promoted and practiced got close to modifying doctrine grounded in divine and natural law, proponents of change sought cover in euphemistic hedges, referring to new departures as "developments," "insights," "approaches," and "perceptions."

Changing the Ground(s) Rules

Anyone who had not kept watch on American annulment trends might understandably assume that prior to the 1970s, when decrees of nullity rose sharply, the Church accepted fewer reasons for declaring marriages invalid. Actually, the number of grounds for annulment has not really changed. Historically the Church has recognized a fairly sizable array of conditions that invalidate marriage.[20] A series of impediments, making a person incapable of validly contracting marriage,[21] have long applied to unions where: (1) the male spouse is not yet sixteen, the wife not yet fourteen at the time of the wedding; (2) the male is impotent, the female frigid, or the marriage never consummated[22] (3) either spouse is still involved in a marriage not properly dissolved; (4) a Catholic and an unbaptized person marry without proper dispensation; (5) the male spouse, a recipient of Holy Orders, is not personally dispensed by the pope; (6) either spouse who publicly vowed celibacy did not receive dispensation to marry; (7) the female spouse is forced to marry by means of abduction or confinement; (8) one spouse kills the other in order to enter a new marriage; (9) the spouses are closely consanguinous; (10) there is prior affinity between the spouses, as occasioned by a widowed person marrying the deceased spouse's parent or child; (11) someone party to a common-law marriage later marries the parent or child of the live-in partner; (12) a person marries a child or sibling he or she adopted; and (13) Catholics enter a marriage "lacking form" and therefore validity because it does not occur before an authorized priest and witnesses.[23]

Annulments continue to be granted to those who qualify under the terms of the Pauline and Petrine privileges, neither of which can be classified under the heading of "impediments." Although the overwhelming majority of ordinary process annulments granted in the last two decades are based on defective consent, it should not be assumed that such annulments were unobtainable in the past. The Church has long looked askance on marriages where either partner's consent to marry was defective. Defective consent can produce the same result as an impediment (i.e., nullity), but it is not simply another kind of impediment. Since impediments are designated by Church law, in certain situations they can be lifted by an appropriate authority. Marital consent also falls within the purview of the law, but it relates to the very nature of contracting marriage[24] "The Church holds the exchange of consent between the spouses to be the indispensable element that 'makes the marriage.' If consent is lacking there is no marriage."[25]. In the past as well as in the present certain situations could be dealt with under the defective consent rubric: where a spouse, short of being confined or abducted, is forced into marriage; a spouse conceals something vital (e.g., homosexuality) from a partner; a spouse enters marriage intending to be unfaithful, interested only in a trial marriage, or is not open to having children; and where one spouse intends, even before the marriage is contracted, to treat the marriage partner in a manner totally devoid of respect and dignity.

Extensive as the Church's pre-1970 inventory of grounds for annulment may appear, the annual number of annulments in America remained in the hundreds. But in keeping with the tenets of the "new pastoralism" it was widely believed that the Church's position on nullity offered inadequate relief for thousands of former and prospective communicants whose marriages had failed. It was especially imperative to devise means by which those divorced and remarried could return to the sacraments. The Church since its founding was acutely aware of the trials and tribulations of failed marriages as well as those that remained intact. But whatever the depth and range of its sympathies, it chose not to ameliorate marital problems by easing strictures on annulment. Over the centuries the Church practiced what now goes under the fashionable name of "tough love." Except in the most obvious cases, such as those involving "lack of form," annulment was never intended to be perfunctory. Moreover, it usually represented a last resort.

Amidst the hue and cry surrounding the need, availability, and propriety of annulment, it is often forgotten that since time immemorial the Church's first concern when marriages fail has been the possibility of reconciliation. Short of that, the Church has always been open to the separation of spouses.[26] These options, still recognized, are consistent with traditional Church policy for processing the majority of annulment petitions. Its rationale resembles the due process model which undergirds the American criminal justice system. Just as the state must hurdle a succession of procedural obstacles to prevent it from convicting the innocent, a tribunal is obliged to traverse a figurative doctrinal and canonical mine field to avoid nullifying valid marriages. The parallels between the two systems can be carried even further. Just as the justice system is bound to the presumption of innocence, the tribunal system is duty bound to assume that marriages are valid until proven otherwise.

Under the terms of what may be called the pre–Vatican II grounds for nullity, the annual number of ordinary process annulments in the United States never reached the one-thousand mark. But with divorce and remarriage among Catholics on the rise, the ecclesial ambience of post–Vatican II generated a logarithmic increase in the pressure to loosen or expand the criteria for nullity. For many theologians and canonists, particularly those caught up in the heady reaches of the Conciliar "spirit" and the "new pastoralism," the volume of annulments was pitifully inadequate. The time had come to put aside the childish strictures of the past and tenderize the Church's "tough love" stance. The generic medium for tenderization was defective consent. In fairly short order, it became the preferential ground of American tribunals, a handy, all-purpose instrument for finding marriages nonexistent through defective consent (Table 2-1).

Table 2–1. U.S. Tribunals Grounds for Nullity in First and Second Instance Sentences by Ordinary and Documentary Process, 1984–1994.

Year	Defective consent	Lack of form	Other	Total decrees of nullity
1984	36,069	12,584	2,585	51,238
1985	37,034	13,663	2,623	53,320
1986	39,534	14,733	3,414	57,681
1987	41,971	15,652	2,947	60,570
1988	41,763	16,187	2,633	60,583
1989	40,879	17,984	2,553	61,416
1990	40,678	19,652	2,494	62,824
1991	42,617	18,679	2,637	63,933
1992	39,753	15,944	3,333	59,030
1993	38,327	13,005	2,315	53,647
1994	38,699	12,595	3,169	54,463
TOTALS	437,324	170,678	30,703	638,705

Source: Adapted from *Statistical Yearbooks of the Church,* 1984–1994.

Neither the *Statistical Yearbook of the Church* nor CLSA's annual statistical summaries for American tribunals provide data on the incidence of defective consent cases prior to 1984. CLSA summaries give tallies on several grounds for nullity, but are curiously silent on defective consent. Figures are given for "lack for form" annulments, for small numbers of cases involving unconsummated marriages, and the Pauline and Petrine privileges. But no data are presented on what is by far the most common ground for annulment in America. The silence suggests heightened defensiveness on the part of CLSA and its statisticians. Leaving aside the "lack of form" and "other" categories, nearly all of the documentary process variety, the Vatican figures show (Table 2-1) that since 1983 the grounds for nullity in over 95 percent of the ordinary process decisions by American tribunals relate to defective consent. When "lack of form" and "other" cases are included, defective consent is still by a wide margin (68 percent) the leading issue facing the question of marital validity.

In all likelihood, defective consent was the basis for a more modest percentage of annulments in the early 1970s. Tribunals had not yet raised determination of defective consent to an art form. Among other things, it was still perceived, quite properly, as more difficult to establish than other grounds. Whether a male spouse was at least sixteen years old at the time of marriage is usually a matter of record. Age can be verified by examining a baptismal certificate or by checking with public agencies that keep vital statistics. But more intensive investigation is required to determine his openness to children, commitment to fidelity, or whether at the time the marriage was contracted he planned to treat his bride as a mere love slave or maidservant. But even those criteria were fairly cut and dried compared to what would follow. Delving into how a person's psyche functioned, often deep in the past, is no mean feat. In fairly short order, however, diocesan tribunals became remarkably adroit at using defective consent as their leading instrument of nullity.

While Vatican and CLSA statistics are silent on the incidence of defective consent annulments in the late 1970s and early 1980s, more recent data verify its place at the apex among the grounds for nullity employed by American tribunals. Of the 638,705 decrees of nullity granted in the United States during 1984–1994, 437,324 (68 percent) dealt with defective consent. Based on Vatican data for ordinary process annulments only, between 1984 and 1994 98 percent of the decrees of nullity granted by American tribunals involved defective consent (the long-term data appear in chapter 4, Table 4-1). Accordingly, as noted in the opening chapter, the study of defective consent nullity is really the study of ordinary process annulment in the United States. That empirical fact, considered together with the total number of annulments, becomes all the more significant when we bear in mind that defective consent as a ground for nullity is nothing new. But obviously it metamorphosed into something different, a ground covering exceptionally wide spaces. Although many defective consent decrees of nullity were granted in the 1970s, their near monopoly on ordinary process annulment was not achieved until promulgation of the revised code of canon law in 1983. How this state of affairs came to pass and the consequences that flow from it are principal concerns of this book.

Emboldened by Vatican II's pastoral rallying cry and anxious to mitigate the plight of Catholics separated from the sacraments, many theologians and canonists redoubled earlier efforts to enlarge the annulment constituency. Their resourceful mission soon bore fruit. In fairly short order the pool of marriages eligible for annulment came to consist of virtually all unions ending in civil divorce, as well as many en route to that destination. As the confessional vignette heading Chapter 1 shows, even marriages not yet ending in divorce were considered fair game. In like manner, the pool of potential petitioners for nullity came to include practically all Catholics whose marital history included at least one failed marriage. The pool includes many non-Catholics, previously divorced, who either seek annulments to marry Catholics on Church terms, or wish to validate marriages to Catholics already entered by having earlier marriages annulled. In some cases, the annulment may be preliminary to conversion to Catholicism. The modification of eligibility demographics was predicated on a series of assumptions in addition to those discussed above in connection with the conciliar "spirit" and the "new pastoralism." Within the American canonical community it was virtually an article of faith that the Council Fathers had modified the Church's position on the essence of marriage. That assumption, as we shall see, was augmented by suppositions drawn from the new code of canon law, from Rotal jurisprudence, and by recourse to the human sciences. Inventive, at times facile, these initiatives led to significant changes in the American tribunals' reckoning of matrimonial consent. Preexisting criteria for defective consent were substantially broadened, giving diocesan tribunals far more latitude if not license to annul.[27]

Procedural Concerns

Apologists for the great upward leap in nullity initially credited much of the early portion of the rise to the American Procedural Norms (APN), twenty-three stipulations which streamlined and shortened the tribunals' handling of annulment petitions. At the urging of the CLSA the National Conference of Catholic Bishops (NCCB) petitioned Rome in 1969 for approval of the APN. When Rome did not respond with anticipated alacrity, the NCCB resubmitted its request. Rome eventually acceded, and the APN took effect on July 1, 1970.[28] Attached to Rome's approval was the proviso that the norms could be used on a trial basis for three years. However, their life span was extended until the revised *Code of Canon Law* became operational in 1983. Perhaps none of the stipulations contributed more to expediting petitions for nullity than Norm 3:

> A collegiate tribunal must be constituted for each case. The Episcopal Conference, in accordance with faculties to be sought from the Holy See, may permit the competent ecclesiastical Tribunal to derogate from this norm for a specified period of time so that a case may be handled by a single judge.
>
> The conditions are that: 1) there be a grave reason for granting the derogation; and 2) no formal opposition be expressed prior to the definitive sentence by either the judge, the defender of the bond, the promoter of justice or either of the parties.

The manifold ramifications of tribunal size will be taken up at length in a later chapter. Suffice it to say for the moment that even under the celebrated APN single-judge tribunals were the (virtually ironclad) rule rather than the exception. Tribunalists in the late 1960s could probably point to a heavy backlog of cases needing attention, but it seems unlikely that was the sort of "grave reason" Rome had in mind when consent was given to launch the APN experiment. Though not proof that it never happened, during the course of my research I did not come upon a single case where a multiple-judge court was impaneled because of formal opposition to a single judge. Based on analysis of how rights of respondents in nullity proceedings have been systematically abridged and dishonored, it is unlikely that many respondents were even told they could request a collegiate tribunal.

Declarations of nullity were also expedited by Norm 23, which dispensed with automatic appeal of an affirmative decision to a higher tribunal. Under the 1917 code such a decision required a conforming decision at Second Instance. Norm 23-II, however, stated that "In those exceptional cases where in the judgment of the defender of the bond and his Ordinary [i.e., the bishop] an appeal against an affirmative decision would clearly be superfluous, the Ordinary may himself request of the Episcopal Conference that in these individual cases the defender of the bond be dispensed from the obligation to appeal so that the sentence of the first instance may be executed immediately." Implementation of this section of Norm 23 by American tribunals adhered to the same minimalism the tribunals applied to Norm 3. Defenders found very few affirmative decisions that lacked merit, and therefore took very few appeals to Second Instance. In effect, their inaction provided the second conforming decision previously required but bypassed by Norm 23. What all this meant was that tribunals adhered to what might be called the Rule of One: a single judge at First Instance issuing a single affirmative decision. The processing of petitions for nullity could occur with unprecedented celerity.

Despite apparent misgivings, Rome's assent to the APN was no doubt given in good faith. A short-term increase in American decrees of nullity might have been nervously anticipated, but it is altogether improbable that Rome was prepared for what ensued. At the very least, agreeing to the APN affirmed the Holy See's commitment to the hoary but noble legal maxim that "justice delayed is justice denied." But Rome's good faith was predicated on the belief that American tribunals would implement the APN with judicious restraint. That assumption proved disingenuous, as the annulment statistics compellingly testify. Given an inch, American tribunals took miles. Under the guise of doing justice with celerity, tribunals developed practices which distorted the original paradigm into "justice hastened is validity denied."

Although the influence of the APN cannot be discounted, most of the radical increase in annulments would have occurred without them. Simplification of the mechanics of trying cases undoubtedly expedited the awarding of decrees of nullity, but the key variables behind the bulk of the increase were substantive rather than procedural. The volume of annulments remained high well after the APN were phased out. The APN bore no substantive responsibility for defective-consent cases almost monopolizing ordinary process caseloads. On the other hand, repeal of the APN did not repeal their legacy. Use of individual judges to rule on petitions for nullity is still the order of the day, and resumption of mandatory review at Second Instance of affirmative decisions, as will be shown in a later chapter, borders on travesty. Perhaps the chief significance of the APN was that they provided the American tribunal system with a procedural running start on what was to come later.

Not to be underestimated, however, is the APN's contribution to the emergence of a preferential option for nullity among the system's theorists and practitioners. When confronted with choices, real or speculative, between firm and loose adherence to Church law and teaching on valid marriage, American canonists became strongly inclined to confer the benefit of any doubt on annulment. The inclination still holds sway in the confines of diocesan tribunal offices.

❖ 3 ❖

Building on
the Groundwork

If in the hierarchy of influences on annulment in America the "spirit of Vatican II" and the new pastoralism vie for top honors, *Gaudium et Spes*, is not far behind. This section of the Council's Pastoral Constitution of the Church in the Modern World deals with the sanctity of marriage and the family.[1] The text appearing on those few pages, it is repeatedly alleged, signals a shift in Church teaching on the nature or essence of marriage. Before examining No. 48, it is instructive to note some prefatory remarks in No. 47. Pointed reference is made to such marital and familial "blemishes" as polygamy, the "plague of divorce," and free love. Dishonor, we are counseled, accrues to marriage through "selfishness, hedonism, and unlawful contraception." Neither the marital stigmas cited nor the sociocultural and psychological conditions that threaten marriage and the family are discussed in words suggesting that the Council Fathers were preparing to promulgate a substantial change or, for that matter, any change in Church teaching. In fact, No. 47 asserts that what follows is intended to *clarify* certain key points in that teaching. There is not the slightest hint that it is about to be amended or expanded.[2] Besides pondering the content of No. 47, it is important to remind ourselves that the basic theme of Vatican II was pastoral, not doctrinal and legal.

The most frequently cited portion of No. 48 states:

The intimate partnership of life and love which constitutes the married state has been established by the creator and endowed by him with its own proper *laws*: it is rooted in the *contract* of its partners, that is, in their irrevocable personal consent. It is an institution confirmed by the divine *law* and receiving its stability, even in the eyes of society, from the human act by which the partners mutually surrender themselves to each other; for the good of the partners, of the children, and of society this *sacred bond no longer depends on*

29*

29

human decision alone. For God himself is the author of marriage and has endowed it with various benefits and with various ends in view[3]

Stylistically, the language here is typical of that found in the rest of No. 48. As with many official Church documents, the English translation of the Latin can strike a lay reader as being rather stilted, perhaps ponderous. But otherwise the text is quite straightforward. Critical ingenuity on the order of the deconstructionism currently in vogue on many campuses[4] is required to discern in the passage a "spirit" at odds with the explicit meaning of the text. Perhaps that is why the Flannery translation seems to be out of favor among those who profess to find new departures in No. 48.

American commentators appear to prefer the translation of the same passage as it appears in the volume of edited by Walter M. Abbott:

> The intimate partnership of married life and love has been established by the Creator and *qualified by His laws.* It is rooted in the conjugal *covenant* of irrevocable personal consent. Hence, by that human act whereby spouses mutually bestow and accept each other, a relationship arises which by divine will and in the eyes of society too is a lasting one. For the good of the spouses and their offspring as well as of society, the existence of this sacred bond no longer depends on human decisions alone[5]

Readers not exegetically minded might find scant difference between the two translations. But theologians and canon lawyers are not given to casual perusal of Church documents. Donald R. Campion's sanguine introduction to the Abbott version illustrates the difference a translation can make. The Council Fathers, he maintains, "set forth a Christian understanding of marriage that emphasizes the centrality of conjugal love and of the concept of a *covenant* relationship between two persons. Christian marriage is seen, moreover, as a reflection of 'the loving *covenant* uniting Christ with the Church.' The stress on conjugal love and the strongly *personalist* tone of the entire section on marriage carries us far beyond *legalisms* and philosophical abstractions indeed."[6] While both the Abbott and Flannery renditions appear to convey the same basic message, closer scrutiny reveals some interesting differences. Flannery puts more emphasis on law and omits what has been accorded critical significance by many American theologians and canonists, the term *covenant.* The presence of that term in Abbott, along with the "personalist" theme he discerns in the document, helps account for the enthusiasm evinced by Campion.

The Flannery compilation of the Vatican II documents was published in 1975, nine years after the Abbott volume went to press. Cardinal John Wright's preface to the former cautions that the rapidity with which early translations were made assured "frequent infelicities, not to say inaccuracies, in translation." Some of the first translations, he contends, "were frequently accompanied by commentary or reactions usually friendly and helpful to further lines of independent thought, but frequently irrelevant and even confusing to one seeking to learn exactly what the Council said rather than what someone outside the Council *thought* about the matter."[7]

Lacking fluency in Latin, I cannot attest to the comparative fidelity of the two translations of No. 48. Judging from Cardinal Wright's remarks, the Flannery translation would seem to have the edge. Given its later publication date, the translators were probably less susceptible to errors that frequently attend a rush to print. It is instructive to note that the English edition of the *Catechism of the Catholic Church* relies solely on Flannery when it cites or quotes Council documents, including *Gaudium et Spes*, No. 48. On the other hand, a priest who is a Latinist assures me that both Abbott and Flannery take questionable liberties with an important condition the original Latin attaches to the sacred bond. Flannery states that the bond "no longer depends on human decision alone." But for "decisions" in lieu of "decision" the Abbott rendition of the clause is identical. According to my Latin expert, the primary source reads "*non ex humano arbitrio pendet.*" "No longer" and "alone" are appendages. Far more important, they consign the Creator to an almost ancillary role among guarantors of the integrity of the bond. The Council Fathers stated that there is *no* room for *any* human decision. A recent decision by the Church's highest marriage court lends support to that rendering of the passage, deeming the the Abbott translation "tendentious in the direction of watering down the dogma of indissolubility."[8] The same charge of bias, of course, applies to Flannery. Perhaps that is why the English edition of the new catechism, despite using Flannery throughout, departs from its characterization of the bond. The relevant passage states that

> *the marriage bond* has been established by God himself in such a way that a marriage concluded and consummated between baptized persons can never be dissolved. This bond, which results from the free human act of the spouses and their consummation of the marriage, is a reality, henceforth irrevocable, and gives rise to a covenant guaranteed by God's fidelity. The Church does not have the power to contravene this disposition of divine wisdom.[9]

Plainly, the *Catechism* recognizes the impervious character of God's authority and wisdom over that of any mortal who deliberates on the sacred bond. The rigorous strictures enunciated in the *Catechism* are much the same as Christ's (Matthew 19:6).

Literal adherence to these conceptions of the bond would seem to mandate radical changes in the American tribunal system's approach to the dissolution of marriage. Theoretically, the number of annulments would plummet. But as unequivocal as the *Catechism* teaching appears to be, it really contains a critical loophole in that "marriage" refers to *valid* marriage. The American tribunals have succeeded in enlarging the loophole into a bay window. The tendentious fealty paid to the seminal character of *Gaudium et Spes*, No. 48 by American canonists is an example of how this has occurred. Their understanding of the document is unflinching, unlikely to waver in the face of demonstrable mistran-

slation of a key portion of the document. A good deal more will be required to
upset America's annulment applecart.

Letter and "Spirit"

Campion's commentary on No. 48 succinctly states what are now widely held
views in the United States on marriage and law. For Campion as well as many
other analysts of Vatican II there is an abiding aversion to legalism, or indeed
any Church policy or teaching even suspected of being tinged with it. Commitment to the "spirit of Vatican II" practically presupposes repugnance for
legalism. Invocation of the term often serves as a signal for freewheeling interpretations of Conciliar documents and for dissent, particularly with respect to
Church's rules and her mode of governance. It also has an secondary function
as a rhetorical weapon for curtailing or terminating debate. "Letter" and "spirit,"
along with such pairings as "pastoralism" and "legalism," and "grace" and
"law," are often treated like components of Hegelian dialectics. But their opposition seldom produces any specific synthesis of the kind supposed to emerge
when concepts conflict with each other. More important, neither are they likely
to be granted even theoretical potential for complementarity. Instead, the tendency is to regard them as mutually exclusive, juxtaposed in order to force an
either-or resolution. The ideologically congenial variable is crowned with un-
disputed hegemony and rectitude, while the other member of the pairing is
downgraded, denigrated, or summarily dismissed.

An example of one-sided resolution of the allegedly irreconcilable conflict
between pastoralism and law is provided by Häring in a recent discourse on
pastoral care for the divorced and remarried.[10] Like countless parish priests and
laypersons, Häring can recall heartrending anecdotes about the plight of Catholics whose marriages failed. Such cases become especially poignant when one
party to marital breakup appears innocent, and when divorced Catholics, in
apparently happy remarriages, wish to return to full communion. Their woe can
bestir compassionate urges in the most hard-hearted listener. For Häring and
others, when pastoral needs are stymied by law, the law must yield. "The great
danger for the Church's marriage tribunals is of turning into courts of law where
the healing love of the Redeemer can only with difficulty gain admission and
where the Church's servants charged with a ministry of healing cannot, despite
all their good will, find the atmosphere that would be favourable for the work
of helping and healing."[11] Not unexpectedly, Häring places freedom and law as
well as pastoralism and law in almost hopelessly adversarial relationships. In
his view, while the postConciliar Church has dispensed with much of its past
legalistic rigidity, it has not gone far enough to reduce the "tension between law
and freedom in the case of the extremely doubtful validity of a marriage that
has collapsed beyond hope."[12]

Unquestionably law has manifold potential. It can be an instrument of op-
pression, and, as Dickens argued, it is often an ass. But it can also educate,
inspire, protect, liberate, and ensure justice. Church teaching and pastoral

measures, as well as Church law and the spirit behind it, need not be construed as forming dualisms signifying unresolvable conflicts between opposing forces that refuse to enter a truce. Nor is it necessary to posit a continuous tug of war between freedom and law. Commenting on their interconnection, canonist Cormac Burke points out that "The simple reflection that to be a Christian has always meant to be someone who is subject to the law of Christ—who freely subjects himself to the law of Christ—already suggests that an anti-law mentality fits poorly in Christian life and Christian society. One becomes, or lives as, a Christian not to be freed from law but to be freed by law: Christ's law."[13] In an ecclesial context, the tensions generated by law when it is paired with pastoralism, "spirit," grace, and freedom are more usefully regarded as paradoxically complementary. Cicero stated that "In the end we are all of us slaves to the law, for that is the condition of our freedom."[14] From the standpoint of the Church, Cicero's statement might be reworded to read "In the end we are all of us slaves to Christ's law, for that is the condition of our sanctification."

It is a safe bet that John Paul II would agree with Cicero. He stresses the harmonious relationship that obtains between the Magisterium and Church law, and between the law and pastoralism. In proclaiming the revised code of canon law, he commented that "the Code . . . fully accords with the nature of the Church, particularly as presented in the authentic teaching of the Second Vatican Council seen as a whole, and especially in its ecclesiological doctrine."[15] Recognizing that it may not always be possible to transpose with perfect fidelity "the image of the Church described by conciliar doctrine into canonical language," the pope nevertheless insists that the "Code must always be related to that image as to its primary pattern, whose outlines, given its nature, the Code must express as far as is possible."[16] Put somewhat differently, canon law is designed to mirror closely Church teaching. The mirror is not to be made over into a canonical prism. A mirror reflects images, perhaps with some imperfections, while a prism distorts what is projected through it.

Paradoxically, while revisionist theologians seek to purge Vatican II of legalism, canonists often seem obsessed with infusing Council documents with juridic meaning. At times they seem so absorbed with legal minutiae that they lose sight of the larger magisterial whole. Legalism, of course, must be integral to the canonist's calling. But legalism is not univocal. It can take the form of relatively mechanical application of the law, with little concern for questions of equity or extenuating circumstances. From another perspective, it can consist of probing the law for loopholes to further nonlegal or extralegal agendas. Those two options by no means exhaust all the possible functions of legalism in its capacity to serve several masters. In the hands of resourceful tribunalists, it can work toward either denying or granting annulments. As will be shown below, leading American canonists have indulged their legalism to vitiate or even defy the wishes and instructions of the Church's highest courts and of the Holy Father himself. At all events, legalism within the American tribunal system clearly operates in the service of maximizing the number of decrees of nullity.

Contract versus Covenant

As we have seen, the Council Fathers are credited with pronouncing marriage a covenant rather than a contract. Among America's most influential canonists, the covenant conception of marriage has been embraced with eagerness approaching acclamation. If there were any demurrals within the canonical community, they were mild, drowned out by the hosannas of the majority. Paul F. Palmer, in an oft-cited article, claims that the shift from contract to covenant represented a return to the Church's roots. "In the first millenium of the Church's history, all marriage, pagan as well as Christian, was discussed almost wholly in terms of covenant." But for the "last six centuries, Christian marriage has been discussed almost exclusively in terms of contract." Palmer's view is predicated not only on his examination of Church history but also on the observation that "the Fathers of Vatican II never use the word 'contract' in discussing Christian marriage."[17] The well-published canonist Ladislas Orsy, though not himself fully wedded to the contract-to-covenant transition and its ramifications as seen by others, reports that the covenant characterization of Christian marriage became virtually axiomatic in canonical and theological circles after Vatican II.[18] Orsy, however, does not delineate how expansive are the circumferences of those circles. In poring over the literature, one gets the impression that English-speaking canonists and theologians have read more into the convenant characterization than their counterparts in other Church precincts. Parenthetically, it can be noted that while the covenant conception of marriage might be traceable to the early Church, no prominent American canonist emphasizes the historiographical corollary that restrictive annulment is also rooted in Church antiquity. Even among scholars who contend that the Church has always had the power to dissolve marriages, none would maintain that the incidence of dissolution in the past came close to its current level.

Exegetically the contract-covenant dichotomy may be problematic, quite possibly an example of what Cardinal Wright warned against when questionable translations of Conciliar documents are blindly accorded authenticity.[19] Neither Palmer nor Campion before him advert to the possibility that what they construe as a watershed change might simply be an artifact of translation. Palmer is partly correct in noting the Council Fathers' avoidance of *contract* and reliance on *covenant.* But his observation, like Campion's commentary, is based on the Abbott version of *Gaudium et Spes,* No. 48, where *covenant* appears five times and *contract* not at all. In the Flannery translation, however, we find that marriage "is rooted in the *contract* of its partners, that is, in their irrevocable personal consent."[20] Subsequently the text states that "Just as of old God encountered his people with a *covenant* of love and fidelity, so our Saviour, the spouse of the Church, now encounters Christian spouses through the sacrament of marriage."[21] It would not be terribly farfetched to take the first passage to mean that the agreement between spouses is a contract, the second to denote that the agreement between the spouses and Christ a covenant. However that may be, neither *contract* nor *covenant* appears more than once in the Flannery translation of No. 48.

The contract-to-covenant transition American canonists and theologians seek to institutionalize, dogmatize, and load with significance may ultimately be a distinction without difference. Had the Council Fathers intended to declare Christian marriage a covenant instead of a contract, and if the change was one of substance, presumably they would have identified it as such and given a rationale for it. But that does not happen, either in Abbott or Flannery, and probably in no other translation as well. If a real modification of Church teaching had been mandated without comment, the void would likely have been at least partially filled in the revised *Code of Canon Law*. Church law, as John Paul II stipulates, embodies the Magisterium. Since the new code appeared eight years after the Council ended, there was ample opportunity to ensure that the law would incorporate the intended meaning of No. 48, clarifying any doctrinal ambiguity associated with it. Let us now examine relevant portions of the new code to see whether it yields any enlightenment on the contract-covenant issue.

Contract versus Covenant: The Code

Title VII of the *Code of Canon Law*, consisting of 112 canons, is the Church's body of statutory law on marriage. It begins with C. 1055, 1 "The marriage *covenant*, by which a man and a woman establish between themselves a partnership of their whole life, and which of its own very nature is ordered to the well-being of the spouses and to the procreation and upbringing of children, has, between the baptised, been raised by Christ the Lord to the dignity of a sacrament."[22] The very next subsection of C. 1055 specifies that "a valid marriage *contract* cannot exist between baptised persons without its being by that very fact a sacrament." C. 1057, 2 defines matrimonial consent as "an act of will by which a man and a woman by an irrevocable *covenant* mutually give and accept one another for the purpose of establishing a marriage," while C. 1058 declares that "All can *contract* marriage who are not prohibited by law." C. 1063, 4 refers to spouses "observing and protecting their conjugal *covenant*." Thenceforth, from C. 1064 through C. 1165, 102 canons in all, the term *covenant* does not appear. *Contract*, or one of its variant forms, is used twenty-eight times, either as a noun, verb, participle, infinitive, or adjective. Indeed, C. 1095, the statutory wellspring for the overwhelming majority of ordinary process annulments granted in the United States, begins by stating: "The following are incapable of *contracting* marriage." The new code makes no effort whatever to explicate a difference between *covenant* and *contract*. Neither term appears in C. 1056, an important defining statute, which stipulates that "The essential properties of marriage are unity and indissolubility. . . ." Based on this simple exercise in what sociologists call content analysis, a solid case can be made that the terms are, in fact, used interchangeably.

Contract and *covenant* belong to the genus *agreement*. That is not to say Christian marriage, if termed a contract, is of the same mold as agreements covering an installment purchase of a household appliance or the settlement of collective bargaining negotiations. The marriage agreement has everywhere been accorded special status. No society in history—primitive or advanced, Christian or pagan—has looked upon marriage as a garden variety agreement. In the United States even "quickie" marriages performed by justices of the peace or by cruise ship captains are thought to touch upon compelling state interests. Ordinarily licenses and blood tests are required, and the ceremony itself must be witnessed or conducted by functionally specific persons. Catholic couples, to marry with Church blessing, must be of reasonably sound mind, free of impediments, and satisfy a variety of administrative prerequisites. These same conditions plus others apply to mixed marriages occurring in the Church. Whether the union is labeled a contract or a covenant, a couple planning even the most modest Catholic church wedding would have to be brain dead not to sense that they are entering an extraordinary agreement, one substantially different from other kinds of agreements. This would seem all the more obvious in a society boasting what are reputedly the world's best educated Catholics.

In American legal parlance, *covenant* often denotes a binding contract, a meaning fully consistent with Church usage. The binding character of Christian marriage has been a given since the time of Christ's earthly ministry. The traditional vows exchanged by prospective spouses provide powerful, objective affirmation of that altogether-basic Church position. For those outside the pale of the niceties of canon law it seems incongruous that so much is made of the one word *covenant* in *Gaudium et Spes*, No. 48, while entire passages such as the "sacred bond no longer depending on human decision alone" seem to be glossed over and perhaps mistranslated as well.

Based on the foregoing textual analysis, one is tempted to dismiss the contract-covenant matter as mere semantic quibble. Common sense suggests treating the words as synonyms. But that would apparently be detrimental to the cause of permissive annulment. Despite vulnerability to the charge of linguistic nitpicking, assertions that *covenant* replaced *contract* provide apparent corroboration to the contention that the Council Fathers, without saying so, changed the Church's conception of marriage. *Covenant,* moreover, is easily made to imply a higher marital ideal, out of reach for a large percentage of couples who merely "contract" marriage. Over-idealization of valid marriage is a common unstated strategy among those favoring relaxation of the Church's criteria for annulment. Marriages falling short of idyllic covenantal stature, as most do, form an almost inexhaustible constituency for nullity. Still, the comparative ease with which the alleged contract-to-covenant transition became encrusted as received wisdom was a theological and canonical tour de force. A new reality was created by the simple expedient of substituting one term for another. What was at bottom a euphemism became transmuted into a matter of doctrinal substance which continues to profoundly influence how American tribunals deal with broken marriages and petitions for nullity.

Expanding the Essence

A hoary cliché tells us that change, real or imagined, has a way of generating its own momentum, one variation begetting others. Once satisfied that *Gaudium et Spes*, No. 48 was an instrument of change, American canonists lost no time mining the document for other departures from the past. A similar extractive process would occur later with the new *Code of Canon Law*. The discovery— or rediscovery—of marriage as a covenant was accompanied by other revelations and claims. Among the latter was the thesis that the Council, and subsequently the new code, expanded upon the traditional views on the essence of marriage.

The expanding-essence thesis is perhaps best exemplified in the work of Lawrence G. Wrenn, a prolific and influential canonist. Wrenn's views on marriage and annulment enjoy wide currency in the American canonical community.[23] In general, they may be fairly said to represent, with minor variations here and there, the conventional wisdom among American canonists. Becker, a canonist sharing Wrenn's positions on the covenantal nature of marriage, marital consent, and the message of No. 48, asserts that "It is peacefully accepted at this time that these paragraphs represent on the one hand a distinctly new approach to the canonical considerations of marriage consent, and on the other hand a faithful incorporation of the insights of the Second Vatican Council." Whether the peaceful acceptance Becker proclaims has occurred in the Church universal or is mainly peculiar to the Church in the United States is more problematic than he admits.[24] If Vatican nullity statistics are used as a gauge, the "distinctively new approach" has yet to achieve distinctiveness in much of the Catholic world or in the highest reaches of that world.

Wrenn's *Annulments* and *Decisions*, both published under the auspices of the CLSA, have gone through several editions. Together with his *Procedures*,[25] they serve as standard references for many if not most diocesan marriage tribunals[25] Using C. 1081, 2 of the 1917 *Code of Canon Law* as a baseline, Wrenn informs us that

> until the 1960s, the essence of marriage was considered to be the right to the joining of *bodies*, or more specifically, the right to those acts which are per se for the generation of offspring.
>
> Since the late 60s . . . the essence of marriage has been expanded to include what may be called the right to the joining of *souls*, i.e., the right to spousal communion, a community of life. . . .
>
> [inclusion of] . . . the personal element as well as the physical element was immediately precipitated by . . . *Gaudium et Spes*, which defined marriage as an "intimate partnership of life and love" in which "the partners mutually surrender themselves to each other" . . . and also by the encyclical letter *Humanae Vitae* which said, "through the mutual giving of themselves . . . the spouses seek to attain that communion of persons, by which they perfect one another."[26]

Wrenn's body-count portrayal of the preConciliar conception of marriage comes close to caricaturing what the Church taught long before convening Vatican II crossed John XXIII's mind. While C.1081, 2 in the 1917 code might have served as the narrowest legal test for the existence of a marriage, it certainly did not embody the fullness of the Magisterium's position on the nature of marriage.

It should be superfluous to underscore that assertion by harking back to Saint Paul's enjoinder to Ephesian husbands (Ephesians 5:21–33). The admonition to love their wives as Christ loved the Church and as they loved their very selves encompasses considerably more than the conjugal act. Wrenn's chronology designates the late 1960s as the point at which the essence of marriage came to include the right to the "joining of souls." Supplementation of the physical element by the personal element is credited to *Gaudium et Spes* and *Humanae Vitae*. Wrenn's historiography would have benefited by consulting the words of one of Paul VI's forebears, who instructed the faithful as follows:

> By matrimony . . . the *souls of the contracting parties are joined and knit together more directly and more intimately than their bodies*, and that not by any passing affection of sense or spirit, but by a deliberate and firm act of the will; and from this *union of souls* by God's decree, a *sacred and inviolable bond* arises. Hence the nature of this *contract*, which is proper and peculiar to it alone, makes it entirely different both from the union of animals entered into by blind instinct of nature alone in which neither reason nor free will plays a part, and also from the haphazard unions of men, which are far removed from all true and honorable unions of will and enjoy none of the rights of family life. . . .
>
> [T]he *sacred partnership* of true marriage is constituted by the will of God and the will of man. From God comes the very institution of marriage, the ends for which it was instituted, the laws that govern it, the blessings that flow from it; while man, through generous *surrender* of his own person made to another for the whole span of life, becomes, with the help and co-operation of God, the author of each particular marriage, with the duties and blessings annexed thereto from divine revelation.[27]

These two passages are from *Casti Connubii*. Pius XI's great encyclical appeared more than thirty years before Vatican II was convened, thirty-eight years prior to *Humanae Vitae*, fifty-three years before publication of the revised *Code of Canon Law*. Although Pius XI refers to marriage as a contract, it is abundantly clear that it is an absolutely unique kind of agreement. That matter aside, every last allegedly new departure contemporary canonists cite as having altered or expanded the essence of marriage was articulated, explicitly and eloquently, in *Casti Connubii* The point is made all the more forcefully by quoting another of the encyclical's memorable passages:

> This mutual inward moulding of husband and wife, this determined effort to perfect each other, can in a very real sense . . . be said to be the chief reason

and purpose of matrimony, provided matrimony be looked at not in the restricted sense as instituted for the proper conception and education of the child, but more widely as the blending of life as a whole and the mutual interchange and sharing thereof.[28]

Gaudium et Spes, No. 48 obviously draws heavily on Pius XI's words. It would not be overstatement to consider it a reprise of *Casti Connubii*, which enjoys singular prominence in No. 48's documentation. Moreover, the rest of the documentation scarcely suggests that those who drafted No. 48 were in an innovative frame of mind when they put it together. Besides embodying the legacy of *Casti Connubii*, the text's footnotes are larded with references to Augustine, Aquinas, four Old Testament writers, and ten New Testament passages, including three citations from Ephesians. Apart from a single footnote referring to three sections of *Lumen Gentium*, which say nothing specific about the nature of marriage, every source cited in No. 48 predates Vatican II, often by centuries or even millennia.

Gaudium et Spes, No. 48 is hardly a manifesto for spouses to unite while casting off their legalistic, impersonal chains. Essentially it is a scrupulous reiteration of what had gone before. It may clarify Church teaching on marriage, as the Council Fathers themselves say in No. 47, but it does not proclaim the changes many canonists read into it. One must confess a certain bewilderment at how learned canonists, in their references to *Gaudium et Spes*, seem oblivious to the seminal character and staying power of *Casti Connubii*. Along with other voices from the past, its palpable ties to No. 48 are often glossed over or simply ignored. The encyclical's significance is not limited to mere historical curiosity. Rather, it can fairly be regarded as articulating the very core of No. 48 and authentic contemporary Church teaching on marriage.

Personalism and Interpersonalism

Post–Vatican II Christian marriage, leading American canonists assure us, is seen as essentially "personalist" or "interpersonalist." As Wrenn puts it, "The essence of marriage includes two elements, the *personalist* element, the joining of souls, and the *procreational* element, the joining of bodies . . . :[S]ubstantial ignorance regarding either element can invalidate a marriage."[29] Doyle, writing in an authoritative source, asserts that "The essential concept of marriage proposed by Vatican II is personalist in nature. . . ."[30] As might be expected, the interpretations of marriage minted by such prominent canonists became the coin of the realm for most American diocesan tribunals.

Those not conversant with the occasionally esoteric turns taken by canon lawyers might well ask: When and where has marriage not been personalist or interpersonalist? A sociologist, psychologist, or social psychologist would be astonished to hear anyone venture an analysis of marriage without taking into account its personalist dimension. However, members of those disciplines, unlike canonists and theologians, do not usually concern themselves with essences.

To a behavioral scientist specializing in the study of the family, representing personalism or interpersonalism as a new insight into the essence of marriage is akin to reinventing the wheel, or, like Molière's *bourgeois gentilhomme*, suddenly discovering that one is speaking prose. It would seem that not even the pre–Vatican II Church was unmindful of the personalist element in marriage. More than a century ago Leo XIII spoke thusly: "If, then, we consider the end of the divine institution of marriage, we shall see very clearly that God intended it to be a most fruitful source of *individual benefit* and of public welfare. Not only, in strict truth, was marriage instituted for the propagation of the human race, but also that the *lives of husbands and wives might be made better and brighter*."[31] It may be argued, of course, that Leo XIII's pronouncement relates to the ends, not the essence, of marriage. Still, his words do reveal some awareness of a personalist element in Christian marriage. However that may be, let us examine more recent conceptions of personalism and interpersonalism.

Wrenn cites C. 1096 in support of his view that the personalist component in the essence of marriage is the union of souls.[32] The canon in question reads as follows

> 1. For matrimonial consent to exist, it is necessary that the contracting parties be at least not ignorant of the fact that marriage is a permanent partnership between a man and a woman, ordered to the procreation of children through some form of sexual cooperation.
> 2. This ignorance is not presumed after puberty.

The wording of the statute gives rise to questions about the meaning Wrenn and others glean from it. The phrase *union of souls* does not appear in the canon, though it might arguably be inferred from "permanent partnership." But as examination of *Casti Connubii* shows, the concept of marriage as a union (or communion) of souls did not originate with Vatican II or with the revised code of canon law. Whatever its derivation, however, it is nonetheless debatable whether it is integral to the essence of valid marriage, or more appropriately to the essence of *ideal* marriage. Paul VI's statement that "husband and wife *tend* towards the communion of their beings" does not suggest that the Church requires a "communion of souls" for valid marriage.[33] Tendencies are not essences. Nor does it suggest that spouses have a *right* to a "communion of souls."

Beyond doubt the fusion of two souls in holy matrimony is a splendid, uplifting ideal. Yet it is an ideal exceedingly difficult for couples this side of utopia to live, and just as vexatious for canonists to operationalize. Empirically and juridically, how do we gauge whether a given marriage is truly a "union of souls"? Does it mean that the spouses must be soulmates as well as bedfellows? Must they see eye to eye on most matters, sharing the same values and interests? Must they attend Mass and pray together for a tribunal to rule that canonically the marriage is valid? Similar difficulties obtain when one attempts to operationalize interpersonalism.

The permutations and combinations of thoughts, attitudes, and behaviors that can be symptomatic of the presence or absence of a union of souls approach infinity. Doyle admits as much after reviewing Rotal decisions he finds compatible with the communion of life prerequisite. He concedes that in none of the rulings "does one find an exhaustive and detailed list of the elements essential to the community of the whole of life."[34] He makes reference to Rotal sentences that essay to provide the concept with more content and specificity. But these are almost as ambiguous as the phrase they are supposed to clarify. One of the "most succinct expressions" of the meaning of the capacity for community of life, Doyle believes, is found in a commentator's contention that "It is the will to treat one's spouse as a spouse should be treated."[35] But that appears to be a matter of trying to answer one question by raising another equally imponderable: How should a spouse be treated for the marriage to be considered valid? Moreover, *should* is not synonymous with *must.* There is no "exhaustive and detailed" inventory of the items that that are "essential to the community of the whole of life" because it is humanly impossible to put one together.

Undaunted by Rotal judges' inability to provide a definitive listing of the components that form a community of the whole life, Doyle ventures that in a true covenant marriage the spouses must be capable of fulfilling at least two essential obligations: (1) the heterosexual side of marriage and (2) a "true intertwining of . . . personalities."[36] The first obligation, of course, is as old as Christian marriage. Doyle tries to infuse the second with content by claiming that it includes the capacity to give one's self and accept the other as a distinct person, to be "other-oriented," and to develop an adult personality.[37] In the final analysis, however, the "intertwining of personalities" and "adult personality" are no less difficult to operationalize than communion of life (or souls) At the very least, on the other hand, Doyle's contention that spouses must be other-oriented is considerably more compatible with the idea of Christian marriage than efforts by other canonists to cast interpersonalism in terms of the palpable narcissism of self-theory. Nonetheless, questions remain as to whether it can be deemed a new departure in Church teaching. Although today's more strident feminists would like it excised from the body of Scripture, Saint Paul's instruction to spouses surely refers to what can reasonably be termed an "intertwining of personalities" and to the desirability of being "other-oriented." Similar sentiments are present in many papal commentaries on Christian marriage.

The exchange of selves as an essential obligation of marriage is not peculiar to Doyle. It goes the the core of the interpersonalist version of marriage many canonists find in *Gaudium et Spes*, No. 48. Commenting on the emergence of this view, Egan concedes that the Council Fathers "on more than one occasion referred to marriage as a mutual gift of self by the married; and lest perchance anyone fail to appreciate the patently non-legal character of these references, the Fathers . . . reminded one another over and again . . . that they were not in the Pastoral Constitution speaking in 'juridical' terms or categories."[38] The mutual giving of selves can be accomplished only figuratively, not literally or existentially. Rhetorically, it ties in neatly with the Christian marriage ideal, but the self, unlike a kiss or caress, cannot be actually given or bequeathed to one's spouse. Furthermore, Egan holds, such giving is not essential to valid marriage.[39]

Although *Gaudium et Spes*, as Egan contends, is not expressly juridical, there is no gainsaying the fact that it has juridical consequences. The Council Fathers' pastoral vision is embodied in the new code, and canonists have tried since the Council adjourned to infuse *Gaudium et Spes* with juridical content. The consequences have not always been felicitous. John Paul II, in his January 27, 1997 address to the Rota, confronted this issue in a discussion on the *"juridical effects of the personalist aspects of marriage."*

> ... there still exist symptoms which show a tendency to oppose the personalist aspects to those more properly juridical, without the possibility of a harmonious synthesis: thus, on the one hand, the concept of marriage as a reciprocal gift of the persons would seem to justify a vague doctrinal and jurisprudential tendency to broaden the requirements for capacity of psychological maturity and for the freedom and awareness necessary to contract marriage validly; on the other hand certain applications of the tendency, by bringing out its inherent ambiguities, are rightly perceived as conflicting with the principle of indissolubility, no less firmly stressed by the Magisterium.[40]

Interpersonal relations between spouses involve justice, and therefore have juridical dimension. But the pope counsels that "a priority source for understanding and correctly applying canonical marriage law is the Church's ... Magisterium, which is responsible for authentically interpreting the word of God concerning this reality ..."[41] In other words, efforts to mine *Gaudium et Spes* for legal ramifications, and relate personalist factors to marriage must take place within the context of established Church teaching.

Obviously, developing a checklist of marital referents—behavioral and psychological—for the phrase *communion of life* is a forbidding challenge for learned canonists. That being the case, is it realistic to expect the average couple, unschooled in the fine points of canon law and theology, to know what goes into that standard and what must be done to make their marriage conform to it? In view of the uncertainties surrounding efforts to define what a communion of life really is, it seems chimerical to regard it as an essential obligation of marriage. Would it not be more appropriate to treat it as an inspiring ideal, much like sainthood, rather than as a critical test for valid marital consent? At all events, it seems anomalous to hold that marriages can be nullified for failure to achieve a communion of life when tribunalists themselves are unsure about what that "essential obligation" represents.

Adding to the difficulties that inhere in making communion of life an essential obligation of marriage is the question of retroactive application of that supposedly new teaching. A large though indeterminate number of marriages contracted prior to Vatican II have been annulled by American tribunals. Who has not heard of a wayward middle-aged husband deserting a marriage contracted before Vatican II to take up with a younger woman, obtaining a divorce and annulment, and then remarrying in the Church? A fair assumption would be that at least some annulments of that genre were based on a communion-of-life test which did not exist when those marriages were contracted. To what extent may tribunals licitly rely on a post–Vatican II conception of marriage to invalidate, ex post facto, marriages contracted prior to the Council? Some canonists address this issue by declaring more or less summarily the new code's specifications on valid consent to be manifest dictates of natural law. Thus Mendonça writes that "It is now unanimously acknowledged in doctrine and jurisprudence that the 'incapacity' of canon 1095 is an expression of natural law. Therefore, it is applicable retroactively to any marriage . . . celebrated or contracted before it was inscribed in the 1983 Code. . . ."[42] Mendonça's documentation in support of this claim is impressive, pointing to strong consensus, but appears to fall short of proving unanimity. Natural law, traditionally, is defined as God's law inscribed in the minds and hearts of humans. To a layperson, it seems curious that this natural law principle remained hidden from canonical scrutiny until it was perceived as integral to one of the most problematic portions of the revised code of canon law.

Formidable as providing behavioral referents for it may be, and whatever the questions surrounding retroactive application of newfound norms to older marriages, the real problem with incapacity for communion of life as an authentic test for marital validity cuts more deeply. In many American nullity proceedings the communion of life desideratum is treated as a right to a successful marriage. Ideals do not necessarily become rights by canonical alchemy or fiat. Personal sanctification is an ideal of Christian living, but no one has a right to it. Furthermore, how can there be a right to something when the guardians of that right are incapable of specifying what it consists of? If indeed a "communion of life" is a right, the typical Catholic spouse is unaware of its existence. "Communion of life" is not ordinarily among the explicit terms of the marriage contract to which prospective spouses consciously give their consent. Nonetheless, American tribunals persist in using it as a criterion for the validity of marriages and marital consent. As a consequence, eligibility for nullity grows ever wider.

In fact, C. 1096 deals primarily with the cognitive capabilities of spouses. Do prospective spouses know marriage is a permanent relationship marked by fidelity and oriented toward procreation? In other words, the statute is not concerned with whether a marriage is, experientially, a union of souls or, legally, the right to such a union. What spouses-to-be must comprehend is simultaneously crucial and minimal. Their level of awareness, as the second part of the canon makes clear, requires no canonical or theological sophistication. It is assumed to be present in any reasonably normal postpubescent human being.[43] The cognitive elements of matrimonial consent are well within the grasp of a very broad gamut of human types. They are accessible not only to graduates of Catholic institutions of higher learning, but also to Third World peasant teenagers, high school dropouts, and many whose IQ scores are well below Mensa level. Beyond question those components were known—often well known—to thousands of petitioners granted annulments on grounds of defective consent.

With American tribunals this simple cognitive test is not uncommonly transformed into a compatibility test for marital validity. Instead of focusing on whether the petitioner and respondent actually knew the rudimentary cognitive components of marriage when they exchanged consent, tribunals often direct their attention to facets of the rarely realized ideal—intimacy, effective communication, shared fulfillment, enrichment, self-esteem, and harmony. If marriage is indeed essentially personalist (or interpersonalist), and if the personalist or interpersonalist elements listed above are vital to the communion of souls, the only marriages immune to annulment vulnerability are really hypothetical. Interpersonal difficulties are legion, as much a part of marriage as the titles Mr. and Mrs. For many couples kissing and making up is a marital high, perhaps even a sign of growth toward a new level of connubial bliss. For others the outcome of seemingly trifling differences can lead to one pitched battle after another, and eventually divorce. If petition for annulment follows, the tribunal has virtual carte blanche to find for nullity on the ground that the marriage was not a "communion of life." In effect, incompatibility, once the last vital sign in the life of Hollywood marriages, becomes a leading measure of the validity of Christian marriage.

If the cognitive requirements for valid marriage are so elementary, why the canonical community's preoccupation with the essence of marriage? The reason for their acute concern becomes apparent when we examine the role of the will in relation to marital consent. For ages the Church has taught that the will is engaged in every human act that is not merely visceral or physiological. Presumably the decision to enter marriage falls within that volitional pale. It is the will that moves the individual to consent to what should be a lifetime relationship of fidelity to one's spouse, a relationship permitting sexual behavior open to the conception and rearing of children. The volitional aspect of consent is addressed in C. 1057:

> 1. A marriage is brought into being by the lawfully manifested consent of persons who are legally capable. This consent cannot be supplied by any human power.
> 2. Matrimonial consent is an act of will by which a man and a woman by an irrevocable convenant mutually give and accept one another for the purpose of establishing a marriage.

The will and intellect combine to forge a sacramental decision, ostensibly one well within the capabilities of the overwhelming majority of human beings. But therein lies the rub. If valid matrimonial consent entails awareness of the essence of marriage and the ability to fulfill it in some measure, modifying the essence can attach nullificatory riders to the seemingly simple ground rules. Expanding the essence necessitates spelling out conditions and behaviors indicating whether the new portion of the essence has been honored. Accordingly, those entering marriage must know more, do or avoid doing more, for the union to be certifiably valid. Failure to measure up to the enlarged essence and the manifold rights and obligations it subsumes can indicate lack of due discretion, incapacity, or simulation. In the American tribunal system the invariable result of this sort of tinkering with the nature of marriage is that sacramental marriage becomes less feasible for all but the elect, and annulment is placed within easier reach of those unable or unwilling to measure up to new standards.[44]

❖ 4 ❖

The New Jurisprudence

America's annulment output does not spring solely from the "spirit of Vatican II," the "new pastoralism," suppositions about the essence of marriage, and its return to covenant status. Additional justification derives from the body of appellate court decisions referred to as Rotal jurisprudence. The term *jurisprudence* has more than one meaning. It may refer to the science (or art) or philosophy of law, the study of the structure and principles of legal systems, or the study of the development of judicial decisions and rationales undergirding them. Church jurisprudence pretty much adheres to the third of these meanings. Secular jurisprudence in this day and age concerns itself almost exclusively with positive (human-made) law. Church jurisprudence deals not only with positive law, such as the mandatory retirement age for clerics, but also with divine and natural law. Much effort is expended analyzing and implementing Church doctrines and pronouncements for their legal implications.

Whether civil or ecclesial, jurisprudence gives most of its attention to decisions by appellate courts. The Sacred Roman Rota, practically speaking, is the Church's highest court for marital litigation. The Rota is answerable to the Apostolic Signatura and the Holy Father, though its decisions are seldom appealed to higher authority. Its jurisdiction is not limited to marriage cases, but these constitute the bulk of its docket. It functions in some respects as an ecclesial counterpart to the United States Supreme Court, which, in contrast, almost studiously avoids domestic relations cases. As an appellate tribunal, the Rota has power of *certiorari*, the authority to order cases decided by lower Church courts (i.e., First and Second Instance tribunals) sent up for review. It can rule on whether lesser courts correctly applied the law and adhered to proper procedures. Like the Supreme Court, it is empowered to reverse lower court decisions (sentences) or remand them for further consideration. But parallels between the two courts should not be overdrawn, because they operate within different legal traditions.

The Signatura is at the pinnacle of the Church's pyramidal judicial structure, as that body's full official title—Supreme Tribunal of the Apostolic Signatura—suggests. While C. 1443 designates the Rota as the tribunal for receiving appeals, in some situations the Signatura acts as the highest appellate court. It too is authorized to hear cases involving nullity, as well as recourses against Rotal judgments, and recourses in certain cases the Rota refuses to examine. Recourse, however, is not identical to appeal, though it may have a similar effect. Often it involves seeking legal redress after deadlines for filing an appeal have expired. It is more on the order of reopening and retrying a case instead of simply reviewing it. The Rota must accept appeals properly filed, but can exercise discretion in deciding whether to grant a petition for recourse.

The Church's judiciary may be regarded as consisting of First, Second, and Third Instance tribunals and the Apostolic Signatura. First Instance tribunals are the trial courts for most ordinary process cases and are responsible for attending to chores associated with documentary process cases. Each diocese is supposed to have a First Instance tribunal. Technically, the chief First Instance judge is the bishop himself, though seldom does he actively engage in the processing of cases.[1] The bishop is required to name a judicial vicar (*officialis*) and share with him the power to judge.[2] Other judges with titles such as associate judicial vicar, vice judicial vicar, and adjutant judicial vicar can be appointed to assist the judicial vicar. Second and Third Instance tribunals ordinarily function as appellate courts. In the United States Provincial or Interdiocesan tribunals adjudicate cases at the Second Instance level. Ordinarily the Rota is thought of as the Third Instance tribunal, but it can also serve as tribunal of Second Instance. One striking difference between Church and common-law appellate courts is that the latter rarely function as trial courts. The Rota and Second Instance tribunals, in contrast, are authorized to retry cases previously decided by lower Church tribunals. Appellate courts in both systems can also remand cases appealed from lower tribunals.

A Study in Contrast

Church law and procedure grew out of the *civil-law* system, which owes much to Roman influence. American law and procedure are largely progeny of the English *common-law* system. Civil-law jurisdictions typically organize legal rules into codes, each governing a fairly specific area of human conduct, such as marriage. The laws themselves are mainly statutory, enacted by a ruler or by legislative bodies. Similar agents and bodies are empowered to enact laws in common-law societies, but the courts enjoy a degree of hegemony not shared by their civil-law counterparts. Not only can they overturn statutory law, but their decisions, particularly on the appellate level, become part of the body of law called *case law*. A court's ruling in a particular case may provide a legal principle that will be controlling in similar cases heard at some future time by other courts. In this manner a precedent is established, and other courts in that jurisdiction may be just as beholden, or even more so, to that precedent as they are to rules enacted by legislative bodies. The generally binding character of precedent, like the jury, is peculiar to common-law systems. Occasionally precedents are abandoned in subsequent court actions, but ordinarily the courts are quite circumspect about departing from earlier decisions. The power of precedent flows from the common-law doctrine of *stare decisis*, that is, standing by that which was previously decided. The doctrine is a kind of legal analog to the folk wisdom that warns, "If it ain't broke, don't fix it."

Common law is by nature rather chaotic, its very name born of a state of confusion. When the Normans conquered England they found a society with very few written laws and without a body of national law. One notable vestige of that situation is that England still lacks a written constitution. For centuries after the Battle of Hastings (1066), legal rules remained localized, based on decisions by judges who tried to have them to reflect parochial customs and interests. Eventually, their rulings came to reflect prior actions taken by themselves or other judges. As time wore on, the Crown's control of judges became more centralized. Itinerant judges would be dispatched to various parts of the realm to hear cases. These mobile jurists would make a circuit, as it were, to dispense justice in various parts of the kingdom. That circuit judges still abound in the United States is yet another vestige of the early development of the common-law system. Today, however, they are less likely to be on the road. More often than not, their circuit is circumscribed by the extent of their jurisdiction rather than by a propensity to travel within a specified geographic area. Due in no small measure to the fact that England's traveling judges were appointed by the Crown and therefore sensitive to the king's interests, a fairly uniform set of laws developed for the entire kingdom. Thus, instead of each small community or unit of government being governed solely by its own rules, there were now laws common to everyone, laws often formulated by judges.

Today even so-called common-law societies have statutory laws aplenty. In the United States there are huge bodies of federal, state, and local laws, while the Church has but one set of statutory laws for its governance. To understand the law fully in a common-law system it is theoretically necessary to search through volumes of published appellate court cases as well as the relevant statutes. Case law's coexistence with statutory law does not diminish its significance within the American system. The case-study method of instruction, established at Harvard Law School toward the end of the nineteenth century, continues to dominate legal education in the United States. Law students devote countless hours to studying, analyzing, and discussing appellate court decisions as a means toward becoming familiar with legal reasoning and the development of legal principles.

Church tribunals, including those on the appellate level, operate under a different set of jurisprudential parameters. The boundaries of Rotal authority as well as those of other Church judicial bodies are dealt with in C. 16.

1. Laws are authentically interpreted by the legislator and by that person to whom the legislator entrusts the power of authentic interpretation.

2. An authentic interpretation which is presented by way of a law has the same force as the law itself, and must be promulgated. If it simply declares the sense of words which are certain in themselves, it has retroactive force. If it restricts or extends the law or resolves a doubt, it is not retroactive.

3. On the other hand, an interpretation by way of a court judgement or of an administrative act in a particular case, does not have the force of law. It binds only those persons and affects only those matters for which it was given.

The third section of the canon attests to the inability of the Rota to establish hard-and-fast precedents. Taken in its entirety, the canon shows why the Rota, as opposed to common law appellate courts, does not make law in the strict sense. Nor is it empowered to nullify a Church law or any part of the Magisterium. Unlike the U.S. Supreme Court, which can make law at variance with the wishes of Congress and the president, the Rota must defer to the "Legislator." Within the Church's legal system, the ultimate "Legislator" (as well as chief executive) is the pope, fittingly referred to on occasion as the Supreme Pontiff.

It hardly needs saying that diocesan tribunals as well as the Rota are subject to the authority of the Legislator. The pope delegates power to Church tribunals without abdicating it. Exercise of delegated power must be prudent and faithful. Thus John Paul II cautions that

> In this regard it seems appropriate . . . to recall *some hermeneutical principles*, when they are disregarded, canon law disintegrates and ceases to be such, with dangerous results for the Church's life, for the good of souls, and particularly, for the inviolability of the sacraments instituted by Christ.
>
> If ecclesiastical laws are to be understood first of all 'in accord with the proper meaning of the words considered in their text and context', it would, as a result, be totally arbitrary, even patently illegitimate and gravely culpable, to attribute to the words used by the Legislator, not their 'proper' meaning but one suggested by disciplines different from the canonical one.[3]

The pope, in his reference to other disciplines, probably had theology and behavioral science in mind.

As with America's civil trial courts, Church tribunals examine evidence and testimony in light of the legal rule (or rules) covering the specific case under consideration. The code does not want for statutes dealing directly with marriage. Not counting subclauses, marriage is covered by 112 substantive and 37 procedural canons. Apart from canons related to defective consent, it should seldom be necessary for First Instance tribunals to look to the Rota for direction. Some key canons dealing with defective consent could use more specificity, but they are not as vague as they are made out to be. However, finding ambiguity where none may exist gives reason to consult ostensibly relevant Rotal jurisprudence when it probably could be avoided.

What the Rota did in similar cases is of more than passing interest, to be sure, but not binding, even on the Rota itself. Special notice is supposed to be given to patterns shown in a series of Rota rulings that deal with the same issue or same type of case. Strictly speaking, Rotal interpretations become authentic only when they concur with the mind and will of the pope. Thus, even when the Holy Father delegates authority to the Rota, it does not have license to act with complete autonomy. Rather, its exercise of that authority is valid to the extent that it is consistent with papal views on the matter at issue.

By and large, the Rota concerns itself with particular cases, though its rulings in such cases provide models for lesser tribunals deliberating on similar cases. Ultimately, therefore, "the true authentic interpretation which declares the general meaning of the law for the entire community is reserved to the legislator [i.e., the pope]. . . ."[4] Given the structure of the Church's legal system, the significance of the pope's annual addresses to the Rota cannot be overstated. They represent occasions where the Legislator himself is formally instructing the Rota and lesser Church tribunals in his understanding of the law. One cannot get any closer to the horse's mouth. It is as if James Madison were to rise from the dead to explain to contemporary American jurists what the Founding Fathers had in mind when he wrote the Constitution. If, within the Church, a situation other than a penal matter arises which is not covered by any existing law, the Rota can render a judgment by drawing upon a principle found in the body of general ecclesiastical law, though not necessarily one apparently found in another Rota ruling.[5] But given the scope of Church law on marriage, the need for this type of Rotal action is likely to be restricted to extraordinary circumstances.

A Right Is Born

Comparing Church and common-law legal systems is not idle digression. The comparison is necessary to show how American canonists have manipulated the law to facilitate permissive annulment. They have done this by conferring on selected Rotal cases the level of authoritativeness that American jurisprudents bestow upon landmark Supreme Court decisions. An important example is offered by the canonical community's treatment of *coram* Anné. Wrenn's commentary is almost reverential:

> In a decision of February 25, 1969 . . . which history may regard as the most influential of our century Lucien Anné noted that . . . the essence of marriage includes not only the *biological* element (the right to procreative intercourse) but the *personal* element as well (the right to the community of life). In light of this now generally accepted insight, the phrase "lack of due competence" . . . took on a whole new meaning, and now refers both to the right to procreative intercourse and to the right to a caring, interpersonal relationship.[6]

As noted earlier, the "communion of life" concept of marriage was articulated at least as far back as *Casti Connubii*, thirty-eight years before Anné incorporated it into his sentence. The idea of a "caring, interpersonal relationship" is even older, a reprise of Paul's letter to the Ephesians.

Anné was surely aware of the origin and history of these standards. But that did not dissuade him, a number of other canonists, and not a few theologians from probing *Gaudium et Spes*, No. 48 for new juridic substance. From the vantage point of someone outside the canonical community, that in itself is somewhat difficult to comprehend, given the pastoral, nonlegal thrust of this particular Conciliar document. Nevertheless, Wrenn and many others credit Anné with breaking new ground by speaking of the "communion of life" as a right. It may be argued that he simply enunciated a right long implied in natural law and Church teaching on marriage. Natural law, given to the world at the creation, is "nothing other than the light of understanding placed in us by God; through it we know what we must do and what we must avoid."[7] The divine inspiration behind the enjoinder to do good and avoid evil—the primary principle of the natural law—is practically self-evident. The basic precepts of the natural law are embodied in the Decalogue. Nonetheless, human beings facing moral choices are often confused about what, specifically, is good and evil. The potential for ambiguity increases as one moves from the primary principle to secondary and tertiary principles. The Church, relying mainly on Scripture and conciliar deliberations, attempts to remove the blinders produced by Original Sin. Such efforts apply to canon law. "Where are these rules written," Augustine asks, "if not in the book of that light we call the truth? In it is written every just law; from it the law passes into the heart of the man who does justice, not that it migrates into it, but that it places its imprint on it, like a seal on a ring that passes onto wax, without leaving the ring."[8] Although Augustine and Aquinas wrote extensively on marriage, it may well be that neither penned the final word on the sacrament. Yet it seems unlikely that the implication drawn by Anné eluded them. Nor is it likely that he envisioned that cosmic jurisprudential significance would be conferred on his ruling, foreseeing precisely how his discernment of the right would be amended by the protean "law of unintended consequences" and misused within the American tribunal system. Anné's insight is not shared by all his fellow Rotalists, and it has not yet received an imprimatur from the highest reaches of the Church. Accordingly, the authoritativeness of his view does not extend much beyond the strength of his arguments.

Assertion of a right to the "communion of life" has led to far more questions than answers in marriage jurisprudence. Most fundamentally, solid consensus on the meaning of the expression is absent. For some it is simply a collective term for Augustine's triad of the goods of marriage, an amalgam of fidelity, openness to children, and permanence.[9] Others see it as interchangeable with the idea of an interpersonal relationship. Many, however, regard it as a new addition to Augustine's listing. Seventeen years after Anné the uncertainties had not been dispelled, as seen in a 1986 Rota ruling that "The capacity to assume the duty of a communion of conjugal life, considered in itself, refers to a *number* of essential elements of that communion whether in reference to the genital or sexual relationship or in reference to the interpersonal relationship."[10] Nearly three decades have expired since Anné's discovery, yet the cloud of ambiguity surrounding the communion of life has yet to lift. One Rota sentence granted that "up to this time a clear notion of a communion of life of this kind in its substance has not been handed down."[11] In a more recent decision, a Rotal panel candidly acknowledged the ongoing futility of efforts to endow the right with substantive and juridic content.

> Sometimes the right "to a communion of life" or "to a partnership of life" is placed as an essential right among the terms of canon 1095. No one, however, as far as we know, has ever done any truly scientific analysis of this right in order to demonstrate its substance or autonomous identity. Truly the right in question is properly to be identified as "the right to a communion of *conjugal life*" or to "a *conjugal* partnership of life" and as such it is not other than "the right to marriage." Nothing new is brought to our knowledge when one says, without any further analysis, that such a right is to be exchanged in marital consent. For this is evident: If a communion or partnership of this kind begets some autonomous right it is necessary to explicate the nature of this right clearly. . . . To demand as essential what is not clear does not savor of prudence.[12]

Nor does it savor of sound law.

Whatever the right to the "communion of life" consists of, the extent to which it must be fulfilled to signify validity or invalidity is also a somewhat open question. One Rota decision suggested that the right is given at the time of consent even though the "communion of life" is not realized during the course of the marriage.[13] Within the Rota the prevailing view seems to be that fulfillment and the parties' capacity for it need only be minimal. Whatever the doubts shrouding the meaning and application of the right to a "communion of life", it has undeniably muddled the task of reckoning consent and made it easier for many tribunals to annul. The shift from simplicity to mischievous complexity is succinctly stated by Egan.

> If a male and female can consent to marriage by exchanging a permanent and exclusive right to perform the marriage act, they can marry validly; and there is no point whatever in attempting to complicate the matter by claiming that they must also be able to exchange a right to marriage (nonsense) or even a right to a marriage relationship *which is understood to mean a successful marriage, even if this is never said out loud.* For, while there are things in life which can be effectively obscured through artfully manipulated absurdities and tautologies, marriage in its essentials is not one of them. It is just too common and everyday a reality.[14]

Egan is not explicitly denying the right to a "communion of life," but what many tribunals have made of it: the right to a successful marriage.[15] While it is true that this spurious derivative of the right is not publicly broadcast by its adherents, the annulment statistics tell the story. The American tribunal system has been peerless in manipulating Anné's discovery. Within the system, as now constituted, "communion of life" might just as well be defined as "happy marriage."

Those convinced that Vatican II changed Church teaching on the nature of marriage see Egan's position as inordinately narrow. By focusing on the conjugal act, it excludes or diminishes the interpersonal dimension of marriage. That conception of marriage is now passé, pre–Vatican II, or, worst of all, medieval. But a modicum of reflection shows that the traditional goods of marriage are inseparable from the conjugal acts performed under the mantle of Church teaching. Restricting sex to spouses married to one another is the very meaning of fidelity, and the exclusivity is supposed to endure throughout the marriage. Each act must be open to the possibility of procreation. Plainly, from the Church's standpoint, the conjugal act involves much more than the pleasurable release of sexual urges. Finally, unless spouses are inhuman or subhuman, moved solely by primal instincts, the conjugal act invariably includes behavior that is interpersonal as well as physical and biological.

The singular importance of the conjugal act in the Church's conception of the nature of marriage is seen in the sanctions imposed on Catholics who divorce and remarry outside the Church. They are regarded as being in "a situation that objectively contravenes God's law." They cannot receive communion or "exercise certain ecclesial responsibilities. Reconciliation through the sacrament of penance can be granted only to those who have repented for having violated the sign of the covenant and of fidelity to Christ, and who are *committed to living in complete continence*."[16] Statistically, second marriages are more likely to fail than first marriages. Yet a substantial number feature qualities sadly lacking in previous marriages broken by divorce—fulfillment, intimacy, harmony, communication, enrichment, and so on. In other words, they display the marks of what many canonists associate with the "communion of life." But sanctions on Catholics divorced and remarried without benefit of annulment do not require them to separate, terminating their new-found "communion of life." The Church does ordain, however, that they abstain from the conjugal act. It may be countered, of course, that requiring couples "living in sin" to abandon their "communion of life" would be cruel and impractical, yet the same can be said of prohibiting those in that situation from engaging in sexual activity. Contrary to assertions of many theologians and canonists, the Church, as a result of Vatican II, has not used newly discovered interpersonalism within marriage to downgrade the centrality of the conjugal act in the nature of the sacrament.

Valid marriage requires consent freely given and awareness of the objects of consent. The vagueness surrounding the right to a "communion of life" suggests a fundamental question that may be framed as follows: If learned canonists, toiling in the sometimes ethereal reaches of Church law and theology, are unsure of the meaning of the "communion-of-life," how can ordinary laypersons be expected to know in reasonably full measure that particular clause of the contract they are entering? But the mischief created by the ambiguity that inheres in the "communion of life" standard does not end there. If the very meaning of the right is so hazy, how can diocesan tribunals sensibly use it to reckon the validity of marriage? In sociological terms, how can its presence or absence be operationalized? Behaviors, whether committed or omitted, inimical to a "communion of life" defy accurate tally. They range from divorce and spouse abuse to arguments on whether toilet tissue is properly dispensed over the top or under the bottom of the roll.

The judicial vicar of Duluth, nine years after the Anné ruling, reported using Germain Lesage's enumeration of "concrete elements" to determine whether the right to the "communion of life" was honored. Taken into account were other-directed love, respect for conjugal morality and the spouse's conscience in sexual activity, respect for the spouse's heterosexual personality or "sensitivity," establishing conjugal friendship, joint responsibility for material well-being of the home, moral and psychological responsibility for childbearing and child-rearing, mature personal conduct, self-control or temperance, control of irrational passions or desires that would threaten the relationship, evenness in conduct and the ability to adapt, gentle and kind character and behavior, effective communication, fairness and realism in evaluating the elements that go into conjugal or family life, and lucid choices in setting and realizing goals.[17] No doubt other tribunals use similar compilations. How many of these elements must be lacking before a marriage qualifies for nullity is a question not broached. A marriage with all Lesage's "concrete elements" would truly be a marriage made in heaven. Unless the spouses were bona fide candidates for beatification, it would also be a fiction. That matter aside, the inventory is more germane to compatibility than validity. Duluth's vicar, echoing Anné and Lesage, showed restraint by acknowledging that granting annulments due to "communion of life" failures would not be easy.

Perhaps no American canonist has done more than Wrenn to propagate Anné's "insight" as a signal change in Church teaching on the nature of marriage. Having authored under CLSA auspices several books on annulment that are standard references in most tribunal libraries, his reading of Anné carried much weight. But Wrenn did not lack company in the right-to-a-communion-of-life vanguard. Many other influential canonists, including members of the Rota,[18] effectively assigned landmark significance to Anné's "insight." Within the American canonical guild, that portion of the Anne' decision has been virtually dogmatized as a critical test for the validity of marriage. Canonists toiling in the diocesan tribunals now had a Rota decision with potential as a canonical elixir for annulling marriages.

Egan puts the aftermath of Anné into a pithy and eloquent nutshell. One canonist after another, he notes, writes with unconcealed delight that a "wondrous, new discovery" has occurred "regarding the nature of marriage," to wit, "Whereas theologians and canonists had for centuries held that Titius and Titia consent to conjugal acts on their wedding day, in our more enlightened times we have come to know that to which they actually consent is marriage itself."[19] Flowing from this discovery were theological and jurisprudential conclusions Egan summarizes as follows:

> (1) The "merely physical," "carnal," even "animal" view of marriage which so long stalked the unhappy path of Catholic theological and canonical thinking has at last been abandoned; (2) In its place we are now to admit a more "spiritual," "human," and "personal" understanding of marriage in which the central issue is the relationship between the partners, their mutual fulfillment, "completion," integration, and enrichment; (3) Hence, we are finally in a position to acknowledge that a marriage in which such a relationship has not been achieved or at least could not have been achieved in appropriate measure is invalid and susceptible of being declared such by tribunals of the Roman Catholic Church.[20]

Despite having served on the Rota and taught canon law to Church judges at the Pontifical Gregorian University, Egan is not among the American canonical community's significant others. Rota cases over which he presided do not figure prominently in the documentation or commentaries on Rota jurisprudence by American canonists. Such is the fate of Rotalists ill-disposed toward easy annulment. They are regarded more as mavericks than mainstream jurisprudents.

Actually, Anné was not given full measure by the American canonical community for his historic decision. In their eagerness to anoint the right to a "communion of life" with landmark status, the American canonists shrugged off not only counterarguments but also restrictive caveats advanced by Anné himself. LaDue, for example, maintains that the ruling "is not particularly significant for its resolution of the case, but . . . because of its explanation of marriage as a *consortium totius vitae* and of the juridical implications which flow therefrom."[21] This reading of Anné reflects the pick-and-choose Rota jurisprudence American canonists are inclined to practice. As Anné pointed out, there were other noteworthy juridical implications in his ruling.

> The abnormal conditions of the spouses-to-be that *radically* impede the establishment of any kind of community of conjugal life—so that the elements for establishing it are lacking—are either the *most grave deflection or perversion* of the sexual instinct as, for example, in cases of *full-blown homosexuality* if and insofar as it *extinguishes* the activity of the natural heterosexual instinct, or the abnormal *paranoic perturbation* of the mental faculties or an equal perturbation.
>
> With reference to other cases, the inability of the spouse-to-be to assume the substantial conjugal burdens—except in a case of *true amentia* or *dementia* because of which consent itself is already to be considered invalid—exceeds the ability of judges to define the nullity of a marriage with moral certainty since only God searches hearts and minds. Indeed, the judicial investigation

about the intentions of the spouses-to-be, as in cases of the exclusion of some property of marriage, already turns out to be very difficult. How far more difficult or even impossible would be the judicial investigation of the disharmony of frames of mind and characters because of which one might contend that the spouses-to-be were incapable of establishing a communion of life. The handling of this kind of marriage case would present the picture of the rescission of a marriage rather than the declaration of its nullity.[22]

These cautions are casually shunted aside by American tribunals. The sentence was minimalist to its core, as were other Rota decisions where the right to a "community of life" came into play. The right is narrowly circumscribed. Anné, furthermore, warns that proving prospective spouses incapable of a "communion of life" is quite difficult, infinitely harder than American tribunals subsequently made it out to be. Unlike American tribunalists, Anné insisted that only serious disorders preclude the capacity for the minimal level of "community of life" required for marital validity. It is also interesting how those who wax so enthusiastically over the jurisprudential implications of Anné's pathbreaking decision pass over the fact that the petitioner was denied an annulment. But neither the outcome of the case nor the fact that the respondent was bisexual tempered the pronullity ideological spin American canonists have lavished on the decision.

In the debate over the standing and significance of the right to a "communion of life," two additional considerations are worth pondering. First, while several popes referred to marriage as a "communion of life," no occupant of the Chair of Peter has spoken of it in legal terms or proclaimed it to be a right. Both Paul VI and John Paul II, the only popes to reign for protracted intervals since the Anné decision, issued many statements on marriage without entering this particular doctrinal and jurisprudential thicket. It would be especially interesting for John Paul II to provide clarification. While still an archbishop he drafted *Gaudium et Spes*, the Conciliar document from which Anné mined the right. Second, one searches the new code in vain for mention of the "communion of life", to say nothing of it being enunciated as a right.

"Communion of life" and similar phrases appear in several places in the new *Catechism of the Catholic Church*. It is found in a direct quotation from *Gaudium et Spes*, No. 48, sometimes mentioned in the context of family rather than marriage. Thus, the family is defined (2201) as the "conjugal community . . . established upon the consent of the spouses." One section (1607) refers to the complementarity of the sexes as the "original communion of man and woman." Nowhere in the catechism is the "communion of life" portrayed as a right exchanged at the time of the wedding. Section 1631 does specify that "Marriage introduces one into an ecclesial *order*, and creates rights and duties in the Church between the spouses and towards their children. . . ." That marriage spawns rights and duties is not the same as marriage itself being created by an exchange of rights and duties.

Such considerations, however, received scant attention from the American canonical community. Through resourceful canonical efforts a cautious and rather tentative Rotal statement on Church law and marriage is transformed into what is purportedly an authoritative legal principle. From the right to a "communion of life" the right to a happy marriage is commonly inferred. Default on these rights by either spouse often signals what amounts to a right to an annulment. A single Rota decision and a number of concurring Rota actions have been shaped into a legal instrument alien to the canon law system—a virtually binding precedent. They are accorded places of honor at the jurisprudential table. The inappropriateness of this seating arrangement is incisively addressed by Egan.

> There exists no canonical jurisprudence in the precise and proper sense . . . according to which valid marriage consent requires the exchange of a right to a successful, conjugal, interpersonal relationship, an exchange of the spouses in whole or in part, or any other exchange which is in fact, even if not in expression, the same as one of these. For, no matter whether one holds that in a sufficient number of decisions of a tribunal of the Roman Curia it has been affirmed that any or all of these exchanges are required for a valid marriage, and affirmed over a sufficiently long period of time, it nevertheless remains an "existential" reality that *such affirmations have always been and still are under challenge by other decisions of the same tribunal.*[23]

We have already seen that Egan contends that the only right a couple need exchange to enter valid marriage is the permanent and exclusive right to the conjugal act. Juxtaposing that contention with the passage just quoted, we see Egan challenging three assumptions treated as settled law by most American canonists. First, he implicitly denies there are newly discovered rights, discrete and autonomous, to a "community of life" and an interpersonal relationship, unless those phrases are simply euphemisms for marriage. Those who enter marriage do so "by consenting to something which has never been in doubt among Catholic theologians or canonists, and that something is marriage and nothing else."[24] Second, he rejects the presumption that the right to a successful marriage can derive from the right to a "communion of life." Third, his reference to diverse opinions within the Rota does not square with the claim that Anné's "insight" is "now generally accepted." In fairness to Wrenn and others, the size or locus of the canonical constituency which has embraced the expanded nature of marriage is not usually specified. If the American canonical community is what they have in mind, their words ring true. Wrenn can take much of the credit for having evangelized his fellow canonists. But acceptance is much more tentative or absent elsewhere. As Egan argues, one Rota decision and a number of others following suit doth not necessarily make a body of binding Rotal jurisprudence. Egan's firsthand experience with contrary points of view within Rota chambers suggests that American canonists are selective in their embrace of Rotal jurisprudence. Decisions compatible with the practices of American tribunals are highlighted, while rulings that might disrupt or prohibit what is occurring in America are downplayed or simply passed over.

Enter Case Law

To a considerable degree American canonists have in effect quietly superimposed the case-law model of jurisprudence onto the Church's legal system. There is nothing inherently wrong with case law. Some jurisprudents consider it one of the glories of the American legal system.[25] It is a legal pragmatist's delight, facilitating decision-making when a court faces a case not covered by the Constitution or any known statute. Having sought statutory authority and found none, the court may venture a decision resting on "unwritten" common-law tradition or general standards of equity. Thus the judge creates a law. Later, another court, asked to resolve a similar case, encounters the same constitutional and statutory void. Learning of the earlier case that resembles the one now before him, the judge probes it for a legal principle that can be reasonably applied to the instant case. Stripped to essentials, that is how case law works. It involves reasoning by analogy, looking for legal principles in cases that are partly the same and partly different. In the main, case law has well served the American legal system. It offers a great deal of flexibility, adapting the law to changing conditions in a highly dynamic society and to the juridical commonplace that no two cases are absolutely identical.

But this type of legal reasoning can take bizarre and unpredictable turns. In 1965, Associate Justice William O. Douglas of the U.S. Supreme Court searched for a legal principle to determine the constitutionality of a Connecticut law forbidding the sale, use, and prescription of contraceptives. Much as Anné found in *Gaudium et Spes*, No. 48 a right to the "communion of life" in marriage, Douglas discovered a right to privacy in a "penumbra" emanating from the Fourth Amendment's prohibition against illegal search and seizure. The right Douglas discerned in *Griswold v. Connecticut* to legalize contraceptives was invoked eight years later in *Roe v. Wade* by Harry Blackmun, author of the court's majority opinion, to give legal blessing to abortion, an issue that has rent the body politic ever since. More recently, in 1994, a U.S. District Court judge in Seattle struck down the state's law prohibiting assisted suicide on the ground that it violated the constitutionally guaranteed right to privacy.[26] The ruling was overturned by a three-justice panel of the U. S. Court of Appeals for the 9th Circuit,[27] but later upheld by the same court's justices sitting en banc.[28] The right to privacy is likely to be debated by constitutional scholars well into the next century.

Canonists are quite aware of the possibilities opened by case law intrusions into the canon law system. Brundage, for example, writing in the early 1970s, perceived canonical creativity as an instrument of Church reform. His "creative canonists" could satisfy their appetite for judicial activism in a Church legal system on friendlier terms with case law and precedent. Brundage detected "some signs that such a case law revolution has already begun in canon law," and opined that it "ought not merely . . . be tolerated, but positively . . . encouraged by the framers of the revised code of canon law."[29] Brundage's dreams have come at least partly true, particularly in English-speaking countries. Creative canonism is a veritable defining feature of the American tribunal system. His use of the term *revolution* is quite apt, for what he proposes would radically restructure the Church's legal system.

Several indications of case law's infiltration of the canon-law system in the United States have already been seen. Some Rota actions are crowned de facto with precedent-setting power in a legal system that officially regards precedent askance. What purports to be Rotal jurisprudence is often at variance with the intent and language of the code and even with actual Rotal jurisprudence. As will be shown, case-law techniques also surface in the American tribunal system's administration of canon-law procedures. By amending official Church norms or attaching riders to them, the system often operates under its own set of rules. In the language of the sociology of deviance, there is patterned evasion of papal instructions, "unfriendly" Rota decisions, Signatura directives, and the plain meaning of the code's text. Case-law intrusions already occurring leave little doubt that full-scale transition to case law by the Church would undermine the authority of the Supreme Legislator, the Signatura, and even the Rota itself. Conceivably, that is precisely what is sought. Joining the case law approach to the canon law system would create a juridical counterpart to the Second Magisterium so assiduously pursued by many dissident theologians. Unification would add dramatically to the divisiveness already created by parallel magisterial claims.

Law does not apply itself. That task is in the hands of mere mortals, whether tribunal judges, pastors, or laypersons. While law is supposed to be applied objectively and dispassionately, even the best judges occasionally allow personal predilections to influence the process. In such situations it might be loosely said that the judge makes law. Canon law, by design, is far more resistant to judge-made law than common law. It is also substantially less susceptible to change not statutorily authorized.[30] Although most Church positive law is not immutable, some of it embodies divine and natural law as well as other ageless verities which not even the pope can modify or abrogate. Thus in *Ordinatio Sacerdotalis*, John Paul II declared that "the Church has no authority whatsoever to confer priestly ordination on women and that this judgment is to be definitively held by all the Church's faithful." Further, if Church law is to be amended, a collegiate panel of Rotal judges, randomly chosen, is not the preferred instrument for doing it. With common law, in contrast, even supposedly core legal principles are malleable. American civil appellate courts, employing phrases such as "evolving standards of decency," can make the law mean whatever a simple majority of justices want it to mean. Using Rotal jurisprudence for leverage, American canonists indulge in similar judicial adventurism. As the annulment statistics proclaim, they have developed "evolving standards" of their own, on the subject of matrimonial consent.

One of the great conceits of American canonists is manifested in their nonplussed reactions to Rotal conceptions of defective consent which do not coincide with their own. LaDue, for example, considers it "somewhat surprising that the rotal decisions in the years immediately following the promulgation of

Gaudium et Spes do not seem to have been affected by the council's teaching at all."[31] What is really implied here is that many Rota judges do not share American interpretations and applications of the message of *Gaudium et Spes*. LaDue apparently assumes that the canonically correct position on what the Council taught is the one embraced by a plurality of American canonists. He is by no means the sole American canonist with that mindset.

That nearly seven decades separate the old and new codes of canon law attests to its stability. For those champing at the bit for change such an interval must have seemed like an eternity. The canonical literature appearing between Vatican II and the new code is generously salted with hopes and speculations on changes that the revised code would incorporate.[32] Even before its promulgation, significant shifts from days of yore were being prophesied or read into *Gaudium et Spes*. It was all but a foregone conclusion that many changes already assumed to have occurred would be incorporated into the new code. But even when expectations related to the validity of marriage and indissolubility were not fulfilled statutorily, the tribunals proceeded as if that had really happened. In that vein, John Paul II recently cautioned that "in interpreting the Code currently in force one cannot hypothesize about a break with the past, as if in 1983 there had been a leap into a totally new reality. In fact, the Legislator himself positively and unambiguously asserts the continuity of canonical tradition, particularly where his canons refer to the old law."[33] Since canon law reflects and embodies the Magisterium, the Holy Father's statement implies doctrinal as well as canonical continuity. Thus doctrinal changes imputed to *Gaudium et Spes* might well be delusory, unwarranted attempts to abrogate old teachings still very much in force. John Paul II's words have special relevance for an issue that frequently rears its head in today's Church: the contention that statutes in the 1917 code not repeated in the 1983 revision are ipso facto dead letter this argument was often used to validate the use of altar girls prior to Vatican approval. More relevant to this study, the pope's statement raises serious questions about claims that the new code's specifications on marital consent differ substantially from those in the old code.

Disparate Jurisprudence

Apologists for America's annulment output are wont to maintain that what the tribunals are doing is fully in accord with Rotal jurisprudence. An element of truth dwells in their contention. The right to a "communion of life" was indeed unearthed by a panel of Rotalists and seconded by other Rota tribunals. But as already noted, Rota canonists place a much narrower construction on the right than their American counterparts. However, this is by no means the only way in which American tribunals part company with the Rota on the determination of defective consent. Strong empirical evidence shows that the Rota's Rotal jurisprudence and American Rotal jurisprudence are poles apart on this critical issue. The radical expanse of the gulf is seen in studies of Rotal decisions on American cases conducted by Varvaro and Hettinger. In the first of his two

Table 4–1. First and Second Instance U.S. Ordinary Process
Defective Consent Annulments, 1984–1994

Year	Ordinary process	Defective consent	Percent of total
1984	36,461	35,762	98
1985	37,032	36,803	94
1986	40,117	39,210	98
1987	42,503	41,584	98
1988	41,325	41,039	99
1989	40,685	40,401	99
1990	41,123	40,239	98
1991	43,104	42,051	98
1992	40,676	39,753	98
1993	38,280	37,597	98
1994	38,868	38,969	99
TOTALS	440,174	433,138	98

Sources: Adapted from *Statistical Yearbooks of the Church,* 1984–1994.

studies Varvaro examined forty-seven Rota decisions on cases appealed from
American tribunals between 1980 and 1985.[34] During that interval the Rota
adjudicated forty-seven cases originating in the United States. Varvaro had access to the full text of only twenty-seven sentences, but the outcomes of all
forty-seven cases were available.

Data on defective consent annulments were not available until 1984, when
the Vatican's *Statistical Yearbook of the Church* began specifying in more detail
the various ways annulment proceedings are concluded. CLSA's annual statistical summaries do not give totals for annulments granted, much less those
granted for defective consent. Varvaro considered the "specific grounds" of
nearly all of the forty-seven American cases he examined to be "psychological
in nature."[35]. Using Varvaro's observation and Vatican defective consent figures
since 1984 as yardsticks (Table 4-1), we can reasonably estimate that over 90
percent of Varvaro's cases turned on defective consent. From 1984 to 1994, 98
percent of the ordinary process annulments granted by U.S. tribunals were based
on defective consent. The differences between First and Second Instance totals
are due mainly to time lag. Second Instance tribunals had simply not gotten
around to ratifying all the annulments granted by their First Instance brethren.
The data leave no doubt that during those years defective consent and ordinary
process annulment were practically synonymous.

In forty-two of Varvaro's forty-seven cases the Rota reversed the American
tribunals, upholding the validity of the marriages. Among the five cases where
the Rota affirmed nullity, two involved "lack of form," another impotence.
Given the fact that the forty-four remaining cases were "psychological in nature," the Rota and the American tribunals were at odds in 95 percent of the
cases where grounds were related to defective consent. Four cases involved

marriages annulled after 11–27 years' duration. Commenting on one, which lasted twenty-five years before a petition for nullity was filed, the Rota noted that "It seems almost impossible to conclude with certainty, after many years have lapsed from the celebration of the marriage, when the spouses never approached psychologists or psychiatrists during this time to help them with their difficulties, to conclude that an anomaly of psychic disturbance existed at the time of the celebration of the marriage."[36] American tribunals often try to finesse the problems that inhere in nullifying long-term marriages by using collegiate rather than single-judge tribunals. Although resort to a three-judge panel is supposed to signify more scrupulous adjudication, the change is essentially cosmetic. A multiple-judge court ostensibly lends legitimacy to granting annulments in what should be hard cases. There is no evidence that collegial panels differ from single-judge courts in granting or denying annulments.

Varvaro, updating his earlier study, reports ten of eleven American cases decided in 1986 being reversed, one on procedural grounds. In 1987 the Rota overturned ten of twelve American cases, including a decision involving the rejection of further appeal. Although Varvaro does not indicate the nature of the rejected case, in all likelihood it dealt with an annulment denied.[37] Varvaro's findings were generally replicated by Hettinger's examination of Rota decisions on cases heard in 1986, when eight of ten American annulments granted were overturned.[38] He reports that the Rota reversed all ten of the American cases it heard in 1988, eighteen of twenty in 1991, and nine of ten in 1992.[39] But no matter which set of figures is used to arrive at a combined total for the ten years they examined, at least 92 percent of American defective consent cases reviewed by the Rota were overturned. By any measure that is a stunning rate of reversal. In legal systems throughout the world it is practically unimaginable that trial courts would be overruled on appeal in more than nine of ten cases. So huge a margin of error for civil trial judges would constitute humiliation on a grand scale. The judges would likely be regarded as either incompetent, corrupt, ripe for impeachment, or, if elected, as prime candidates for being voted out of office in the next election.

Approximately 440,000 ordinary process annulments were decreed by American tribunals during the eleven years covered by the Varvaro-Hettinger reviews.[40] The ninety-five (or ninety-six) U.S. defective-consent cases adjudicated by the Rota in those ten years are an infinitesimally small fraction of the total tried by the American tribunals. How confident can we be that so small a sample is representative of hundreds of thousands of defective consent cases? In terms of statistical theory and methodology, sample size is not as critical as representativeness. In general, enlarging a sample adds to its reliability, though a point of diminishing returns can be reached much sooner than most people would expect.[41] Depending on how chosen, huge samples can be notoriously biased, while at the other extreme, theoretically, a sample of one can typify a large universe. For example, Consumers Union, which publishes *Consumer Reports*, purchases a single automobile to rate tens of thousands of similar models produced by the same manufacturer. The magazine's ratings are taken quite seriously by consumers and manufacturers alike.

It may be argued, of course, that marital consent cases where the Rota denies that nullity is proven are atypical, or that occasional mistakes are bound to happen when tribunals are adjudicating about forty thousand cases a year. A persuasive rebuttal, far more compatible with the evidence, is that the only significant difference between American decrees of nullity voided on appeal or by recourse and nearly all allowed to stand is that the former were scrutinized by the Rota. If the cases surveyed by Varvaro and Hettinger are even crudely representative of all cases adjudicated by American tribunals, we can safely conclude that an immense gap exists between Rota rulings and the Rotal jurisprudence American tribunalists employ to nullify marriages.

Let us put the disparity into more specific quantitative terms. Between 1984 and 1994, American First and Second Instance tribunals granted 440,174 ordinary process annulments (see Table 1.1, p. 4). We know that 98 percent (433,138) of those annulments were based on defective consent. In recent years the Rota has been deciding about two hundred cases a year. But let us assume that the Rota, by some providential stroke, reviewed all 433,138 defective consent annulments decreed by U.S. tribunals. The Varvaro-Hettinger reviews of Rota decisions on American defective consent cases show that at least 92 percent of them are overturned. It is worth stressing here that the 92 percent reversal rate was not a statistical fluke, based on examination of Rota decisions during a few freakish years. Rather, it was obtained by reviewing the Rota's performance in ten of twelve recent years. Applying the 92 percent reversal rate only to defective consent annulments granted from 1984 to 1994 means that a staggering 398,847 of them should never have occurred. If ever figures could be said to speak for themselves, this would be a historic example. Is it any wonder that the sacrament and institution of marriage are thought by some to be in mortal danger?

Once one of the most loyal and orthodox precincts, the Church in Holland has become a hotbed of dissent. Departures from the Magisterium abound in the infamous Dutch Catechism. The postConciliar Dutch Church is to Rome what the pesky Corinthians were to Saint Paul. Even before the Dutch condoned putting the terminally ill out of their misery, their tribunals were practicing canonical euthanasia on marriages. In a letter dated December 30, 1971 the bishops of Holland were sternly reprimanded by the Apostolic Signatura for what was occurring in their tribunals. The bones of contention included: (1) regarding the "indissoluble unity of marriage sanctioned by Christ" as "the ideal" rather than the norm; (2) viewing marital consent as a process, not as something conferred at the time of the wedding; (3) treating annulment as though it is the spouses themselves "who can establish by their own judgment if the marriage was valid because it was happy or else null or dissolved because it ended in failure"; (4) misuse of psychology to determine incapacity for interpersonal relationships; and (5) superficial pastoral concern which "completely lacks any theological foundation and is more concerned with aid, in one fashion or another, to human situations rather than with conserving the revealed Faith."[42] The Signatura's closing remarks are quite pointed.

It is clear that a particular or local church cannot act in a manner contrary to the procedure and doctrine of the universal Church, taking account only of the particular church. The one holy catholic and apostolic Church is made present in the life and activity of all particular churches. Even where a certain pluralism is admitted, there remain essential points in which it is not permitted for any particular church to separate itself from the universal Church and from the other particular churches. . . .

[T]he [Dutch tribunal] judges themselves recognize that their judgments are accepted with difficulty in other regions. In their own country, they are challenged by certain of the faithful who are scandalized to see with what audacity even fundamental rights are wronged. . . .

[W]here a judge should refuse to conform, he ought to be dismissed from his charge by a competent authority . . . and the task of administering justice should be given without delay to a more proven man.[43]

The Signatura's 1971 critique of conditions in Holland would lose little relevance if, a quarter-century later, it was addressed to the American hierarchy and canonical community.

Varvaro, commenting on the results of his second survey, makes some remarkable revelations that could also raise Signatura eyebrows.

One can easily conclude . . . that the Roman Rota does not appear to be very supportive of United States cases which reach that high level of adjudication and does not easily decide in favor of the nullity of the marriage based on *our jurisprudence*. I still remain convinced that we must continue to present our cases to the Rota for further consideration provided that they are procedurally correct so that they will have to address the substantive issues we have experienced in our own deliberations.[44]

Varvaro's candor is commendable. For all intents and purposes he acknowledges that despite ritual homage paid Rotal jurisprudence by American canonists, their version of it is significantly different from the Rota's in the area of marital consent. In that vein, it is refreshing to find a respected American canonist who openly admits that he and his confreres live and function in their own jurisprudential world. Yet his frankness also betrays troubling hubris. What can be ascribed to the legal reach of "our jurisprudence"? A potent force within the reaches of the American tribunal system, Yankee jurisprudence has infiltrated other English-speaking societies. But within the remainder of the Church universal, especially in Rome, its authenticity and legality is not highly valued. To say that a 92 percent reversal rate by the Rota "does not appear to be very supportive" minimizes the intensity and scope of the highest marriage court's jurisprudential rebukes. Yet Varvaro's implies that American canonists should persist in their efforts to convert the Rota from the error of its ways. The jurisprudential impasse with the Rota evokes an expression, much in vogue these days, that captures the situation of American canonists: they just don't get it.

❖ 5 ❖

Psychologizing Annulment

Perhaps no modern society is more thoroughly smitten with psychology than the United States. A society that prizes individualism and the discipline that specializes in the study and treatment of individual behavior were made for each other. Psychology's influence runs broad and deep. Psychologists pontificate with total aplomb on innumerable facets of human behavior. Their pronouncements are taken quite seriously, despite frequent gaping chasms between what they say and what they really know.[1] Psychotherapy ("talk-therapy") has tapered off in popularity in recent years, but counseling is a leading growth industry, surprisingly resistant to vagaries of the business cycle. Recourse to therapy in one form or another was given a huge boost when state agencies and private insurance companies mandated or widened eligibility for treatment. Simultaneously the number of personal problems considered amenable to psychological intervention seemed to grow grew relentlessly.

The days of public and private largess may have peaked, however. Andrews reports that, beginning in the 1990s, cost-containment measures have created unprecedented economic disruption in the mental-health industry.[2] Health Maintenance Organizations are no longer as willing to foot the bill for protracted talk-therapy by psychiatrists, psychoanalysts, and clinical psychologists. Retrenchment reduced the income of many therapists, especially those in the upper echelons of the profession. The median income of psychiatrists has fallen to the level of general practitioners. Many in the profession have moved from talk-therapy to medicalized practice, particularly psychopharmacology, which relies more on medication than doctor-patient interaction. Some have reacted to the shortfall by taking on more substance-abuse cases, where earlier funding levels have been sustained or increased.

The economic downturn, while forcing some therapists to reduce caseloads and fees, has not led to a corresponding decrease in the public's appetite for psychology. In what Andrews considers an extraordinary turn of events, religious organizations have taken up much of the slack by offering psychological as well as spiritual counseling.[3] Actually, these two approaches to mental health have been intertwined for some time, a necessary effect of the psychologization of religion. Even if religious organizations had not filled the breech, the therapy industry would not want for clientele. Media talk shows are low level forms of group therapy. Newspaper advice columnists and similar media types assiduously promote counseling for the lovelorn and forlorn. They may account for more counseling referrals than telephone directory listings. Therapists are as common at scenes of tragedy as ambulances and paramedics. Grief counselors often arrive at disaster sites before personal-injury lawyers. Once the private reserve of priests, ministers, rabbis, family, and friends, consolation and commiseration have lost ground to the ministrations of psychological experts. Throughout the educational system, psychological theory animates textbooks, lesson plans, and teacher-student relationships. The National Defense Education Act, passed in 1958, created sixty thousand positions for school guidance counselors. Hardly an American alive has not been subjected to psychological tests that purport to measure such phenomena as intelligence, job fitness, mental disorders, and aptitude for college or graduate and professional training. Support groups, offering therapy for the masses, are legion.[4]

Religion-sponsored therapy and therapists as grief counselors merely touch on the extent to which religion and psychology have melded. Some scholars see psychology functioning as religion, others as actually supplanting it[5]. At many seminaries pastoral psychology is as requisite as theology. Depending on the priest, confession may be structured as a therapy session rather than a mere recitation of sins and plea for absolution.[6] The penitent is more client than sinner. Where priests of yore thought in terms of saving souls, many are now primarily concerned with "healing." Not unexpectedly, in a society awash in psychology, the tribunal system did not escape its influence. The assumption that *Gaudium et Spes*, No. 48 modified the essence of marriage by adding a personalist component offered a wide opening for psychological intervention. "Personalism," of course, is practically a synonym for the formal object of general psychology.

Canonists and Behavior Science

PostConciliar canonical discourse is generously larded with references to behavioral science. On closer inspection, it becomes evident that when canonists talk of behavioral science they almost invariably have psychology in mind, especially psychiatry and abnormal or clinical psychology. The other behavioral sciences—anthropology, economics, and sociology—are largely disregarded. But even when behavioral science is narrowed to—if not equated with—psychology, there is singular absence of specificity. The extraordinary diversity within the psychological community is blithely ignored. The unsuspecting may be led to believe that tribunals have at their fingertips the principles and research findings of hard science. Psychology is a house with mansions galore, the scientific claims of its specializations ranging from probative to provocative to pretentious. If the field as now constituted were to be stratified according to scientific purity, biological, molecular, and experimental psychology would be at the top. Since Vatican II there have been spectacular developments in hard behavioral science, particularly in cognitive psychology and molecular biology. Toward the other extreme, any number of the field's branches compete for marginal scientific respectability.

Tribunals do not ordinarily rely on members of the rigorously scientific branches of psychology for consultation. There have been no published reports of tribunals contracting for the services of cognitive psychologists or molecular biologists to ascertain the quality of marital consent. Mental-health experts retained for that purpose are usually members of the "helping professions"—psychiatrists, clinical psychologists, counselors, or even social workers. Psychiatrists, to be sure, receive intensive scientific training in medical school, but if they practice as talk-therapists the very nature of their work inclines them toward soft science. That inclination is even more pronounced among clinical psychologists and counselors, especially those of humanistic persuasion. Many of the latter openly disavow the hard science approach to psychology, relying instead on clinical experiences, impressions, and intuition.[7] At present, they form the dominant wing of the helping professions. Asked about the quality of graduate training in psychology, a former president of the American Psychological Association's clinical psychology division responded that "One of the fundamental problems is that I don't think we are graduating thousands of psychologists. We are graduating thousands and thousands of practitioners who are peripherally acquainted with the discipline of psychology."[8] Membership figures for the American Psychological Association lend support to his assessment. Of approximately eighteen thousand members in 1959, 14 percent claimed special competence in clinical or counseling psychology. Within thirty years 59 percent of sixty thousand members allied themselves with those specialties.[9] The general public tends to assume that every professional doing psychology is ipso facto a scientist, and the canonical community appears to follow suit. But much of what passes for the psychological analysis of marital consent is not based on meticulous research.

Time and again defenders of America's outpouring of defective consent annulments contend that it was made possible not simply by behavioral science but by *advances* in behavioral science. Despite a comprehensive though admittedly not exhaustive search of the canonical literature in English, I did not come upon a solitary bona fide identifiable advance, recognized as such within psychology, which bears directly on the issue of defective consent. In the voluminous annulment literature, passing references are occasionally made to acknowledged titans in the fields of psychology and psychiatry. But in these rare instances it is never shown, with any depth and specificity, how the theories and research of figures such as Freud, Jung, Adler, Erikson, Frankl, Watson, and Skinner relate to determining the quality of matrimonial consent. When a prominent psychiatrist or psychologist is cited, it typically amounts to little more than canonical name-dropping. To paraphrase of a remark by the late legal scholar-anthropologist Karl Llewellyn: Whenever canon lawyers speak of new departures in the behavioral sciences, they are usually referring to unspecified "advances" made by unspecified somebodies, in unspecified directions for reasons that are unclear.[10] The paucity of references to developments with even a semblance of breakthrough status vis-à-vis defective consent does not deter canonists, however, from claiming significant ties between the annulment process and psychology.

Among tribunals in the United States, probably the most systematic reliance on psychology is found in the tribunal serving the archdiocese of Hartford. ordinary process cases in Hartford are routinely examined by a panel of psychologists. Not surprisingly, Wrenn, the Hartford tribunal's leading light, evinces high regard for what psychology can contribute to tribunal deliberations. The can be seen in the latest edition of *Annulments*, where Wrenn argues that C. 1055, 1 of the new code added a fourth element to the essence of marriage— the well-being of the spouses (*bonum coniugum*)—to the traditional three: fidelity, permanence, and openness to children. He later adds the qualification that he means the *right* to spousal well-being rather than *bonum coniugum* itself is proper to the essence of marriage.[11] That claim is debatable, as we saw in the preceding chapter, and need not concern us now. Our interest lies with his use of psychology. Suffice it to say here that *bonum coniugum* is no easier to operationalize than communion of life. Conceding that obstacle, Wrenn seeks help from several sources, including Aquinas. The most important modern psychologist Wrenn turns to is Rollo May, a humanistic psychologist who theorizes on self from an existential perspective.[12] In the pantheon of self-theory May belongs with such luminaries as Erich Fromm, Carl Rogers, and Abraham Maslow. The school of thought they developed has many disciples in the helping professions. It influences such therapeutic approaches as transactional analysis, encounter groups, est, and assertiveness training. Self theory, as might be expected, plays a major role in therapies that focus on self-awareness, self-actualization, self-help, self-realization, self-esteem, self-fulfillment, self-expression, intimacy, feelings, and "becoming." Perhaps the most recent addition to this list is self-forgiveness, a concept with potentially profound implications for the sacrament of penance. This school of thought has no doubt contributed to the preoccupation with self many find so salient in American culture.[13]

How the ideas of humanistic self-theorists can be relevant to determining grounds for annulment is something of a mystery. Rarely is it mentioned that their multifaceted approach to the self seems not to extend to self-denial, a *sine qua non* of authentic Christian life and marriage. Truth be told, no prominent self-theorist is favorably disposed toward organized religion. Generally speaking, religion's influence on the psyche is considered essentially deleterious. It contributes to personal malaise, mainly through its power to inhibit freedom, assign blame, and engender feelings of guilt.[14]

Self-theory tenets undergird many assumptions held dear by contemporary marriage counselors. Self-esteem, effective communication between spouses, especially with respect to expressing feelings, and intimacy, are routinely set forth as hallmarks of successful marriage. That may well be the case. However, successful marriage cannot be equated with valid marriage. A "lack of form" marriage considered idyllic by counseling is nonetheless canonically invalid, while a marriage entered with Church approval that later comes apart might well be altogether valid. Similarly, qualities such as self-revelation might contribute to the mutual psychological well-being of spouses. It does not follow, however, as Wrenn and others propose, that they are truly essential obligations of marriage as conceived by the Church, or litmus tests for the validity of marriage. Self-revelation, it should be added, is a two-edged sword. It can enhance compatibility in some marriages but weaken or destroy the harmony of others. Much depends on which portions of the soul are bared and how one's spouse responds to the disclosures. With many marriages revelation of the innermost workings of the soul is prudently reserved for the confessional or for private dialog with the Lord. Apart from its questionable relevance for marital consent, self-theory as science is low on the behavioral-science totem pole. There are psychology departments at major universities where humanistic and experimental psychologists, operating in their respective academic fiefdoms, are barely on speaking terms.

None of this is meant to deny the real need to draw on behavioral science in efforts to gauge matrimonial consent. But canonists' use of the massive body of psychological theory and research has been generally superficial and tendentious. One upshot of this state of affairs is that phantom changes in Church teaching and law are wedded to phantom advances in behavioral science. This, in turn, is responsible for relegating untold but substantial numbers of valid marriages to phantom status.

Generally speaking, tribunals seldom need to probe the psyche to decide documentary process cases. The forces leading baptized Catholics to marry outside the Church, for example, are catechetically but not canonically relevant. In the Church's scheme of things, intellect and will guide human behavior, playing especially critical roles in the exchange of marital consent. This presents a problem for canonists who rely heavily on advances in behavioral science. Precious few hard behavioral scientists advert to the existence of willed behavior. The deterministic postulates of hard behavioral science notwithstanding, however, for valid marriage to occur there must be free and informed exchange of consent. Consent becomes defective in four general ways. It is improper when there is (1) ignorance of the essential properties of marriage; (2) willful refusal to accept one or more of those properties; (3) a serious psychological disorder rendering one or both parties incapable of free and informed consent; and (4) some external agent or condition that vitiates free and informed consent, even though neither party is psychologically incapable of exercising it.

Some thirteen canons in the new code deal specifically with matrimonial consent. The entry at the head of that chapter of the code, C. 1095, is first in far more important ways than order of appearance. By any measure it is the statutory foundation for the overwhelming majority of ordinary process annulments granted by American tribunals. Put another way, it accounts for approximately two thirds of all decrees of nullity issued by the tribunal system. C. 1096 is an important defining statute, specifying what those entering marriage must know. For reasons that should be self-evident, Cs. 1095 and 1096 require fuller discussion and will therefore be treated in more detail below.

The remaining canons account for relatively few annulments, but in the interest of thoroughness they are briefly listed here. Cs. 1097–1107 concern error in one way or another. Error about a person but not about a quality of that person can render a marriage invalid if the quality is directly and principally intended.[15] An example would be a case where an individual mistakenly marries a twin of the person chosen for marriage. Invalidating error can occur when consent is obtained by deliberate deceit, if the party deceived is unaware of having been manipulated into marriage.[16] Error on the essential properties of marriage impairs consent if it moves the will to enter a marriage devoid of those properties.[17] Simply knowing or believing that a marriage is invalid does not necessarily rule out marital consent.[18] Internal consent is presumed to concur with the words or signs of the marriage ceremony. But if it can be shown that in spite of the appropriate words or signs there was wilful rejection of some essential aspect of marriage, the consent would be regarded as "simulated" and therefore invalid.[19] Consent based on a future condition is invalid; consent based on some past or present condition is valid only with the local bishop's approval.[20] Consent is invalid if it is plainly the result of external force of fear of such magnitude that one must enter marriage to escape the force or fear in question.[21] Ordinarily the contracting parties must be present at the same time when consent is exchanged and express their consent in words or appropriate signs. Under some circumstances marriage can be entered into by proxy.[22] An interpreter may be used to convey consent, but only if the priest witnessing the marriage is assured that the interpreter is trustworthy.[23] Consent given to an invalid marriage is presumed to persist until revocation of that consent is proved.[24] Cs. 1097–1107 can scarcely be regarded as loopholes. If anything, they enumerate and narrowly circumscribe ways in which error invalidates marital consent. The strictures they impose make C. 1095 all the more inviting as the favored instrument for nullity.

Since proper exchange of consent is absolutely essential to making a valid marriage,[25] proponents of more permissive annulment correctly perceived it as the cornerstone in need of loosening. The older parameters governing defective consent did not meet the new pastoral imperatives for healing those victims of failed marriages wishing to give marriage another try or already in a subsequent marriage. An updated model for consent became a vital need. Several components were already in stock—the revisionist conception of the nature of marriage, the "new pastoralism," and the American strain of Rotal jurisprudence. Particularly useful was the assumption that the Church, in *Gaudium et Spes*, had finally proclaimed Christian marriage as essentially "personalist" or "interpersonalist." That assumption, along with a more nebulous version of valid marital consent, all but dictated the enlistment of behavioral science to augment the emergent perspective on valid marriage. In this way, tribunal deliberations would be modernized and decrees of nullity given an aura of scientific certitude.

The Loose Canon

It is beyond dispute that C. 1095 is responsible for the vast majority of defective consent annulments granted by American tribunals. During its relatively short life this canon has not only been the most important statutory basis for annulment on psychological grounds, but also one of the most controversial statutes in the history of canon law. Here is what the canon says:

> The following are incapable of *contracting* marriage:
> 1. those who lack sufficient use of reason;
> 2. those who suffer from *grave* lack of discretionary judgement concerning the *essential* matrimonial rights and obligations to be mutually given and accepted;
> 3. those who, because of causes of a psychological nature are unable to to assume the *essential* obligations of marriage.[26]

At the risk of belaboring the point made earlier, let it be noted that the canon does not refer to incapacity for "covenanting" a marriage. It relates to marital consent considered defective or invalid because at least one of the parties simply lacks the necessary wherewithal to enter Christian marriage.

C. 1095's first subsection, for obvious reasons, accounts for very few annulments. Those permanently lacking sufficient use of reason rarely marry. Severely retarded persons are often institutionalized or, if not, excluded from the pool of eligible spouses by prevailing American mate-selection patterns. Borderline intelligence need not be a disqualifying condition. Notwithstanding efforts by some canonists to add layers of complexity to the rights, duties, and properties of marriage, there really is not that much one must know and will to enter a valid union. The statute may also be applied to those whose absence of sufficient reason is only temporary. An example would be a groom still so inebriated from the previous night's bachelor's party that he is out of touch with reality throughout the wedding ceremony. In short, C. 1095, 1 covers relatively objective situations in terms of marital consent.

American civil lawyers refer to some laws as bright-line rules. They are clear, understandable, and rather easy to apply to the average case they are designed to cover. They are comprehensive, covering nearly all relevant cases, and objective, so different judges can be expected to make the same rulings. Bright-line rules make court actions predictable, enabling judges to focus on cases that are not mainstream and keep ordinary cases from going to trial. The language of subsections 2 and 3 in C. 1095 falls considerably short of meeting the criteria for a generally trouble-free, bright-line statute.

The Holy Father himself is said to have remanded the proposed C. 1095 to its drafters several times, apparently anticipating the ease with which imaginative canonists could find loopholes for decrees of nullity. Conceding that the canon had been "necessarily formulated in a generic way" and awaiting "further determination," he noted that "qualified jurisprudence of the Rota" could contribute to its clarification and proper application.[27] As later developments would show, particularly in tribunals in English-speaking countries, his initial fears were not groundless and his hopes for reduction in the vagueness that inheres in sections 2 and 3 perhaps a bit too sanguine. The Rota, assisted by papal allocutions, has labored mightily to provide the sections with more precise legal content. Yet not even the distinguished canonists on the Church's highest marriage court speak with one voice on the troublesome portions of the canon. While they inch toward broader jurisprudential consensus on how the statutes should be interpreted, they are never likely to elevate them to bright-line status. Uncertainty surrounding C. 1095 is inevitable as long as its applications depend on the psychology of mental disorders, an area of study notoriously subjective and volatile. Rota efforts to imbue *Gaudium et Spes* with juridic content are almost child's play compared to casting the psychology of abnormal behavior into legal terms. Nonetheless, the Rota's approach to the canon is more narrowly and cogently structured than the approach prevailing in the American tribunal system.

Tribunals in the United States have exploited the ambiguities of "lack of due discretion" and "lack of due competence" to invalidate hundreds of thousands of marriages. Such wholesale production of decrees of nullity could hardly have been intended by the statute's framers. Nor can it be reconciled with the Rota's cautious efforts to distill from the canon fairly cogent, standardized legal principles that embody authentic Church doctrine and the wishes of the Supreme Legislator. As shown in our discussion of Rotal jurisprudence, there is evidence that over 90 percent of American defective-consent annulments are, by Rota standards, probably objectively valid. The evidence, furthermore, suggests a curious irony: canonists acutely sensitive to the pervasive "spirit of Vatican II" are less discerning of the "spirit of 1095," a spirit embracing Christ's enjoinder against divorce and remarriage and the subsequent incorporation of that teaching in Church tradition. As statements by the Holy Father and Rota rulings attest, the spirit of the canon hardly sanctions its use as a fulcrum for mass annulment. In their rush to annul, American tribunals have lost sight of the doctrinal forest for the pastoral trees.

Overidealizing Marriage

If indeed the Church's position on the nature of marriage has taken a new turn, familiarity with the change is limited to theologians, canonists, and a handful of lay scholars. By and large, the laity is not privy to what had occurred. The new catechism deals at length with the sacrament of marriage but does not announce any substantial modifications on the nature of marriage and eligibility for annulment. Precious few couples, whether already married or planning to be, were alert to postConciliar revisions alleged to have occurred in the terms of the marriage contract. The typical couple, at the moment of the exchange of consent, believed that they were taking one another to have and to hold, from that day forward, for better, for worse, for richer, for poorer, in sickness and in health, till death did them part.

The language of nuptial vows may have varied from one ceremony to another, but the sentiments were much the same. Now, however, the contractants, past or present, risk being parties to an agreement with hidden clauses. The covert provisions might be discovered by studying canonical literature, hiring a canon lawyer, or involvement in an annulment proceeding. I have not heard of any premarital instruction program telling participants that they will be exchanging the right to a "communion of life," or that failure to achieve a "communion of life" might negate the validity of a marriage. Personal research and expert assistance might be preliminary necessities for signatories to a complicated business transaction, but such measures are inappropriate for doing what countless Catholics have done over the centuries: entering a valid marriage contract. Even if the postConciliar modification of the nature of marriage is taken as authentic, settled law, the change cannot be taken to transform marriage from what Egan terms a "magnificent commonplace" into a "casuistic oddity."

The machinations of American tribunals have placed valid Christian marriage on an almost Olympian pedestal. Inordinate idealization of Christian marriage is an all-but-inevitable consequence of the evolving criteria for matrimonial consent. The average married couple would be surprised to learn that the vows they exchanged did not have to be taken literally. Special grace would be needed to achieve a "communion of life" impervious to tribunal executioners. Divorce, practically speaking, has for the tribunals already become a kind of weather vane pointing toward misdirection in the infusion of grace, signifying marriage falling short of the ideal. It is seen as a veritable smoking canonical gun, showing beyond reasonable doubt either lack of due discretion or lack of due competence when the marriage was contracted. The canonical community has idealized marriage to a Calvinistic juncture whereby only the "elect" are capable of valid marriage.

John Paul II, in one of several commentaries on misapplications of C. 1095, was moved to observe that "another and not infrequent source of misunderstanding in the evaluation of psychopathological cases . . . arises not from an exaggeration of the extent of the illness but . . . from an unjustified overvaluing of the concept of capacity to contract marriage. . . . [T]he misunderstanding can arise from the fact that the expert declares that a party is incapable of contracting marriage while referring not to the minimum capacity sufficient for valid consent, but rather to the ideal of full maturity in relation to happy married life."[28] In more pedestrian terms, when reckoning the validity of consent, tribunals frequently confuse what marriage is with what it ought to be. This is accompanied by a tendency to infuse marital rights and obligations with a variety of supplemental normative expectations that extend the reach of apparent incapacity.

Operationalizing the Ideal

We see this idealizing tendency in Wrenn's attempt to define essential obligations of "personalist" marriage, deemed so because they refer to traits and behavior necessary to "sustain the marital partnership." These obligations are:

> *Self-revelation*—a psychological state wherein "a person must first of all enjoy a basic ego identity, i.e. he must see himself as one fairly consistent person, have a reasonable degree of respect for that person, and convey a knowledge of himself to his spouse."

> *Understanding*—a person must see his spouse as a separate person, and appreciate her way of feeling and thinking, without distorting it excessively by his own attitudes, needs or insecurities.

> *Loving*—a person must be capable of being a loving person to his spouse, i.e he must be able to give to his spouse and receive from her an affection that bonds them as a couple. [29]

Wrenn's "essential obligations," adapted from psychologist Eugene C. Kennedy's thoughts on marriage, are "the basic practical skills one must enjoy in order to enter a stable, intimate relationship."[30] It is incumbent upon the tribunal, with the assistance of an expert, to examine pre-and postmarital behavior. If the judge concludes that "the person *did not fulfill* essential responsibilies and indeed *could not,*" it is then ruled that "the person was unable to assume those obligations, since it is axiomatic that one cannot assume what one cannot *fulfill.*"[31]

Wrenn's scheme is problematic in a number of ways. First, the personalist "essential obligations" he lists do not appear in C. 1095. Nor are they present in the following canon, which specifies that those contracting marriage simply must know that it is a permanent partnership "ordered to the procreation of children through some form of sexual cooperation." Second, the authenticity of Wrenn's "essential obligations" turns on his interpretation of C. 1055. But that canon deals with the nature of marriage, while C. 1095 relates to the mechanics of consent. Third, when Wrenn essays to operationalize his essential obligations, he faces the same formidable obstacles as those who try to articulate the "communion of life" in behavioral terms. As we saw, even Rotalists who write approvingly of the communion of life acknowledge that it is very difficult to translate into specific behaviors. Wrenn's venture into this shadowy area reads more like a helpful if platitudinous set of guidelines to be dispensed by marriage counselors than doctrinal and canonical imperatives. Essential obligations of that genre give tribunals still greater maneuverability for finding marital consent wanting. Fourth, "self-revelation" is more attuned to tenets of self-theory and counseling than Church teaching on marriage. Fifth, Wrenn, to his credit, concedes that his essential obligations need not be manifested in the behavior of the spouses. Rather, they must have the capacity to perform them. That being the case, those who lack the capacity to engage in "self-revelation," "understanding," and "loving" and to "exchange the perpetual right to them" cannot be parties to valid marriage.[32] But anyone utterly lacking in these capabilities would have to be practically inhuman or in the throes of a serious mental disorder. Thus, except as ideals, Wrenn's standards for incapacity have little relevance for the overwhelming majority of spouses involved in annulment proceedings where the grounds preferred are psychological. Finally, in practice tribunals are inclined to equate "did not" with "could not."

Wrenn correctly notes that the language of C. 1095, 3 is quite broad, stating that "causes of a psychological nature" can preclude assumption of the essential obligations of marriage and render consent defective. He is disposed to confuse correlates with causes, notwithstanding the fundamental behavioral science axiom, "Correlation does not necessarily mean causation." Republicans might win national elections whenever hemlines are long, Democrats when they are short, but that does not warrant the conclusion that skirt length causes specific election outcomes. *Cause* implies a much higher level of certitude and truth than *correlate*. The level of moral certitude Church teaching requires of tribunals in the issuance of annulments lies closer to *cause* than *correlate*.

Taking advantage of C. 1095's breadth, Wrenn asserts that "psychological reasons" for incompetence "include psychoses, neuroses, personality disorders, . . . homosexuality" and even the "situation where neither party to the marriage suffers from a true disorder but they still remain incapable of establishing a marital relationship with each other."[33] It is difficult to imagine who might not properly qualify for a defective consent annulment under the latter rubric. Incompetence sans mental disorder supposedly derives from a Rotal decision handed down in 1973,[34] a decade before the new code took effect. Whatever its source, Wrenn's conception of incompetence is much closer to incompatibility than incapacity.

By expanding upon what must be attained in valid marriage, Wrenn's interpretation of C. 1095 makes it all the more unattainable. As if this were not enough, he then allows virtually any spousal interpersonal deficiency to indicate incapacity to fulfill what he believes marriage should be. Yet his understanding of the canon has carried the day in the deliberations of American tribunals. It is precisely this sort of interpretation that has proved capable of producing annulments at the drop of a petition.[35] The wide variety of conditions, psychological or otherwise, that can negate valid consent may account for the tendency of many American canonists to shorten C. 1095, 2 to "lack of due discretion." Deleting "grave" from "grave lack of discretionary judgement" stretches the statute's boundaries to such an nebulous extreme that mental problems of any kind, from full-blown psychoses to personality quirks, can be used to "prove" incapacity. In one case known me two tribunals maintained that the petitioner had not really married the respondent. Rather, she had exchanged rings and vows with a "fantasy." Neither tribunal produced a shred of evidence suggesting that the petitioner was given to fantasy, delusion, or hallucination at any other time in her existence. Yet it was somehow determined that she fell prey to fantasizing the moment she decided to marry. Accordingly, the marriage was annulled for "lack of due discretion."

Similar looseness infects interpretations of C. 1095, 3, which is often shortened to "lack of due competence." Wrenn's bird's-eye view of the canon visualizes that "According to the present code . . . a marriage is rendered null by any psychological reason (even though it is not a 'disorder' or 'anomaly') whenever that reason or cause renders a spouse incapable of assuming the essential obligations of marriage, especially the obligation of engaging in an interpersonal relationship."[36] This reading of C. 1095 gives tribunals virtual carte blanche to use any untoward social or psychological condition, including missteps in the flow of spousal interaction, to arrive at a finding of incapacity. But that construction placed upon the statute contains the seeds of its own refutation. It raises questions as to whether real incapacity to interact with a spouse is not ipso facto symptomatic of severe mental disorder, and whether those afflicted with such incapacity are likely to marry at all. Paraphrasing Walter K. Olson, children and the mentally unsound can be let out of contracts for lack of "capacity," but that is a rather insulting ground on which to excuse a reasonably normal adult.[37]

These nebulous guidelines for assessing incapacity become all the more conducive to nullity in light of the tendency of mental-health professionals to regard everyone as abnormal to some degree. It is often said—and not entirely in jest—that the surest way to convince a psychiatrist that something is wrong with you is by insisting on your normality.[38] A similar mindset is reflected in the medical profession's unwritten rule that it is more blameworthy for a doctor to dismiss a sick patient than to keep treating a healthy one. Thus, when in doubt a doctor will continue to suspect or diagnose illness.[39] This is really a commendable defensive stance, if only to protect against malpractice suits, but it does not establish the existence of a malady.

Belief in the universality of mental illness was forcefully articulated by Karl Menninger, late dean of American psychiatry. "Gone is the notion that a mentally ill person is an exception. It is now accepted that most people have some form of mental illness at some time and many of them have a degree of illness most of the time. This should not surprise us, for do not most of us have some physical illness some of the time and some of us much of the time?"[40] Inadvertently, perhaps, Menninger was propounding what can easily be construed as a psychological counterpart of Original Sin. In any event, a tribunal operating under premises akin to Menninger's, and not insisting on a clear clinical showing of *grave* mental disorder, is giving itself warrant to attribute lack of due discretion or lack of due competence to either spouse in every case it tries.

As the term *grave* in C. 1095, 2 clearly signifies, the Church does not mandate perfect mental health for those about to contract marriage. Few souls would qualify, and it would be next to impossible to identify those who did. The normality-abnormality issue elicited the following instruction from John Paul II:

> [W]hile for the psychologist or psychiatrist every form of psychic illness can appear the opposite of normality, for the canonist, who is inspired by the . . . integrated vision of the person . . . the normal human condition in this world . . . includes moderate forms of psychological difficulty. . . . Where such an integral vision . . . is lacking, normality on the theoretical level can easily become a myth, and on the practical level, one ends up denying to the majority of people the possibility of giving valid consent.[41]

If proper consent demands complete normality, valid marriage is the exception rather than the rule. To protect against invalid marriages, premarital preparation would have to be radically restructured. In addition to the usual pastoral and catechetical instructions and inquiries, intensive psychiatric screening would be required, lest the Church allow a host of prime candidates for annulment to contract marriage.[42] On the other hand, if all but the thoroughly normal were ruled ineligible for valid marriage, there would be less anxiety among those wishing to reserve churches for June weddings, because few couples would be found psychologically fit to marry.

John Paul II's efforts to curb misuse of C. 1095 have had minimal effect on most American tribunals. Defective consent annulments continue at an unprecedented level, as tribunals make full use of the canon's extraordinary versatility for voiding marriages. Its magical powers are attested to by one vice-*officialis* who writes: "Tribunal judges adjudicate many marriage annulment cases by applying the far-reaching insights of canon 1095. This is a remarkable canon."[43] Indeed it is, possibly the most versatile canon of all. It is a veritable canonical Swiss Army knife, an instrument with manifold uses in the hands of American tribunals.

Judging Incapacitation

The pope has declared, in unmistakable terms, that only *severe* mental disorders render people incapable of valid consent to marriage. "For the canonist the principle must remain clear that only *incapacity* and not *difficulty* in giving consent and in realizing a true community of life and love invalidates a marriage. Moreover the breakdown of a marriage union is never in itself proof of such incapacity on the part of the contracting parties. . . . The hypothesis of real incapacity is to be considered only when an anomaly of serious nature is present which, however it may be defined, must substantially vitiate the capacity to understand and/or to consent."[44] The following year he instructed the Rota that "only the most severe forms of psychic illness reach the point of impairing substantially the freedom of the individual. . . ."[45] In neither allocution does the pope distinguish between consensual incapacity relative to "due discretion" and "due competence." In other words, nothing less than severe psychopathology can justify use of C. 1095, 2, 3 to invalidate consent.[46] It hardly needs saying that since the Holy Father is the ultimate earthly legislator, the authenticity of his interpretation of C 1095—or, for that matter, any canon—supersedes interpretations found in Rotal jurisprudence and in the commentaries of individual canon lawyers. Yet on a daily basis the pope's direction is finessed, undermined, countermanded, or simply ignored within the U.S. tribunal system.

In *The Jurist* article cited above, the vice-*officialis* proposes "to illustrate how . . . 'toxic shame' can *distort* a person's decision to marry."[47] This contention will be examined more closely in the chapter that follows. For now, it may be noted that "toxic shame" is an allegedly key emotional disorder which is prominent in the lexicon of the recovery movement. It is associated with codependency and defective self-esteem. Forbidding as it sounds, few psychiatrists place it on the same level with such psychopathologies as schizophrenia and bipolar (manic-depressive) disorders. It is considered essentially emotional in character, one of many feelings harbored by human beings. Without denying or minimizing the emotional component in our psychological make-up, the principal canonical considerations in assessments of matrimonial consent are cognitive and volitional.

Furthermore, there has probably never been in the entire course of history a case where a prospective spouse's decision to marry was entirely free of distortion. In truth, innumerable phenomena are capable of distorting the decision to marry. A young man's proposal might be influenced—but not completely determined—by starry-eyed expectation that his girlfriend's figure will be as svelte and winsome in twenty years as it is when he slips the engagement ring on her finger. The comely bride-to-be who accepts the ring might similarly anticipate that her virile, athletic fiancé will be paunchless and have a full head of hair when he passes forty. In any event, the introduction of concepts such as toxic shame and distortion is clearly meant to qualify more marriages for nullity by reason of defective consent.

Geoffrey Robinson, an Australian bishop and canonist whose views have found favor in America, is more cautious than Wrenn in explaining the applicability of C. 1095, 2 and 3. Yet with respect to our understanding of defective consent he considers lack of due discretion and lack of due competence to be two major developments in twentieth-century Church law. With respect to the latter, he writes:

[I]ncapacity to fulfill and therefore to assume the essential obligations of marriage . . . refers to those people who are simply unfit subjects for marriage, who were never meant for marriage, who cannot possibly live that life-style, people of whom even their relatives and friends would say, "He/she should never have married." It is based on the principle that no one can bind himself to the impossible. It can also apply when in a particular marriage there is such a clash of deep-seated needs that the harder the couple try to build a marriage, the worse it will become.[48]

Robinson does not, however, specify precisely how his hypothetical spouses are "unfit subjects for marriage." Unless their unfitness derives from a serious mental disorder, his idea of incapacity diverges from that of the pope. For the Holy Father, grave psychopathology is the sine qua non of invalid consent owing to lack of due discretion and lack of due competence.

On a sociological as well as a canonical level, Robinson's definition of incapacity in terms of relatives and friends saying "He/she should never have married" is not persuasive. Perhaps the expression carries a different meaning in Australia, but in the United States and, more important, in Rome, it does not signify incapacity. Usually it is offered as an expression of condolence when a marriage fails, or as a rationalization for the propriety of the break-up. More precisely, the statement should read "He/she should never have married that person," or "They should never have married one another." Those who utter such phrases are frequently among the first to encourage the spouse to let go of the past and remarry. Juridically, whether "He/she should never have married" is somewhat beside the point. The words are more descriptive of an unhappy or unfortunate marriage than an invalid one. Furthermore, while relatives and friends may give useful depositions in an annulment proceeding, they are not the ones to determine incapacity. That responsibility resides with a Church tribunal, presumably with the assistance of a competent expert.

Although Robinson, unlike many American canonists, discounts immaturity and incompatability as grounds for nullity, he appears to flirt with the latter in his reference to a "clash of deep-seated needs." In today's America it is virtually a commonplace that women have an abiding need for intimacy that many if not most husbands do not satisfy. Are such men "unfit subjects for marriage," incapable of entering into a valid union? Or can they give valid consent only when they wed a woman whose desire for intimacy is feeble? And what if a wife refuses to tolerate her spouse's deep-seated need to take off from work every fall to hunt deer, consume beer, and bond with male friends? In fairness, Robinson published these views before John Paul II, in successive addresses to the Rota, elucidated the circumstances under which C. 1095, 23 permits nullity. Still, Robinson's position on defective consent is generally consistent with views held by most American canonists.

Several Rota decisions examined by Varvaro do faithfully embody the teachings set forth in the papal allocutions. In one case the Rotal judges write that "The medical experts claim beyond doubt that the respondent was affected by nervous disturbances both before and after the marriage. . . . None of them claims there were serious anomalies in the exercise of the intellectual or volitional faculties, and so none assert any limitation on the sufficiency of discretionary judgment."[49] In another case the Rota held that "Personality disorders do not support the nullity of marriage unless they are so serious—with aggravating circumstances—that they clearly impede sufficient deliberation about entering a marriage and so clearly take away that discretion of judgment which is required to bring about a valid conjugal relationship."[50]

Varvaro's commentary on the Rotal rulings is, in a sense, as instructive as the decisions themselves. At one point he states that "The [American tribunals'] understanding of the relative gravity of personality disorders still seems to remain hidden and even unacceptable to some rotal judges."[51] He seems to imply that certain Rotal judges have not progressed to the level of psychiatric enlightenment attained by American canonists. Varvaro also apparently regards as bothersome if not inexplicable the Rota's insistence that personality disorders must be truly grave before they can be taken to invalidate a marriage. Finally, like most American canonists, he appears to be wedded to the interpersonalist conception of marriage. Indeed, he expresses wonderment that the twenty-seven decisions examined in detail in his first study are devoid of "any consideration of the relational difficulties that two individuals can experience rather drastically in a relationship, despite the 'seriousness.' Can the 'seriousness of the illness' [insofar as it affects consent] be determined without consideration of the relational aspects so pertinent to marriage?"[52] He notes that in at least one case where nullity was denied "the ground for incapacity on the part of the man [was] for interpersonal relationships. . . . [T]he Rota was not too happy with this phraseology."[53]

Varvaro's earlier survey shows that well before Pope John Paul II's 1987 and 1988 allocutions to the Rota there was already in place considerable Rotal jurisprudence at variance with the practices of American tribunals. It also shows that American canonists, for all their veneration of Rotal jurisprudence, are selectively deferential. Almost invariably their choices clear the way to annulment. One might think that the Rota's expressions of displeasure and the Holy Father's admonitions would have put the rein on the production of decrees of nullity, but that has hardly been the case. Vatican statistics show that no sharp downturn in the number of defective consent decrees of nullity granted through ordinary process has occurred since 1984.

At times canonists and theologians lose sight of the more mundane dimensions of human existence. Egan, it bears repeating, while conceding the mystery of marriage, notes that it is nevertheless a "magnificent commonplace," "part and parcel of the ordinary flow of things this side of eternity."[54] The Church's prerequisites for ordinary mortals to contract valid marriages are really quite minimal. To marry validly a person need not be a Rhodes scholar, steeped in the theology of marriage, conversant with the latest Rotal jurisprudence, and the recipient of prenuptial psychiatric clearance from an experienced clinician. To say that the requirements are simple is not unduly simplistic. Much the same understanding appears in Rotal decisions and papal instructions. But with the majority of American tribunals not even the most impeccable qualifications for matrimony rule out a decree of nullity. In applying C. 1095 to petitions for annulment tribunals have shown great ingenuity in creating defective consent scenarios. However, not by ingenuity alone did the volume of annulments for the 1980s come to exceed the total granted by the Church since Catholics first set foot in North America. Through it all psychology, in one form or another, provided vital assistance, enabling tribunals to claim apparent scientific basis for their discovery of a phenomenon previously undetected: an epidemic of defective consent among Americans desiring annulments.

Let us pause here to recapitulate the developments that brought the American tribunal system to its current state. Doctrinal and canonical. changes attributed to Vatican II and evolving Rotal jurisprudence allegedly altered the Church's age-old stance on the nature of marriage. Amending the nature of marriage led to perceived changes in the nature of the marriage contract. Generally speaking, the terms of the new contract were more complex and more difficult to fulfill than those of the old contract that was supposedly abandoned. Added to this mix were generous dashes of the "new pastoralism" and psychological twists and turns made feasible by C. 1095 and unidentified advances in behavioral science. The upshot was that as properties of valid marriage were enlarged, capability for realizing them narrowed. For American diocesan tribunals, these developments effectively constituted a master blueprint for an assembly line geared to maximizing defective consent annulments and "healing." The line's productivity has surpassed the most sanguine expectations among those committed to loosening eligibility for annulment. For Rome, the engine of nullity derived from the American reading of the blueprint has produced a chronic headache. It cannot be overemphasized that the blueprint was crafted mainly by American canonists. Although it incorporated elements drawn from Conciliar documents and Rotal decisions, its purpose was alien to authentic Church teaching and counter to the Rota's efforts to sustain strictures on the availability of annulment. But what Rome and its Rota never intended has become nightmare reality. Dreams and nightmares are fair game for many therapists. Let us now turn to some of the specific ways in which what passes for behavioral science contributes to America's nullity nightmare.

❖ 6 ❖

Systemic Abuse
of Psychology

"That system of law is best which confides as little as possible to the discretion of the judge." Although the author of that ancient legal proverb is consigned to anonymity, the wisdom of the principle lives on. Judicial discretion can undermine the rule of law. In this way, American tribunalists contorted C. 1095, 2, 3 to create additional leeway for ruling for nullity. Theoretically, new powers of discernment afforded by behavioral science would narrow the ambit of tribunal discretion and provide reliable bases for making objective determinations in defective consent cases. If anything, however, psychology enabled the tribunals to exercise more discretion.

Psychology, in its helping-profession precincts, is notoriously equivocal. Equivocation can come in the guise of eclecticism, pragmatism, or trial and error, either singly or in combination. Practitioners may be committed to a specific theory or school of thought, but when the chips are down they will shift to whatever seems to work. When tribunalists and psychologists combine forces in defective consent cases, the outcome is often an exercise in improvisation.

Flexible, shifting standards work to the advantage of tribunalists seeking to grant annulments. They offer relief from the constraints of onerous legalism, the *bête noire* of many post–Vatican II progressives. The species of legalism many canonists find bothersome is not confined to the strictures of canon law itself. Official doctrinal prescriptions and proscriptions are also major sources of annoyance. They too are often subsumed under the heading of "legalism." Like the "spirit of Vatican II," psychology offered non-or extralegal means by which the law could be administered and the needs of pastoral healing accommodated. Tribunals could be agents of therapy as well as justice. As a consequence, there was added risk that the primary concern of the Church's marriage courts—dispensing justice based on truth—would be confounded by therapeutic initiatives outside the law.

Law and Psychiatry

Historically, psychiatry's relationship with law has been checkered, even when the two fields appeared to have fairly common interests. Letting bygones be bygones, most tribunals have thrown out the welcome mat to a variety of therapists and diagnosticians. The resulting bedfellowship has led to a strange blend of confusion and harmony. Psychiatry has been averse to punishment since its inception. For much of the nineteenth century there was little difference, in conditions and care, between prisons and asylums.[1] Philippe Pinel (1745–1826), considered the "father of psychiatry," agitated for more humane institutional treatment of the insane. Modern canonists also display a certain antipathy toward measures that smack of punishment. Church sanctions on divorce and remarriage are seen not only as instruments of blame and impediments to pastoralism and healing, but as denials of the right to marry and the need to keep the sacraments as accessible as possible. The God they worship stresses mercy at the expense of justice. But in the Church's scheme of things, that is a false ascription of priority. Justice is tempered by mercy, not supplanted by it. Neither is the handmaid of the other. If they are to be weighed, it must be done with respect to truth. This aspect of Church teaching is rather neatly summed up in the new catechism's treatment of the common good: The order of things is "founded on truth, built up in justice, and animated by love."[2]

Law presupposes human choice, while psychiatry tends toward determinism. Attempts to narrow the range of human accountability appear early in the development of psychiatry. Sir Isaac Ray's treatise *The Medical Jurisprudence of Insanity*, published in 1838, was an early effort to limit criminal liability. Five years later the treatise was a factor in enunciation by the Queen's Bench of the House of Lords of the historic *M'Naghten* rule, still the basis for modern formulations of the insanity defense in much of the English-speaking world.[3] Cesare Lombroso (1835–1909), an Italian army psychiatrist usually credited with founding scientific criminology, sought to use a variant of biological determinism to explain criminal behavior. These early examples deal with crime, but the emergent approach to accountability soon extended to other activities as well. Psychiatry's antipathy toward regarding human beings as free moral agents persists to this very day, and is also evident in cognate disciplines within the larger field of psychology.

Free will and accountability are key postulates in the Church's conception of human nature[4]. They have always figured prominently in how the Church looked at sin and at marital consent. Even before Vatican II and the new code annulments were granted for those who could prove they did not enter marriage freely. To the extent that psychiatry encourages added strictures on freedom of choice, it has provided more grist for the annulment mill. The reluctance to hold individuals responsible for their actions is closely related to the widespread taboo against judgmentalism. Contemporary helping-professionals and religionists are inclined to regard judging the behavior of others askance. The Church's position on judgmentalism is not absolute. Condemning sinners is frowned upon, while sin itself is fair game. Many therapists, however, are likely to proscribe both forms of judgment. The ban is found perhaps in purest form in the "nondirective" therapy of Carl Rogers, which might just as aptly be termed "nonjudgmental" therapy. Rogers considered his work "client"-centered rather than "patient"-centered because the latter term is not sufficiently neutral. It signals that the therapist finds something wrong with the "client's" person or behavior. Rogerian nonjudgmentalism is global, applying to the self as well as others. Carried to its logical extreme, the Rogerian approach would inhibit if not eliminate a host of everyday activities—jury service, voting, grading students, allocating pay increases and job promotions, to name but a handful. For Catholics, examination of conscience before confession would be counter to the taboo against judging the self. Christians, moreover, would be prevented from responding to the obligation in charity to help sinners mend their ways (Matthew 18:15).

Within the modern American Church avoidance of judgmentalism is manifested in widespread disbelief of the existence of Hell, fading belief in sin, the decline in confession, and the perceived irrelevance of penance. Tribunals stress their assiduous nonjudgmentalism while taking and processing testimony and conducting trials. One tribunalist of my acquaintance maintains that the 1917 and 1983 codes differ in that the latter makes no assignments of blame. In fact, however, Book VI of the new explicitly deals with Church sanctions, which are not earmarked for the blameless. In any case, it is an interesting experience to receive a lecture on nonjudgmentalism from someone whose very job is to render judgments on such matters as the credibility of witnesses and experts, and the validity of marriages.

Nowhere is the tension between psychiatry and law more apparent than in the insanity plea, the ultimate denial of personal accountability. *M'Naghten* and derivative rules, far from making it easier to determine the state of mind of a person who commits a legally harmful act, have been the bane of judges, juries, and psychiatric experts. A century and a half of sparring between legal scholars and psychiatrists has brought the issue no closer to mutually acceptable resolution. Similar tensions often surface in commitment proceedings. Psychiatrists wish to institutionalize many persons with severe mental disorders in order to provide them with a secure environment and therapy. Lawyers, on the other hand, are reluctant to have the loss of freedom depend solely on psychiatric diagnosis without at least vestiges of due process. Conflict over the commitment and retention of mental patients has festered for decades. Psychiatrists fault lawyers for the court-ordered exodus of mental hospital patients who now consititute a sizable percentage of the homeless. Lawyers, in turn, oppose the loss of freedom without serious cause.

Finessing Accountability

Just as psychiatry grapples with the criminal intent (*mens rea*) of those who break the law, tribunals must reckon with consent among those who marry.

While criminal intent and invalid consent are neither the same nor altogether unrelated, they have at least one important feature in common: both are very difficult to establish by psychiatric methods. Each determination entails gauging a person's state of mind during the commission of some act or series of acts that occurred in the past. There are, however, important differences in the practices of civil courts and marriage tribunals in this context. American secular courts are less likely than tribunals to rely on a single expert. In addition, they are bound by a higher level of proof than the diluted degree of moral certitude American tribunals require of themselves. Attorneys on either side of criminal and commitment proceedings are typically more skeptical than tribunalists about psychiatric findings. Civil courts are fortunate in that only a small percentage of their cases involve insanity pleas. Tribunals, however, spend most of their time on defective consent annulments.

From the end World War II until roughly 1970 it was considered a badge of legal enlightenment to grant psychiatry entree into criminal court proceedings Lawyers, much like today's canonists, were sold on the ability of psychiatrists to explain human behavior and its foibles. But eventually disenchantment set in. For one thing, attorneys for defendants found not guilty by reason of insanity came to realize that incarceration in a mental hospital might last longer than a prison term. With the exception of mandatory life sentences and the death penalty, prison confinement has statutory limits. Confinement in a mental hospital can be completely open-ended. Unless court-ordered, discharge depends on whether the patient, in the opinion of the staff, is "cured" or able to function in the community. Progress to either of these therapeutic levels might take forever. Attorney skepticism was heightened by awareness that living conditions in many state mental hospitals were not much better than what prisons offered. On top of all this, in criminal proceedings the defendant's statements to a psychiatrist would sometimes be revealed in open court, effectively neutralizing the constitution's protection against self-incrimination. This understandably gave defense attorneys second thoughts about the utility of psychiatric experts. One might expect the psychiatric pitfalls associated with the insanity plea and commitment to give pause to diocesan tribunals wrestling with defective consent. But tribunals anxious to annul have little trouble reconciling the vagaries of psychiatry with rulings for defective consent. To be sure, parties to annulment proceedings are not being dispatched to mental hospitals and prisons. But from the Church's standpoint, the stakes are much higher. Specious decrees of nullity are undermining the integrity of a sacrament instituted by Christ.

Methodologically, psychiatists often indulge in logical circularity, a tendency also observable in tribunal judges. Consider the case of a serial murderer whose victims are young children. Many psychiatrists almost reflexively assume that anyone who commits such heinous and apparently senseless acts must be mentally ill. Well and good, up to a point; they may be right. But unless that conclusion is backed by solid clinical evidence, it is nothing more than impressionistic inference. Empirically, all the psychiatrist really knows is that the offender perpetrated some inexplicable horrendous deeds. Given the evidence, it would make just as much sense to assume that our hypothetical murderer is sane and evil. But that is not how psychiatrists typically view human nature and grossly deviant behavior. It is far more likely that mental illness will be inferred from that behavior; then, with circularity almost too obvious to mention, the inference is often used to explain the behavior from which it was inferred. Marriage tribunals routinely engage in similar logical gymnastics in defective consent cases. A history of unhappy marriage followed by divorce impels the presumption that something psychological had to be amiss when the parties consented to marriage. A finding of lack of due discretion or incapacity is virtually assured. Such reasoning is more decisive in annulment proceedings than in civil trials because there are fewer legal and psychological checks and balances.

Some of the American canonists' enthusiasm for psychiatry is attributable to naiveté and exaggerated faith in the discipline's diagnostic and explanatory powers. All the same, it is intriguing that canon lawyers, so adroit at nuancing and hair-splitting, neglect to apply their keen analytical powers to the company they keep. Perhaps their uncritical receptiveness to psychiatry stems from the desire to demonstrate the compatibility of faith and science, a sign of their coming to terms with modernity. Or perhaps apparent credulity is disingenuousness, dictated by awareness of the usefulness of psychiatric leverage in nullifying marriages on grounds of defective consent. This not to say that psychiatry should be drummed out of tribunal procedures. Properly used, psychiatry can be an effective tool in helping tribunals carry out their responsibilities. But to date, the American tribunals' romance with psychiatry has been intellectually shallow and generally destructive of Church teaching on the permanence and indissolubility of marriage. Erstwhile spouses—husbands and wives—cast into the roles of petitioners and respondents, are examined directly or from afar by psychiatrists and psychologists whose findings, authentic or superficial, enable tribunals to wave their nullificatory wand. Tribunalists become more concerned with therapy than justice, and less sensitive to how their work should contribute to the common good.[5]

Ironically, the history of psychiatry shows that few of the field's leading lights held congenial views on religion. Freud's antipathy against religion went far beyond renunciation of his Jewish background. As Freudian sociologist Philip Rieff puts it, Freud believed that being religious was the same as being sick, inasmuch as "religious questions induce the very symptoms they seek to cure."[6] Carl Jung, son of a minister, may loosely be considered an exception. Jungian psychology has quite a few devotees in Catholic circles, despite the fact that one of Jung's primary missions was to free himself of the Christian myth.[7] Jung's God is more an inner psychic phenomenon than a heavenly Father. At all events, thanks in no small measure to the legacy of pioneers such as Freud, Jung, Fromm, and others too numerous to list here, psychiatry's coexistence with law and religion remains precarious.

Mysterious New Developments

The annulment literature is almost devoid of efforts to show, other than by assertion, precisely how behavioral science "advances" (or "insights") afford canonists and tribunals with heretofore-unknown mappings of the mysteries of human interaction, the workings of the mind, and the psychodynamics of marital consent.[8] Let it be noted, first of all, that insights have a role in behavioral science, mainly as sources of hypotheses, as plausible commentaries on inconclusive evidence, or as new perspectives on fairly solid research. But they cannot to be equated with established findings, with firm conclusions and hard proofs the findings sometimes make possible. The canonical literature reveals few citations, discussions, or even names of specific developments in behavioral science that break new ground in a way truly germane to gauging the quality of discretion and the amount of capability necessary for valid matrimonial consent. There have undoubtedly been new developments in the human sciences, but their connection with consent is established by presumption and fiat rather than by research.

Reaching for Incapacity

Loosely speaking, Wrenn's use of self-theory in an attempt to provide some content to the *bonum coniugium* aspect of marriage qualifies as a valid effort to bring behavioral science and canonical deliberations together. Self-theory has interesting things to say about personality and the ebb and flow of small group interaction. It can contribute to understanding marital success and failure, but says little about what is germane to validity. Moreover, it ranks low on the science continuum for psychology. If Wrenn's recourse to behavioral science is feeble, what can be said of Garrity's exploration into the dire consequences toxic shame might have for valid marriage? Using the rhetoric and claims of the Recovery Movement, Garrity hypothesizes causal connections between defective consent and toxic shame and dysfunctional family background.[9] Toxic shame is usually described as an extreme lack of self-esteem, a condition once called an inferiority complex. Designating shame as toxic makes it sound all the more grave and scientific, a disorder caused by an indentifiably poisonous substance or condition. Actually, the "toxin" is the family whose members have unmet needs and who are therefore deemed dysfunctional. Of course, only mythical families are without unmet needs. Some critics liken family dysfunction to "family influenza," since it is a disorder without boundaries or a specific target population. Every human being has—or had—a family. Indeed, estimates for the number of Americans in dysfunctional families range from 100 million to the entire population. Thus, saying that defective consent is caused by family dysfunction has all the etiological discriminatory power of saying it is caused by breathing.

As if the pandemic level of dysfunction morbidity were not alarming enough, its impact is exacerbated by the codependency and addictions it spawns. Originally, the term codependent referred to an addict's spouse or relatives. It was assumed that codependents not only were affected by the addicts' behavior but also unintentionally contributed to it. The reach of addiction was extended to a host of behaviors other than drug and alcohol abuse. Any habit thought to have untoward consequences—eating, fasting, sex, money, candy, prayer, daily communion—can be relegated to the realm of addiction.[10] Those who dare maintain that they have been untouched by dysfunction and codependency are said to be in denial. Thus, from the standpoint of epidemiology, the United States is suffering societal mental disorder not seen since the Tulip Madness in sixteenth century Holland.

Toxic shame has yet to be anointed by the American Psychiatric Association (APA) as an identifiable disorder. That in itself is significant, given the APA's readiness to add new disorders to its already comprehensive inventory. The conditions Garrity seeks to tie in with defective consent are closely associated with the Recovery Movement which swept America in the 1980s and still remains very much in vogue.[11] In some respects the movement is an offshoot of self-theory, insofar as it stresses "feelings," especially positive ones about self, nonjudgmentalism, and avoidance of guilt. The readiness of alleged victims of dysfunction to bare their souls (or feelings) publicly is standard fare on television talk shows. The movement has strong links with self-help counseling techniques. Few of its leading proponents have appropriate scholarly credentials and research experience, depending heavily instead on personal experiences with some form of dysfunction, codependency, or addiction. Indeed, the movement's prototypical recovery model, Alcoholics Anonymous, with its twelve-step program for abstinence, studiously rejects the ministrations of professional clinicians. Lacking a distinctive body of theory and research, the Recovery Movement is at best on the outer fringe of the human sciences. The "evidence" it gathers is impressionistic and anecdotal. It is rarely organized and presented in a form amenable to scientific analysis, and rarely held up against studies of control groups. Its contribution to authentic behavioral science is roughly the same as what astrology offers to astronomy.

Garrity's thesis exemplifies how many American canonists look upon behavioral science. Despite professions of fealty to psychiatry, psychology, and cognate disciplines, there is usually failure to differentiate reasonably scientific subspecies from unscientific pretenders. Indeed, the attempt to build a case for toxic shame as a cause of defective consent attests to unfamiliarity with behavioral science research, or to unwillingness to abandon preconceptions rendered useless by its findings, or to desperation to dredge.up psychological arguments for defective consent.

In 1986 California commissioned a task force to encourage self-esteem throughout the state, especially in the educational system.[12] Despite professing to know that low self-esteem acts as a potent independent variable in causing major behavior problems, the researchers' curious goal was to determine if what they took for granted was scientifically true. Low self-esteem was examined for its influence on academic performance, unplanned teenage pregnancies, criminal and violent behavior, long-term welfare dependency, alcoholism, and drug use.

All these dependent variables had such weak correlation with self-esteem that a causal relationship was ruled out of the question. A search of the literature by one of the authors covered more than 6,500 studies with titles that included the term *self-esteem*. Altogether there were in excess of thirty thousand scholarly articles and dissertations which used a variety of concepts related to self-esteem. For the most part, correlations between self-esteem and other variables were statistically unimpressive. Some studies showed higher correlations with respect to narrow forms of self-esteem but they could have been confounded by other factors. There is, for instance, fairly strong correlation between academic performance and self-esteem. But as one scholar who studied the question concedes, the relationship could be entirely due to students' effort rather than self-esteem as such.[13]

As near as can be determined, the connection between self-esteem and matrimonial consent has not been subjected to rigorous scientific scrutiny. Perhaps that is because marital consent cannot be studied as objectively as academic performance, family violence, and other dependent variables examined by researchers. We really do not know whether and how self-esteem relates to consent. But in view of the weak correlations obtained in research on self-esteem, no great leap of faith is required to posit that even extreme lack of self-esteem, as in toxic shame, is unlikely to be causally related to defective consent. Still, neither the absence of appropriate research nor the voluminous studies of self-esteem already conducted deter Garrity from maintaining that in some cases toxic shame and codependency are capable of causing lack of due discretion when marriages are contracted. No doubt many American tribunal judges would agree.

The logic behind the toxic-shame hypothesis is seen daily in tribunal efforts to relate personal problems to invalid consent. This is especially the case when the marital histories of parties to annulment include references to episodes of child abuse, alcoholism, and family violence. Frequently it is taken for granted, quite uncritically, that such experiences necessarily influence the quality of consent. It matters not whether they occurred during the pre-or postmarital periods. Their occurrence at any phase of the individual's life span leads to the presumption that their influence was felt at the moment consent was exchanged. Theoretically, even factually, that may be true. But rare is the case, as Anné himself suggested, in which tribunals have the investigative wherewithal to transform what is a tentative hypothesis into the kind of certitude one expects in the determinations of a court of law.

In trafficking with behavioral science as it might apply to marital consent, canonists often repeat one of its common fallacies. Put in simple terms, the fallacy has it that "bad" inevitably comes from "bad." Untoward antecedents must have untoward consequences. Methodologically, it often amounts to begging the question at hand. As an explanation of undesirable behavior, the principle is deeply ingrained in folk wisdom as well as in behavioral science. The premise is integral to Freudian theory on the significance of early childhood. Led on by Freud's free association techniques, his patients often uprooted previously forgotten but painful childhood experiences. Although he believed many of these experiences never actually happened, he reasoned that by reliving them later in life patients could ameliorate their neurotic symptoms. Freud theorized that childhood fantasies were resurrected to accommodate unfulfilled sexual needs. Early unresolved sexual conflicts ("bad") are repressed into the "seething cauldron" of the unconscious, where they continually seek expression in the face of prohibitions imposed by social convention. Repression is not foolproof, however, and seemingly dormant conflicts are acted out through a variety of defense mechanisms during puberty and adulthood as abnormal behavior ("bad"). Inadvertently, Freud helped lay the groundwork for the recent wave of litigation on sexual abuse that allegedly occurred in the distant past. Aided by "recovered memory" therapists, victims purport to be able to recall childhood trauma long after it was supposedly experienced. Recollection of early dark chapters apparently forgotten is a prominent feature of the Recovery Movement and has had tragic consequences for objectively innocent priests and others charged with pedophilia. Psychologists have mixed views on the ability of therapists to plumb the remote recesses of the psyche for accurate information on childhood abuse. So many have been falsely accused that a False Memory Syndrome Foundation has been established to aid innocent victims of such charges.

The bad-to-bad sequence is not peculiar to psychoanalysis and psychology. Economists, politicians, and the public at large, for example, see no redeeming qualities in poverty. Nothing good can come of it, not even otherworldliness, incentive to improve one's station in life, a measure of happiness, or even a widow's mite. The reductionism of the bad-begets-bad paradigm practically precludes individuals rising above personal flaws and handicaps imposed by social structures and the winds of fate. From a scientific perspective, it fails to explain how many who experience Toxic-shame, family dysfunction, child abuse, alcoholism, and so on, enter into marriages that remain intact and ostensibly valid. At the same time, it illustrates how American canonists forage in psychology to build cases for incapacity and defective consent. Conversely, one searches in vain for accounts of how behavioral science, even the pop variety, might be used to demonstrate the validity of marriages.

Diagnostic Pitfalls

American canonists' use of even mainstream behavioral science leaves much to be desired. Their enthusiasm for the analytical and diagnostic powers of psychiatry is seldom tempered by healthy skepticism and judicious restraint. The widespread reliance on the *Diagnostic and Statistical Manual of the American Psychiatric Association (DSM)* by tribunals weighing psychological grounds for nullity is a case in point. Canonists treat the manual as the equivalent of a psychiatric bible providing the definitive phylogeny of mental problems.[14] There seems to be little awareness that *DSM* is but one of several classifications of mental disorders, albeit the most widely used, or that it has undergone major changes from one edition to the next. *DSM II* attempted to classify disorders etiologically; *DSM III* switched to a typology based on symptoms. In another notable change, *DSM II* but not *DSM III* considers neurosis a disorder.

DSM-III-R lists nineteen diagnostic categories, including one for "Conditions Not Attributable to a Mental Disorder That Are a Focus of Attention or Treatment."[15] The latter category, as it happens, includes "Marital problem[s]," "Other specified family circumstances," and "Other interpersonal problem[s]." This could be a fitting repository for such conditions as codependency and Toxic shame. The manual catalogs 296 conditions which presumably fall under eighteen diagnostic categories related to mental disorders. No fewer than twenty-seven forms of schizophrenia are delineated. The manual certainly testifies to psychiatry's ability to make ever finer distinctions in classifying mental disorders. This may be the sort of thing canonists have in mind when they refer to behavioral science advances. It may also be a sign of American society's ongoing psychologization, or even a mark of confusion, rather than evidence for path-breaking developments. In truth, many conditions previously considered mildly deviant or harmless are now classified as mental disorders. The helping professions have increasingly narrowed the meaning of "normality." There is hardly a soul alive who is immune to one or more of the 296 mental conditions in the manual. Properly distributed, that large and varied a storehouse of mental conditions can provide at least one disorder per lifetime for every man, woman and child in the United States, and confirm Menninger's contention that mental illness is as universal as physical illness.

The need to revise successive editions of *DSM* shows that psychiatry's quest for diagnostic and etiological principles and certitude remains incomplete. The field is in a constant state of flux. Like a manuscript going through several drafts, the *DSM* is subjected to additions and deletions. Behaviors newly regarded as bizarre or undesirable are elevated to mental-disorder status, while other behaviors are shorn of their abnormal stripes. Inclusion in the manual need not depend on inexorable growth in psychiatric understanding. It may be due to considerations which are political and cultural rather than clinical in nature. Until 1973 homosexuality was considered a sexual disorder by the American Psychiatric Association (APA) membership. Overnight, as it were, homosexuals were voted normal, a change not based on new medical or clinical evidence.[16] In the opposite direction, compulsive gambling was declared a mental illness by the association in 1980.[17] Smoking, once common among psychiatrists, has become a mental problem called "Nicotine dependence." Those who try to quit smoking may incur another disorder called "Nicotine withdrawal." Currently, serious consideration is being given to including premenstrual syndrome (PMS) among the disorders to appear in *DSM-IV*. Canonists seem oblivious to the dynamic and tentative character of psychiatric diagnosis. Instead, diagnostic categories in *DSM-III* and *DSM-III-R* are taken as psychiatric Holy Writ, even though their worth has been challenged by reputable scholars within the discipline.[18]

Canonists' almost blind trust in the diagnostic powers of *DSM* is not shared by the manual's very own editors. *DSM-III-R* is prefaced with a "Cautionary Statement" that reads:

The purpose of DSM-III-R is to provide clear descriptions of diagnostic categories in order to enable clinicians and investigators to diagnose, communicate about, study, and treat the various mental disorders. *It is to be understood that inclusion here, for clinical and research purposes, of a diagnostic category... does not imply that the condition meets legal or other non-medical criteria for what constitutes mental disease, mental disorder, or mental disability.* The clinical and scientific consideration involved in categorization of these conditions as mental disorders may not be wholly relevant to *legal judgments,* for example, that take into account such issues as *individual responsibility, disability determination, and competency.*[19]

This comprehensive disclaimer is an exquisite and prudent hedge or, more important, an expression of honest humility. It signifies that the APA has learned from experience the hazards confronting those who try to incorporate clinical and diagnostic materials into legal proceedings. Especially noteworthy is the statement that such materials may have limited relevance when "individual responsibility, disability determination, and competency" are at issue. These are precisely the kind of considerations that must be factored into tribunal deliberations on defective consent.

A recent issue of the *Journal of Abnormal Psychology* is devoted entirely to efforts under way to prepare *DSM-IV.*[20] Each contributor, implicitly or explicitly, desires having the new manual avoid the shortcomings of previous editions. Concerned with what he sees as undue emphasis on reliability (agreement among diagnosticians) at the expense of validity (how the diagnostic categories fit reality), Carson comments that the tradeoff has failed to lead to "an enhanced rate of genuine progress on the fundamental issues of the field, nor has it significantly reduced the rampant confusion that characterizes the research literature. The clear and present danger is that the *DSM-IV* will result in merely more tinkering on a superficial level with operational diagnostic criteria that tend over time to approach the status of revealed truths, notwithstanding their often patently arbitrary nature and the unproductiveness of their outcomes."[21] Carson is by no means the only contributor with reservations about the faith clinicians should place in current or future editions of the manual.[22]

Labelists and Mental Disorder

Psychiatrists' doubts on the *DSM* series are minor cavils compared to how labelists look upon psychiatric type-casting. Since the early 1960s labeling-theory has been a major force in the study of deviant behavior. Its disciples have been especially active in the fields of crime, delinquency, and mental disorder. From the labelist perspective, most mental disorders found in psychiatric classifications cannot be scientifically authenticated. This is particularly true of functional disorders which by definition have no apparent physical basis. Thomas Szasz, a maverick psychiatrist, carries this contention to an extreme by arguing that mental illness is a figment of imagination.[23] What most psychiatrists consider mental illnesses he prefers to call "problems in living." While Szasz does not formally identify himself as a labelist he would agree with labelists who deny the authenticity of psychiatric diagnostic categories. Verifying them is not feasible because we cannot be confident that those examined by psychiatrists are representative of the general population, or, more specifically, those in the general population with mental problems. This is more than a methodological quibble. Psychiatrists themselves question the reliability and validity of diagnoses based on *DSM-III-R*. Labelists contend that low reliability and validity are inevitable because clinical data are by their nature selective, seldom checked against control group data. Accordingly, the only thing we can be sure that schizophrenics, for example, have in common is the experience of being labeled schizophrenic by psychiatrists and other clinicians. Using such postulates, labelists argue that most mental disorders are nominal rather than objective behavioral entities, clinical pigeonholes as it were. Putting it in terms Szasz himself might utter, mental illness is pretty much whatever psychiatrists say it is.

Bestowing formidable titles on apparently deviant—or inexplicable—behavior does more than create difficulties with pronunciation, spelling, and understanding. The names take on a life of their own, often with serious consequences. Because they are coined by those whom labelists call "moral entrepreneurs"—in this instance, psychiatrists—the names often operate as stigmas. Their prestigious sources and the disorders they purport to represent affect how others perceive the bearers and how the bearers perceive themselves. Once the label is affixed by someone with sufficient status to make it stick, two important changes may occur. Those who associate with a person thus stigmatized modify their interaction with that person in accordance with the label. A coworker known to purchase large numbers of lottery tickets is now a "gambling addict," a sick person, because a clinician said so. The differential treatment can set in motion a self-fulfilling prophecy. Now dealt with by others according to what the label is supposed to signify, the person's self-perceptions and behavior take on the terms of the label. The label, therefore, can be simultaneously a cause and effect of what has been defined as a mental disorder.

Labelists refer to this phenomenon as "secondary deviance." Bizarre or illegal behavior not responded to by others is termed "primary deviance." Since there is no response and therefore no effective labeling by an external agent, such behavior may never be repeated. But if there is reaction on the part of a person whose status gives assignment of a label staying power and significance, secondary deviance can ensue. Those who implement or enforce the label are called "gatekeepers." They may be police officers, social workers, teachers, counselors, and the like. Actually, the weight given to this aspect of social interaction is not peculiar to labelists. It is implied in our culture's present taboo against judgmentalism. Aversion to judgmentalism is apparent in countless euphemisms which supposedly soften the blows that go with names considered capable of diminishing self-esteem or inflicting emotional damage, particularly in the form of guilt. We saw this in Carl Rogers's use of the neutral term *client* to avoid the stigmatizing connotations of the term *patient*. Similarly, *crippled* has given way to *disabled* or *physically challenged, convicts* or *inmates* are called *residents, sinners* become *victims.*

Obviously, the willingness of clinicians to acknowledge the difficulties in developing reliable and valid diagnostic categories reinforces the labelist position.[24] The labelist perspective on mental disorders becomes less persuasive when disorders have a clear-cut physical basis. Even there, however, the interactionist theme cannot be completely discounted. Deterioration of the central nervous system plays a critical role in the behavior of those afflicted with paresis, but the person's abnormal mannerisms might also be influenced by how the condition is perceived by that individual and others. Recent developments in molecular biology showing irregularities in the brains of some schizophrenics pose problems for labelists. But the connection is irregular enough to raise some doubt about the tendency of biological psychiatrists to assume that schizophrenia is primarily a form of brain disease. Even if it were, a disease of the brain is not necessarily a disease of the mind. In any event, whatever its level of plausibility, labeling-theory is a bona fide behavioral-science development. Unlike "advances" alluded to by canonists, it has a specific identity, and has generated a body of theory and research reported in a massive literature. Despite its contribution to the study of human deviance, canonical commentaries on behavioral science as an instrument for determining defective consent seldom allude to its existence.

This brief discourse on labeling theory is not meant to suggest that its adherents have all the answers. Besides its problems with disorders with a physical basis, labeling needs more research on differential reactions to the labeling process. Nevertheless, assuming that the perspective has something to offer, little imagination is needed to see what it does to classifications like those of *DSM-III-R.* Granting even modest credibility to the labelist perspective would lead to more cautious usage of diagnostic labels to establish psychological grounds for nullity. We might also see fewer tribunal sentences making casual use of terms such as *sociopath, psychopath, histrionic personality, passive-aggressive, dependent, compulsive, mixed, anxiety disorder, affective-disorder, avoidant, narcissistic,* and *borderline.* To the labelist, such terms are largely metaphorical. A further question arises as to whether they represent *grave* disorders. Yet they are commonly employed in efforts to establish defective consent.[25]

The fallibility of psychiatric diagnosis was dramatically demonstrated in a famous study by a Stanford University psychologist. The researcher and several associates were able to get themselves committed to mental hospitals by faking a single symptom. They complained of hearing voices uttering such words as "thud," "empty," and "hollow." In all but one of twelve attempts they were admitted after being diagnosed as schizophrenic. Once admitted, they behaved normally, yet none was unmasked by the hospital staff for having faked mental disorder. In one of the study's more fascinating twists, some of the hospital patients were not as easily deceived as the staff. They told the pretenders that they were not mentally ill, and voiced the suspicion that they were investigating hospital conditions.

The study provoked disbelief among mental-health professionals, which led to a follow-up study where a mental-hospital staff was forewarned that some fake patients would try to be admitted to the facility. Of 193 people admitted to the hospital, 41 were identified as "fakes" by at least one staff member, while 19 others were deemed "suspicious." The second study actually reinforced the results of the first, inasmuch as the psychologist who conducted both studies did not try to have anyone admitted to the hospital.[26] The studies point to more than the fragility of psychiatric diagnosis. They illustrate, in addition, the tendency among mental-health professionals to assume, in the manner of Menninger, that virtually everyone is at one time or another caught in the throes of mental illness. They also reveal how easily mental illness can be feigned. Finally, it is well to note that the counterfeit illness in the first hospital study was not some relatively benign disorder. Rather, the researcher's confederates were diagnosed as having schizophrenia, one of the most serious of all mental illnesses.

It is instructive to examine, in this context, John Paul II's insistence that only serious psychological disorders can be used to build a case for defective consent. The National Institutes of Mental Health (NIMH) estimates that 4.5 percent of all Americans suffer from "severe mental illness," and that more than 25 percent have some "psychiatric disorder."[27] Let us make the improbable assumption that all of the latter have serious disorders, not merely behavioral peculiarities on which a convenient label has been pinned. Let us further assume, even more improbably, that the disorders are chronic rather than episodic. That gives us, hypothetically, 30 percent of the population with ongoing mental disorders ranging from serious to severe. Leaving aside annulments granted administratively, we know that 98 percent of the ordinary process decrees of nullity granted in the United States between 1984 and 1994 were based on defective consent. Let us estimate that 8 percent of those decrees were based on error rather than C. 1095. Juxtaposing the 90 percent figure with the NIMH estimates suggests that parties to nullity are about three times as likely to have serious mental disorders as the general population.[28] While Catholics may differ from other Americans in many ways, no reputable study has ever suggested that they are substantially more prone to mental disorder. A much more plausible explanation for the disparity is that the tribunals do not require serious or severe mental disorders to arrive at a finding of defective consent. Putting this more bluntly, the pope's directions on the proper application of C. 1095 are studiously ignored by the American tribunal system.

John Paul II's instruction on mental illness and defective consent was publicly enunciated in his 1987 and 1988 addresses to the Rota. His interpretation of the law was probably anticipated in the American defective consent decisions reviewed by Rota between 1980 and 1985. Varvaro's study of those cases was published two years after the pope's 1988 allocution to the Rota. Yet Varvaro reacts with disbelief to "comments made by the judges in actual print." He is particularly taken with one judge's contention that antisocial persons need not be psychopaths. They may be antisocial for reasons other than psychopathy.

Perhaps unaware that psychopathy is often referred to as a diagnostic "waste basket" category, Varvaro wonders how the judge's position "would withstand criticism from experts in the field of psychology or psychiatry. Even if it is admitted as true would not an antisocial person be a poor marital choice for a partner; it would seem that a case for nullity would not be too difficult to build for any anti-social personality."[29]

Varvaro's incredulity bespeaks innocence, if not gullibility, about the capriciousness of psychiatry. It also illustrates why there has been an ongoing tug of war between American canonists and Rome. The tribunal system's pick-and-choose Rotal jurisprudence extends to the content and use of psychiatric expertise. Tribunalists in the United States seem bent on resisting Rome's oft-stated instruction that only serious mental disorders warrant a holding of defective consent. Few would deny that an antisocial person is not an optimal candidate for marriage, but it does not follow that such a person is incapable of entering a valid marriage. To be sure, a case for nullity could be built for such a marriage, and quite likely tribunals have done so hundreds of times. But building a case is not to be confused with acting in accordance with Church teaching and law. If anything, tribunals that feel obliged to build cases for nullity should at least give equal time to exploring ways to uphold validity.

Annulment and the Expert

Not surprisingly, tribunal reliance on psychiatric consultants increased as nullity on psychological grounds became more common. C. 1574 specifies that "The services of experts are to be used whenever, by a provision of the law or of a judge, their study and opinion, based upon their art or science, are required to establish some fact or ascertain the true nature of some matter." This is tantamount to mandating use of experts in matrimonial consent cases, since few tribunalists have appropriate training in psychology. The mandate, however, is not always honored. Furthermore, when experts are called upon their role is supposed to be essentially advisory. Experts propose, tribunals dispose. The implication is that assessments by experts are not to be accepted uncritically, but there are strong indications that is often exactly what happens when their findings can be used to support incapacity.[30] The canon, unfortunately, does not specify the nature of the expertise the experts should bring to the task. Depending on the diocese, the expert could be a psychiatrist or a social worker.

By the late 1970s nearly all hearings held by the Archdiocese of Hartford's tribunal, for example, took place in the offices of seven psychiatrists serving as tribunal adjuncts[31] Other tribunals use experts on an ad hoc basis when their services are necessary "to establish some fact or to ascertain the true nature of some matter." While the new code sets standards for the qualifications of tribunal staff, there are no specific guidelines for determining who is a qualified expert. Regrettably, we lack systematic research on the personal attributes of tribunal experts, their professional credentials, and on how they influence annulment proceedings. It would be helpful to survey which disciplines they represent and in what proportions, their religious affiliations, theoretical perspectives, and attitudes toward divorce and remarriage, the average amount of time spent on each case, and their going rates for consultation. How are they selected? Does each tribunal have a preferred list, or are they chosen randomly from a referral directory? Do some tribunals put more weight on their findings than others?

Ideally, tribunal experts would be psychiatrists or holders of doctorates in clinical psychology. Though it may be asking too much, the model for tribunal work would be a practicing Catholic with a more than nodding acquaintance with Catholic theology, philosophy, and canon law. Many tribunals, unable to afford the best but cautious about tapping their own staffs for expertise, fall back on the lesser helping professions. Accordingly, the expert often turns out to be someone with a master's degree in counseling or social work, which is probably not what those who drafted C. 1574 had in mind when they referred to expert consultants.

The available evidence indicates that tribunals typically rely on a lone expert when they contract for psychological consultation. Canon law allows, at the judge's discretion, more than one. But given fiscal constraints, plus heavy tribunal caseloads, the cost of additional experts would be prohibitive. Outlays for experts' fees are not publicized, but if they are even half what is charged by experts who testify in civil court proceedings, tribunal budgets would explode. In civil courts $200 an hour fees are considered modest, although some experts charge a flat fee for each case. In 1991, a fairly representative year, American tribunals nullified 42,617 marriages on grounds of defective consent.[32] If, as C. 1574 seems to require, an expert assisted in each case, at the bargain rate of $100 for a one-hour session, the total cost to the country's tribunals would have exceeded $4 million. The $100 would not only be a bargain in terms of prevailing fee schedules, but also with respect to the services expected by the code. "Experts must clearly indicate the documents or other appropriate means by which they have verified the identity of persons, places or things. They are also to state the manner and method followed in fulfilling the task assigned to them, and the principal arguments upon which their conclusions are based."[33] Fees, of course, would be lower if clerics trained as clinicians served as experts, but the pool of such clerics is small. There are indications, however, that budget limitations hinder both the hiring of experts and performance of those who serve. Owing to the cost factor, it is not unusual for tribunals to dispense with expert consultants, even when annulment grounds are psychological. In those circumstances the tribunal judges, in effect, wear two hats, one canonical, the other clinical. Diagnoses ventured by the wearer are likely to be exercises in cocktail-party psychiatry, dangerously analogous to the practice of medicine without a license.[34]

The following passages, taken verbatim from an actual sentence (the names alone are fictional), illustrate what can happen when a judicial vicar plays psychiatrist:

[The Court concedes that] many of the factors that motivated Stella to marry were good and proper. Unfortunately, the Court sees that Stella was marrying not Steve but an imagined person she "thought" would provide her with the things she wanted. Stella never really knew the Steve she was marrying. She hardly knew herself. She married to satisfy her perceived needs, not to love and accept the *person* of Steve. She did not truly appreciate who Steve was, nor who she was!

Stella did not marry the flesh and blood person of Steve. She married a manufactured image of someone who she thought could meet her needs as she perceived them to be at that time! . . .

[I]t has been determined after a careful study of this case that Stella did suffer from a serious lack of judgmental discretion. That grave lack of discretion was such that it invalidated the consent she exchanged with Steve despite the good intentions of both of them.

This finding, more than a decade after Stella and Steve married, does violence to C. 1095, 2 and paints a sorry picture of tribunalist psychiatry. The decree of nullity was formulated without the assistance of an experienced clinician. Nary a word adverts to the essential qualities of matrimonial consent spelled out in C. 1096. Was Stella "ignorant of the fact that marriage is a permanent partnership" between her and Steve, "ordered to the procreation of children through some form of sexual cooperation"? The vicar's account of the marriage suggests that Stella was hallucinatory and delusional when she exchanged vows with Steve. Given the "serious lack of judgmental discretion" credited to her by the vicar, one wonders how she managed to make elaborate preparations for the wedding and arrive at the church on time on her nuptial day wearing conventional bridal garb instead of a bed sheet.

The vicar's reconstruction of the wife's mental condition when she contracted for marriage elicited no concurrence from a professional clinician for the simple reason that the tribunal did not solicit input from one. Nor did the petitioner's own witnesses give any testimony lending credence to the judicial vicar's portrayal of her. Somehow, it appears, Stella's false perceptions and "serious lack of judgmental discretion" had escaped the attention of Steve, of the priest who conducted the prenuptial investigation, two priests familiar with the couple who witnessed the marriage, relatives, members of the wedding party, and guests well acquainted with the bride. Besides illustrating what can happen when an *officialis* assumes the role of psychological expert, the sentence shows how flimsy a finding of "lack of due discretion" can be. C. 1095 deals with matrimonial rights and obligations. It does not speak to motivation and perception. No one entering marriage is privy to all can be known about a prospective spouse, or, for that matter, sees with inerrancy one's own makeup.

Presumably one expert is better than none. Use of a solitary expert is not without risk, however. Second opinions are no less advisable in psychiatric than in medical diagnosis. In secular court trials, when mental condition is at issue, the usual format calls for one or more experts to testify for each of the opposing sides—prosecution versus defendant or plaintiff versus respondent. At times the experts on each side concur. Frequently, however, their relationship is adversarial, the testimony of one neutralized by that of the other, and the court or jury must try to tease truth and justice from the standoff. Use of multiple experts in an annulment proceeding might produce only a marginal increase in diagnostic reliability. Except with extreme mental disorders, psychiatry is usually unable to provide the law with the yes-or-no answers it desires. For many psychiatrists, mental disorders are processual and not amenable to simple affirmation or denial.[35] When dealing with a person's past state of mind, psychiatrists tread uncharted waters. Their findings are inherently exploratory and, no matter how plausible, scarcely in keeping with rigorous scientific methodology. Willard Gaylin, professor of psychiatry at Columbia University's medical school, refers to forensic psychiatrists as "storytellers." The term is not used to suggest mendacity or incompetence. Rather, it signifies that however skillfully they conduct themselves in a forensic role, they seldom provide the law with definitive, unconditional answers. Although Gaylin's insights deal with attempts to determine criminal intent, they lose none of their relevance when applied to matrimonial consent. And Gaylin's storytellers ordinarily spend far more time with their subjects than tribunal experts spend with theirs.[36] At the very least, the extensiveness of their investigations of their subjects is likely to produce more credible "stories" made public in open court.

If caseloads remain at current levels, second opinions would reduce many tribunals to insolvency. But while the reliability increment would be small, it would at least enhance public confidence in tribunal decisions on defective consent annulments. It seems almost superfluous to note that no matter how impressive a lone expert's credentials or reputation for probity, unless the diagnosis passes muster with at least one other expert—a kind of peer review—the expert risks the appearance of being a hired gun. Another positive effect of using two experts would be to pressure tribunals to be more discriminating in accepting petitions for nullity. Smaller caseloads would reduce tribunal income from petitioners' fees and simultaneously lessen the need for experts. They might also give experts more time to study each case and avoid making flash diagnoses that ill serve truth and justice.

As noted, the expert's findings are supposed to be advisory, the decision to annul being the exclusive prerogative of tribunal judges. But given the direction in which most American tribunals lean, a diagnosis of any mental disorder will almost invariably lead to nullity. Nevertheless, even when acting in a strictly advisory capacity, the expert's task is daunting. It necessitates determining here and now, sometimes decades after the fact, the mental state of either or both spouses during the courtship period, and, far more important, at the time they married. The crucial importance of pinpointing mental states when the exchange of consent occurs has long been a concern of the Rota. As one Rotal decision put it, "the core problem, the nut we must crack open and examine, is the question if these psychodynamics permitted the expert to state that at the time of the celebration of the wedding they impeded the placing of a decisional act sufficiently free."[37] The Rota here adverts to a very tough nut. Cracking it open and analyzing its contents is an undertaking that pushes to the limit the talents of any clinician claiming psychohistorical skills. Strictly speaking, three basic facts must be established before annulment on grounds of defective consent is canonically warranted. First, it is necessary to prove that either the petitioner, respondent, or both, at one time or another suffered from a severe mental disorder. Second, it must be shown that the psychological condition was present before or at the time of marriage. Third, a causal relationship between the psychological condition and defective consent must be demonstrated. Nowhere have I found published data on how often these fundamental requisites are satisfied, but my discussions with dozens of individuals who were party to annulment strongly suggest that their presence is seldom established in accordance with the basic methodological standards of behavioral science and the requirements of canon law.

Junk Science

It scarcely needs saying that psychological experts, to perform their job properly, are obliged to examine their subjects and whatever ancillary evidence there is before making a clinical judgment. It is hard to conceive of a more fundamental obligation. In practice, however, many if not most tribunal experts seldom conduct a direct, face-to-face examination of either spouse. Only three of my informants had the pleasure of meeting a tribunal expert, and for two of them the psychiatric examination lasted less than ten minutes. One reported that the psychiatrist simply reviewed material covered during the initial interview conducted at the tribunal office. Such clinical celerity is reminiscent of the perfunctory psychiatric processing of World War II draftees. Responses to a handful of questions, usually sex-related ("Do you like girls?"), were used by psychiatrists to certify inductees and enlistees for active duty. Few subjects failed the test.

Similar expeditious superficiality often marks psychiatric intervention in annulment proceedings. Cases have come to my attention where the expert not only failed to examine the petitioner and respondent or pore over the evidence and testimony, but arrived at a diagnosis of defective consent solely by means of a telephone conversation with a tribunal judge. In most judicial systems, attempts to introduce into evidence expert diagnoses of that nature would be laughed out of court.[38] One Rotalist expressed vexation with experts who do not conduct direct, personal examinations of the ex-spouses. "The evaluative work provided by the doctors," he noted, "can hardly be called a formal expert testimony; Dr. R. inspected neither the respondent nor the acts of the case and heard only the petitioner prior to the introduction of the case. . . ."[39]

The case of the ten-minute diagnosis mentioned earlier provides additional clues on how tribunals and their experts so readily find for defective consent. The psychiatrist had at his disposal, in addition to a transcript of the intake interview, access to the tribunal questionnaire completed earlier by the petitioner whose answers gave no hint that his twenty four-year marriage, which produced four children, was marred by defective consent. He and his former spouse, he maintained, intended to remain together for life and be faithful to each other. Although the questionnaire was not designed to tap attitudes on the "communion-of-life" conception of marriage, plainly the spouses grasped the fundamentals of the magisterial view of matrimony. The questionnaire included items designed to probe marital difficulties related to in-laws, finances, gambling, drinking, drugs, physical spouse abuse, religious differences, family background, and ability to deal with every day problems. Except for acknowledging financial difficulties associated with putting four children through college, the petitioner denied that there were problems in any of these areas. Asked to explain why the marriage failed, he attributed the divorce to his wife's "constant nagging." Two years into the marriage he developed ulcers which ruptured twenty-two years later, nearly causing his death.

The tribunal's expert never identified any specific psychological disorder. Although the petitioner, without providing any details, mentioned that he and his ex-wife had briefly sought help for unspecified marital problems, neither the tribunal nor the expert made any effort to contact the psychiatrist the couple had seen. Nevertheless the tribunal issued a decree of nullity based on "grave lack of due discretion" and "incapacity." Evidently the judges pieced together a kind of psychiatric-juridical collage, whereby a bleeding ulcer, spousal bickering, and the fact of divorce pointed to defective consent. This annulment was granted by an archdiocesan tribunal that often advertises itself as one of the Church's most efficient.

Despite obtaining what he sought, the petitioner was dumbfounded and offended to learn that he supposedly lacked due discretion when entering his prior marriage. Raised as a Lutheran, he found the proceeding both incomprehensible and farcical. Largely as a result of the experience, his desire to become a Catholic was abandoned. The oddity of this case pales in comparison to one where two psychiatrists found a respondent suffering from a "paranoid personality" because of his extraordinary efforts to save a marriage of twenty eight years' duration. The experts' diagnosis was based in part on the respondent's "rigid adherence" to the quaint notion that marriage is a permanent commitment. The marriage was annulled but later ruled valid by the Rota, which noted that the two American tribunals hardly performed in the service of truth.[40]

In annulment proceedings the expert is called upon to engage in what is essentially a form of psychohistory. The task may be less dramatic than delving, Freud-like, into the psychic recesses of such historical luminaries as Moses, Leonardo daVinci, and Napoleon. But however nondescript the subjects may appear be—this housewife petitioner or that blue-collar respondent—canon law requires the expert to evaluate their states of mind when their marriages were contracted. A common assumption is that mental and behavioral problems manifested during the marriage were present, if only in latent form, on the wedding day. Then an even greater leap of faith occurs: the assumption that such problems precluded valid marital consent. In most defective consent cases the process can be characterized as a presumptive psychiatric chain consisting of nothing but tenuous links.

Consider a hypothetical husband whose social drinking after fifteen years of marriage degenerates into acute alcoholism leading to spousal abuse. Unable or unwilling to tolerate his behavior, the wife obtains a civil divorce and petitions for annulment. If the expert's investigation shows that the man's father was a heavy drinker who occasionally struck the mother, it all but assures that the tribunal will assume that the respondent's own misbehavior had premarital antecedents. On the other hand, even if the respondent's father was a model husband, a teetotaler who always treated his wife with loving care, the chances are that the tribunal and its expert will still decide that the respondent's problems were present in incipient form prior to the marriage.[41]

Peter Huber has written a penetrating analysis of the growing tendency of American trial courts to provide a forum for marginal "experts" who testify in liability suits.[42] What he and others term "junk science" is accorded a mantle of undeserved probity and used to secure trial outcomes that are both unscientific and unjust. In exchange for their willingness to open the witness stand to ostensibly scientific testimony unworthy of the name, the courts became sounding boards for "a hodgepodge of biased data, spurious inference, and logical legerdemain. . . ."[43] " 'Junk science'," he contends, "is the mirror image of real science, with much of the same form but none of the same substance."[44] Safe products have been driven off the market and litigants awarded millions of dollars in damages on the basis of scientific testimony that would never withstand peer review.

American canonists would profit by examining recent efforts by the U. S. Supreme Court to come to grips with expert scientific testimony. In remanding a case involving claims that Bendectin, a drug often prescribed to combat morning sickness during pregnancy, was the cause of birth defects, the U.S. Court of Appeals for the Ninth Circuit was asked to reconsider an earlier ruling in light of *Federal Rule of Evidence 702*. The circuit court was instructed to ensure that expert testimony actually reflects scientific knowledge, derives from scientific method, can be termed "good science," and is relevant to the case at hand.[45] To help with these determinations, the court was advised to look into whether the expert's theory or method is regarded as acceptable by the scientific community; whether it underwent peer review or was published; whether it is testable or has already been tested; and whether it has an acceptable margin of error. And it should be stressed that the Daubert case involved a medication, not psychological conjecture. Commenting on the role of junk science in prolonging Bendectin litigation for more than a decade, the circuit court noted that "It's as if there were a tacit understanding within the scientific community that what's going on here is not science at all, but litigation."[46] It is difficult to rule out the possibility that the same sort of understanding occurs among experts who testify in defective consent cases.

The Rota can be quite sensitive to the problems created by junk science.

[T]hose experts are to be roundly criticized who proceed with a certain pseudo-scientific ambiguity, who are totally unconcerned for the truth of the facts alleged, who rush to conclusions that will be pleasing to the parties or their advocates, who give no basis for their opinions, who seem to presume facts rather than prove them, sometimes exaggerating certain elements, sometimes overlooking other elements, proceeding without any logical connection or without a sufficient linking together of factors, sometimes confusing the chronological elements of a case, sometimes confusing the cause and effects of situations, and sometimes attributing to one party what should be said of the other. The opinion of the expert, which is not founded on information contained in the acts of the case but comes from some theoretical or aprioristic approach, cannot be accepted by the judge.[47]

One could not ask for a better description of junk science on the tribunal level. This bit of Rotal jurisprudence enjoys little favor among American canonists, judging from how seldom they cite it. Yet it bears directly on much of what commonly taints tribunal deliberations and decisions. Minimally, sentences are supposed to reflect moral certitude as well as fidelity to Church teaching and law. Moral certitude, canonically, is supposed to hinge on proof beyond reasonable doubt, not on the preponderance of evidence. Defective consent cases, by their very nature, often put moral certitude out of reach and cut against the Church's position on valid marriage. Rotal rulings like the one cited here, the statements of spouses whose marriages were annulled, tribunals' budget limitations, and analysis of the expert's role combine to suggest that many annulments given on psychological grounds are based on what might charitably be called semieducated guesses. Junk science is a vital accessory to the guesswork.

A quantitative species of junk science is manifested in CLSA's annual statistical summaries of tribunal activities. For more than two decades the primary mission of American tribunals has been adjudicating annulment petitions. But while the CLSA's statistics provide some useful information, they do not reveal with any precision several fundamental aspects of tribunal operations—how many decrees of nullity are issued, how many denied, and the various grounds for annulments granted. The summaries are reasonably accurate with respect to cases decided by documentary process, but ordinary process statistics do not include exact tallies on decrees of nullity and denials. No figures are given for how "Cases Decided" are distributed according to outcome. It is like reading election returns that fail to specify the number of votes received by the candidates and the winner's margin of victory. The kinds of data Catholics and the general public would like to see are what reasonably diligent bishops should insist on seeing. As now constituted, the statistical summaries generate obfuscation, cynicism, and suspicion. On the other hand, full disclosure would be tantamount to advertising the havoc being wrought on Christian marriage by the American tribunal system. It would add quantitative corroboration for what is qualitatively one of the great scandals in the history of the American Church.

Nonetheless, CLSA data are used to defend America's eminence in the declaration of decrees of nullity.[48]

Defective Consent and Remarriage

Problems associated with C. 1095 annulments do not vanish after nullity is granted. If the First and Second Instance tribunals rule for nullity, the ex-spouses can usually remarry in the Church. There are some notable exceptions, however. Execution of First and Second Instance sentences for nullity is suspended if a respondent appeals to Third Instance for review. For petitioners already remarried one or more times, a decree of nullity ratified at Second Instance usually makes their second or latest union eligible for Church blessing. The process is called convalidation. In serial-monogamy situations the canonical problems can get complicated.[49] Even if not appealed, a defective consent annulment does not automatically place the parties beyond the pale of tribunal intervention. Formidable psychological and pastoral concerns should be reckoned with before remarriage is permitted. The burning question is what must be done to ensure that the psychological condition that provided grounds for nullity is not still present at remarriage?

In many dioceses the right to remarry is not always conferred carte blanche. The bishop or tribunal can impose a *vetitum*, which prohibits remarriage until certain conditions are satisfied.[50] If more drastic action seems appropriate, remarriage can be proscribed permanently. One survey showed that 130 of the 176 tribunals canvassed made use of the *vetitum*, but the number of cases where it was ordered is not given. Nor are there data on the frequency of its use when grounds for nullity are related to defective consent. Tribunals responding to the survey indicated that the prohibition is used most often when there is "severe mental illness," "personality disorders," "alcoholism or drug addiction," and "physical brutality." To a lesser extent it is applied when candidates for remarriage refuse to support children from a previous marriage and when remarriage might generate scandal. For the prohibition to be lifted, the tribunals' modal prerequisite was counseling.[51]

Throughout our discussion of the helping professions, the terms psychology and psychiatry have been used inclusively. Much of what has been said about those two fields applies to such other specialties as counseling and social work. Yet certain summary observations are germane to what follows. Proliferating at an explosive rate, counseling is almost universally regarded as an unalloyed good. As suggested earlier, problems of every stripe—crime, natural disaster victimization, drug addiction, spouse abuse, alcoholism, overeating, codependency, and so on—are considered responsive to counseling. As a result, it is often prescribed almost reflexively. Since counselors are dedicated to doing good, their efforts are regarded by many as invariably beneficial. Seldom is it noted that despite the swelling number of counselors, problems they address persist or become more widespread. When members of the healing professions are confronted with this disturbing fact a stock answer is "Without us things would be a lot worse." Besides being self-serving, the answer is safe and reassuring, partly because most counseling is not subjected to follow-up study.

Despite ministering to an ever-larger clientele, the helping professions have never really delivered all they were thought to promise. Expecting cures, Americans had to settle for "coping," and sometimes not even that.[52] What evaluative studies there are of psychotherapy show moderate success at best, not terribly much better than a placebo effect or doing nothing at all. A therapist who does little more than hold hands with patients might get results almost as good as one who spends years trying to make sense of their dreams and free associations. The gap between promise and results probably explains the eclecticism of many psychiatrists. Instead of painting themselves into an unproductive corner by overcommitting to a particular psychiatric theory or an approach that is obviously not working, therapists turn pragmatic, using any method that seems to help. The gap might also partly account for many psychiatrists shifting from psychotherapy to pharmacological measures. But the openings the transition created has been filled by helping professionals with lesser qualifications, often counselors and social workers. Undeniably the replacements help some clients, though it is unlikely that they are better at it than the psychiatrists they replaced. Patients as well as disorders can put up stiff resistance to treatment. No matter how skilled or well trained, therapists have tremendous difficulty helping those who have no real inner desire to be helped.

Well established but woefully underpublicized is the fact that an indeterminate but sizable number of clients are simply not suited for therapy. For many in that category, its effect is neutral at best. For others the condition under treatment actually worsens. The differential effects of counseling are clearly shown in studies of efforts to rehabilitate criminals and delinquents.[53] These findings are not inconsistent with the results of the the *vetitum* survey cited above. Tribunals reported that postannulment counseling had mixed results. Slightly more than half said it was "very effective," while nearly as many found it ineffective or confessed inability to judge the results.[54] The tribunalists' assessments of counseling were more impressionistic than scientific. But similar evaluations occurred elsewhere. Psychiatrists working with the Brooklyn tribunal were reported as believing that the practice of *vetitum* counseling in that jurisdiction was "largely useless."[55]

That the fruits of *vetitum* counseling are frequently barren or bitter is understandable. Diagnosing a mental disorder is one thing, treating and bringing it under control another. Often treatment does not run its full course, ceasing shortly after remarriage occurs. Often the treaters are in over their heads, especially when dealing with serious disorders. Or they may be tilting at diagnostic windmills, questionable disorders identified through junk science. A judge in a tribunal that prides itself for efficiency and thoroughness states that removal of a *vetitum* is "usually a matter of going through a marriage-readiness evaluation which consists of counseling services provided by Catholic Social Services."[56] The statement all but shouts that the tribunal knowingly grants defective consent annulments in cases where no grave disorder exists. Counseling is scarcely an appropriate strategy for schizophrenia or manic-depression. This sort of implementation of the *vetitum* signals that use of junk science to nullify marriage is often followed by junk therapy to enable a Church blessing to remarriage. Both steps involve misuse of psychology, both trivialize marriage itself.

Based on what evidence we have, *vetitum* in the United States is irregularly imposed, poorly monitored, and generally ineffective. The right to remarry is given precedence over the risk of another divorce and another defective consent annulment. It is analogous to the situation in which the state allows a divorced father, thousands of dollars in arrears on child support payments, to remarry and bestow his financial irresponsibility on a second family. Despite its manifold inadequacies, the *vetitum* has certain symbolic value. It may suggest to the unwary the existence of a psychological disorder of sufficient magnitude to warrant nullifying the previous marriage on grounds of defective consent. Mandating counseling, however ineffective it may be, allows the tribunal to point to good-faith effort to prevent the grounds for an annulment from carryings over to a subsequent marriage. It can enhance the impression conveyed to the world that tribunals annul with the disinterested assistance of behavioral science. Finally, requiring even useless counseling before remarriage salves the tribunal's collective conscience and legitimizes its pastoral impulses. Petitioners released from the shackles of unhappy marriages can face matrimony anew in remarriage and return to full communion with the Church. Lost sheep are returned to the fold. Samuel Johnson pithily observed that "second marriages represent a triumph of hope over experience." Most remarriages permitted by American tribunals via defective consent annulments embody a similar hope, along with the vanquishing of Church teaching and law by counterfeit psychology and misdirected pastoralism.

❖ 7 ❖

Promoting the Blueprint

Thus far our primary emphasis has been on the conceptual basis for America's rise to the pinnacle of the annulment heap. The American experience shows, in thoroughly convincing fashion, the truth of the hoary cliché that ideas have consequences. The ruminations of revisionist theologians and canonists, augmented by what passes for behavioral science, led to alleged changes in the essence of marriage, in the role of Rotal jurisprudence, and to broader psychologization of the annulment process. The new vision of Christian marriage provided a conceptual blueprint for reorienting the American tribunal system, a grand scheme for softening if not melting its traditional hard line on nullity. Blueprints, of course, can languish on the drawing board unless there are mechanisms for enabling them to leap from paper to action. The modernized approach to marriage and nullity had to be transmitted from the theological and canonical intelligentsia to those staffing the diocesan tribunals. From there it could be transfused into the consciousness of the laity.

It was not necessary for the agents of change to draft elaborate plans requiring radical restructure or replacement of the existing judicial machinery. A national network of diocesan tribunals was already in place. But in terms of productivity, the system performed at cottage-industry level, denying considerably more annulments than it granted. The blueprint called for moving the tribunals from preindustrial to post-Conciliar modes of production. The handicraft approach would have to be replaced by an assembly line. The introduction of the American Procedural Norms (APN) in 1970, streamlining adjudication of ordinary process annulments, worked toward that end. Single-judge trials and suspension of the requirement for conforming decisions by Second Instance tribunals undoubtedly facilitated more decrees of nullity. Many of the norms found their way into the new code. The new code makes no provision for procedures peculiar to tribunals in the United States. Tribunals throughout the world are supposed to play by the same rules. Yet there are canonists who persist in crediting some of America's unmatched production of declarations of nullity to procedural changes.[1] In any event, procedural changes were not nearly as important as winning the minds and hearts of those staffing the diocesan tribunals. For many incumbent tribunalists aggressive indoctrination was unnecessary. They too were caught up in the heady atmosphere of Vatican II renewal, primed for relaxing the traditional strictures on annulment.

The less eager were quite easily brought into line, though pockets of resistance prevented achievement of a perfectly solid front. Canonists responsible for the new blueprint dominated the principal English-language forums. Many were tenured professors of canon law, strategically positioned to spread the word in books and scholarly journals, in the classroom, and as source persons for the media and the hierarchy. They set the terms of whatever debate occurred on the annulment situation in the United States. Their publications and utterances shaped and reinforced the views of incumbent tribunalists, and they were responsible for training the new recipients of licentiates and doctorates in canon law. Students they mentored were sent out to staff diocesan tribunals, where they could evangelize their sitting colleagues and reform the annulment process. A generation of canonists steeped in the gospel of easy annulment now staffs the diocesan tribunals, ready and willing to engage in "healing" by nullity. Once the tribunals themselves were in the fold, the system had the necessary ideological and organizational components for setting up a canonical counterpart of that unique American creation, the assembly line. Just as Henry Ford's genius led to mass manufacture of the Model-T, America's theologians and canonists fashioned an assembly line of their own to mass-produce decrees of nullity.

Spreading the Word

The theological, canonical, pastoral, and psychological premises animating the American tribunal system seldom come under serious challenge from within. Publications on annulment, whether scholarly or journalistic, present a veritable pronullity common front. Ritual homage is paid to the permanence and indissolubility of Christian marriage, frequently as a prelude to defending and praising a system that seems bent on undermining it. I surveyed all articles relating to annulment that appeared in *The Jurist*, flagship publication of the CLSA, between 1970 and 1996. Generally well written, the journal's selections reflect favorably on the canonical erudition of their authors. Typically they are well documented, some as heavily footnoted as articles in prestigious law reviews. Much of the documentation consists of references to like-minded canonists, each with a pronullity ax to grind. Rota citations, as we have seen, lean heavily in the same direction. References to the work of foreign canonists and theologians are commonplace, indicating that many contributors and readers are at home in at least one language other than English, particularly Latin. Dissenting views and articles occasionally appear, but in the context of all the written material on annulment they function as a form of tokenism. The English literature on annulment comes very close to being monolithic.

Poring over a quarter century of *The Jurist* sensitizes the reader to a variety of themes. First, most articles deal with issues other than annulment. Among those that do, one cannot help but be taken with how many contributors regard Rome as a negative, meddlesome influence. For all the talk of curial authoritarianism and interference, American canonists do not look to the Vatican with fear and trembling. Outwardly at least, respect and civility are shown. But the external facade often masks indifference or subtle defiance. Practices generating Vatican concerns are often staunchly defended or glossed over. Not infrequently the impression is conveyed that Vatican criticism of the tribunal system is based on misunderstanding of American culture and failure to relate to the efficiency of American marriage tribunals. Functionally, then, the Vatican is merely nominally despotic, and treated as if none too enlightened.

Another theme, discussed at length in preceding chapters, is the American canonical community's deferential praise of the role of behavioral science in ordinary process cases. Since Vatican II the system's relationship with behavioral science has gone from dalliance to what approaches obsequious acquiescence. But the encomiums for psychiatry are not matched in *The Jurist* by the allocation of space to contributors from the healing professions. Occasionally an article by a clinician appears. Also, canonists sometimes cite Census data or allude to unspecified advances and insights of behavioral science. In fairness, Varvaro's surveys, including one coauthored by Guarino, flirt with engaging in social science research. They are useful though methodologically weak. Their work notwithstanding, a sizable assortment of annulment issues yearns for empirical study. To name some obvious topics: an updated examination of cases appealed to the Rota; the outcome of Church remarriages made possible by annulment; the premarital instruction received by recipients of annulments; the socioeconomic background and religiosity of petitioners for nullity; the pastoral measures of First Instance tribunals to reconcile petitioners and respondents. This brief listing merely scratches the surface. Despite the dearth of research, the impression conveyed is that scientific angels are on the side of tribunals, enabling them to deal as never before with the knotty problem of marital consent. Finally, among canonists who publish, there is a discernible urge to see how much further the frontiers of defective consent nullity can be pushed.[2]

The Jurist articles on annulment chronicle a remarkable level of consensus on the fundamentals of the American approach to nullity. The shared perspective is all the more notable in light of the reputed disputatiousness of legal theorists and practitioners. There is, to be sure, debate on finer points and occasional mild misgivings on the interpretation and application of Church teaching and law. A few isolated voices express concern with the number of annulments granted. But overall, American contributors to the journal do not present any serious criticism of the premises and policies that govern the adjudication of defective consent cases.[3] The manifold assumptions that provide the system with ideological and canonical substance are treated as settled law, virtually impervious to any theological and canonical counterarguments, however compelling or authoritative. When the assumptions are compatible with change, the modification is almost always in the direction of expanding eligibility for declarations of nullity. There is little fault-finding of the administrative policies and procedures of the diocesan tribunals. Threats of criticism from Rome are usually met with sanctimonious defensiveness, professions of innocence, and assurances that departures from Church teaching and law are exceptions. Many of Rome's concerns, as one judicial vicar put it, indicate that the Vatican is unduly influenced by a small, vocal, fundamentalist minority that is opposed to change. The system's efficiency is routinely lauded, and few questions are raised about precisely how the efficiency is achieved and what it brings forth. The commendations often strike an arrogant ethnocentric note. If only tribunals elsewhere resembled ours, it is said, the gap between America's production of annulments and that of other societies would be narrowed, and the Church universal would be better for it.

Responding to the oft-stated concern that the United States, with five percent of the world's Catholics, grants eighty percent of all Catholic annulment, the Director of the Office for Canonical Affairs for the Diocese of San Diego, remarks, "I frankly feel that this is the shallowest of all tribunal criticisms. Americans make up 6% of the world's population, but they account for 100% of the men on the moon. So what? America functions. Much of the rest of the world does not."[4] One wonders if the Director would use similar logic to explain why the United States has more jail and prison inmates per capita than any other democratic society.

The impact of material in scholarly journals like *The Jurist* on the judicial and administrative activities of the diocesan tribunals cannot be measured. Yet surely it is considerable, if only because it is the CLSA's house organ. Contributors include professors of canon law and leading tribunalists in the field. Their influence goes beyond the pedagogical power inherent in teaching and authorship. Some are officers in the CLSA, while others serve on *The Jurist*'s editorial board and referee manuscripts submitted for publication. Prestigious professor-canonists are often called upon to interpret sticky legal problems by formulating "unofficial" opinions which may be accorded more de facto authenticity than those formulated by high-ranking Church figures. Their expertise on the legality of such issues as church closings, liturgical variations, and dissent is seen as carrying over to questions arising from declarations of nullity.

Publications like *The Jurist, CLSA Proceedings*, and *Studia Canonica* (Canada's foremost canonical publication) are essential resources for those processing annulment petitions and for keeping abreast of where the system and the law are headed. But the CLSA does not rely solely on scholarly periodicals to disseminate information on marriage and annulment. Under its sponsorship Wrenn has published a series of titles that grace the reference shelves of most if not all tribunal libraries. His *Annulments*, now in its fifth edition, covers as well as any reference in print the American canonical community's approach to ordinary process annulment. If we count the revision of the second edition separately, his *Decisions* was published in three editions. His *Procedures* is a lucidly written handbook that treats ordinary process cases from start to finish, including possible postsentence appeals.[5] Relevant statutes are listed by number. Instead of giving the official English translations of the laws, Wrenn explains them succinctly in simpler language. For tribunals pressured to process cases as expeditiously as possible, as most American tribunals are, a more convenient short reference book would be difficult to find. It includes samples of letters sent to the parties and witnesses, a copy of the Archdiocese of Hartford's brochure, forms for the *libellus* (the document containing the petition) and for requesting a marital history. No samples of sentences are provided, but they can be found in Wrenn's *Decisions*, which offers model formats and rationales. The availability of such material no doubt expedites the processing of cases. But it can also lead to impersonal substitutes or shortcuts for deliberation, judiciousness, and diligence. In one case examined by Varvaro the Rota noted that the "defender of the bond did nothing more than sign a prepared declaration of one page which could have been used for any marriage nullity case without specification."[6] The defender's misfeasance makes one wonder how often tribunalists, like civil attorneys or paralegals drawing up simple wills, accelerate the awarding of decrees of nullity by choosing canned arguments, inserting new names and dates, and filling in the blanks with examples of legal reasoning thought to be appropriate for those kinds of cases. A veteran tribunalist confides that these practices are fairly common, dictated by the need to process large caseloads within time frames specified by law.

Reaching the Laity

Quite understandably, the views purveyed by canonical academicians in scholarly journals and books are source material for authors of popular publications. Several books on the market, aimed at laity and clerics unschooled in canon law, spread what the authors regard as the good news on annulment. In general, the books cover the same territory. Owing to Vatican II, the Church reputedly modified her teaching on the nature of marriage and on the grounds for nullity. Tribunal staffs were not only enlarged, but also driven to process cases more efficiently. Thanks to such developments, annulment is now a more viable option and the procedure for obtaining one more expedient. There is almost invariably assurance that all this was accomplished without compromising commitment to the permanence and indissolubility of marriage. Typically, some space is devoted to cost and time factors. Capsule case studies and citations of Rotal decisions are occasionally included to provide prospective petitioners with examples of situations that might parallel their own.[7] Those who read any of the books written for popular consumption are unlikely to come away with an understanding that the approach to annulment purveyed is largely peculiar to the United States, other English-speaking countries, and western Europe.[8]

For many years the *Catholic Almanac*, a parish and household staple, has faithfully echoed the American canonical community's annulment perspective. Readers are provided with annual repetitions of the personalist, "communion of life" conception of valid marriage. Decrees of nullity based on such grounds "do not indicate any softening of the Church's attitude regarding the permanence of marriage. They affirm, rather, that some persons who have married were really not capable of doing do." To its credit, the *Almanac*, using Vatican data instead of CLSA figures, tacitly acknowledges that American tribunals have a knack for identifying large numbers of incapacitated "some persons." Here, too, no effort is made to explain why the rest of the world's tribunals do not discern similar levels of incapacitation, or why the United States accounts for so disproportionately high a number of defective consent annulments. Bypassing explanations, the *Almanac* refers to a "landmark decree of nullity issued in 1973 by the Roman Rota," apparently preferring it to the 1969 ruling by Anné. It then cites John Paul's January 26, 1984 allocution to the Rota, which makes reference to "grave lack of discretionary judgment" and incapacity to fulfill the "essential matrimonial rights and obligations" the most common grounds for defective consent annulments. The *Almanac* does not delve into how these sections of C. 1095 come into play, or the confusion that attends their proper interpretation and application. The unsuspecting reader, particularly one who is not apprised of the pope's later allocutions on these issues, can easily believe that the Holy Father has given his stamp of approval to the American usage of C. 1095 in granting decrees of nullity based on defective consent.[9]

Nullity tidings are also contained in diocesan newspapers, parish bulletins, and pamphlets. Most include a brief statement on how divorce and annulment differ and how the Church's outlook on nullity has changed. A series of questions and answers may be designed to serve the same purpose. Invariably there are assurances that revelations made during annulment proceedings will be kept in strict confidence and that fees can be waived for those of lesser means. Frequently, an effort is made to soothe anxiety among potential petitioners through the assurance that an annulment has no effect on the legitimacy of children. Some parish bulletins simply announce a lecture-discussion presentation by a tribunal staff person. All are welcome, but the real target audience is parishioners who are either separated, divorced, or divorced and remarried. Whether or not it is remotely possible that their marriages are invalid, they are encouraged to contact the tribunal to see if they might qualify for an annulment. The tone of the invitations usually suggests that a visit to the tribunal office will at least set a nullity proceeding in motion. Some invitations practically promise an annulment to all who apply. The promotional efforts, like cigarette and beer ads not meant for minors, may evoke responses from constituents not directly targeted, such as spouses who dream of greener marital pastures but would not seriously consider separation and divorce were annulment not presented as a convenient and acceptable alternative. The potential these expositions have for ending such troubled marriages is simply not addressed in the annulment literature.

The role of the secular press in the dissemination of the American annulment gospel is not to be underestimated. Hardly an urban daily newspaper or weekly newsmagazine has not at one time or another run a feature article on the local or national annulment picture. Frequently the coverage is inspired by a public figure, perhaps a politician or popular entertainer, who is somehow involved with annulment. The stories follow a rather standardized pattern, usually starting with mention of annulments sought or obtained by celebrities, or reference to the high incidence of annulment in the United States. A tribunal spokesman, hewing scrupulously to the American nullity party line, will explain and defend the system, typically in a very cursory manner. Assurances that annulment is not guaranteed for the rich and famous, that the Church remains committed to permanence in marriage, and that advances in psychology have given us new means for probing marital consent are de rigueur. Without identifying the parties, a few case histories may be summarized, documenting how annulment has provided divorced Catholics with healing and more fulfilling remarriages.

Although there is sometimes reference to Rome's dissatisfaction with the volume of American annulments, usually the only canonists interviewed are solidly behind what America's tribunals are doing. A recent *Chicago Tribune* story refers to Vatican traditionalists directing "heavy criticism" at the American Church, and quotes Archbishop Vincenzo Fagiolo, a Rotalist for many years, as charging that the "high numbers of Catholic annulments in the U.S. is scandalous."[10] The archbishop's viewpoint is juxtaposed with that of the adjutant judicial vicar for the Chicago archdiocesan marriage tribunal, who states that "the increase in annulments is primarily due to rewriting of canon law since the Second Vatican Council."[11] Presumably the adjutant judicial vicar knows something about canon law that has eluded the archbishop. Statements attributed to tribunalists are uniformly self-serving, if not self-congratulatory. Of course they are no more likely to concede publicly the fraudulent nature of thousands of decrees of nullity than is the neighborhood supermarket to admit that its produce is not fresh. Privately, however, some will confess that they are engaged in a sham.[12] By and large, press accounts on annulment are straightforward, more descriptive than analytical, and utterly dependent on the accuracy of information conveyed by interviewees. Some accounts include statistics more accurate than those published by the CLSA. Ironically, the most telling criticism of the system may come from those who have had marriages annulled. For example, one petitioner, although pleased by the annulment of his marriage, nevertheless questioned how a tribunal can decide what is almost impossible to decide: whether a couple's marriage was sacramental.[13]

Despite earnest efforts and the best intentions, even seasoned newspaper reporters have difficulty filing stories on annulment that are both balanced and accurate. For one thing, hardly any reporters in the United States, including those specializing in religion, are well-versed in the intricacies of Church law and procedures relating to annulment. Quite sensibly reporters enlist the assistance of canon lawyers. And what better canonists to interview than the heads of diocesan marriage tribunals and the leaders of the CLSA? Interviews with such figures will likely be reported with great fidelity, but their content will almost surely be tainted with bias. Finding a judicial vicar or a CLSA official who is not sold on the American way of annulment is no simple task.

An enterprising reporter might seek out laypersons who have gone through annulment. They, too, are not necessarily altogether reliable informants. No matter how cooperative, they are not always able to relate many things that a diligent reporter would like to know. If once involved in a Documentary Process annulment, they can probably describe what it entailed. But parties to Ordinary Process cases are usually at a loss to explain precisely what occurred and to articulate the tribunal's rationale for its decision. They also tend to be incapable of discussing the significance of their cases in a larger ecclesial and canonical context.

Another roadblock is the fact that all who participate in annulment proceedings are bound by rules of confidentiality. The situation is analogous to confession, however. The penitent might relate matters that transpired in the confessional without facing stern sanctions; the confessor does so under pain of excommunication. Quite a few former petitioners and respondents are willing to talk, despite having been pledged to secrecy. Tribunal personnel honor the prohibition against discussing specific cases as assiduously as they adhere to the seal of the confessional.

If reporters had access to ordinary process sentences affirming or denying nullity they would learn considerably more about annulment than they gain from interviews with American canon lawyers. But the only sentences published are the Rota's, which happen to be written in Latin. Rota sentences cover the relevant law and jurisprudence, proper application of each, and the evidence, testimony, and arguments bearing on the question of validity. The names of the parties, witnesses, and experts are included. But any material that might reveal the identities of those involved in the case is expunged when Rota sentences are translated into English. Some translated sentences considered noteworthy are published in canonical journals that are completely unknown even to dedicated bibliophiles. Publication of translated sentences is meant to help canonists keep abreast of Rotal jurisprudence, but there are indications that not all canon lawyers read them regularly or take them seriously.

Given these constraints, reporters have difficulty preparing balanced, in-depth articles that look beyond what their informants tell them. By focusing on judicial vicars and CLSA officials, television and newsprint reporters inadvertently provide the system with a forum that would delight any public relations expert: Free exposure to expound and defend their views on the propriety of annulments granted by American tribunals, with minimal chance of effective rebuttal. It is a forum entered with little trepidation. Although dissent within the Church in the United States is certainly not unknown, few American canonists are disposed to publicly take issue with what is purveyed by the system's spokesmen. Any who dare voice opposing views must usually express them in media outlets that are not in the mainstream. Critical or querelous letters to editors written by laypersons might appear after canonists have had their say, but they carry little weight in the debate on annulment. The upshot of all this is that press coverage of annulment conveys to the public at large and Catholics in particular a slanted perspective that casts the American marriage tribunals in a light more flattering than is deserved.

It Pays To Advertise

Tribunal outreach efforts often walk a thin line between pastoral solicitude and canonical barratry. In common law barratry refers to inciting groundless litigatim. In nonlegal parlance it is more picturesquely termed "ambulance chasing." Solicitation of business by lawyers was traditionally frowned upon in the United States, a taboo that still holds in several other societies. In many jurisdictions attorneys actively stimulating litigation could be punished by jail sentences or by suspension of their licenses to practice law. Perhaps the most important reason behind the legal and ethical proscription was the desire to keep a lid on litigation, especially frivolous actions undertaken for the purpose of generating fees. To ensure that the ban against promotion of legal services would be observed, lawyers were not allowed to advertise.[14] The ban, never completely effective, lost most of its bite in 1976 when the American Bar Association, fearing antitrust actions, tempered its rules against advertising. Virtually all restrictions were lifted a year later when the Supreme Court, in a 5–4 decision, ruled that lawyers have a constitutional right to advertise.[15] Americans can now see or hear attorneys promoting their services on billboards, in full-page ads in the Yellow Pages, and in television and radio commercials.

Canon law is silent about tribunals promoting their services. While it may be legally and ethically permissible for civil attorneys to solicit cases, there is something unseemly about ecclesiastical judicial bodies engaging in similar behavior. Common sense suggests that it is tantamount to proclaiming an interest in the outcome of the case. Tribunals, it may be argued, solicit for pastoral and educational purposes, while lawyers in the secular legal system do it primarily for fees. But the contrast in terms of altruism versus pecuniary gain cannot be so neatly framed. Before the U.S. Supreme Court's 1977 decision, lawyers often maintained that advertising stimulated competition which, in turn, would reduce attorneys' fees, making their services more affordable to the needy. But tribunals also charge fees, though they do not operate at a profit. Their promotional efforts are questionable because they introduce an element of structural bias where none should exist. The office of an attorney in private practice who spends lavishly on advertising might overflow with clients. Some of their cases might wind up in court, leading to even larger fees. But private attorneys lack the authority to decide the outcome of trials they initiate. In stark contrast, a tribunal reaching out for petitioners is also the court that will sit in judgment on their cases. There is, at the very least, the appearance of a conflict of interest. Judges in the civil legal order would be expected to recuse themselves from cases they helped into court. If tribunalists were angels it would not be a problem for them to mete out evenhanded justice under such circumstances. Even if it is assumed that all tribunalists are dedicated and holy, however, they operate within a system where evenhanded detachment is difficult for them to attain. For all intents and purposes the American tribunal system has removed Justice's blindfold, tipped her scales in the direction of annulment, and used her sword to undercut Church teaching on the permanence and indissolubility of marriage.

Recruitment of prospective petitioners by means of a question and answer format is regarded as especially suitable for the limited space available in diocesan papers, parish bulletins, and tribunal brochures. The questions are usually those considered most rudimentary or most frequently asked by laypersons. While the format may appear to serve pastoral and canonical concerns, it is not problem free. Space constraints limit the number of questions and the expansiveness of responses. Consequently, the information conveyed can be glib, cryptic, partially true, or even misleading. Readers who find the material applicable to their situation, or wish for clarification or an opportunity to pose questions of their own, are advised to contact the tribunal office. A breakthrough in this mode of promoting nullity occurred recently when one resourceful tribunal spread its message beyond the readership of parish and diocesan publications. To increase the chances of making contact with potential petitioners a half-page ad was placed in *The Florida Times-Union*, a Jacksonville daily.[16]

The ad, as Marshall McLuhan might have said, illustrates how the medium can confound the message. One question asked: "Thirty years ago couples could not get annulments; now they can. Why now and not then?" The reply

> Tribunals were established in the 11th century. Twenty years ago the U.S. Catholic bishops requested from the Holy Father simplified procedures. The bishops also expanded tribunal staffs and allocated a great deal of financial support. Since then, the Church in the U.S. has developed considerable expertise and with the use of modern technology has increased by one-hundred fold the number of petitions and resolutions.[17]

The question itself is poorly framed, since it can easily be taken to mean that annulments were unavailable thirty years ago. As an example of advertising puffery, the answer merits a passing grade, but it fails to meet the question head on and misleads the reader. It alludes to the APN without revealing that technically they have been defunct since 1983. Some of the norms, it is true, appear in the new code. But others, such as the waiver of mandatory review at Second Instance of decrees of nullity, are replaced by procedures emanating from the 1917 code. Conspicuously absent is any hint of the Vatican's position on the volume of American annulments. Credit for the annulment upsurge is also attributed to factors one might associate with an increase in the output of widgets: money, personnel, "expertise," and technology. The terms are compatible with the lingua franca of production management, but they do not articulate the real reasons behind the availability of annulments. Actually, the principal modern technological contributions to tribunal offices are telephones, recording machines, and word processors. Some tribunals are blessed with fax machines. Such devices undeniably enhance a tribunal's ability to process petitions and attend to paperwork. But their role in the output of defective consent decrees of nullity is secondary to the tribunal's conception of the nature of marriage, how it chooses to implement canon law, its use of expert opinion, and its judges' vision on the propriety of annulment. The reply, finally, understates where the new expertise and technology have taken us. Petitions and "resolutions" (read: decrees of nullity) have actually increased closer to one-thousandfold since the early 1970s.

The response to another question in the ad suggests that the authors are more attuned to *Advertising Age* than the *Code of Canon Law* or pronouncements by the Holy Father.

Q. What are grounds for obtaining an annulment?

A. Most often they are "lack of due discretion." By that we mean, What was the degree of emotional maturity of both parties at the time that they gave consent (since marriage comes into being by the consent of the parties)? How did this affect their judgment about getting married and choosing each other as spouses?

In marriage you have two people who are attempting to give themselves totally to one another while at the same time they are accepting each other. So you have a giving and an accepting by two persons, which is really four distinct acts. A person's emotional maturity will determine the capacity to give himself or herself in the interpersonal relationship of marriage and to consent to a lifetime union.

Analyzing at length the flaws in this answer would necessitate repeating discussions found in earlier chapters. A few brief comments will suffice. How tribunals are able to gauge emotional maturity/immaturity is left to the reader's imagination. While the argument from emotional immaturity persists as an instrument of nullity among American tribunalists, it does not set well with John Paul II and members of the Rota. In his 1987 allocution to the Rota the Holy Father complained that "psychic maturity which is seen as the goal of human development ends up being confused with canonical maturity which is rather the basic minimum for establishing the validity of the marriage."[18] In addition, the answer omits the word *grave* before "lack of due discretion," fails to specify that emotional immaturity must be caused by some serious mental disorder, and relies on a simplistic "interpersonalist" approach to the essence of marriage and a minimalist conception of incapacity.

The general tenor of the ad rather unmistakably conveys the impression that annulment is no big deal. It is as though the ad aims to inform readers that filing for an annulment resembles opening a checking account at a neighborhood bank—safe, easy, convenient, and affordable. Similar assurances appear in every annulment ad I have seen. The impression conveyed is that an annulment proceeding is part and parcel of life's normal routine. It comes as no surprise that in 1989 and 1990, the tribunal responsible for placing the *Times-Union* ad accepted for trial every last one of 389 petitions presented to it. The following year 176 cases were presented, 158 accepted. The modest reduction in cases presented might account for the subsequent placement of the ad. During the three-year interval, 575 cases were decided by sentence, which can be safely taken to mean that virtually every case accepted by the tribunal resulted in an annulment.[19]

What has been written in English on annulment is overwhelmingly skewed in the direction of permissiveness. The prevailing views within the academic wing of the canonical community are faithfully mirrored in publications intended for general consumption. Books, magazines, newspapers, pamphlets, and ads form an almost solid front for easy annulment. Theological and canonical subtleties may be lost or muddled in the trickle-down process to the popular level, but the basic message and thrust remain the same. Articles dissenting from the conventional American wisdom on annulment occasionally appear in publications labeled "conservative," "reactionary," and "fundamentalist," but almost never in the mainstream media, either secular or religious.[20] Interestingly, such publications are almost never referred to as "orthodox." Books criticial of the awarding of decrees of nullity by American tribunals are practically nonexistent. Books critical of the American tribunal system are practically collectors items. Two authors cited earlier considered the system too restrictive and hypocritical. Kelleher argued for dispensing with diocesan marriage tribunals, and for the Church to abandon her position on permanence and indissolubility and allow divorce and remarriage for those in marriages irretrievably broken.[21] Brunsman did not go quite that far. Tribunals simply could not keep pace with the pent-up demand for annulments, partly due to restrictions imposed by Rome. To avoid or moderate tribunal gridlock, there should be more extensive reliance on the "internal forum" solution.[22]

Ground for criticism from the opposite direction was broken in 1978 by William H. Marshner's slim volume, *Annulment or Divorce?* His principal concern was the theology of marriage, particularly with respect to how some developments in that field facilitated annulment. The ground he broke remained fallow for nearly twenty years, until publication of Sheila Rauch Kennedy's *Shattered Faith.* Using seven case histories, including her own, Kennedy documents the reactions of those on the receiving end of unwanted annulments. Her subjects report outrage and bewilderment. None mentioned coming under the influence of the "healing" power so often attributed to annulment. Indeed, some parted company with the Church which in their minds abandoned their vision of valid marriage. After twelve years of marriage that produced twin sons, Sheila and her husband, Congressman Joseph Kennedy II, divorced. Joseph remarried outside the Church, then petitioned the Archdiocese of Boston's tribunal for an annulment, preliminary to having the second marriage validated. The annulment was granted on the ground that the petitioner lacked due discretion. Angered and stunned by the tribunal's finding that she was never really married, and distraught over the annulment's effects on the children, Sheila became a contentious respondent in the fullest sense. Besides writing the first book-length critique of the American species of annulment in nearly two decades, she appealed the tribunal's decree of nullity to the Rota. The outcome of the appeal is still pending.

Since Kennedy family affairs are front-page news, the case received considerable national attention. Predictably, canon lawyers were sought out for commentary. Quite rightly none of those interviewed would discuss the details of the case or the merits of the annulment. However, they rise to the defense of the tribunals in familiar ways. "This is a very important ministry, given the society we live in where there are so many divorces," said Monsignor Desmond J. Vella, judicial vicar for the Metropolitan Tribunal for the Archdiocese of New York. "We see our work as dealing with two competing values. On the one hand, we're defending and upholding the Church's teaching on the indissolubility of marriage. On the other hand, we're reaching out to Catholics who cannot enjoy a central position in the Church because of divorce and remarriage. What are these people to do? Where are they to go? We just can't ignore them."[23] Taking a different tack, Patrick Cogan, Executive Coordinator of the CLSA, stated "The courts in Rome began to take into account the findings of behavioral sciences and apply that to understanding the qualities necessary to exchange consent in marriage. It told us much about how the human psyche works. There may be a basic incompatibility in the beginning, and the couple didn't realize it."[24] Cogan makes no mention of the sharp differences between Rome and American tribunals on the nature of defective consent.

Perhaps the most compelling indicator of the pronullity slant of the literature may be discerned in a topic on which the tribunal system maintains studious silence. Reams have been written on why annulment is more available and how to get one, but there is nary a book, chapter, article, pamphlet, or newspaper ad attempting to show how to defend the validity of a marriage. No American canon lawyer rides a diocesan circuit, appearing in this parish hall and the next, to explain how Catholics might contribute to the defense of marriages existing in the shadow of nullity.

Promotion of annulment has not depended solely on propagation via words written or spoken by canonical scholars, Church functionaries, lay authors, and the media. The influence of informal networking between those who have been granted annulments and relatives and acquaintances who may be tempted to seek one cannot be underestimated. The most astute and creative advertising professionals have always been sensitive to the significance of word-of-mouth testimonials. Nowhere is this principle better illustrated than in the spread of the faith in the early Church. Those dispatched by Christ to "teach all nations" did not interact directly with the countless thousands who elected to embrace Christianity. Moreover, they were fourteen centuries removed from Gutenberg's invention of movable type. Converts themselves became agents of conversion, and as their numbers increased, so did the reach of their evangelism. A similar dynamic surely occurs as annulled marriages become common. The sheer volume of annulment creates additional demand, and what was once a last canonical and pastoral alternative becomes a desirable and fashionable method for administering last rites to "bad" marriages.

❖ 8 ❖

Screening and Docketing Cases

Few Catholics today have not heard of the American Church's change of heart in granting annulments. Those entertaining thoughts of an annulment probably first broach the matter with friends and relatives. At this stage, an ideal informant would be a person who had a marriage annulled. The first Church functionary with whom an annulment proceeding is explored will probably be a parish priest. Some test the waters more directly by calling or visiting the tribunal office. In these times most priests approached by a candidate for annulment are inclined to defer to the diocesan marriage tribunal. Some, before making a referral, venture a tentative assessment of the person's chances. But that response is probably based more on what is known about the diocesan tribunal's annulment policy than on a canonically informed judgment. Generally speaking, today's priests are not as well versed in canon law as clerics of the past, since seminaries place less emphasis on the subject. But their unfamiliarity with the finer points of Church law on marriage and nullity is offset by the experience factor. The parish priest who does not know at least a dozen parishioners who have had marriages annulled has been asleep at the pastoral switch. If the priest is on good terms with both spouses, by referring the would-be petitioner to the tribunal he can avoid the appearance of taking sides.

Some tribunals use field advocates to screen applicants for annulment. In those dioceses parish priests are advised to make referrals to field advocates instead of directly to the tribunal. Briefly trained in canon law workshops, field advocates attempt to discern whether there are grounds for nullity. Discernment comes easily with most documentary process cases. But in practically all ordinary process cases determining whether there are psychological grounds for nullity is a more complicated undertaking. If either spouse has a history of mental disorder, that alone could be probable cause for defective consent. Absent that sort of evidence or diagnosis by an expert, the field advocate is involved in a guessing game. Field advocates for one midwestern tribunal, concededly unable to diagnosis mental disorders, are instructed to prepare a *libellus* if they believe the marital relationship was "sick." But any marriage ending in divorce or separation can be deemed sick. Interpersonal sickness is not necessarily a sign of mental disorder, especially one grave in nature. Still, the advocate's guesswork may result in the presentation of a petition to a tribunal judge who decides whether to accept the petition and have the case go to trial. Ostensibly, properly trained field advocates help tribunals keep their caseloads at manageable levels. The size of the tribunal system's caseload indicates that far more cases are accepted than rejected, however.

No matter which form tribunal outreach programs take, few prospective petitioners boast even a modicum of knowledge on the procedural and juridical mechanics of annulment. Unless cued by a field advocate or the intake person at the tribunal office, most cannot articulate canonically acceptable grounds for nullity, especially grounds psychological in nature. Ordinarily grounds are supplied by a tribunal staff person (a notary or auditor) and later found justiciable by a judge. The typical applicant crossing the tribunal threshold knows little besides the fact that he or she is divorced or estranged in some other way, that full-fledged membership in the Church for those divorced and remarried requires an annulment, that a friend or relative got an annulment, and that the tribunal is the place to get one.

Petition-Friendly Tribunals

The right to petition for annulment is practically absolute. With some tribunals, that right for all intents and purposes presupposes an implied right to a decree of nullity. But tribunals are under no obligation to accept every petition tendered. A petition can be rejected if the judge or tribunal lacks competence (i.e., jurisdiction), the petitioner is without canonical standing, the petition does not contain certain information (e.g., home address), or if the petition itself is baseless.[1] But the likelihood of the last option is diminished by the fact that a member of the tribunal helps draw up the petition. Moreover, within the American system the odds are that the tribunalist who helps put the petition together is favorably disposed toward annulment. No doubt this is one reason for the high acceptance rate for petitions. Most American tribunals, however, do not accept petitions unless the marriage or marriages in question led to divorce.

The petition is to be accepted or rejected within thirty days.[2] The percentage of petitions accepted for further processing, or adjudication, varies from one diocese to another. In 1989, for example, the Archdiocese of Denver accepted less than half the cases presented, while no fewer than 66 of the 165 diocesan and archdiocesan tribunals submitting data to CLSA decided to go to trial with every petition presented.[3] Overall, however, the rate of acceptance by American tribunals is extraordinarily high (Table 8-1). That same year all First Instance tribunals reporting accepted 42,092 of 48,702 petitions presented, an acceptance rate of 86 percent. If there is a discernible trend, it is in the direction of higher

Table 8–1. Presentataion and Acceptance of Petitions by U.S. First Instance Tribunals, 1980–1992.

Year	Tribunals reporting	Cases presented	Cases accepted	Percent accepted
1980	163	70,970	43,773	62
1981	166	58,475	46,519	80
1982	168	56,002	46,145	82
1983	171	57,528	50,695	88
1984	160	47,243	40,468	86
1985	160	49,608	43,838	88
1986	168	49,340	41,541	85
1987	170	49,587	42,723	86
1988	158	38,389	39,361	100.30
1989	179	48,702	42,092	86
1990	171	49,182	44,516	84
1991	168	48,992	43,939	90
1992	166	46,451	41,845	90
TOTALS		670,469	567,725	85

Source: CLSA Proceedings, 1981–1993.

acceptance rates. The thirteen-year interval covered began with a 62 percent acceptance rate and ended with the rate at 90 percent. In 1992 the number of tribunals accepting every petition fell to 59, but several others came within a petition or two of "perfect" scores. For each year between 1986 and 1992 many tribunals turned nary a petition aside. All these figures, it should be stressed, are for cases that go to trial (ordinary process). Documentary process cases are not included. Until 1986 figures were given for cases "Abandoned." Between 1980 and 1985 39,471 cases were Abandoned, that is, dropped at the initiative of the petitioner or respondent.[4]. Time of "Abandonment" is not specified. Allowing for cases "Abandoned" by petitioners after presentation but before acceptance would raise the rate of acceptance by tribunals beyond 86 percent.

It must be noted that the annual and aggregate totals understate the volume of activity by the tribunal system. Each year an average of twenty tribunals send no data to the CLSA, with archdioceses as well as dioceses unaccounted for. The thirteen years examined include no data from the Archdiocese of Philadelphia. There were years when Detroit and St. Louis failed to report. Furthermore, among tribunals reporting some sent data on "Cases Presented" but not on "Cases Accepted" and vice versa. Although there are no data to offer proof, it may not be unreasonable to hypothesize that since 1970 American tribunals have adjudicated more ordinary process cases than were tried by the universal Church since its founding.

Archdiocesan and diocesan variations in acceptance rates cannot be attributed solely to regional demographic differences. More plausibly, tribunals do not share equally in the mainstream American canonical views on the nature of valid Christian marriage, on how marital consent should be reckoned, and therefore on what constitutes a justiciable case. Obviously, some screen petitions with greater care than others. Tribunals placing a stricter construction on the law would be more inclined to deny standing to would-be petitioners whose grounds for nullity are tenuous, unprovable, or patently nonexistent. Despite a handful of tribunals that reject more petitions than they accept, however, the typical American tribunal agrees to try most petitions submitted. If there is any serious screening of applicants, it occurs before petitions are presented to tribunal judges.

Keeping the Door Open

Plainly, with many tribunals rejection of petitions is anathema. There is always room at the tribunal inn, a situation that prompted one well-informed priest to comment: "The tribunals are out looking for business." It hardly needs saying that the exceptionally high acceptance rate is part of a much larger problem. Acceptance is merely the opening act of a juridical drama which usually lacks dramatic tension inasmuch as the denouement—nullity—is so easily anticipated. The annulment brochure of one medium-sized midwestern diocesan tribunal asks, "Does everyone who seeks a Church annulment get one?" The answer corroborates the point made here: "Usually once a request for annulment is accepted, a favorable decision is given. However, a careful review is made before a request for an annulment is accepted." In the year the brochure was released, the diocese in question accepted 379 of 430 cases presented, an acceptance rate of 88 percent. The record would not seem to substantiate the exercise of "careful review," particularly if, as is likely, the bulk of the cases accepted fell under the defective consent rubric. The text of the brochure and the tribunal's acceptance rate suggest an eagerness to solicit candidates for nullity. A "favorable decision" is synonymous with nullity; evidently upholding the validity of marriage is "unfavorable." The frame of reference here is supposed to be the interests of the petitioner, not those of the tribunal.

Patrick R. Lagges, adjutant judicial vicar for the Chicago Archdiocesan marriage tribunal, is reported as stating that of about 3,000 who apply each year for decrees of nullity, approximately 1,900 "drop out before going beyond the first, cursory steps of making out an application. Another 150 drop out once the process reaches a tribunal judge."[5] The 1,900 or so dropouts are probably not serious applicants. They may be likened to browsers who enter a store, look around, and leave without making a purchase. For many, the resolve to seek an annulment evaporates when informed of the initial interview fee charged for drawing up a petition. Others withdraw upon learning that an annulment involves a bit more than the asking. Given the CLSA data on Chicago's hospitality toward petitions, the vicar's figures do not necessarily signify canonical vigilance. During the five years preceding the vicar's interview, 5,438 of 5,448 petitions presented to the tribunal were accepted.[6] In other words, it is a safe bet that most of the 1,900 dropped out of their own accord and not because they were officially turned away. Had petitions been filed in their behalf and accepted for trial, their cases would have been counted under "Abandonment." CLSA's statistical summaries show that between 1987 and 1991 the Chicago tribunal reported 82 "Abandonment" and 195 "Tribunal Abatement" cases. Every tribunal, of course, has its share of dropouts. In some instances they are people who decide to resume conjugal life with estranged spouses.

Virtually any priest or layperson privy to the annulment grapevine can identify at least one "open door" tribunal. Presumably a tribunal's readiness to accept petitions bears a direct relationship to its inclination to annul. Petitioners residing in restrictive dioceses have been known to file for annulment in a diocese with a more hospitable tribunal. A trouble-free decree of nullity is probably the most common reason for such shifts in venue, although in some instances they are motivated by the fear of having dirty marital linen aired too close to home. Choice of tribunals can result from ambiguities in the determination of which Church court has competence (i.e., jurisdiction). Competence is supposed to belong to the tribunal where the marriage occurred, where the respondent lives, where the petitioner lives (provided that it is in the same Episcopal Conference), and where most of the evidence will be collected.[7] In our mobile society, ex-spouses often reside in different states or different dioceses within the same Episcopal Conference. As a result, implementation of norms regulating competence is not always clear-cut, especially with respect to establishing where most of the evidence will be gathered. If competence is sought by a tribunal in a diocese other than the one in which the respondent lives, the judicial vicar can consent to that arrangement only after consulting with the respondent.

One method used to give apparent legitimacy to a change in venue involves little more than establishing a mailing address in the diocese with the friendlier tribunal. That alone may suffice for the host tribunal to designate itself as the competent forum. Such is the renown of American tribunals for granting annulments that foreign nationals have on occasion filed petitions for nullity in the United States. Petitions, like guided missiles, are directed toward whichever tribunals enjoy (or suffer from) a reputation for freewheeling annulments. Varvaro notes that Spanish advocates in particular were known to seek transoceanic venue changes on the expectation that annulments in the United States would be more obtainable and cheaper. Two of forty-seven cases Varvaro examined in one study followed that scenario. Both were accepted by American tribunals, both resulted in annulment, and both decrees were nullified by the Rota. One case was tried by a tribunal long considered America's leading annulment mill.[8] The reasons the Spanish petitioner had for seeking that tribunal as the competent forum do not appear in the acts (the case file). But as the Rota quite pointedly commented, they "are easily understood by all."[9] The competence question appears to be diminishing in significance, inasmuch as the majority of American tribunals are annulment-friendly. What is left of the competent forum issue depends largely on how hard or soft a line tribunals draw on annulment.

Comparative Court Administration

Speaking as one who has conducted and directed research on court administration, I find the aggregate acceptance rate of petitions by the American tribunal system astounding. Some perspective may be gained by using the American legal system for comparison. With an estimated two-thirds of the planet's lawyers, the United States is said to be the most litigious society in history. Our legal system, more so than most, gives life to the law's potential to intrude into any human relationship. Yet despite the profusion of lawyers and the citizenry's inclination to rely on courts to resolve a boundless variety of problems, approximately 90 percent of the civil suits filed in America never go to trial. Thus in one fiscal year only slightly more than 7,500—1.3 percent—of the 584,300 cases filed ("presented," in canonical terms) in California's superior courts went to trial.[10] The low percentage obtained despite California's reputation as a plaintiff's paradise. On the federal level, during fiscal 1989–1990, 9,263 (4.3 percent) of 213,429 civil cases terminated in the U.S. district courts were resolved through trial.[11] Full-dress litigation in these and other jurisdictions is avoided by pretrial settlements, jurisdictional roadblocks, dismissal of cases as frivolous, denial of standing to plaintiffs, prohibitive costs, and suits simply withdrawn.

Diversion from trial often results from pleadings, which usually precede civil lawsuits as means of informing the court of the specifics at issue. Pleadings are allegations, or bills of particulars, about factual matters that represent the plaintiff's basis for action and the defendant's grounds for defense. They are supposed to be grounded in law and in fact. Their purpose is to help the court and the contending attorneys decide whether cases should be tried. Without such screening mechanisms the federal and state court systems, already pushed to the limit, would be overwhelmed by tidal waves of litigation. As matters stand, years can pass before civil actions go to trial. In terms of standard judicial administrative procedures, the folk belief that everyone is entitled to a day in court is really a theoretical and often fanciful ideal. In practice, there is many a slip between the desire to sue and actually going to court. But with many American tribunals there are very few slips or none at all.

Tribunals, if they desire, can exercise discretion in responding to petitions, accepting or rejecting them as they see fit. The canonical counterpart of pleadings is the *libellus*, specifying the grounds for nullity. However, while pleadings are drawn up by the opposing attorneys, the *libellus* is the handiwork of a tribunalist who may be a field advocate. Often it is prepared by an auditor or notary sparsely trained in canon law, and based solely on information provided by the petitioner. For many if not most tribunalists, a narrative account of a troubled marriage followed by divorce signifies "lack of due discretion" or incapacity for a "communion of life" and warrants a preliminary presumption of defective consent. Properly speaking, there should be at least indications that some grave psychological disorder was present at the time of consent if the case is to be accorded standing. If the petitioner, orally or in written response to a tribunal questionnaire, reports any experience even vaguely related to mental health problems—counseling, psychiatric treatment, bizarre behavior, childhood abuse, and the like—that will usually be regarded as probable cause for defective consent. It is very unlikely that the tribunal at this point will make any effort to verify independently what the petitioner relates. In short, there are comparatively few instances when tribunals, before accepting ordinary process cases, have solid evidence that marital consent may have been invalidated by a serious mental problem.

Certain large dioceses contribute disproportionately to the high national acceptance rate of petitions. In 1987, for example, the Archdiocese of Boston accepted every one of 1,197 cases presented, the Archdiocese of Seattle all 604 presented, and the Archdiocese of Chicago 1,074 of 1,078.[12] It is difficult to comprehend how only 4 of 2,879 petitions presented to the three archdiocesan tribunals were turned aside. But this was not an isolated occurrence. Two years later, six archdiocesan tribunals accepted all 4,454 cases presented.[13] Such carte blanche maximization of the docket cannot be found in any other court system in the Western world.[14]

One could argue that American bankruptcy and divorce courts are exceptions. A bankruptcy proceeding, however, is not a trial in the usual sense of the term. If voluntary, an insolvent debtor petitions the court to declare him bankrupt. If involuntary, it is an attempt by creditors to seize all an insolvent debtor's assets, distribute them equitably, and release the debtor from liability. Bankruptcy under Chapter 11 enables a debtor to defer payment on liabilities while trying to reorganize personal finances. In contrast with an annulment proceeding, which seeks to determine whether spouses are married, the basic question in a bankruptcy proceeding is not whether a debtor is insolvent, but how the debtor's property will be distributed.

Nor is a petition for divorce treated in the same way as a petition for nullity. While it is true that courts in no-fault jurisdictions must accept practically all cases, many divorces are uncontested or mediated and therefore whether a marriage existed is not an issue to be resolved at trial. Under canon law, ordinary process annulments must be tried. Were that not the case, the defender of the bond would be a passive bystander and mandatory Second Instance review of First Instance decisions merely ceremonial. There are other significant differences between no-fault divorce and annulment proceedings. Instead of adjudicating specific grounds, no-fault divorce typically requires nothing more than an assertion by either party that the marriage is irretrievably broken. The courts might devote considerable effort to issues surrounding custody, visitation rights, child support, and the division of marital assets. But there is rarely any juridical and psychological agonizing over whether the spouses properly gave their consent to marry. As a consequence, divorce courts are hardly ever called upon to determine whether a legal marriage ever existed.[15]

The fact that tribunals find the vast majority of petitions justiciable is counter not only to sound court management, but also to the laws of chance and the findings of psychological research. We know that about 98 percent of petitions presented and accepted for trial will be adjudicated under the aegis of C. 1095. Since the national acceptance rate is 86 percent, and since nearly all ordinary process cases turn on defective consent, about ninety-five of every one hundred cases that go to trial involve petitioners or respondents, or both, who were ostensibly afflicted with serious mental disorders when they consented to marry. As noted earlier, such a level of psychological morbidity indicates that applicants for annulment are far more prone to mental disorder than the general population. But even if that were so, it is quite unlikely that applicants put their psycho-pathology on display during the initial interview with a field advocate or a tribunal notary. Unless their symptoms are acted out in plain view, it is doubtful whether the intake tribunalist would be capable of even a tentative diagnosis of mental disorder. It is also extremely improbable that only 5 percent of petitioners for ordinary process annulments and their erstwhile spouses appear to be normal when cases are first presented to tribunals. In short, the mere fact of divorce is treated as warrant for the assumption that a mental disorder afflicted the peti-tioner or respondent, or both, when marital consent was exchanged. If there is such a disorder its existence cannot ordinarily be firmly established until the case goes to trial.

Probing for Grounds

At intake the vast majority of prospective petitioners provide tribunals with little information truly germane to a C. 1095 action. Not everyone, apparently, ap-proaches the tribunal totally uninformed. In my talks with petitioners, respon-dents, and tribunalists, there were reports of annulment-seekers who were instructed by priests on how to ensure acceptance of their petitions and a likely decree of nullity. Besides routine identification material—name, address, place of birth, baptismal data, marital status, and so on—applicants may volunteer an unsworn account of marital difficulties. Depending on how verbal the petitioner is, some relevant information may be developed in the personal and marital histories many tribunals request. Some tribunals, instead of requiring oral or written background material, insist on completion of a questionnaire before a *libellus* is prepared. The questionnaire format is more structured than autobio-graphical case histories. Both types solicit information on common topics, such as family background, the courtship, married life, and the break-up of the mar-riage. The questionnaire affords clearer focus on responses pertinent to marital validity and is less amenable to rambling, free-association types of responses that often fail to address the real juridical issues. On the other hand, question-naires do not permit the kind of probing that can be done by a skillful inter-viewer. Mailed questionnaires have a singular drawback, routinely ignored by many tribunals. Contrary to the requirements of canon law, there are no fool-proof provisions to ensure that the addressee is the person who completes the questionnaire.

Instructions on marital history used by the Archdiocese of Hartford include a narrative section asking from petitioners and respondents alike information on a variety of topics. One segment of the history relates to the "background of each party." The material to be covered is supposed to fit the following outline, with examples given where applicable:

> *The character of your parents, an assessment of their relationships, who was the dominant one in the home, your relationship with them. The personality* [sic] *of your brothers/sisters and your relationship with them. Your educational background, attitudes toward school. your sense of accomplishment. Social activities and ease in forming friendships.* Mental health problems or unusual physical problems. Any behavior problems in school. Unusual fears in childhood or later. *History of dating, any other serious romances: if so, why terminated.* Attitudes toward sex and related problems. *Life goals and personal standards of achievement,* religious practice. *Number of jobs, reasons for terminating.* Problems in adult life, e.g., alcohol, drugs, *gambling, handling money,* arrests. Evaluation of personal strengths and weaknesses: Ex. *Are you sensitive to the needs of others, nervous, quick tempered, moody, jealous, selfish, ungrateful?* Would others consider you to be honest and truthful? Would others have reason to consider your conduct *erratic or unpredictable,* outlandish or fantastic? *Would others consider you to have good judgment in everyday situations?*[16]

I have taken the liberty of italicizing portions of the guidelines which have no apparent proximate and persuasive relevance to the current inventory of Church-approved grounds for nullity. A lot of psychological chaff is mixed in with the juridically relevant wheat. Some of the material could possibly be linked to defective consent, but much of it is extraneous, far more germane to marriage counseling than to a Church tribunal investigating marital consent. Taken as a whole, the instructions are a psychological exploration, on a grand scale, for personality and behavior traits that may be employed to initiate and justify a trial. There are tens of millions of validly married spouses who at one time or another are insensitive to the needs of others, quick tempered, moody, jealous, selfish, and ungrateful. In the section on courtship the instructions touch on the essential properties of marriage—permanence, fidelity, and openness to children—but overall the guidelines are geared to unearthing material that might somehow be incorporated into a C. 1095 annulment based on interpersonal failures and inability to establish a "communion of life" signifying successful marriage. Whoever formulated the instructions was well aware of the side of the law on which permissive nullity lies. A notary tossing a dart at a wall papered with the marital history could be confident of hitting a word or passage that could be used as the basis for a *libellus.*

Marital histories, oral or written, often follow one of two recurrent themes. Many supplicants for annulment characterize the failed marriage as a mistake. Although mistaken marriages are not necessarily invalid, there is some warrant for the tribunal to pursue the matter further. The second theme involves metamorphic marriage. The would-be petitioner volunteers that after *n* blissful years, sometimes adding up to decades, the marriage soured or flew apart. In effect, the person has conceded the absence of any disqualifying mental condition at the time consent was exchanged and therefore waived consideration for a petition to be accepted by the tribunal for a possible C. 1095 annulment. In practically all such cases the tribunal could spare itself time, effort, anguish, and temptation by expressing regret and commiseration, and showing the person out of the office. Yet many tribunals not only allow such cases to go to trial, but find a way to annul. Perhaps it is well to note here that in most documentary process cases this sort of screening is inapplicable. If a baptized Catholic married outside the Church, the marriage is ipso facto invalid from its outset, no matter how long it was harmonious afterward.

Simply from reading Hartford's marital-history directions, a behavioral scientist could reasonably hypothesize that the tribunal issuing them would be hospitable to petitions for nullity. Tribunal statistics for the archdiocese uphold the hypothesis. In 1987, the year the CLSA published Wrenn's book, the Hartford tribunal accepted 412 of 466 (88 percent) cases presented. The following year the tribunal reported 468 cases presented and 579 cases accepted.[17] Obviously, many cases accepted in 1988 were backlogged from previous years. No further hypothesizing is needed to estimate that at least 90 percent of the 991 cases accepted over the two-year period eventuated in nullity.

The Archdiocese of Philadelphia requires petitioners to complete a lengthy questionnaire. It covers much the same general territory as Hartford's marital history, but with less emphasis on psychological minutiae. The instrument's questions are more direct, designed to elicit fairly objective responses. Several items are open-ended, providing space for the subject to explain answers to questions. Nevertheless, portions of the questionnaire solicit information that relates more to compatibility than validity. It asks for brief descriptions of any difficulties before or during the marriage in the following areas: jobs, finances, loans or debts, gambling, drinking, drugs, in-laws, fidelity, physical violence, coping with everyday problems, and religious beliefs. At best, no more than five of the items can be realistically tied to defective consent without straining, though probing religious beliefs can bear on cases that involve the Pauline or Petrine privilege, neither of which relate to defective consent.

At the very end of the questionnaire the tribunal perhaps tips its hand by asking for an explanation on why the person's "first marriage was not a successful one." Unless the response touches on specific grounds for nullity, the question has only tangential concern for a tribunal. Tribunals are charged with determining the validity of marriages, not why they failed. Successful marriage and valid marriage are not necessarily one and the same. In one recent case a petitioner before the Philadelphia tribunal was sent a revised version of an article that originally appeared in the July 1980 edition of the *St. Anthony Messenger*. Written by Jeffrey Keefe, a clinical psychologist and consultant to the Syracuse (New York) tribunal, it is titled "Why the Church is Granting More Annulments." The article is a well-written summary of practically all the theological, canonical, and psychological shibboleths used to rationalize annulment in America. The Philadelphia tribunal does not submit data to the CLSA, so the percentage of petitions it accepts cannot be cited here. But if the Philadelphia tribunal adheres to Keefe's conception of validity, the acceptance and favorable-decision rates are probably high.

Marital histories, questionnaires, and initial interviews at tribunal offices seldom develop solid evidence of serious mental disorders. They can, of course, provide leads which stimulate further investigation. In that respect, they help the tribunal decide whether preparation and acceptance of a *libellus* is appropriate. Seldom is there at this stage of the proceeding a smoking clinical gun pointing to incapacity in the form of grave lack of due discretion or lack of due competence. But for many American tribunals, even the slightest signs of mental disorder and failure to achieve the successful marriage version of a "communion of life" suffice as probable cause for improper consent. It cannot be overemphasized that at the moment a *libellus* is accepted the tribunal usually has nothing to go on other than the petitioner's recounting of the marriage. The respondent, witnesses, and the expert have not yet had their say.

The readiness with which American the tribunals accept petitions has not escaped Rotal attention. In one decision it was noted that "Cases are coming before ecclesiastical tribunals which from the very outset evidently are without any juridic foundation. This would be avoided if they were not introduced at all or if the defender of the bond exercised greater care and diligence. . . . The judges are also obliged . . . to persuade parties not to present a *libellus* if it does not have the *fumus boni juris*."[18] The absence of juridic foundation does not stay the hand of the new pastoral activism, which cannot abide the pains of divorce, divorce and remarriage, and denial of the sacraments. The tribunals' healing mission is unfulfilled unless efforts are made to provide client-petitioners with the means to return to "wholeness." With such a cast of mind, many tribunals routinely accept petitions almost indiscriminately as a necessary first step toward lifting the heavy yoke of unfortunate marriages. Church doctrine, Church law, papal exhortations, Signatura concerns, Rotal instructions, and justice yield to the urge to heal. The best pastoral and therapeutic intentions do not repeal the rule against using the end to justify the means. The Church has methods other than annulment for mitigating the suffering that goes with broken marriage—spiritual direction, prayer, pastoral counseling, and penance. When, as often happens, such methods fall short, there remains the lesson of the Cross.

If 86 percent of petitions for annulment are docketed for trial, tribunals in effect are assuring about 90 percent of successful petitioners that no juridical or psychological stone will be left unturned to find a way to annul. Put more succinctly, the nullity die is cast once a petition is accepted. The means used by tribunals to keep the assembly line supplied with cases are illustrated in one advocate's discussion of her role in processing petitions. At intake, she explains, one must be alerted to conditions that can contribute to a "non-marriage," such as problems in the family of origin, alcoholism, homosexuality, psychological difficulties, and emotional instability. Her responsibility is to show that because of such factors the marriage "never worked" (i.e., was not successful). Invoking without much discrimination the debatable supposition that valid marriage must be a "community of life," she notes that pregnancy, deceit, and recent bereavement can also negate free consent.[20] Combining any incapacitating variables drawn from so broad a gamut with her twofold premise that valid marriages must be a community of life that works, the advocate has a surfeit of material for a *libellus*. CLSA statistics strongly suggest that screening applicants for annulment in this mode is standard procedure in many American tribunals. C. 1060's unequivocal enjoinder notwithstanding, even before trial the benefit of doubt is tilted in the direction of nullity. The canon reads, "Marriage enjoys the favour of the law. Consequently, in doubt the validity of a marriage must be upheld until the contrary is proven." This is a verbatim reiteration of what the 1917 code stipulates, except that the earlier version includes reference to the Privilege of Faith. If C. 1095 is indeed the most abused statute in the new code, C. 1060 is just as surely the most unused in terms of its plain meaning. Either it is studiously ignored or turned on its head, with the benefit of doubt routinely bestowed on nullity.

Consequences of Intake Policies

Overcrowded court calendars lead to unrealistic demands on the energies of tribunal staffs, shoddy processing of cases, and, not least, specious decrees of nullity. Paradoxically, what are really unmanageable caseloads are instrumental in enhancing the tribunals' public image. Most obviously, they proclaim that the tribunals really care, that they are trying their utmost to give aid and comfort to petitioners wishing to return to the sacraments. There is also a more subtle way in which they work toward favorable public relations. Petitioners are often forewarned not to expect speedy resolution of their cases. Bringing a case to conclusion may take a year or longer. Thus, the impression conveyed is one of a tribunal working assiduously to gather testimony and evidence, then examining it from every angle before reaching a decision. Undoubtedly the process can be time consuming, but long delays are due in no small measure to needlessly overloaded dockets. Time that should be devoted to cases with genuine juridic merit is allocated to petitions that should have been summarily rejected. As a result, productivity takes on a life of its own, becoming as important a priority as judicious deliberation.

Tribunals that are properly circumspect about weighing and accepting petitions have a public-relations cross to bear. Justifiable hard-line screening, well within the norms of canonical procedure, is perceived as hard-heartedness. Unsuccessful petitioners cannot fathom denials by their own diocesan tribunal when similar cases accepted by neighboring tribunals lead to annulments. Tribunals striving to uphold indissolubility pay a price set by other tribunals' laxity. They must frequently explain to irate petitioners, socialized into the world of easy annulment, why they are out of step with the larger tribunal system. It is not unheard of for such tribunals to be called on the carpet by other Church judicial bodies for their diligence in upholding what the Church actually teaches. One canonist relates how his diocesan tribunal was reprimanded by the provincial tribunal for refusing to adjudicate any and all petitions. Petitioners denied standing appealed to Second Instance, whereupon the provincial tribunal remanded their cases for trial with the lesser tribunal. But the First Instance tribunal stuck to its guns. When it offered to allow Rome to mediate the intertribunal differences, the provincial tribunal backed down. This potentially ugly situation has supposedly been eliminated by personnel changes in the provincial tribunal.

Systemic Considerations

Analysis of tribunal dockets has qualitative as well as quantitative significance. The very size of the system's caseload is critical to understanding the character of its operation. Among other things, the open-door policy of most American tribunals does more than sustain the nullification mill. In terms of organizational theory, it suggests a derivative of Parkinson's Law, which asserts that "Work expands to fill the time available for completion." With tribunals the number of petitions accepted expands to fill the time needed to maximize nullity. More insidiously, it pressures tribunals into circumventing or stretching the law in order to expedite the flow of trials. Finally, it necessitates processing cases with improperly credentialed personnel, a matter more fully discussed in chapter 9.

Most respondents, for whatever reasons, do not challenge petitions for nullity or decrees that ensue. Nonetheless, even when respondents are utterly passive, ordinary process cases are by law and definition contentious.[20] Otherwise they would not require trials and the scrutiny of the defender of the bond.[21] These requirements are frequently glossed over or simply ignored by tribunalists. In a recent interview, the adjutant judicial vicar for Chicago's archdiocesan tribunal, one of America's busiest, equates respondent passivity with the absence of contentiousness. "For the most part, you don't have disagreement on the cases. A lot of parties just don't care, so long as they don't have to do anything. *We're trying to make sure they aren't contentious cases.* We want it to be a process where people can be healed."[22] Perhaps the vicar meant "adversarial" instead of "contentious." As the statement stands, however, it is an explicit denial of the code's mandate that ordinary process cases must be regarded as contentious, irrespective of the parties' lack of rancor and the tribunal's pastoral urge to heal. Canonically speaking, "amicable annulment" along the lines of "amicable divorce" is oxymoronic. Although American civil courts and tribunals both often deal with complicitous spouses, their respective roles differ sharply. In "friendly divorce" the judge is basically a disinterested spectator. The court might intervene when couples have young children whose interests and well-being are threatened, but otherwise the judge simply watches the marriage dissolve, then signs papers proclaiming its legal demise.

With ordinary process annulment, however, no matter how congenial the parties may be toward each other, tribunal judges are not merely neutral observers. It is incumbent upon them to determine whether a marriage is valid before consigning it to oblivion. The code specifies that contentious cases dealing with the bond of marriage are "reserved to a collegiate tribunal of three judges, any contrary custom being reprobated. . . ."[23] Reference here is to ordinary process cases *tried* in First Instance, since the statute specifies that reservation of such cases to multiple-judge tribunals is to occur "without prejudice to canons 1686 and 1688." These two canons concern documentary process cases, which lead to trials only in exceptional situations.[24] If at First Instance it is impossible to empanel a collegiate tribunal, the Episcopal Conference can allow the bishop to have cases tried by a single clerical judge for as long as the impossibility persists.[25]

The three-judge requirement is not a radical departure from the past. Indeed, it is strikingly similar to Norm 3 of the celebrated APN. The latter rule, quoted in its entirety earlier, may be summarized here as requiring collegiate tribunals for all cases, unless Rome consented to use of single-judge trials for a specific time interval. Such dispensation was supposed to be granted only for a grave reason, and only if no formal objection was made by the judge, defender, promoter of justice, or either party. Objections had to be made before a definitive sentence was handed down. There is scant difference between the APN requirement that every ordinary process case *must* have a collegiate tribunal and the provision in C. 1425, 4 mandating such a tribunal unless it is *impossible* to form one. The revised code, if anything, is more insistent on collegiality. Compared to APN 3, C. 1425 offers tribunalists less room to maneuver.

But the ability of American canonists to deflect or circumvent the clear meaning of the law is not to be underestimated. We have already seen how "*grave lack of discretionary judgement*" in C. 1095, 2 is often transmuted to "lack of due discretion." The "grave" in APN 3 was similarly excavated and backfilled. There is no evidence that parties in proceedings governed by Norm 3 were routinely apprised of the right to express "formal opposition" to single-judge trials. While suspension of the collegiate rule was permissible for designated intervals, nothing shows that those intervals were ordained publicly by Episcopal Conferences. Thus the language of Norm 3, practically speaking, was inverted to make single-judge trials the rule and collegiate trials rare exceptions. As previously noted, I have yet to meet any party to an annulment who was told of the right to a three-judge panel. Some forthright canonists have told me it is almost never done.

Despite the new code's unequivocal preference for collegiate panels at First Instance, American tribunals generally restrict three-judge courts to small numbers of so-called hard cases, such as marriages of long duration. This does not necessarily mean prolonged, agonizing deliberation even in such cases, however. The panel might not devote any more time to the case than a single judge. In other words, a trio of judges might be empaneled simply for the sake of appearance. However that may be, analysis of the aggregate caseload and staffing of American tribunals before and after the new code took effect provides compelling evidence for systemic avoidance of three-judge trials. Evasion of code requirements is shown by comparing CLSA tribunal data for 1982, 1987, and

1991 (Table 8-2). Two methodological considerations are behind the choice of those years. First, not until 1982 did the CLSA's annual statistical summaries include data on tribunal personnel. Second, using data from the years selected made it possible to control for the number of tribunals reporting and the number of cases "Decided by Sentence." Figures for each variable were pretty evenly matched in the years chosen.

Several caveats are in order to help make sense of the data. Because not every diocese and archdiocese submits data to the CLSA, all figures in the table are on the low side. The 1982 "Part-time Professional" total is skewed sharply upward by the 200 to 300 persons reported in that category by the Military Ordinariate. That same year the Ordinariate also claimed two Full-time Professionals. Thenceforth, under the headings "Military Vicariate" and "Military Services," no more than six full-time professionals and one part-time professional were listed. Evidently the 1982 figure is either inaccurate or a one-time anomaly. It should be kept in mind that the specific tasks performed by the professionals cannot be determined from the CLSA summaries. As is the case with statistics on cases tried, the figures on tribunal personnel do not reveal as much as we would like to know. Some of the informational void on tribunal staffing can be filled by turning to another source.

A random check of tribunal rosters in *The Official Catholic Directory* shows the division of labor varying from one tribunal to another. To cite but two examples, the 1993 *Directory* shows the Diocese of Belleville (Illinois), with a judicial vicar, an adjutant judicial vicar, four judges, four defenders, and two advocates. The Diocese of Joliet, at the other end of the state, has a judicial vicar and five judges who also serve as advocates and defenders. While the *Directory* designates roles within tribunals, it does not indicate whether they are held on a part-or full-time basis. Of course, if a tribunal has but one professional, full-or part-time, that person would be the judicial vicar. Another opaque feature of the CLSA data is that some tribunals might count expert consultants among their professionals. Finally, neither the CLSA summaries nor the *Directory* permit an accurate count of tribunalists according to whether they serve at First Instance, at Second Instance, or at both levels. *Directory* listings show that some personnel routinely shift from one type of tribunal to the other, but we have no statistics on precisely how their services are distributed in terms of caseload and man-hours. Accordingly, our figures on professional staffing combine First and Second Instance personnel.[26]

These cautions aside, the data reveal much about the system's productivity. For the three years covered, tribunals averaged 36,795 ordinary process cases "Decided by Sentence." Because defective consent cases are the primary concern of this study, the table does not show tribunal activity with respect to documentary process cases. But for the purpose at hand it should be noted that CLSA data for the years covered by the table show that tribunals reporting concluded more than twenty-seven thousand documentary process cases in each year. Conservatively, 90 percent of ordinary process cases decided by sentence eventuate in nullity, while the percentage of documentary process cases resulting

Table 8–2. Trial Caseload and Staffing, 1982, 1987, and 1991.

Year	No. tribunals reporting	Decided by sentence	Full-time Professionals	Part-time Professionals
1982	154	36,788	531	1,641
1987	160	37,851	440	911
1991	164	35,747	418	819

Sources: CLSA Proceedings, 1983, 1988, 1992.

in nullity is even higher. Thus, First Instance tribunals in the years examined here accounted for about sixty thousand annulments a year.

Doing More with Less

The most striking revelation is that the number of cases decided by sentence remained fairly constant despite substantial *reductions* in full-and part-time professionals.[27] In other words, annulment production levels were sustained with fewer personnel. The maintenance of the annulment output becomes even more remarkable in light of the new code's requirement that ordinary process First Instance decrees of nullity must be appealed to Second instance. During the APN experiment, annulment proceedings were expedited not only by single-judge tribunals, but also by suspension of the rule that First Instance defective-consent nullity decrees did not take effect without a conforming sentence at Second Instance. Appellate review would occur only if it was initiated by the respondent, defender of the bond, or promoter of justice. Restoration of automatic Second Instance review was a major disappointment for American canonists. Yet even with a reduced complement of professionals, the system sustained the pre-1983 level of ordinary process First Instance annulments at the pre-1983 level, and ratified 26,891 decrees of nullity in 1987 and 37,060 in 1991. In addition, Second Instance tribunals processed 269 formal appeals in 1987 and 265 in 1991. To paraphrase Winston Churchill, "Never have so many annulments been granted by so few."

Throughout the 1970s and into the 1980s it was fashionable to cite tribunal staff increases to help explain America's disproportionately high volume of annulments. An example of this was seen in the *Florida Times-Union* ad cited in the preceding chapter. Such explanations were no doubt meant to placate Rome, some American bishops, and concerned laity.[28] Perhaps due to stabilization in tribunal staffing, the canonical community has since fallen comparatively silent on ties between productivity and personnel increases.[29] Conceivably, the system's pace was partly maintained by additional secretarial assistance and office modernization. But the number of full-and part-time secretaries was roughly the same in each of three years examined. Perhaps holding the size of the secretarial force constant in the face of additional responsibilities was made possible by improvements in hiring practices and office management. Word processors and computers can expedite the considerable paperwork associated with annulment. References to better office procedures and equipment are part and parcel of the oft-repeated contention that tribunal efficiency contributes significantly to the United States being the world's annulment epicenter. American tribunals, needless to say, are not the only ones in the world with word processors and other state-of-the-art office equipment.

Efficiency, properly speaking, refers to optimal use of personnel and resources to produce a specific product or service. But it becomes an empty goal if it is achieved at the expense of quality and adherence to established rules. To what avail are record numbers of shoddy widgets if the company producing them operates under sweatshop conditions and fails to abide by laws governing worker safety and wages? Similarly, what benefits accrue to the Church universal if diocesan tribunals, to keep the annulment assembly line humming, turn out unworthy decrees of nullity? The efficiency of American tribunals may permit handling documentary process cases with great dispatch, but efficiency in the service of truth is vastly more elusive in the adjudication of ordinary process annulments. It is one thing to determine whether a baptized Catholic married outside the Church, but quite another to establish that either party to the marriage is lacking due discretion, is incapable of "communion of life" or is mentally impaired. These determinations do not become more feasible simply by streamlining and computerizing tribunal office routines, or by hiring more competent secretaries.

CLSA data are silent on the incidence of single-judge trials since the APN became defunct. We know they were the order of the day prior to 1983. We also know that under the new code the production of annulments remained fairly stable, despite a decrease in the number of tribunal personnel a id despite mandatory appeals to Second Instance. Given those conditions, a reasonable inference is that single-judge trials continue to be the norm, C. 1425, 1 notwithstanding. Canonists publicly concede the prevalence of single-judge cases, often with qualifying statements that "complex" or "difficult" cases are heard by collegiate panels.

Additional evidence for the prevalence of single-judge trials is provided by a more detailed examination of CLSA data for 1991. Statistical summaries for that year list forty-three diocesan tribunals with one full-time professional, presumably the judicial vicar.[30] Those full-time professionals are assisted by 196 part-time professionals whose official titles are not specified. Another twenty-four dioceses, lacking full-time professionals, depend on ninety-three part-timers, including judicial vicars. Although tribunal divisions of labor are not the same throughout the system, a team of part-time professionals will probably include a judicial vicar, one or more defenders, judges, and advocates. Part-timers who are religious, it should be noted, usually have ministries not directly related to tribunal work. Some are retired priests with backgrounds in canon law or with what is perceived as special competence in marital issues. It is not uncommon for younger clerics to be thrust into tribunalist roles, perhaps after brief training in the rudiments of annulment canon law. They will likely be assigned to documentary rather than ordinary process cases. Experts who consult for tribunals can be classified as either full-time or part-time. At all events, it is important to keep in mind that not all professionals are judges, which makes it even more difficult to impanel collegiate First Instance tribunals.

What this means, of course, is that canonical expertise for trying cases is stretched thin. To take one example, the *officialis* of the Diocese of Saginaw's tribunal is a priest with a masters degree in chancery affairs, the defender a monsignor with no degree in canon law. Of the four priests who serve as judges, one has a doctorate in canon law, another a master's degree in an unspecified field, and the remaining two no relevant degrees. The tribunal advocate is a priest without an advanced degree in canon law.[32] Apart from the issue of canonical competence, the Saginaw arrangement exemplifies the difficulties faced—or reluctance shown—by dioceses in bringing the training of tribunal personnel up to the code's standards, now more than ten years old.

The sixty-seven tribunals under discussion, each with but one full-time professional or only part-time professionals, constitute well over one third of all First Instance tribunals in the United States. Despite skeletal staffing, in 1991 they accepted 8,634 petitions for nullity and decided 7,338, some carried over from the previous year. They accounted for approximately 20 percent of the ordinary process cases accepted and decided by sentence by the 168 tribunals submitting data to the CLSA.[32] Assuming they conformed to the pattern that prevails for American tribunals as a whole, these lesser tribunals were responsible for about 6,600 (15 percent) of all ordinary process nullity decrees granted in the United States in 1991. Put another way, the sixty-seven dioceses averaged just under one hundred annulments per full-time tribunalist.

Data for selected tribunals (Table 8-3) do not point to a tidy linear relationship between tribunal size and judicial activity. In 1991 the Archdiocese of New York, with seventeen full-time and seven part-time professionals, decided 759 cases. That same year, four tribunals (Arlington, Baton Rouge, Grand Rapids, and Portland), with only three full-time and seventeen part-time professionals, decided the fate of 1,008 marriages. One cannot help but marvel at the comparative productivity of these diocesan tribunals. Operating with few personnel, singly and collectively they processed an extraordinary number of cases. The Diocese of Brooklyn's tribunal, with eight full-time and thirteen part-time professionals, decided 570 cases in 1991, not even one fourth as many as decided by the eight full-time and forty-one part-time professionals in the tribunals represented in Table 8-3. The latter tribunals, it would appear, got incredible mileage out of their part-time professional help.

Discernment of the original intent of those who frame law can be a tricky and unending business. Many a political scientist and law professor in the United States has built an academic career on pondering what the Founding Fathers had in mind when they wrote the Constitution. That said, I contend that the reasoning behind the canonical provision for single-judge trials when a three-judge panel is impossible is not difficult to discern. Drafters of the code undoubtedly knew that in some parts of the world dioceses did not even have tribunals. They also real-

Table 8–3. Trial Caseload and Staffing for Selected Tribunals, 1991.

Archdiocese/diocese	Full-time	Part-time	Cases decided by sentence
Arlington	1	4	221
Baton Rouge	1	5	257
Grand Rapids	1	6	296
Kansas City (Kansas)	1	2	349
Portland (Oregon)	0	2	234
Saginaw	1	8	220
St. Augustine	1	3	195
San Bernardino	1	6	272
Wichita	1	5	221
TOTALS	9	45	2,435

Source: CLSA Proceedings, 1992.

ized that some diocesan tribunals would temporarily lack enough trained canonists to conduct collegiate trials. This awareness is clearly implied in C. 1439, 1 which recognizes that a single First Instance tribunal might have to serve several dioceses. But that acknowledgement in no way signifies a weakening of the code's strong resolve for collegiate trials at First Instance.[34] Presumably, too, the drafters believed there would be safety and reliability in numbers, yet with collegiate panels limited to three members, there would not be too many cooks to spoil the broth. Theoretically, each panel member would be subject to the scrutiny of fellow panelists. The interplay among the judges should yield a collective judiciousness that would neutralize any one panelist's idiosyncrasies, bias, or propensity to grant or deny nullity on whim. Finally, it would not stretch matters to suppose that the drafters' distaste for single-judge trials was tacit repudiation of what such trials had helped produce under the aegis of the APN—an unprecedented outpouring of decrees of nullity. But if there was any one thing the drafters of the code did not anticipate it was the continuous resistance of American tribunals to collegiate First Instance trials.

Despite passage of eight years since the new code took effect, there was little evidence that American tribunals have moved closer to the law's specifications. The truth of the matter is that single-judge trials are essential to the American tribunal system. Broad-scale conversion to collegiality would be profoundly disruptive. Processing cases with a modicum of collegiality and collegial judiciousness would require a sharp reduction in tribunal caseloads, staff increases, and willingness to live with a radical drop in the output of decrees of nullity. Keeping caseloads at current levels without tripling the number of qualified judges would either lengthen delays in the disposition of cases or force the collegiate panels to try cases even more summarily than they now do. The present economy of scale would be diminished. The cost of processing cases would rise, perhaps to an intolerable level for bishops and litigants alike.

Summary proceedings are especially inappropriate for defective consent cases, which by their nature call for intensive investigation and judicial soul-searching. Indubitably, whether tribunals find it impossible to abide by the three-judge norm depends on caseload size, the number of judges available to try cases, and premises regarding the nature of marriage and viable grounds for nullity. Those variables, of course, are functionally intertwined, change in one inducing change in the others. Thus, on the basis of logistics alone, tribunals must rely on single-judge trials to affirm their conception of valid marriage and prevent long-term slowdowns, perhaps even periodic shutdowns, in the production of annulments.

Keeping the Line Going

Assembly lines are designed to have higher output than other modes of production while being less labor-intensive. The tribunal system's line turns out decrees of nullity at a rate considered impossible three decades ago. It does so with skeletal staffing in many of its branches. Like assembly lines everywhere, the tribunal system's is sensitive to a variety of external forces. Its productive capability is especially dependent on a reliable source of raw material, that is, petitions for nullity. If, as some canonists assume, the pool of potential petitioners for annulment has scarcely been tapped, a plentiful supply of raw material may be assured for decades to come. Should divorce among Catholics continue in its current pattern, the system will have the benefit of a renewable resource. But the availability of raw material is controlled to a considerable extent by systemic standards governing the acceptance of petitions.

Labor to operate the line is provided by the professionals and secretaries who staff the tribunal offices. While the system is labor-intensive, production costs are relatively modest. The managerial class consists almost exclusively of clerics, usually well-trained but low-salaried, without stock options or golden parachute retirement benefits. Use of part-time professionals further minimizes operating expenses. Some lay employees have legal responsibilities, but for the most part their duties are essentially clerical. Expert consultants for defective consent cases may be more generously remunerated than those who hire them. Usually, however, they too are part-time employees. The system is free of union problems or any threat of competition. Its management and labor force are almost exclusively "true believers," ideologically and pastorally committed to the rectitude of its goals. Morale should be high and the threat of labor strife remote. Organizationally, the system has features that most American corporations and factories would find enviable.

The primary sources of capitalization are the American hierarchy and user fees. American canonists frequently cite the bishops' largess as a major reason for the system's matchless productivity. Given other pressing needs, such as the care of retired religious and litigation costs arising from the recent spate of sexual-abuse charges against clergy, the bishops' support is munificent indeed. Tribunals reporting to CLSA have annual expenditures totaling slightly more than $20,200,000. Roughly half that amount comes from diocesan subsidies, the remainder from fees paid by petitioners. Allowing for tribunals not reporting, total annual operating costs of for the American tribunal system may be conservatively estimated as $25 million. Although that sum is not of Fortune 500 magnitude, neither is it pocket change. In most annual diocesan budgets the tribunal allocation is among the larger line items. A high volume of cases is probably construed as a sign that the tribunals are earning their keep.

Each tribunal sets its own fee schedule and each waives fees for those unable to pay. Nonetheless, some prospective petitioners of adequate means are frightened off by fee requirements. The Archdiocese of Detroit reportedly waives fees for all comers, which may account for the fact that on a per capita basis its production of decrees of nullity is second to none. Many tribunals have incremental payment plans, each step in the annulment process requiring remission of a fee before the case advances to the next phase. Thus, a formal petition will not be drawn up until the charge for the initial interview is paid; ordinary process cases will not go to trial until the formal petition fee is remitted. Yet another fee must be paid for the trial itself. At least one large tribunal requires payment in full before arrangements for an expert opinion are made and before the outcome of the case is unveiled to the parties.[34] If, as is likely, a decree of nullity is granted, some tribunals require payment of a ratification fee before the parties are given official notice of the tribunal's decision and before the case is sent to Second Instance for mandatory review.

Outsiders frequently—and erroneously—see this sort of payment scheme as evidence that annulments are purchased. The tribunal system has manifold flaws, but the sale of decrees of nullity is not among them. Tribunals, for good or bad, perform services, which must be paid for whatever the outcome of cases. Because the overwhelming majority of petitions accepted lead to nullity, if petitioners denied annulment were not expected to pay, suspicion that annulments are for sale would acquire a measure of credibility. Some tribunal fee arrangements are analogous to those used by many colleges and universities, whereby grades and degrees are withheld from students who either fail to pay tuition balances and requisite fees or neglect to work out an acceptable payment plan.

Contrary to popular belief, tribunals are not profitable. If they were, subsidies would be unnecessary. Tribunals have always been subsidized, but never on the scale prevailing since Vatican II. Actually, many of the details of tribunal finances are not made public. Budget figures do not mention salaries and expert consulting fees. As near as can be determined, fee schedules do not differentiate between ordinary process and documentary process cases. If that is so, except for add-ons for expert consulting fees, petitioners whose cases require trials probably pay the same amount as those petitioners whose cases are handled administratively, enabling the tribunal to "omit the formalities of the ordinary procedure."[35] In documentary process cases the court, without a trial, can rule for or against nullity in an action resembling what would be termed a default judgment or a declaratory judgment in an American civil lawsuit. There is little or no need to depose witnesses, transcribe testimony, pay expert consulting fees, or incur the costs of Second Instance review. Accordingly, a petition based on "lack of form" ordinarily requires appreciably less time and effort than one where the grounds are defective consent. It might be asked whether a hidden subsidy is at work here, with fees from documentary process cases helping to underwrite some of the costs of cases that go to trial, especially those where fees are waived.

Tribunals, like most social and religious agencies, wish to convey a favorable image to the public. This may be manifested in assurances relating to fair treatment irrespective of the petitioner's station in life, confidentiality, healing, and adherence to Church teaching. No doubt similar signals are directed toward the bishops, particularly claims that the diocese is getting a fair and orthodox return on its investment. Despite such efforts, the image projected draws mixed responses from the public. For many Catholics the tribunals are ecclesial divorce mills. There is widespread and largely groundless fear that an annulment is invariably an embarrassing experience, one that pries into such private areas as the conjugal bedroom. Then, too, tribunals have not successfully disabused many Catholics of the conviction that annulments are always available to those with money. Indeed, one occasionally hears Catholics as well as non-Catholics liken today's annulment proceedings to the sale of indulgences.

The day-to-day operations of American tribunals bear witness to the theological and canonical premises that animate the system as a whole. The wholesale acceptance of petitions in many dioceses and subsequent adjudication of the petitions by single-judge courts are causes and effects of caseload size. Ultimately, however, heavy tribunal dockets are an inevitable by-product of the conceptions of marriage, matrimonial consent, and the rectitude of nullity which now rule the American canonical roost. Revisionist marriage theology, pronullity jurisprudence, the pastoral imperative, psychologization of the annulment process, and tribunal administrative policies have been formed into a canonical apparatus designed to euthanize thousands of marriages.

❖ 9 ❖

Tribunal Personnel

The analysis of any social system benefits from examination of its role structure. A role consists of a bundle of rights and duties associated with a specific position—a status—within a group or organization. Roles comprise both normative and behavioral components. Some roles are narrowly circumscribed by special rules and expectations, while others allow individuals more leeway. But no matter how scrupulously the rights and duties are spelled out by custom and law, the person playing the role may define them differently. As a result, discrepancies arise between official and personalized definitions of roles and between prescribed and actual behavior. Deviation from formal role prescriptions, while common, is not always tolerated by the designated guardians of the rights and duties built into a role, or by one's peers. On the other hand, many roles allow for some improvisation while simultaneously calling for rigid conformity. For example, a confessor may use a psychological, doctrinal, or scriptural approach to counsel penitents, but whatever the approach the duty to honor the seal of the confessional is absolute.

Formal role prescriptions for tribunal personnel are found in canon law, and often refined by pronouncements emanating from the pope, the Apostolic Signatura, the Rota, and perhaps in some instances by bishops. There is ample prescriptive material to allow us to judge how faithfully the behavior and qualifications of American tribunalists conform to Church specifications. While the official definitions of tribunalist roles are a matter of record, the behavioral components of tribunal roles are seldom in plain view. Annulment proceedings are private affairs, primarily for reasons of confidentiality. Unless one personally experiences an annulment as a petitioner, respondent, or witness, or serves as a tribunal member, direct observation of tribunalists' behaviors and the internal dynamics of tribunal deliberations is not feasible. Nevertheless, such matters are not beyond the reach of empirical study.

Tribunal procedures as well as personnel qualifications are set forth in the code. How tribunalists fulfill their prescribed roles and whether tribunals adhere to proper procedure are reflected in annulment statistics published by the Vatican and the CLSA. By their statistical fruits we can learn a good deal about tribunal personnel. Some material on the inner workings of tribunals and the fitness of tribunalists can be gleaned from Rota decisions and from the canonical literature on annulment. Additional material on the role behavior of tribunalists can be obtained from interviews with subjects who have been through annulment proceedings in one capacity or another.

Tribunal Role Structure

Few lay Catholics are familiar with the make-up and functions of their own diocesan tribunal. There is nearly universal lack of awareness of how the new code sharpened tribunal role definitions, generally upgrading and standardizing the requisite qualifications. Drafters of the code stressed legal and clerical credentials required of tribunalists, although some positions are open to qualified laypersons. Judicial vicars, associate judicial vicars, judges, and defenders of the bond are to have a doctorate or at least a licentiate in canon law.[1] Judicial vicars and associate judical vicars must be clerics at least thirty years old, while laypersons can serve as defenders and, in some instances, as judges. Nothing is said about the defender or any other tribunalist needing training in behavioral science. A singular recent development in tribunal staffing has occurred with respect to women. In the past they were relegated to clerical duties. Today women trained in canon law can serve as judges, advocates, defenders, and promoters of justice.[2] But the role of judicial vicar (*officialis*) is limited to priests.

Our discussion of tribunal personnel will focus mainly on judicial vicars,[3] who often serve as judges, First and Second Instance judges, and defenders of the bond. They are the key figures in the majority of tribunals and annulment proceedings in the United States. Some attention will be given to a special category of judges designated as synodal, prosynodal, and diocesan. Tribunal rosters include full-or part-time advocates, procurators, procurator-advocates, and promoters of justice. Advocates are canonical trial lawyers who are available to represent parties to an annulment proceeding. Unless the bishop grants a waiver, the advocate must be a Catholic. A doctorate in canon law is recommended but the role can be filled by a person "otherwise well qualified."[4] Procurators act as proxies for the parties, capable of exercising what in civil law would be called the power of attorney. A party to an annulment proceeding can appoint an advocate and procurator,[5] but rare is the petitioner or respondent who knows exactly what advocates and procurators do. Even rarer is a party personally acquainted with anyone who serves in either of those capacities. Accordingly, choosing an advocate or procurator almost invariably boils down to accepting representation by a tribunal nominee. In smaller dioceses, no more than one person is nominated. The situation is much the same as a court assigning a public defender to a person accused of a crime who cannot afford counsel.

Very few parties to an annulment proceeding retain a canon lawyer on their own. Seldom are they given a list from which they can make a choice. Nor is any party likely to be told of the right to request removal of an advocate or procurator.[6] Promoters of justice are sort of canonical ombudsmen charged with ensuring fairness, especially with respect to procedure, during Church legal actions. They can also act as defenders, but not in the same case. In any given case, the judge can name an auditor who may be another tribunal judge or a person approved by the bishop.[7] The auditor is responsible for gathering evidence, then submitting it to the judge. In the process, the auditor decides "what evidence is to be collected and the manner of collection."[8] The auditor prepares the case, as it were, for deliberation by the judges. Another member of the tribunal team is the notary, essentially a clerk who must be present at all hearings and sign whatever documents the hearings produce. In many tribunals the notary has a degree in canon law.

There are many signs that in the United States, parties to annulment, particularly respondents, are very seldom accorded full disclosure of their rights. Among those with annulment experience interviewed for this study, none could articulate any of the rights mentioned here. Perhaps tribunals assume that acceptance of an advocate or procurator is tantamount to a waiver of certain rights, or that the parties, typically incapable of personally vindicating their rights by canonically approved means, are best served when assertion of rights is left to members of the tribunal. Neither of these possibilities, however, seems consistent with the code's stipulations. Full disclosure would occasion staff increases, delay, and probably more unwelcome contentiousness.

Defender of the Bond

Few Church functionaries bear titles denoting more resolute commitment to vigilance than defenders of the bond. Truly they may be likened to Defenders of the Faith, albeit with narrower responsibilities. On its face the title suggests a resourceful and courageous guardian of sacramental marriage whose scrupulous devotion to truth and justice will ensure against unjustified decrees of nullity. The name evokes the image of a staunch vindicator, determined to conserve marriages with even a glimmer of validity. Those familiar with television portrayals of litigation might visualize the defender as a skillful trial lawyer, a forceful courtroom presence, whose cleverness and dedication practically guarantee a proper outcome of the proceeding. The actual duties and behavior that go into the role of defender, however, belie this dramatic conception of the defender's contribution safeguarding the validity of marriage.

An operative definition of the defender of the bond's role was enunciated by Pius XII in his October 2, 1944 allocution to the Roman Rota. Basically, the defender is responsible for investigating, presenting, and clarifying everything that "may be adduced in favor of the bond."[9] The pope cautioned, however, against a combative adversarial relationship between the defender and the judges. Since the Church's legal system is generally more inquisitorial rather than adversarial, the defender is more consultant than foe. Ideally, the defender's input will be taken seriously and have an impact on how the tribunal rules. In practice, however, defenders may discharge their duties aggressively, though not with the courtroom histrionics of many trial lawyers, or they may be more-or-less passive bystanders. Another striking difference between defenders and trial lawyers is that defenders do not ordinarily interact directly with the litigants but instead engage in what is essentially a paper chase, focusing on the acts and proofs of the case, examining them in light of the Church's position on marriage and canon law.

Pius XII did not spell out in detail the qualifications the defender should bring to the position. The defender was expected to have "experience of life and mature judgment." Nothing was stipulated with respect to academic preparation. Evidently it was assumed that defenders, minimally, would be devout Catholics, conversant with theology and canon law relevant to marriage. In days of yore, older priests relate, defenders were typically relentless in their efforts to uphold the validity of doubtful marriages. An elderly canonist tells of an intervention, legendary in proportion, of the defender in a pre–Vatican II "dispensation from the marriage" case. The technical name for such case is *ratum non consummatum*, a term referring to a sacramental marriage never consummated. In defense of the bond the defender investigated in painstaking detail the activities of the bride and groom during the time between the wedding and the reception. Witnesses accounted for the couple's activities throughout all but a single half-hour of that interval. Whether they engaged in a conjugal act during that half-hour was not established. What was established in the mind of the defender, however, was enough doubt to support validity. The petition for nullity was denied.

In post–Vatican II America such perspicacity in the application of C. 1060 would be unheard of. The role of defender now seems to be filled by a mélange of well-meaning types who fall virtually anywhere from top to bottom on scales of juridical and doctrinal competence and on their handling of the benefit of doubt. The academic preparation of defenders was perhaps not a major concern in Pius XII's day simply because there was not as much for them to do. It was, after all, a time when defective consent annulments in America numbered in the hundreds and were just as infrequent in other societies. Defenders, like judges, had ample time to deliberate on their relatively small caseloads. Little could Pius XII imagine that within thirty years after he broadly defined the defender's role, American tribunals would be cranking out annulments almost as fast as America's factories turned out guns, planes, and tanks during the war years of his papacy.

Defenders as well as promoters of justice are appointed by the bishop. Under the 1983 code they are supposed to be "clerics or lay persons of good repute, with a doctorate or licentiate in canon law, and of proven prudence and zeal for justice."[10] Neither Pius XII's ukase nor the new code's stipulations appear to have had much impact on the formal educational preparation and the field performance of American defenders. In 1988 John Paul II, elaborating on Pius XII's characterization of the defender's role, warned against recent tendencies to redefine the role "to the point of confusing it with that of others taking part in the case, or to reduce it to some insignificant formality." Put less diplomatically, defenders had become vulnerable to cooptation and sycophancy, often acting as disinterested bystanders or, worse, even as enthusiastic advocates for nullity. Consequently, "this eliminates from the legal argument the intervention of the person qualified really to investigate, propose and clarify all that could reasonably be cited against nullity, with serious damage to the impartial administration of justice."[11] Although John Paul mentioned no tribunal system by name, American defenders must have been among those he had in mind.

The pope's charge, it should be noted, is not limited to defenders who work at cross purposes with the administration of justice. It applies with equal force to advocates, promoters of justice, and judges who are also capable of subverting the magisterial conception of marriage. This presentation to the Rota has particular relevance for the study at hand, inasmuch as the Holy Father carefully delineated the obligations of the defender in cases involving psychic incapacity. In such cases the defender must pay special attention to the "correct view of the normality of the contracting party and the canonical conclusions to be drawn from the psychopathological symptoms. . . ."[12] The pope, in other words, is urging those who serve as defenders in defective consent cases to have some expertise in behavioral science as well as canon law. His instruction adds significant refinements to the rights and duties assigned to defenders by Pius XII and the new code.

Defender Track Record

Defenders are not directly involved in the preparation of the *libellus*, but they can later dissent from the tribunal's decision to accept a petition. There is no evidence on how often this happens, if at all. Tribunal screening of petitions could anticipate the defender's characteristic reactions to certain types of grounds. Theoretically, the reactions can range from staunch opposition to uncritical concurrence. Once a petition is accepted, the defender is able to intervene at any stage of what follows, even to a point of initiating appeals to Second and Third Instance. Most defender activity, however, occurs as ordinary process cases are going through First Instance. Other tribunalists might be in a position to see how defenders acquit themselves in given cases, but are prohibited from discussing their performance outside the confines of tribunal chambers. Petitioners and respondents never see a defender at work in First Instance proceedings. For that matter, there is little if any face-to-face interaction between advocates and the parties. On occasion the Rota comments on how a defender performed in a given case. Thus, an assessment of how effectively defenders defend must be winnowed from Rota material, annulment statistics, and reports from parties to annulment proceedings.

Table 9–1. Outcome of U.S. First Instance Ordinary Process Cases Concluded by Sentence, 1984–1994.

Year	No. concluded	No. for nullity	No. against nullity	Percent nullified
1984	37,450	35,472	1,978	94.7
1985	37,538	36,180	1,358	96.4
1986	40,857	39,175	1,682	95.9
1987	41,443	40,165	1,278	96.9
1988	41,208	39,671	1,537	96.3
1989	41,208	39,845	1,206	97.1
1990	41,374	40,291	1,083	97.4
1991	41,820	41,121	699	98.3
1992	41,414	40,516	898	97.8
1993	37,987	37,123	864	97.7
1994	37,310	36,460	850	97.7
TOTALS	439,812	426,019	13,433	96.9

Source: Statistical Yearbooks of the Church, 1984–1994.

Some feel for their performance is gotten by examining the outcome of First Instance tribunal deliberations. Between 1984 and 1994 America's First Instance tribunals ruled against nullity in 13,433 of 426,019 ordinary process cases concluded (Table 9-1). That nullity resulted in almost 97 percent of the cases tried suggests the sort of product consistency that could evoke envy and admiration among the managers and owners of many modern businesses and factories. Exactly how defenders contributed to the 13,433 sentences against nullity cannot be determined from the data. Nor can we ascertain how many annulments would not have occurred if defenders had been more effective. In civil trials, lawyers can provide brilliant representation yet fail to achieve a favorable outcome for their clients. Secular trial judges sometimes compliment attorneys for skill displayed in arguing a losing cause. In all likelihood, defenders sometimes suffer the same fate, their best efforts going for nought when tribunal judges rule for nullity. Yet even in the improbable event that defenders can take full credit for all of the denials of nullity, a 3.1 percent success rate is not terribly impressive.

If the small percentage of petitions adjudicated without leading to nullity has validity as even a crude measure of their performance, defenders boast only an exceedingly low percentage of triumphs in their attempts to keep marital bonds intact. Their effectiveness is further diminished by the even smaller percentage of nullity decrees reversed by America's Second Instance tribunals. If First Instance tribunal outcome statistics are indeed an embarrassment to defenders, advocates retained by contentious respondents share in their shame. On the other hand, it may be argued that the apparent ineffectiveness of defenders and respondents' advocates is actually a tribute to the soundness of tribunal decisions. But that interpretation is difficult to reconcile with the high percentage of reversals suffered by American tribunal rulings appealed to the Rota.

Our evaluation of defenders and advocates would be less tentative if we knew how often they disagree with tribunal judges, the number of Second and Third Instance formal appeals they initiate, and the outcome of cases where disagreement occurs. Despite the absence of such data, there is reason to believe that their influence on annulment proceedings depends on factors other than how assiduously and resourcefully they discharge their duties. Much, of course, hinges on degree of commitment to the prevailing ideology of easy annulment and on how they reckon valid matrimonial consent. If defenders, advocates and judges "read the same newspapers," the chances are that they will almost reflexively concur in the tribunal's analysis and disposition of cases.

The Great Credential Lag

Besides recourse to annulment statistics, the performance of tribunalists can be approached by examining their credentials. Credentials signify qualifications which in turn are important determinants of behavior. Well-trained lawyers and jurists should practice and apply the law more effectively than lawyers and jurists with less formal legal education. The new code incorporates this common-sense principle by specifying the credentials tribunalists are to bring to their work. Lists of diocesan tribunalists along with their graduate degrees are published annually in the *Catholic Directory*. Each *Directory* contains a wealth of information on the state of the Church during the preceding year. Thus, the 1993 edition shows the make-up of tribunal rosters for 1992. The rosters show that American tribunals have not hastened to staff themselves in accordance with the new code. Their inability or refusal to do so has not gone unnoticed in Rome. Less than two years after the revised code took effect, the Apostolic Signatura wrote to several American bishops about the qualifications of tribunal personnel. Besides reminding the bishops about academic requirements, the Signatura pointedly noted that tribunalists lacking the requisite degrees had no acquired right to tribunal positions simply because they had held them before the new code became effective. The Signatura was especially troubled by the eleventh-hour appointments of several individuals without degrees, apparently made so their presence on the tribunals would be assured after the new code appeared.[13] Anyone familiar with American politics would find such appointments akin to those made by lame-duck officeholders shortly before expiration of their terms. Political supporters are named to public sinecures in appreciation for previous backing and in the hope of ensuring continuation of policies rejected by the electorate.

There can be little doubt that the Signatura's insistence on tribunal staffing being up to code reflected the hope that stiffer credential requirements would help stanch the flow of American annulments. But the American canonical community showed little enthusiasm for applying such a curial tourniquet. Shunning bylines, a group of unnamed canonists publicly responded to the Signatura in the CLSA's newsletter. Conceding that the letter was not the first expression of the Signatura's displeasure with American tribunals, they consigned it to the realm of "advice." While the Signatura was within its competence in dispatching the letter, its content, they held, was technically classifiable as a "private interpretation." Continuing, the canonists proclaimed that it is not within the Signatura's purview to provide authentic interpretations of the code. Such interpretations are reserved to the Commission for the Authentic Interpretation of the Code. The Signatura had merely sided with one school of thought on tribunal staffing and appointments. "[T]his is not an authentic interpretation, but an issue still being debated among canonists. Until the issue is resolved by an authentic interpretation, both opinions remain 'private.' "[14] Having made their stand, the anonymous canonists suggested that American bishops take the issue under advisement. For all intents and purposes, this meant sustaining the status quo. In legal terms, the Signatura's position was in effect rendered obiter dictum, that is to say, a passing or incidental statement unrelated to the disposition of specific cases.

In simpler terms, the canonists were saying to the Church's supreme tribunal: "Hands off! You can tell us what you think, but we are not obliged to do your bidding. Until we hear from what we regard as the proper authority, we will staff our tribunals as we please."[15] In view of the fact that Church law grants the Signatura competence to "oversee the proper administration of justice,"[16] the response of the American canonists came close to insolence. The canonists' position is analogous to that of theologians who do not regard papal directives as binding unless they are pronounced *ex cathedra*. In the meantime, *their* "private opinion," not that of the Signatura, continued to shape the staffing and operations of American tribunals. Among the incongruities marking this exchange is the sight of canonists, so often disposed to invoke the "spirit of Vatican II" to avoid the curse of legalism, themselves resorting to narrow legalism to thwart the will of the Signatura.

Several key differences between the legal systems of the Church and the United States were sketched earlier in the discussion of Rotal jurisprudence. But however much the two systems may vary, they nonetheless have certain features in common. In every system where courts are arranged hierarchically, rulings by the highest court are not ordinarily shrugged off with impunity by lesser courts or by legal practitioners. It is instructive to examine the tribunal staffing dispute in the context of the American legal system. For discussion's sake, let it be assumed that the U.S. Supreme Court rules that henceforth graduates of nonaccredited law schools cannot practice law. Technically, the American Bar Association (ABA) is responsible for accrediting law schools. An ABA committee formed to examine the Supreme Court's decree concludes that it will produce hardship among students attending law schools lacking accreditation. The committee decides that court's pronouncement is merely another opinion, with no more legal or professional force than its own contrary opinion. Should this happen, the consequences would be easy to foresee. Unless the schools in question took prompt measures to merit accreditation, no court in the United States would countenance the practice of law by future graduates. Moreover, attorneys with degrees from unaccredited schools might be charged with unauthorized practice of law by state and local bar associations, and perhaps find themselves in the ranks of the unemployed. The American canonical community's disregard for the efforts of the Church's highest court to enforce standards specified by canon law should come as no surprise. Papal pronouncements on such issues as psychological grounds for nullity and the obligations of defenders routinely receive much the same reception. It seems a bit incongruous, to say the least, that a canonical community which often treats aspects of Rotal jurisprudence as if they were engraved in stone empowers itself to disregard directives from the court that rules over the Rota.

Varvaro's first survey of American cases reviewed by the Rota contains material supporting the Signatura's position on the need to upgrade the credentials and performance of tribunalists. Time and again, for example, the Rota found defenders succumbing to the radical role inversion warned against in John Paul II's 1988 address to the Rota. They became advocates for nullity rather than guardians of validity.[17] In one case the Rota was impelled to remind the tribunal whose decision it reversed that the defender is never to argue against the validity of the marriage. In another, the defender, besides listing all the reasons for nullity he could come upon, used the motivation behind a Mexican divorce to justify a decree of nullity. The petitioner's motives for obtaining the divorce, the Rota held, had no bearing on the validity of the annulled marriage. One defender was taken to task for responding to an advocate's twenty-five-page brief with a canned statement which could have applied to any number of other cases heard by the tribunal. Still another case, not included among Varvaro's, found the defender proclaiming with undisguised enthusiasm his concurrence with the decree of nullity. Never had he seen a marriage more deserving of nullification. The Rota, on appeal, overturned the decree with a definitive sentence showing that the defender, together with the First and Second Instance tribunals, had gotten virtually nothing right. So sweeping was the Rota's critique that it was difficult to understand how the defender could have accepted the findings of the First Instance tribunal with such equanimity. Either he was incompetent or he failed to honor his sworn duty to guard against frivolous declarations of nullity.

The Signatura's frequent "advice," papal enjoinders, scathing Rotal criticism, and explicit requirements of canon law notwithstanding, improvements in the quality and training of defenders and other tribunal personnel have proceeded with glacial speed. This can be deduced from tribunal personnel assignments appearing in *The Official Catholic Directory 1993*. The survey, preliminary to a more comprehensive study of tribunal staffing, covered the first twenty-five of the 188 dioceses listed alphabetically in the *Directory*. While the sampling methodology is not ideal, the dioceses thus chosen are probably fairly representative. The figures presented here, it should be noted, do not include defenders assigned to the three interdiocesan or provincial tribunals in the sample. Instead, they relate to defenders working on the First Instance or trial court level. No defender was listed for two dioceses-Altoona-Johnstown and Camden. The names and credentials of ninety-six tribunalists serving as defenders appear in the rosters of the other twenty dioceses and three archdioceses in the sample. Among the ninety-six defenders, twenty-eight had doctorates (JCDs) or licentiates (JCLs) in canon law. Thus, slightly more than seventy percent of the defenders apparently had no graduate training in canon law. Among those with degrees but not in canon law, several held licentiates in sacred theology (STLs), masters degrees in divinity, and the like. More than half the defenders without degrees were religious, the remainder laypersons.

While the sample's staffing credentials overall are far below code, some tribunals have managed to approximate its requirements. Belleville, a comparatively small diocese in southern Illinois, has four defenders, two with JCDs, two with JCLs.[18] Indeed, a perusal of the entire *Directory* leads to the impression that tribunals within Chicago's Provincial jurisdiction, except for Rockford, may have been the best credentialed in the country. Atlanta, Bridgeport, and Brooklyn also measured up to code. At the other extreme we find dioceses such as Arlington, where none of eleven defenders listed had a canon law degree, though seven had advanced training in other areas. Boise also had eleven defenders without degrees in canon law, none with a degree in what might be termed a cognate area, such as theology.

Earning a JCD or JCL entails studying the entire body of Church law. But tribunals today deal almost exclusively with marriage cases. Quite a few bishops may therefore assume that practically any priest should know enough about marriage to serve effectively as a defender. Such bishops, in effect, may be harking back to the defender's role as defined by Pius XII. That definition, promulgated before the marriage bond became so tenuous, is passé. Quite likely the educational requisites for defenders were raised to help forestall further damage to a bond being made increasingly fragile. John Paul II's call for defender competence in behavioral science as well as law surely had that aim in mind.[19] Defenders are supposed to be capable of matching wits with tribunal judges; when they lack a semblance of parity in canonical expertise, they are tilting at juridical windmills. Any dialogue will be a mismatch, with judges instructing rather than listening to defenders on the propriety of nullity. The defender becomes an unschooled subordinate, not a knowledgeable peer. A similar disadvantage obtains with advocates whose canonical upbringing is wanting. The situation resembles a civil trial where a paralegal would be pitted against a veteran trial lawyer.

Credential lag, as noted, is not peculiar to defenders. Advocates without the JCDs they are supposed to have are commonplace. The Archdiocese of Philadelphia listed fourteen "approved advocates," not one with a degree in canon law. Eleven of the fourteen were credited with master of divinity degrees. In one diocese the *officialis* has no degree in canon law. In the 1993 *Directory* there is no defender entry for several smaller dioceses other than Boise. Apparently defenders are either appointed on an ad hoc basis from among diocesan clergy or borrowed from other tribunals, or else promoters of justice are used as surrogates. The Archdiocese of Boston listed two defenders, each with a degree in canon law, and fourteen psychological consultants. Eight of the fourteen have degrees in social work and only one can possibly be a psychiatrist. Elsewhere, defenders with master's degrees in fields other than canon law are commonplace.

A question that suggests itself is whether defenders and advocates without the legal training explicitly preferred by the code can contribute in any meaningful way to procedural aspects of the "right of defense." They might be fairly knowledgeable about what constitutes valid marriage and grounds for nullity, but they might also be ill-informed on the law's procedural guarantees for contentious respondents. In addition, they are probably less likely to to be familiar with the body of Rotal jurisprudence. Judging from the *Directory* listings, in some dioceses either their roles or the requirements of canon law are not taken seriously, or the bishops lack the wherewithal or motivation to have them properly trained. The latter possibility, however, seems inconsistent with the oft-repeated praise for the bishops' generous funding of tribunals. While defenders and advocates in defective consent cases are supposed to be jacks of two trades—canon law and behavioral science—the *Directory* suggests that several are indeed masters of neither.

The credential lag might also reflect hesitancy on the part of some bishops and judicial vicars to upset the annulment applecart. This possibility is not unrelated to questions raised by the Signatura on the last-minute tribunal appointments made before the new code took force. A defender or advocate vigorously implementing papal and Rotal wishes would be a divisive influence on most American tribunals. Inevitably there would be collegial tensions with permissive judges and perhaps a reduction in the number of "pastorally indicated" annulments. On the other hand, some bishops may remain in the grip of inertia out of fear that additional training will simply reinforce lax views on nullity defenders and advocates already hold. As one troubled ordinary confided, the problem with tribunal staffing goes deeper than credentials, sinecures, and tenure. If defenders and other tribunal officials are compelled to have doctorates or licentiates in canon law, where would the degrees be earned? Aspiring canonists sent to either of the two leading centers of canon law in North America[20] seem likely to emerge as canonical and ideological clones of those currently in the field. What kind of bond would the newly trained defenders be defending? When grounds for nullity are psychological, American canonists have made the marital bond to so vulnerable that, practically speaking, trying to uphold its validity comes close to defending the indefensible.

Tribunal Judges

Thus far, our discussion on credentials has dealt mainly with defenders and advocates. Let us now turn to the tribunal functionaries empowered to grant or deny decrees of nullity. In 1992 the twenty-five tribunals in our alphabetical *Directory* sample employed 188 judges. The judicial vicars were assisted by fourteen vicars who had a variety of official titles. Although most judicial vicars serve as judges, the *Directory* does not reveal whether all forty-one vicars adjudicated cases. Some subordinate vicars could have been restricted to administrative duties, or responsible for attending to documentary process petitions, most of which require no trial. In any event, seven of the auxiliary judicial vicars did not have degrees in canon law. Two of the seven were members of the Diocese of Boise tribunal whose "director" was a nun with a JCL, the sole tribunalist among twenty-six listed who held a canon law degree.[21] Among the tribunalists designated as judges, sixty-three—twenty-five percent—had JCDs or JCLs. Assuming that all vicars judged, the percentage of judges with degrees rises to thirty-four percent. Several tribunalist designated as judges had graduate degrees in fields other than canon law.

These are astounding figures. If the twenty-five tribunals examined here are representative of the 188 in the United States, appreciably less than half judges in the tribunal system meet the new code's specifications. Nonetheless, each year they help to decide at First Instance the fate of nearly forty-thousand ordinary process cases. No less than two-thirds of the judges who kept the assembly line rolling in 1992 lacked the requisite formal training for the job they were called to perform. A university with nearly 66 percent of its faculty inadequately credentialed would soon lose its accreditation. An automobile factory with more than half its workers lacking necessary skills would probably produce cars with an unacceptable number of defects. The American tribunal system has not yet officially forfeited its accreditation; it has lost its credibility. Relying on a labor force with questionable competence, the system continues to grind out many defective consent annulments which are themselves canonically and doctrinally defective. Credential deficiencies were understandable during the first years of transition from the old code to the new, but their persistence nearly a decade after the change seems inexcusable.

Grocholewski contends that an ill-trained jurist tends to rush to judgment and poses the "greatest risk to the pursuit of the truth and consequently the greatest risk to pastoral effectiveness (not to speak of justice)."[22] As Secretary of the Signatura, Grocholewski is well aware of tactics used by diocesan bishops and tribunals to delay or circumvent adherence to the code's staffing norms. Some bishops, pleading a shortage of qualified canonists, sought dispensations. Each request for a dispensation had to be accompanied by the candidate's curriculum vitae and a statement explaining the necessity for granting the candidate a place on the tribunal. The Signatura responded to such requests either by granting a dispensation, sometimes with conditions attached, granting the dispensation for a specified time, or denying the request. Grocholewski concedes that some dispensations were granted to unqualified candidates because without them judicial activity in some dioceses would have become excessively backlogged. It is noteworthy that he does not suggest that all tribunals face an unmanageable backlog of cases. This implies that the pent-up demand for annulments properly granted is not as great as American canonists routinely claim, also that tribunals can make do without unqualified staff members if they exercise tighter control over caseloads.

In 1992 a large but indeterminate number of American tribunal judges were of the prosynodal or diocesan variety. Under the 1917 code judges could be named during diocesan synods, councils of diocesan priests held every ten years. Candidates selected by the bishop would be submitted to the synod for approval that was virtually automatic. Many tribunalists, however, were made judges without benefit of a synod, usually by the diocesan Board of Consultors after deliberating on nominees tendered by the bishop. Such judges were termed prosynodal. More recently, some tribunals include diocesan judges (also called associate judges) who are appointed by the bishops without the advice and consent of a synod or Board of Consultors. Signatura approval of the appointment of all three types was predicated on good-faith efforts by the dioceses to staff their tribunals in accordance with the code's specifications. Such efforts would entail having the appointees work toward a degree in canon law or replacing them with property trained canonists as soon as possible.

Despite differences in their titles and method of appointment, synodal, prosynodal, and diocesan judges are functionally coequal. De jure they are all interim players, thrust into the annulment game when genuine canonists are either unavailable or unable to cope with heavy caseloads. Despite deficiencies in formal canonical training, de facto they have as much power as other tribunal judges to determine the fate of marriages. Some without JCDs or JCLs reputedly brought some competence in Church law on marriage to their stopgap judgeships. Others were expected to acquire competence through on-the-job training.

Interim judges pose a variety of problems. For one thing, the new code makes no provision for them, in effect phasing out these kinds of judgeships. Under the 1917 code, synodal and prosynodal judges had a ten-year term limit and could be removed only for "just cause." But many without reappointments or dispensation from Rome continued to sit on tribunals after expiration of their terms. The new code says nothing about length of tenure, probably because it is silent on the very existence of interim tribunal judges. While the old code limited the number of synodal judges to twelve per diocese, several dioceses exceeded that number without dispensation to do so. Many synodal judges were appointed shortly before the changeover from the old code to the new. Presumably that would give the tribunals a lengthy breathing spell before they would be forced to staff themselves as the new code directs.[23] Their presence on the tribunals would ensure continuity in the production of annulments. No doubt some interim appointees developed into satisfactory judges, yet even at the outset of their experiential training they could rule with the same authority as veteran tribunalists degreed in canon law.

Three of the alphabetical sample tribunals classify their judges as prosynodal. Four of the fifteen prosynodal judges listed lack degrees of any kind. Possibly synodal appointments made shortly before Advent 1983 had not fully run their ten-year course when the 1993 *Catholic Directory* was published. Perhaps dispensations were granted, allowing them to continue to function as judges because the tribunals had made serious efforts, as shown by the twelve judges with proper degrees, to improve the caliber of their judges. Nonetheless, it is curious that all fifteen judges are still considered prosynodal when in fact the code no longer recognizes that designation.

Perhaps even more objectionable to the Signatura than judges without degrees were tribunal appointments, actual and proposed, which resulted in a single appointee performing multiple functions. Some appointments conferred the roles of judge, defender, and advocate on the same tribunalist. Although the tribunalist would not perform in more than one capacity in the same case, the Signatura found such "consolidation of responsibilities" unacceptable. Particularly nettlesome are tribunals where the judge and defender are one and the same person. Five of the twenty-five dioceses had one or more judges serving as defenders. Seven of Albany's twelve judges and four of Belleville's six were also listed as defenders.

In one of his earlier allocutions to the Rota, John Paul II stated that "The same person cannot exercise two functions at the same time—to be judge and defender of the bond."[24] Appearing a year after the pope's address, the new code does not expressly prohibit a given tribunalist from assuming both roles in separate cases. Nevertheless, Grocholewski argues, fusing the two roles in the same person is improper, since each role involves "completely different tasks" which demand "a specifically different perspective. . . ." The judge must weigh arguments pro and con, while the "defender (whose work is analogous to that of the advocate or the promoter of justice) has to research and expound in a clear way all and only those arguments which militate against the alleged nullity of the marriage." Mixing the roles "destroys the necessary constructive dialectic of the canonical process."[25]

To check on progress in the staffing of tribunals, the alphabetical sample was revisited. This time the data source was the 1996 *Catholic Directory*, the latest edition in print. The two samples are not perfectly comparable because the more recent *Directory* does not provide the credentials of the Archdiocese of Baltimore's sizable number of tribunalists. Without Baltimore, the percentage of judges with JCDs and JCLs goes from twenty-five percent to thirty-one percent. When judicial vicars and their auxiliary vicars are counted with judges, the percentage with proper degrees rises from thirty-four percent to forty percent. Defenders with canon law degrees rose from 23 percent to 27 percent, while the percentage of advocates with JCDs or JCLs rose to five percent from one percent. If Baltimore's credentials in 1995 remained much the same as they were in three years earlier, the increases would narrow. Even when regarded in the most flattering light, the data give sober pause. Over half the judges and nearly three-quarters of the defenders do not meet code specifications. The code's preference for advocates to have JCDs "unless otherwise well qualified," and approved by the bishop appears to be at least partially already dead letter.[26]

The 1996 *Directory* takes us more than a decade beyond the new code's introduction, and there would seem to have been ample time for the sample dioceses to get their tribunal houses in order. It is theoretically possible that some or all the five dioceses were in fact operating within the Signatura's guidelines. A bishop who sought a waiver of degree requirements for tribunalists could also be granted, for a limited time, permission for the same person to act as judge and defender. But such dispensations were to be reserved for exceptional cases involving extraordinary circumstances. One tribunalist whose bishop did obtain dispensation from the degree standards informs me that the Signatura, in weighing dispensation requests, takes into account whether the diocese had made good-faith efforts to staff tribunals with qualified personnel. This same source relates that the Signatura is inclined to apply rigorous standards when making judgments on good faith.

Six years after publication of Grocholewski's critique there were still widespread deficiencies in the qualifications and functions of the tribunal system's personnel. The jousting between the Signatura and American dioceses on the staffing and operation of tribunals has been perennial. Frequently it develops out of canonical maneuvering on issues about which the code itself is mute. In such cases, American canonists are seldom at a loss for words. Textual or statutory gaps are almost invariably filled in such a way as to minimize or neutralize strictures on nullity. Grocholewski's position on the issue of tribunalists filling more than one role, presumably that of the Signatura, is also a reminder to his American canonical brethren that merely because the code does not explicitly prohibit something does not mean that it is therefore permissible.[27] Nevertheless, the code's silence on certain matters is treated as an opportunity to legitimize behavior otherwise proscribed.

This tendency on the part of American canonists is graphically illustrated in a recent commentary on divorce and remarriage by one of America's most prominent canon lawyers. James Provost acknowledges that both the old and new codes admonish "those who are in serious sin not to approach Communion until they have been absolved in the sacrament of penance." A footnote to that observation comments that both codes also "note the possibility of making an act of perfect contrition if it is not possible to receive the sacrament of penance at the time and there is grave reason to receive the Eucharist; an act of perfect contrition is said to include the intention of receiving the sacrament of penance as soon as possible."[28] He considers it "remarkable . . . that neither code explicitly excludes divorced and remarried Catholics from the Eucharist, despite the attention given to this topic in the process of revising at least the Latin code, and in two apostolic exhortations by the pope who promulgated both codes." Provost goes on to say that it is "difficult to determine the significance of this silence with accuracy, but it can at least be observed that where the law leaves room for nuance, it is not inappropriate for those who interpret or apply the law to leave room for nuance also."[29] Here a void is filled with canonical sophistry. True, the codes are silent on reception of the Eucharist by Catholics divorced and remarried. It is also true that they make no explicit mention of divorce. But is it not common knowledge the divorced and remarried are denied communion as a consequence of the fact that adultery is a mortal sin? How, one might ask, can there be a perfect or even sincere act of contrition if the penitent does not intend to avoid the occasions of sin that divorce and remarriage provide for violation of the Sixth Commandment?

Although many bishops have degrees in canon law, they seem to wink at the use of Philadelphia-lawyer tactics by their own canonical experts to circumvent and amend the code. The quest for loopholes in Church rules on divorce and remarriage and on tribunal staffing and credentials springs from the same generalized urge to undermine, neutralize, or ignore the law's requirements. Perhaps it reflects a mindset endemic among lawyers, civil as well as canon. More likely, it represents the American canonical establishment's deep-seated aversion to initiatives from Rome that stifle the production of annulments and constrain the establishment's self-bestowed autonomy.

Variations in Productivity

The quality of their performance is a reflection of more than the degrees American tribunalists hold. It is also a function of tribunal caseloads and prevailing conceptions of marriage and matrimonial consent. Grocholewski offers the Regional Tribunal of Lazio, with jurisdiction over 4.5 million Catholics in a large area of central Italy that includes Rome, as an enlightening example of how a tribunal with exceptional credentials performs. In 1985 all twenty-one of the tribunal's judges, its four defenders, and six of its ten notaries had doctorates in canon law. During that year the tribunal's First Instance judges decided 147 cases, while Second Instance judges issued forty-five decrees of ratification and six sentences in cases tried by them. The tribunal complained of overwork and inability to start and finish cases within deadlines specified by canon law.[30] That same year the Archdiocese of Chicago tribunal handed down sentences in 1,360 ordinary Process cases. Assuming the judicial vicar participated in trials, this output was accomplished by thirteen judges and nine defenders, with eight of the latter also serving as judges. The 1986 *Catholic Directory* shows that in 1985 Chicago's complement of judges and defenders included at least five members without degrees in canon law: a master of science in an unspecified area of study, a master of chancery affairs, a master of arts, and two holders of STDs. Thus Chicago's fourteen tribunalists, with jurisdiction over not much more than half as many Catholics as the Lazio tribunal, adjudicated more than nine times as many ordinary process cases as Lazio's twenty-five overworked tribunalists.

A comparison of the productivity of the two jurisdictions suggests a good deal about the judicial dimension of the celebrated efficiency of American tribunals. It is altogether improbable that Chicago's tribunalists work longer hours or are more adept at speed-reading than their counterparts in Lazio. The astonishing productivity differential is better explained in terms of willingness to accept petitions for trial, different criteria for determining validity, and the time and attention devoted to deliberating on the fate of marriages. By 1991 Chicago's First Instance tribunal reduced its level of activity to 1,078 cases decided by sentence, almost 300 fewer than in 1985. The decrease was acccompanied

Table 9–2. Productivity of Selected Tribunals, 1985.

Diocese/ archdiocese	Full-time professionals	Part-time professionals	Ordinary process cases decided*
Lazio	25	NA	147
Chicago	12	6	1,360
Arlington	1	4	199
Columbus	1	6	200
Joliet	3	3	272
Lansing	0	5	294
Saginaw	1	3	248
San Diego	1	7	190
Santa Fe	1	1	168

*All decisions First Instance.

Sources: Grocholewski,and *CLSA Proceedings* (1986–1987),: 299–312.

by a reduction in the number of the tribunalists. Lest that be taken as a sign that the tribunal experienced a change of heart on the quality and propriety of the annulments it was granting, a few additional factors require mention. Chicago's First Instance tribunalists also served on the Interdiocesan Appellate Tribunal, together with canonists recruited from other diocesan tribunals in the province. Besides adjudicating 1078 ordinary Process cases in 1991, they thus also contributed to the Province's 2,378 decrees of ratification and the twenty-four cases retried at Second Instance.

The Chicago tribunalists in 1985 were slothful laggards, however, compared to their counterparts in other dioceses. The virtuoso productivity of some dioceses merits memorialization (Table 9-2). For purposes of convenient visual comparision, figures for Lazio and Chicago are given. The performance of the American tribunals listed, as measured by output, beggars credulity. Leaving Chicago to the side, the modal number of full-time professionals in the remaining American tribunals listed is one, presumably the judicial vicar. No *officialis* had more than seven part-time professionals yet each tribunal tried and concluded appreciably more cases than the Lazio tribunal. Lansing, with no full-time professional and only five part-timers, decided over twice as many cases as Lazio. It would be the height of hubris to suppose that the American tribunalists are so much more energetic and efficient than their counterparts in Italy. Even today there is no diocesan or metropolitian American tribunal with credentials comparable to those of Lazio in 1985. The explanation for the radical disparities lies elsewhere. The Lazio tribunal probably adhered more scrupulously than most American tribunals to the code's preference for collegiate panels. More important, it operated from a different set of premises on the nature of marriage and on what constitute viable grounds for incapacity.

The credential gap goes hand in hand with a performance gap. There is no shortage of anecdotal material to flesh out what has been shown quantitatively.

Cardinal Edouard Gagnon, addressing the American metropolitans (archbishops) in 1989, related that during a visit to Alberta he and several bishops had occasion to examine sentences handed down by an *officialis,* a former theology professor who did not believe in the indissolubility of marriage.[31] Although data are not available, it would be surprising if his tribunal rejected any petitions for nullity and if ensuing trials did not invariably lead to that outcome. Vatican and CLSA statistics and other sources indicate that judicial vicars of similar persuasion are not peculiar to Canada.

One of the stranger tribunal melodramas to unfold in the United States involved a priest-canonist transferred to a midwestern diocese to fill a tribunal vacancy for an *officialis.* While acting in that capacity he terminated the seventeen-year marriage of two parishioners in a rather unusual extralegal manner. The feat was accomplished not through a C. 1095 annulment, but by absconding with the wife and her five children, then marrying her in a civil ceremony in another state. Before the romance reached the elopement phase, the priest spent an extraordinary amount of time at the couple's house. He also filled in for the pastor of their parish, who had unexpectedly resigned. Later the husband recalled how he "had to sit there and listen to him deliver sermons on the sanctity of the family." One can readily deduce how this canonist viewed the permanence and indissolubility of marriage during his prior tour of duty with an eastern archdiocesan tribunal as well as his brief sojourn as a midwestern judicial vicar. But the story may yet have a happy secular ending. The husband, since remarried, plans to petition for annulment of his first marriage. The petition will be filed with the tribunal previously headed by the priest who ran off with the petitioner's wife and children. It would be imprudent to wager against his chances for having the marriage nullified.[32]

In an interview conducted for this study, an erstwhile judicial vicar openly boasted of having presided over more than four hundred annulments during his stint as tribunal head. With obvious pride he recounted having personally directed, much like Teddy Roosevelt leading the charge up San Juan Hill, canonical campaigns to prevent several university professors from successfully challenging decrees of nullity granted to their spouses. The judicial vicar of an archdiocesan marriage tribunal, riding the circuit from one parish to the next to spread the annulment word, told one audience that "the Church has never been challenged before to look and see what a real marriage is." Today's Catholics, unlike previous generations of the faithful, are privileged to have many options for leaving a marriage of questionable sacramental character. As a result, the Church has been forced to "define sacramental marriage and to look at what it means to be married and what it means to separate."[33] His revelations would be news to a variety of saints and popes, not to mention the Signatura and members of the Rota. Church writings on what marriage is would fill a small library, and the new catechism dwells on marriage at some length. What he is really saying, however, without admitting it, is that "the Church has never been challenged before to look and see what a real *successful* marriage is."

Yet another *officialis* characterizes his former archbishop, recently transferred to Rome, as a "leading international advocate of liberalizing annulments," who is said to lobby in Rome for the Church to relax her standards on divorce and remarriage.[34] In the same interview the judicial vicar proclaims that Church law governing the validity of marriage is exceptionally broad. "Both people have to have the capacity to commit to an indissoluble union that can be broken only by death." The vicar's statement easily translates into the view that the mere fact of divorce is sufficient to establish lack of that capacity. It reflects an almost completely amorphous conception of incapacity much in vogue among American canonists but repudiated time and again by the Rota, the Signatura, and the pope. The same vicar holds that the breadth of Church law covers petitioners abused as children who persuade the tribunal that they lacked the emotional capacity to make a lifelong commitment.[35] This loose understanding of incapacity suggests a considerably-less-than-airtight case as sufficient to persuade a receptive tribunal to annul. It also exemplifies how the text and meaning of C. 1095 are trivialized and infused with unintended ambiguity. How the tribunal goes about verifying the claim of emotional incapacity is not explained. Nor is there any effort to elucidate criteria used to gauge the condition. These considerations could establish new directions in the relationship between behavioral science and canon law. Canonists concede their dependence on the human sciences, but if they can show how child abuse causes defective consent, the dependency will be reversed. They will become a major source of enlightenment for behavioral science.

Anecdotes of this nature can be multiplied many times over. Of significance here is the fact that they do not pertain to interim judges or neophyte tribunalists, the ink still wet on their licentiates and doctorates. Rather, they concern veteran judicial vicars, bishops' appointees, who have canonical life-and-death powers over marriage. Their attitudes and behavior, together with the statistical evidence, suggest that the predilections, judicial temperament, and performance of many American tribunalists—judges, advocates, procurators, promoters of justice, and defenders—actually increase the vulnerability of marriage to nullity. The contentious respondent who hopes to uphold the validity of marriage on trial faces an almost insurmountable challenge.

❖ 10 ❖

Respondents and
the Right of Defense

Virtually every facet of the American tribunal system examined thus far bespeaks an orientation toward petitioners and nullity. The proannulment hydra rears its heads even in what should be unlikely places, for example, in the role of the respondent. In practical terms, respondents fit a variety of molds. Tribunals often differentiate between "cooperative" and "uncooperative" respondents. The former are those who participate in the tribunal's investigation, usually by testifying and perhaps by tendering names of witnesses. Many react to a petition for annulment with equanimity, relief, or even ill-disguised glee. For some, already remarried outside the Church, annulment is a bonus they did not actively seek. Quite a few cooperative types are tacitly or overtly in complicity with petitioners, just as anxious as their former spouses to have their marriages voided and, as the familiar cliché puts it, to "get on with their lives." One hears of prospective petitioners attempting to move their exspouses toward complicity even before filing a petition with the tribunal.[1] Many respondents fall into the cooperative category by virtue of their canonical innocence. Their hearts and consciences tell them their marriages are valid, and they naively trust the tribunal to affirm that conviction. It might be more accurate to say that their cooperation is born of ignorance rather than innocence. If they were fully cognizant of tribunals' penchant to annul, and if apprised of how validity can be defended, their apparent passivity might give way to active opposition.

Some respondents are deemed uncooperative because the tribunal cannot locate them, while many who are contacted make no effort to participate in the proceeding. Finally, we have uncooperatives who are contentious from the moment they see the petition for nullity. They, too, are convinced of the validity of their marriages, and angered to see them under challenge. Even if not already familiar with their tribunal's disposition to annul, they realize intuitively that their marriages face extinction. But while they wish to uphold validity, typically they do not know how to be contentious in an effective way.

Although respondents must be given opportunity to uphold the validity of their marriages, canon law does not require them to use it. Common sense dictates that uncontested cases are more likely to result in nullity than those in which respondents mount a challenge. We lack data on how often respondents formally defend their marriage, how vigorously defense is pursued, and the outcomes of contested versus uncontested petitions. But using the rate of success achieved by defenders and the small number of cases that reach the Rota as yardsticks, even contentious respondents seldom stave off nullity.

Futility in Fighting Back

What tribunals take as lack of respondent interest is frequently more apparent than real. Beneath a facade of inertia and resignation there is often rage, triggered by the tribunal's willingness even to consider nullity. Many refuse to dignify the process by becoming part of what they regard as a farce. No earthly power, including the bishop's astute and creative tribunalists, could persuade them of the invalidity of their marriages. Unschooled in how the Church is supposed to have changed her mind on nature of marriage and annulment, they see annulment as Catholic "divorce," an ecclesial appendage to civil divorce. I have met several apparently passive respondents who fit this characterization to perfection. Instead of relying on canonical procedures to challenge annulment, their response occurred outside the pale of tribunal ministrations and jurisdiction. They left the Church, which in their view reneged on what it had solemnly taught them about Christian marriage. For the most part, the "healing" efforts of tribunals fail to reach them. If healing occurs, it will come through the grace of God and what is left of their faith. Not infrequently, the respondent is an innocent victim, at least in the sense of receiving an unwanted divorce after trying to keep the marriage together. A divorce that went against the respondent's most fundamental beliefs is followed by an inexplicable annulment. Respondents are often injured as well as innocent victims, abandoned during marriage by a petitioner now seeking Church approval for a marriage to the very person who may have inspired that abandonment.[2]

In an admittedly unscientific study of pastors, Bowman conducted structured interviews with twenty-nine veteran priests, each a pastor ordained at least twenty years. The interviews provided the basis for a "journalistic essay"[3] which purports to reflect conditions in the modern American Church. Each pastor was asked ten questions, including one on marriage and divorce, which really consisted of two questions: "How often do you run into 'bad' marriages?" and "What do you do about them?" Several first routed bad marriages to the diocesan tribunals. Twenty-four of the pastors admitted to use of the "internal forum," some without requiring confession and spiritual counseling.[4] One pastor expressed amazement "at the number of divorced people who say they don't believe in annulments. . . . [who] take their marriage vows seriously and can't accept it."[5] The pastor's incredulity is shared by many tribunalists who find it difficult to entertain the possibility that an uncooperative respondent's opposition to annulment might be thoroughly principled and justifiable.

Functionally equivalent to a respondent's failure or refusal to respond to a petition for nullity is a situation where the tribunal provides no opportunity for a response. In a number of cases, some acknowledged by tribunalists, respondents received no notice of an annulment action until after the tribunal had issued a sentence for nullity. One woman did not discover until two years after the fact that her thirty-eight-year marriage had been annulled. She only learned the annulment of what she thought was still a marriage through her children. Later she came upon the revelation that the tribunal found an "absence of serious intent and total commitment on the part of both parties due to immaturity."[6] Other erstwhile respondents report tribunal "Iron Curtain" practices that stifle or even suppress the forms of communication that normally occur between judicial bodies and advocates and those they are supposed to serve. Besides failing to provide respondents with timely notice that they are party to an annulment action or that their marriages have been voided, some tribunals have refused to accept, acknowledge, or reply to certified return-receipt letters sent by contentious respondents.

Complaints regarding such practices go back many years. In 1977 Cardinal Pericle Felici, then Prefect of the Supreme Tribunal of the Apostolic Signatura, addressed such abuses in a lengthy memorandum sent to Archbishop John R. Quinn, president of the National Conference of Catholic Bishops (NCCB). The memorandum begins with the statement that "Many of the faithful, in these past years, have quite bitterly made charges, sending complaints to this Supreme Tribunal, affirming that injustice has been perpetrated in cases of nullity before tribunals of North America."[7] Among other charges, the prefect asserts that "It is evident to this Sacred Tribunal . . . that it not infrequently happens that a case is instructed and decided with the respondent left in the dark and ignored, which practice the party frequently deplores."[8]

Apologists for the American tribunal system tend to dismiss such incidents as aberrations, which was precisely one of the points in Archbishop Quinn's response. "The small number of tribunals cited in this memorandum and the minute percentage of their cases involving parties from other countries should be seen in the context of the truly commendable work being done by the tribunals in the United States."[9] My own investigations, however, indicate they are more common than the system's defenders care to admit. The fact that the prefect cited only four tribunals does not necessarily mean that every other tribunal was free of such "aberrations." It stands to reason that not all tribunal missteps are brought to the attention of the Signatura. Few victims are capable of identifying any but the most blatant miscarriages of justice. The sheer volume of cases and shortcomings in the qualifications of many tribunalists practically necessitate error and abuse. Even if they are isolated events, however, such abuses do not reflect well on tribunal efficiency, adherence to Church law, and grasp of the fundamentals of decency and due process. Failure or refusal to contact a respondent is a flagrant denial of the "right of defense." On that ground alone, an appeal to the Rota would likely find the lower tribunal guilty of reversible error. Better-managed tribunals will hesitate to accept petitions for annulment without being informed how and where respondents can be contacted. Petitioners unable to supply such information must give a detailed written account of their efforts to obtain it.

The misery inherent in the contentious respondent's lot often starts building even before the tribunal formally accepts a case. Prior to accepting a petition, if any hope of reconciliation can be discerned, the judge is directed to use pastoral means to encourage the spouses to forgive, forget, and resume their conjugal life.[10] Little can be done if the petitioner has already remarried, though stranger things have happened than a remarriage breaking up in favor of a return to an earlier one that had ended in divorce. Frequently, however, even in instances where remarriage has not yet occurred, tribunal explorations of reconciliation are feebly perfunctory. One midwestern tribunal, for example, after hearing a petitioner plead terminal estrangement, simply lays the case on file for several months. No initiative is taken to solicit the respondent's views on the possibilities for resumption of the marriage. Finally, after passage of a "reasonable" interval during which the spouses have not flung themselves back into each other's arms, the judge assumes the role of marital coroner. The marriage is tentatively pronounced "dead," though it will not officially expire until the tribunal declares it null. In many instances the marriage is dead on its arrival at the tribunal office. Failure to sound out the respondent on whether the marriage can be salvaged is a harbinger of things to come. It is also a sign that the system's vaunted pastoralism is taking a holiday. Healing goes into hibernation, to reappear in the guise of tribunal motivation to annul.

Different Kinds of Evidence

Today the diocesan tribunal's basic responsibility is to determine the validity of marriages. As we have seen, in more than 95 percent of ordinary processs cases validity rides on matrimonial consent. Proper discharge of the tribunal's responsibility in ordinary process cases is contingent upon developing and weighing relevant evidence and testimony—the acts (the entire case file) and the proofs (the portions of the file with direct probative bearing on the issue). Then, like trial courts everywhere, it must hold the evidence (facts) up to the appropriate statutes to arrive at a decision. In the course of gathering facts and seeking truth, heed must be paid to the rudiments of due process. *The Code of Canon Law*, unlike the U. S. Constitution, contains no Fifth and Fourteenth Amendments, but the concept of due process is well-entrenched in Church law. Due process, whether substantial or procedural, is found in all civilized legal systems.[11] The concept is practically synonymous with fairness, and Church tribunals are ordained to be fair in their search for truth. Marriage tribunals must not only seek truth under these constraints, but also defend truth taught by the Church. In the exercise of that two-pronged mission, tribunals are obliged to examine and weigh the testimony and credibility of the spouses, witnesses, and experts. Special attention should be given to documentary evidence, if any exists.

When matrimonial consent is at issue, tribunal standards for the admissibility of evidence and the credibility of witnesses frequently take, if not a holiday, mysterious turns. This is evident in the handling of marriage vows vis-à-vis consent. However earnestly some canonists try to infuse them with complexity, the cognitive components of valid consent, as defined in C. 1096, are really quite simple, and bear repeating here:

> 1. For matrimonial consent to exist, it is necessary that the contracting parties be at least not ignorant of the fact that marriage is a permanent partnership between a man and a woman, ordered to the procreation of children through some form of sexual cooperation.
> 2. This ignorance is not presumed after puberty.

As for the volitional side of consent, the requirements of C. 1096 find their match for simplicity in C. 1101, 1, which states that "The internal consent of the mind is presumed to conform to the words or the signs used in the celebration of a marriage." This canon is countermanded only when a prospective spouse by some positive act either wilfully excludes marriage itself or any of its essential elements and properties.[12] Whether traditional in content ("Do you take this woman . . . ?") or composed for the occasion by the couple, marriage vows are routinely given scant evidentiary weight by American tribunals. Movie magnate Samuel Goldwyn, famed for malapropisms, is supposed to have remarked that "an oral contract is not worth the paper it's printed on." This seems to be the tribunal outlook on the evidentiary and contractual value of marriage vows. They are apparently regarded as mere ceremonial incantations holding little significance for those who exchange them or for tribunalists who rule on the validity of marital consent. Perhaps this indifference toward the vows has something to do with the insistence that marriage is now a covenant rather than a contract. However that may be, in ordinary discourse a contract, oral or written, is nothing if not a means to spell out rights and duties and an instrument holding the parties to promises exchanged. If and when either party fails to live up to the terms of the contract, it cannot be said that a contract never existed.

In terms of value as hard evidence, it might be thought that vows would score high. If anything, however, tribunals tend to regard vows as unreliable indicators of valid consent in marriages with unhappy endings. Especially in short-lived marriages, the mere fact of divorce is taken to signify that one or both spouses did not intend a permanent partnership or a "communion of life." In other words, although the principals might not have consciously willed it, they were in effect entering into a sort of trial marriage. Put more canonically, there would be simulation of commitment to an essential property of marriage, that is, a permanent partnership.[13] That may well be true in some instances, but it ought not be automatically inferred from the length of a marriage or the fact of divorce.

John Paul II has urged tribunals to exercise great caution before nullifying marriages on grounds of simulation. Implicitly, he reminds tribunalists once more that the validity of marriage must be given the benefit of doubt.[14]

Repudiation of marriage vows by either spouse is a form of recantation. Courts everywhere are suspicious of disavowal of testimony given under oath. To concede one's earlier lack of veracity understandably casts doubt on subsequent claims of truthfulness. This logic is turned on its head when divorce is taken as evidence that the vows never bespoke an intention to enter a permanent partnership. But canonically the case for nullity is not easily built upon a single broken promise.

Tribunals also seem unimpressed with prenuptial investigations as sources of evidence bearing on marital consent. Among non-Catholic petitioners who married outside the Church, prenuptial documentary material may be unavailable. When Catholics marry in the Church, however, the prenuptial investigation in many dioceses in the United States is designed to elicit responses that deal directly with consent. Couples are routinely asked whether they have ever received treatment for mental or nervous disorders. If the answer is affirmative, they are usually asked to obtain from a clinician a statement on whether the condition for which they were treated might affect their ability to enter marriage. There are also questions framed to tap attitudes on the permanence of marriage, mutual fidelity, and openness to children. Such questions might well have been posed by Saint Augustine himself, since they embody his thinking as well as the Church's on the essential properties of marriage. Unless the tribunal, at some later date, unearths previously unknown clinical records, the prenuptial investigation ordinarily provides the principal or only documentary evidence predating the marriage that bears on the character of spousal consent at the moment the marriage was contracted.[15] If either spouse-to-be is suffering from a serious mental disorder, the priest conducting the prenuptial investigation would presumably discern some telltale symptoms and call a halt to the wedding plans, pending further investigation into that person's ability to exercise the right to marry.

Even granting the ordinary parish priest's lack of psychiatric know-how, it is difficult to see how tribunals, well after the fact, can establish with confidence what eluded the priest preparing the couple for marriage. The same observation applies to a contentious respondent. As previously noted, grave mental disorders typically scotch a relationship before courtship progresses from dating to betrothal. Unquestionably the spellbinding power of romantic love produces some inexplicable spousal pairings, but seldom do even the lovestruck join hands with someone manifestly deranged. Commitment to a mental institution, not an unusual fate for psychotics, further diminishes their eligibility and availability for matrimony. Of course, serious mental disorders can surface or develop after marriage is contracted, but contrary to what many tribunals and experts routinely assume, it does not necessarily follow that these disorders were operative when consent was given. Nevertheless, in defective consent cases the evidence developed during the prenuptial investigation is often summarily swept aside and supplanted by essentially speculative ex post facto ruminations on the part of the tribunal and its expert, and by the petitioner's recollections of the past.

Tribunals also effectively downgrade the testimony of respondents who elect to defend marriages threatened by nullity for psychological reasons. Such respondents, it might be thought, would warm the hearts of tribunalists seriously committed to the permanence and indissolubility of marriage. After dealing with a parade of petitioners who tender self-serving testimony, respondents in collusion with former spouses, and respondents who refuse to answer tribunal mail or move without leaving forwarding addresses, a respondent who actually contests a petition for annulment ought to be a refreshing change of pace for a tribunal staff. What could be more welcome or laudable than a respondent willing to rise to the defense of the validity of a marriage and the integrity of the sacrament?

But that does not appear to be the usual reaction. On the contrary, those who contest annulment petitions risk being regarded as obstinate, spiteful, uncooperative, or disputatious. One diocesan tribunal pamphlet, after alluding to the respondent's right to be heard, assures the petitioner that "The hostility or lack of cooperation of the Respondent can hamper a case but usually will not keep it from being processed to conclusion." Typically, of course, the conclusion is nullity. Several tribunal brochures contain statements similar to the following: "The law requires us to inform the other party of the process and to invite his or her cooperation. If the other party chooses not to cooperate, we still are able to pursue the process." Cooperation is a recurring theme in tribunal efforts to solicit and reassure prospective petitioners. The tone of these and other pamphlets suggests that any respondent who challenges a petition is uncooperative and unlikely to be acting in good faith. There is no hint that ordinary process annulments are supposed to be contentious. The prevailing emphasis on cooperation can easily lead unwary respondents to believe that they are expected to be complicitous. To the extent that is true, the language used to describe the respondent's role indicates that, come what may, the tribunal will find a way to annul. If tribunals wished to appear assiduously neutral, they would do better to solicit participation rather than cooperation from respondents.

For the sake of discussion, let us assume that a challenge is properly motivated, utterly sincere, and devoid of any trace of vindictiveness. That being so, the respondent's opposition should constitute a strong prima facie case for the validity of the marriage. Admittedly in many court systems a prima facie case need not compel a specific judicial outcome. But at the very least it should give a court of law sober pause. A modest expectation would be for it to tilt the tribunal's deliberations even more toward validity than C. 1060 prescribes, especially if there is any corroborative-witness testimony. The respondent, in the final analysis, is better positioned than the tribunal judges, experts, and witnesses to gauge the quality of the petitioner's consent when the marriage was contracted. The respondent, after all, had costar billing when consent was acted out.

In legal terms, not only was the respondent eyewitness to the exchange of consent, but was also party to the marriage contract or covenant to which consent was given. The respondent was privy to a serious display of the petitioner's disposition to consent when marriage was proposed, when the proposal was accepted, and final, irrevocable consent given at the altar. It seems almost superfluous to state that the respondent's version of the quality of consent has more authenticity and evidentiary value than the ex post facto conjectures of a tribunal judge or psychological expert. On the other hand, the petitioner, also present at the betrothal and outset of the marriage, has probably given the tribunal a conflicting account of his or her mindset when the marriage was contracted. Accordingly, the outcome of the case can turn solely on the issue of credibility, one spouse's word against the other's. There is no research on how tribunals tend to resolve credibility standoffs. But the volume of annulments produced by American tribunals and the rarity of nullity decree reversals at Second Instance scarcely suggest that the benefit of doubt usually goes to the respondent and validity.

Tendentious use of testimony by tribunals is not unknown. In one case the tribunal auditor, sensing serious contentiousness on the part of the respondent, urged the petitioner to seek more witness support. The advice was based on the realization that the testimony of the petitioner's first set of witnesses, if anything, affirmed the marriage's validity. When this development came to the respondent's attention, his request for supplemental witnesses was first resisted and then grudgingly granted by the same auditor. All of the respondent's witnesses, inadvertently perhaps, actually testified to the validity of the marriage. Citing C. 1553, which states that "It is for the judge to curb an excessive number of witnesses," the judicial vicar refused to honor the testimony of seventeen such witnesses, maintaining that it was not "helpful," "necessary," or "insightful." The testimony thus dismissed included a deposition from an archbishop who knew the couple during their courtship, was present at the wedding, and saw nothing amiss about the exchange of consent.

As the Rota would later rule, however, the judge can limit the number witnesses the parties can call but he cannot exclude testimony of witnesses already deposed. Moreover, the Rota held that the material the vicar so cavalierly passed over had substantial bearing on the merits of the case.[16] None of the witness testimony gathered for either party, the Rota held, provided support for a decree of nullity, yet the judge ruled the marriage null for "lack of due discretion." In effect, he suppressed evidence that did not square with his own canonical and pastoral dispositions. Since time immemorial, suppression of exculpatory evidence by the prosecutor in a criminal proceeding has been regarded as illegal and unethical. Granting that a tribunal judge is not a prosecutor and that annulment and criminal proceedings are not the same, nevertheless, disregarding evidence that can have a material effect on the outcome of any trial is a serious breach of the rules of professionalism and fairness.

Downsizing Respondent Status

Sometimes treatment of the respondent in an annulment proceeding comes close to contempt. One canonist, for example, argues that "a plaintiff's successful prosecution of an annulment action cannot have a negative impact on a respondent analogous to his successful prosecution of an action for breach of contract or for possession of property. The real respondent in a marriage case is the marriage. It is the marriage, not the other party, that hinders the plaintiff from exercising her rights."[17] One aspect of the message conveyed by the statement seems clear: in an annulment proceeding the respondent is essentially a bystander, a marginal figure at best. There is an element of legalistic fatuity in anthropomorphizing the marriage while making the respondent little more than a spectator. Marriage is no more a respondent than was the temporarily undelivered commission in *Marbury v. Madison*, probably the single most important decision ever handed down by the U.S. Supreme Court. The respondent or defendant in that historic case was James Madison, the Secretary of State for incoming President Thomas Jefferson. The issue was an eleventh-hour commission as justice of the peace that outgoing President John Adams had given William Marbury. The new administration denied the commission and was sued by Marbury. That Marbury prevailed was of minor moment. The enduring significance of the decision, handed down in 1803, was that the Supreme Court, led by John Marshall, established judicial review of the constitutionality of legislation by all courts. In an annulment proceeding the validity of the marriage is the issue, but the respondent is a living, breathing litigant. The validity of a marriage is an abstraction which is to be investigated, argued, and adjudicated. Unlike a respondent, it cannot be subjected to humiliation for holding strong views on the sanctity of Christian marriage in general or on the sanctity of one marriage in particular. Marriages, furthermore, are not sentient beings, capable of exercising the right of defense.

Cormac Burke writes insightfully on ramifications of an annulment proceeding beyond the narrow legal issue of validity, the similarly narrow prevailing pastoral wisdom, and the personal interests of the parties. There are pastoral considerations which should go hand in hand with the granting or denial of canonical legitimacy to prospective remarriages or to remarriages already contracted without an annulment. In defending the indissolubility of marriage, even one apparently hopelessly broken down, the Church is also defending the right of children of such a marriage to parental unity. Burke contends that "Even if one of the parents refuses to live up to his or her obligations to create and maintain married and family unity, the children still have the right to the fidelity of the other."[18] Obliquely at least, Burke is touching on how children and others are scandalized by divorce and annulment. The Church's defense also embraces

the rights and expectations of other persons . . . outside the immediate family circle: other married couples, people preparing for marriage, young people in general.. . . .Marriage is never a purely personal affair; it is also social. Married couples have rights and duties towards the rest of society, and the rest of society has duties and rights towards each married couple. Concretely, the other members of society have the right to see an example of fidelity in the commitment lived by married people. They have the right to the witness of couples around them whose lives say, "Yes, it is possible to be chaste and faithful; it is possible to get on with someone else despite his or her defects; it is possible to overcome one's own pride, limitations and selfishness."

A society where no one bears witness to this fidelity is a society where no one takes marriage seriously . . . a society heading for collapse.[19]

Improbable as it may seem, says Burke, the Church's position on indissolubility serves to defend the spouses themselves. Among petitioners and advocates of permissive annulment, the dominant pastoral sentiment is that no effort should be spared to secure Church blessing for another chance at happy marriage. For Burke, the sentiment is palpably misguided. The simple but authentic pastoral reason why survivors of failed marriages are not free to seek happiness anew in remarriage is that it is not God's wish that they do so.[20]

American tribunalists seem oblivious to the possibility that respondents might oppose nullity for reasons similar to those Burke gives for the Church's defense of indissolubility. Their concern with the pastoral needs of petitioner-victims of broken marriages seems not to be balanced by an equal concern for the well-being of society—the common good. In an age when marriage grows increasingly infirm, the Church is its chief institutional protector. Its effectiveness to serve in that capacity is diminished when the right and left hands pull against one another. The soft approach to nullity might bring healing to numerous couples and their remarriages, but on the societal level it widens already gaping wounds in the institution of marriage.

Respondents who uphold the validity of the marriage can be wounded in more than conscience, credibility, and faith. For a respondent convinced of the validity of the marriage a finding of defective consent attacks both sanity and self-esteem. The tribunal, in effect, is telling the respondent: You and your wits temporarily parted company when you married. Unbeknownst to you, at the time of the marriage your spouse lacked due competence (or due discretion). Although you thought your spouse was normal in those respects, our investigation shows you were mistaken. Your conjugal mate was really incapable of Christian marriage. We arrived at this conclusion with the help of a behavioral scientist who has a graduate degree in psychology. We admit that neither you nor your former spouse was examined personally by our expert, but we have the utmost confidence in his findings since he has a degree from a famous university, and has worked with the tribunal for many years. It is with sincere regret that we annul your marriage and inform you that everything you thought you knew about Christian marriage, and many things you thought you knew about your spouse, are also null and void. This message, or some variation of it, is conveyed to respondents every day the postal service makes its appointed rounds. What this usually amounts to in the vast majority of defective consent cases is—borrowing Senator Daniel Patrick Moynihan's expression—"dumbing down" the ordinary powers of discernment and choice of either or both parties in order to annul their marriage.

Contentious respondents are often doubly traumatized. After being on the receiving end of an unwanted divorce, there comes the aftershock of an annulment. Betrayal by a spouse who pledged marriage till death becomes all the more crushing when compounded by betrayal by a Church tribunal. Notwithstanding its certainty that the marriage was valid, the respondent's conscience is vanquished and humiliated. Adding to the sense of injury and defeat, many tribunals do not even personalize the notices sent to respondents announcing that their marriages no longer exist. Evidently, form letters are essential to tribunal efficiency and to the thinking behind the *Florida Times-Union* ad, cited above, which asserted that "the use of modern technology has increased by one-hundred fold the number of petitions and resolutions." Once the basic letter proclaiming nullity is stored in a computer's memory or on a floppy disk, it can be customized for hundreds of petitioners and respondents simply by filling in appropriate addresses and salutations.

One of my sources lost her husband of twenty-two years to his secretary, and her eight children lost their father. The husband, a staid and respected businessman, had his second marriage legitimized by a defective consent annulment. Angry and bewildered, the children retaliated by doing to their father what he had done to their mother: they severed their relationship with him. If a conference could be arranged with the bishop, the judicial vicar, a distinguished canonist, the defender of the bond, the ex-wife, and the children in attendance, it would be interesting to watch the *officialis* and canonist nuancing their way through an explanation of how the husband's "emotional immaturity" negated the marriage, and how that disqualifying disorder vanished in time for his re-marriage in the Church. It would also be enlightening to hear them try to disabuse the respondent of the notion that in the eyes of God she was still married to the man to whom she gave herself twenty-two years before.

The "Right of Defense"

Respondents may strive to uphold the validity of their marriages without even knowing that they are exercising what is canonically termed the *right of defense*. No statistics are published on how many respondents exercise that right. Nor are there data on how vigorously the right is pursued, or on the outcome of cases where it is undertaken before American tribunals. Figures for Second Instance review in America, however, show that resort to the right of defense hardly ever leads to a favorable result. Success is most likely to be found in Rome, but few cases are taken that far. There is considerable evidence that within the American tribunal system the right is less sacrosanct than canon law requires. One indication is the scant attention given to the ins and outs of the right of defense in the annulment literature. There are publications galore on how to obtain an annulment, but hardly a book, article, pamphlet, or leaflet explains use of the right of defense to oppose one. Some scholarly references list the rights of respondents, but they are pitched to canon lawyers or persons with some acquaintance with canon law.[21] Few lay Catholics have convenient access to this material. It is as likely to be found in public and parish libraries, church vestibule bookstands, or religious bookstores as copies of the *Harvard Law Review*. Publications such as *The Jurist* and *Studia Canonica* are not even among the holdings of many Catholic college and university libraries.

Nor can respondents expect First and Second Instance tribunals adjudicating their cases to direct them to publications that would help with defending the validity of their marriage. Trial courts everywhere are not given to inviting reversals by advising litigants on how to challenge their rulings. Diocesan marriage tribunals are no exception. Even if they were so inclined they could hardly refer the respondent to any instruction manuals, since none exist. References cataloging the respondent's rights may list canons dealing with the right to an advocate or the right to read the tribunal's sentence, but they are devoid of information on how to challenge the premises on which the annulment was granted. It is altogether improbable that respondents will be advised to consult Rotal decisions dwelling on the manipulations of C. 1095 by American tribunals. Equally improbable is the likelihood that the promoter of justice or one of the tribunal's advocates will provide meaningful assistance for a respondent wishing to ward off nullity. In most tribunals these functionaries are as dedicated to easy annulments as the judges granting them. Further, it is well to bear in mind that a tribunalist who serves as advocate in one case might be a judge in another. And, all this to one side, the respondent who ventures a self-taught crash course in canon law and procedure to become effectively contentious still has only the slimmest chance to successfully defend a marriage before an American tribunal.

Vatican Concerns

Tensions have long festered between between Rome and American tribunals over the right of defense. Cardinal Felici's 1977 memorandum to Archbishop Quinn and the NCCB, mentioned earlier in connection with intercontinental forum-shopping, also dealt with abuses associated with the right of defense. Felici linked the eagerness of several American tribunals to process petitions filed by transients from abroad with adulteration of the right of defense:

> [A] wealthy plaintiff can go from far off to the United States . . . and, after a brief residency, can cite a wife in a case of nullity of marriage. . . . The respondent is more often a wife, remaining in her own country, who must defend herself where she neither knows the language nor the customs, where she cannot designate a trusted advocate nor confer with her procurator, nor take legal counsel for her defense. Whence, the respondent does not know whether the plaintiff is taking an honest . . . course, whether he brings forth witnesses who are worthy or suborned, whether he is excluding witnesses of greater knowledge, whether he is deceiving the members of the tribunal. . . . There is no one,

because of that, who would not consider that this favors the plaintiff, who can be cunning and fraudulent . . . , while the respondent who is trying to defend her marriage in vain, is plunged into anxiety.

[I]n these recent years, almost all called into judgment who have had recourse to the Apostolic Signatura, make the accusation that they, cited by deceit and cunning in a distant place, have lacked the means of defending themselves, that rather their advocates betray this violated right.[22]

In many cases, according to the Signatura, it was doubtful whether "the plaintiff actually does reside in the place of the Tribunal, at least the one having recourse often denies it." In one case "the residency of the plaintiff is highly suspect, since the Officialis does not know it and did not investigate the matter, although residency is necessary in order for the judge to declare himself competent. . . ."[23]

In response to the Signatura's memorandum, Archbishop Quinn cited Norm 7 of the APN: "The first competent Tribunal to which a party presents a petition has an obligation to accept or reject the petition. The competence of a Tribunal of first instance shall be determined by the residency of either party to the marriage, the place of the marriage or the decree of the judge to whom the petition is presented that his Tribunal is better able to judge the case than any other Tribunal." Quinn conceded that "The right of defense should be scrupulously guarded in all cases," but did not explain how this might occur when the respondent, handicapped in ways described by Felici, does not learn of the annulment till after the fact.[24] The Signatura maintained that when petitioner and respondent live in different dioceses, the tribunal where the petitioner resides must obtain the consent of the respondent's tribunal before proceeding with the case.

Quinn apparently regarded this as an unwarranted infringement on American tribunals' exercise of the APN. Although Felici noted that this procedure was established by Paul VI in his prorogation of the norms, Quinn referred to it as an "unofficial interpretation." The latter term, evidently, belongs to the same genus as "private opinion." Both phrases are rhetorical catch-alls for authoritative legal statements by Rome that go against the American canonical grain. The Special NCCB Panel for Procedural Norms, Quinn assured, would strongly urge adherence to the unofficial interpretation when the respondent lives in a foreign country. As for cases where the parties live in different dioceses in the United States, the Special NCCB Panel would take the matter under advisement. Quinn's letter, it is worth noting, ended with the comment that the American bishops urged him to request continuation of the APN. Quinn no doubt received considerable advice from American canonists in framing his response to the Signatura.

The Felici-Quinn exchange, its diplomatic language notwithstanding, is an early example of how American tribunals and Rome do not attach the same significance to the right of defense. The Signatura's "private opinions" on this issue were later incorporated into the revised code.[25] If anything, de jure the new code strengthened the right of defense with respect to determining the competent forum. Before accepting a case from a petitioner whose ex-spouse lives in another diocese, the tribunal must obtain the consent of the *officialis* of the respondent's diocese The *officialis* must then sound out the respondent for objections before giving approval to the request for venue. De facto, however, some tribunals operate as though earlier procedures are still in force. One still hears of petitions accepted by distant tribunals without providing notice to respondents, thus denying them an opportunity to begin exercising the right of defense by objecting to the venue.

Bolstering the Right of Defense

The new code did not resolve with finality issues associated with the right of defense, nor did its implementation by American tribunals cease to be controversial in Rome. As the 1980s came to an end, the pope was moved to reiterate the vital standing of the right. "Even though canon 1982 of the previous Code did not mention the 'denial of the right of defence' among the cases of irremediable nullity of the sentence, it should nevertheless be noted that both the doctrine and the rotal jurisprudence held for the irremediable nullity of the sentence whenever one or the other party was denied the right of defence."[26] What the Holy Father is so anxious to ensure is actually a generic right, encompassing considerably more than residency and competence. One Rota judge listed the principal components of the right of defense as "(a) the faculty of bringing forward proofs to the trial; (b) the faculty of knowing the proofs adduced by the other party; (c) the faculty of exhibiting one's own line of reasoning, one's own allegations and defenses; (d) the faculty to respond, at least once, to the allegations and defenses of the other parties."[27] Exercise of these faculties, at the very least, also presupposes knowing the alleged ground(s) for nullity. Denial of any of the faculties can compromise or render the general right of defense infirm. The right of defense is especially significant in cases involving marital consent. By contrast, if the respondent, a baptized Catholic, married outside the Church, or married a first cousin, or wed a priest not properly dispensed, it would probably be a waste of time and energy to press the right of defense. Such documentary process cases are relatively indisputable, nullifiable without a truly contentious proceeding. In theory, the right of defense remains available, as always it must, but it would be foolhardy to exercise it with much hope of prevailing.

The right of defense is every bit as absolute as the right to petition for annulment. But even when exercised in responsible and principled manner, many American tribunals honor it with Orwellian finesse. Wrenn maintains, for example, that "only when the defender of the bond has been deprived of his or her right has the 'right of defense' been denied."[28] So narrow a construction of the right effectively denies the respondent an active role in defending the validity of the marriage. It also runs counter to the instruction imparted by the Holy Father in his January 26, 1989 Address to the Roman Rota. Indeed, the pope specifies that the right belongs to plaintiffs as well as respondents. Nothing in his remarks suggests that the right can inhere in the defender alone, unless the respondent elects to waive the right.[29] On the other hand, a waiver is not to be construed rigidly.

> Even though one of the parties may have renounced the exercise of the right of defence, the judge in these cases has the grave duty to make serious efforts to obtain the judicial deposition of the party concerned and also of the witnesses whom the party could have called. The judge should weigh each individual case. Sometimes the respondent does not wish to be present at the trial without offering any adequate motive, precisely because he cannot understand how the Church could possibly declare the nullity of the sacred bond of his marriage after so many years of living together. True pastoral sensibility and respect for the party's conscience will oblige the judge in such a case to offer the respondent all opportune information regarding cases of matrimonial nullity to seek patiently the party's full cooperation in the process, for the sake of avoiding a partial judgement in a matter of such gravity.[30]

Here we have not only a rare official expression of compassion for the respondent but a gauntlet thrown down for tribunal judges. Many American tribunals treat renunciation of the right of defense as the elimination of another inconvenient barrier to the pastoral imperative to annul, and a means of sustaining desired production levels of decrees of nullity. While there are routinely pro forma efforts to establish contact with unresponsive respondents, these are only the beginning of the proactive measures the pope's exhortation specifies. He clearly urges tribunal judges to take steps to protect the right of defense rather than simply announce it. The judge is to act as proxy for the respondent, even to the point of soliciting witnesses not called by the respondent who might testify to the validity of the marriage. It is noteworthy that these remarks are addressed to tribunal judges rather than defenders. The implication is that judges, too, are not to be completely neutral agents with respect to protection of the bond. It is also worth stressing that the pope, as opposed to many American canonists, refers to the petitioner's cooperation as a contribution to the *defense* of the marriage, not as a self-serving means of facilitating nullity.

Access to the Acts

The right of defense is reinforced by C. 1598, which grants both parties and their advocates access to the acts. On its face, the statute bears resemblance to rules of discovery that guide the exchange of information between litigants in our secular courts and to "sunshine laws" enacted in many jurisdictions in the United States to make official documents more accessible. The statute aims at greater openness in the service of the right of defense and truth. True, the law allows judges to deal with portions of the acts *in camera* if it is determined that disclosure would pose "very serious dangers" to the "public good." But it also states, quite forthrightly, that the right of defense must always be preserved.

How can the right be assured if the tribunal withholds portions of the acts that have material bearing on the case? The language of the canon clearly suggests that the right of defense is stunted or violated when such withholding occurs. It is a right which admits to fewer exceptions and less discretion than a tribunal's prerogative to shield the parties and the public from certain information. That reading of the canon also seems more consistent with C. 1060's conferral of the benefit of the doubt on the validity of marriage.

The right of defense ensures that evidence and testimony cannot be illegally used or withheld. Whatever tribunals cull from witnesses and experts should be inadmissible if it is concealed from the parties yet will influence the trial's outcome. We find here counterparts of a criminal defendant's Fifth Amendment right to due process and the Sixth Amendment right to confront unfriendly witnesses. Canon law does not provide for personal confrontations in the form of cross-examination. Nevertheless, the language and thrust of C. 1598 is directed toward a similar end, because it assures the respondent access to transcribed testimony given by the petitioner and by unfriendly witnesses. Portions of the acts and proofs which contribute in any way to the tribunal's sentence must be ruled inadmissible if they cannot be inspected by the respondent, the respondent's advocate, and the defender. Otherwise, the right of defense does not remain intact.

C. 1598's provisions strengthening the right of defense received a cool reception from the American canon-law establishment. There were ominous forecasts that they would effectively padlock the tribunal system. Without assurance of complete confidentiality, it was feared, witnesses would be reluctant to volunteer information. This fear extended to the willingness of psychological experts to participate in defective consent annulment proceedings. There was apprehension over the prospect of civil courts issuing subpoenas or discovery orders that would bare sensitive tribunal materials.[31] To date, the perceived threats have not materialized. No tribunal has been forced to give its staff notice and close shop. Sources of information have not dried up and tribunal documents have not been subpoenaed by civil courts.

In 1983, the last year the 1917 code and APN were in force, American tribunals accepted 55,788 ordinary process cases and concluded 56,304, both figures record highs.[32] There are indications that the speed of the assembly line was turned up a few notches before the new code's strictures took hold. During 1979–1982 American tribunals averaged better than 6,500 "Informal Negative Decisions" per year.[33] As explained to me by one judicial vicar, "Informal Negative Decisions" are nondefinitive denials of nullity which might be reopened at some later date. Technically, only death of a spouse brings absolute finality (*res judicata*) to annulment litigation. If new evidence or arguments are adduced, the outcome of an annulment proceeding can always be reconsidered. The vicar indicated that "Informal Negative Decisions" included many cases tribunals hoped to find a way to annul. In 1983 the number of "Informal Negative Decisions" reported to CLSA fell—precipitously—to 805.[34] Perhaps this was a statistical fluke, since more than three thousand were reported for 1984, the final year data on "Informal Negative Decisions" appear in CLSA statistical summaries. The number of First Instance ordinary process cases concluded dropped to 43,464 the following year,[35] but by the end of the decade that figure had risen to 48,471[36] Probably personnel problems created by mandatory appeals to Second Instance had more to do with the decrease since 1983 than problems created by C. 1598. But even if it is assumed that the decrease was entirely attributable to C. 1598 restrictions, the tribunals were still doing a tidy business. The assembly line had not come close to enforced idleness.

A basic social psychological axiom is that situations defined as real will have real consequences. That rule of human perception was exemplified by canonists' fears of C. 1598's strong protection of the right of defense. Their anxiety generated policies and procedures to thwart the canon's safeguards. Proctor's study of California tribunals illustrates the measures taken to withhold material from petitioners and respondents. Only nine of sixteen tribunals canvassed replied to his questionnaire, but their responses are quite revealing. They showed hypersensitivity to confidentiality issues that proved largely hypothetical and benign. Generally speaking, Proctor found that tribunals attempted to dissuade respondents from inspecting the acts. Some tribunals relied on heavy-handed judicial discretion to deny the parties access to material considered sensitive.[37] Similar techniques are still employed by tribunals elsewhere. Johnson reports that many tribunals temper the dictates of C. 1598 by allowing advocates rather than the parties themselves to examine the acts and proofs.[38] The Archdiocese of Atlanta's tribunal set up procedural roadblocks for petitioners and respondents desiring to examine testimony and evidence. Upon receipt of a notice sent by the tribunal, the parties have fifteen days to petition in writing for permission to inspect the acts. Citing C. 1598, 1, the tribunal claims the right to reject the petition or allow examination of no more than selected portions of the material. Before the petition is granted, the party must pledge to use the information only in Church courts, keep it in strict confidence, and not make any copies.[39]

The Atlanta scheme imposes onerous constraints on a contentious respondent. What if the respondent wishes to discuss the material with a canon lawyer who does not sit on the diocesan tribunal, or with a confessor–spiritual director? Can a respondent, unable to take notes and relying solely on power of recall, put together an intelligent rebuttal? If the tribunal ruled for nullity and the respondent was denied access to the acts for refusing to take the pledge on the ground that the rules prevented full exercise of the right of defense, it is virtually certain that the respondent would prevail on appeal to the Rota. Indeed, five years after publication of Proctor's study, the Rota reversed a decree of nullity granted by a tribunal that routinely shielded petitioners and respondents from testimony taken by the tribunal. It is significant that the tribunal evidently justified its policy on the ground that it was simply following the example of many other American tribunals.[40]

We shall never know precisely how often portions of the acts to which petitioners and respondents are denied access are incorporated into tribunal sentences. What little evidence we have suggests that it is quite common. But if the "forbidden fruit" has any bearing whatever on the outcome of a case, both the spirit and letter of C. 1598 are flouted. This would be especially true in defective consent cases where, as one tribunal reported, the parties are automatically denied access to expert testimony.[41] Patently, the expert's input in such cases could well be crucial. Along with its content, how it was obtained and used could be decisive considerations in an appeal. If, as often happens, an expert did not directly examine a petitioner who is granted an annulment on psychological grounds, a respondent-appellant would have a strong argument for reversible or irremediable error. One tribunal reports an intriguing method for preventing petitioners and respondents from examining expert testimony. Whatever the expert says is regarded as a report by a "specialized assessor," and not treated as part of the body of evidence and testimony.[42] This ploy is of a piece with abuses already seen, such as respondents not given written notice of the petitioners' grounds for nullity or not officially told their marriages were annulled.

The California tribunals canvassed by Proctor successfully resisted the few attempts to use civil discovery procedures to obtain access to annulment information. In those instances the courts and plaintiffs' attorneys yielded to the tribunal's claim of privileged privacy or to the threat of litigation challenging the subpoena. One tribunal relied on the position taken by the Archdiocese of Chicago, which states in part: "This ecclesiastical decision . . . is a purely religious matter and has no civil effects in the United States."[43] Authoritative as the archdiocese's statement sounds, it might be seen as disingenuous. Little legal imagination is required to see possible ties between what surfaces in annulment proceedings and issues that often arise, for example, in child-custody disputes. Up to now, plaintiffs' attorneys have generally not pursued such disclosure. But in some circumstances a resourceful, aggressive attorney will probably have an excellent chance of securing a broad discovery order from a sympathetic judge. Church affairs are no longer as sancrosanct as in the past. In the United States the civil courts, not the Church, decide which ecclesiastical decisions have civil effects. This is one of the lessons tragically driven home in many priest-pedophile cases, the secular courts overriding efforts by dioceses to reserve for themselves the right to deal with alleged offenders solely by pastoral and psychological means. The threat of civil court intervention in annulment proceedings nevertheless remains remote and hypothetical. But even if the threat becomes more real, it should not be allowed to serve as a rationale for putting rein on the right of defense.

Some American canonists believe that tribunals should be shielded by the same principle of confidentiality that applies to the lawyer-client privilege and the seal of the confessional.[44] That may be well and good in theory, but the right of defense cannot be fully exercised if any material thus protected is used to determine the fate of a marriage. C. 1544 directs that "Documents do not have probative force at a trial unless they are submitted in original form or in authentic copy and are lodged in the office of the tribunal, so that they may be inspected by the judge and by the opposing party." This would seem to apply to oral testimony shielded from the respondent, including the diagnoses of "specialized assessors."

Muffling the Right

Ordinarily the right of defense is triggered when the tribunal notifies the respondent that his or her former spouse has petitioned for annulment. The notice may or may not cite grounds or be accompanied by a partial enumeration of the respondent's rights. The respondent might be offered an advocate or procurator. To the best of my knowledge, however, no tribunal provides a complete enumeration of those rights. The right to a collegiate tribunal is in fact one of the best kept secrets in annulment proceedings. Nor is there any indication that the respondent might have been able to nip the annulment process in the bud by challenging the validity of the petition itself. A priest who serves on an archdiocesan tribunal which claims to be "one of the best staffed and run Tribunal operations" was asked, "What rights does the former partner of the person applying for the annulment have?" His response illustrates how the right of defense is often trivialized, diminished, or treated with disdain. "The former spouse has three basic rights: the right (1) to be interviewed only, (2) to be interviewed and provide further cooperation, or (3) to simply do nothing—in a sense, to be in contempt of court."[45] There is not even the barest allusion to the right of defense, probably the most basic right of all, or to such ancillary rights as the right to an advocate, the right to an advocate of one's choice, and the right to examine the acts and sentence. Later in the interview the tribunalist does note, without going into detail, that either party can file an appeal to the Second Instance tribunal. Neither the automatic appeal to Second Instance nor the right to appeal to the Rota acting as Second or Third Instance is mentioned.

As we have seen, the percentage of respondents conversant with what little canonical literature there is on their rights approaches zero. Even if given copies of relevant material and the *Code of Canon Law*, with all the relevant statutes highlighted, the average respondent would not know how to begin putting together a viable defense. It would be akin to handing the defendant in an American criminal proceeding a copy of the Bill of Rights and expecting that to equip the person to contribute toward winning an acquittal. Poll upon poll shows American Catholics ignorant of many of the Church's most basic teachings and rules. If they are unfamiliar with the rudiments of the faith, it is completely unrealistic to expect them to be knowledgeable about canon law and procedure. If petitioners cannot even articulate viable grounds for nullity, respondents can hardly be expected to cope with the complexities of mounting an effective defense of their marriages. In any type of litigation, civil or ecclesial, there can be a huge divide between knowing one's rights and vindicating them. For all intents and purposes, without meaningful assistance, exercising the right of defense at First or any other Instance is simply beyond the ken of the average respondent. Lacking help, the respondent is practically forced to imitate the proverbial fool who represents himself in a legal case. Practically speaking, the respondent's fate and that of the marriage are consigned to the mercies of the judge, an advocate or procurator, and the defender.

Obtaining Counsel

Usually the respondent does not *choose* an advocate or procurator. Nearly every American knows a lawyer, but few American Catholics know a canon lawyer, much less one available to serve as advocate or procurator. Tribunalists are not listed in the telephone directory, nor is there such a thing as a canon lawyer reference service. Even if such directories existed, the average person would be unable to make an informed choice. Little if any information on the relative competence of advocates, procurators, and defenders can be gained by questioning those who have been party to an annulment. Nearly everything these functionaries do is behind the scenes and not a matter of record unless the tribunal's definitive sentence takes note of their initiatives. By then, of course, the game is usually up. What really happens in virtually every contested case is that the respondent agrees to be represented by an advocate or procurator nominated by the judicial vicar. If the offer for representation is made by letter, it is without any explanation of what procurators and advocates do, or how one differs from the other. In one case that came to my attention, a respondent was expressly prohibited from retaining a canon lawyer with a JCD who was not among those on the judicial vicar's approved list. In short, a contentious respondent will typically have to settle for a court-appointed advocate or procurator.

Ideally, even court-appointed advocates and procurators, combining forces with defenders, should be able to effectively assist in upholding the validity of marriages. The statistics give no grounds for optimism, however. As the American tribunal system now operates, the advocate assigned to the respondent might well be a judge in other cases. Similar double duty occurs with defenders. If the advocate and defender share the prevailing vision of valid marriage, the respondent has little hope of an aggressive defense.

Respondents in annulment proceedings have less room to maneuver than their counterparts in civil actions. Generally their options are circumscribed by canon law itself, by personal ignorance, and by tribunal policies and biases. The respondent can testify, submit evidence, name "friendly" witnesses, and try to rebut the testimony of the petitioner and "unfriendly" witnesses. The rebuttal, loosely speaking, functions like cross-examination in a civil proceeding. But there is no opportunity for probing exchanges or for the sort of interrogation possible in face-to-face courtroom encounters. Nor is any questioning of the petitioner and proofs conducted in the respondent's presence by the defender and by the respondent's advocate or procurator. Presumably the respondent's testimony, evidence, and arguments, along with that of friendly witnesses, will be transcribed, and studied by the defender and advocate before they plead the case before the judge. The respondent is seldom privy to any discussions that occur among tribunal figures. At this stage there are no opportunities to observe how well or ineptly the case for validity is argued and received. Such information might be winnowed from the First Instance sentence or from sentences prepared by an appellate tribunal.

Petitioners are more likely than respondents to have been introduced to the basics of an annulment proceeding by tribunal outreach measures. Otherwise, they are probably equally uninformed about canon law and procedure. Ordinarily they can relive their ill-fated marriages in poignant detail. Tribunal offices are tearful places. Although few petitioners can set forth canonically acceptable grounds for nullity, particularly when the only grounds are psychological, tribunals will obligingly provide them. During a presentation to a large class of undergraduates at a Catholic university, one tribunal staff member, when asked what happens when a petitioner without grounds appears before the tribunal, replied, "If there are no grounds, we'll find some." The tribunalist's search-and-find response probably represents standard procedure in most American tribunals. From a tribunal's perspective, accepting borderline cases and forcing grounds onto them may be the essence of pastoral solicitude. Their compassion bodes ill, however, for the contentious respondent's interests and the right of defense. It not only portends a conflict of interests but has the potential to give rise to an insidious self-fulfilling prophecy. The tribunal, having identified grounds and found the petition justiciable, then breathes life into its creation. The cause for nullity becomes almost self-evident as well as self-fulfilling. In civil litigation the respondent has a voice in defining the issues, but with annulment the respondent reacts to what has been defined by a subordinate of the very judicial body responsible for determining the merit of what is at issue. Putting it in common-law terms, the tribunal functions, in effect, as accuser, prosecutor, judge, and jury. The search-and-find approach to grounds becomes a search-and-destroy mission with respect to the marriage.

By design, canon law is biased in the direction of validity. Bias is not inherently evil or dysfunctional. It can operate in the service of some higher good. As exemplar of the due-process model, the American criminal justice system is structured against convicting the innocent even at the expense of effective crime control and public safety. As the folklore of due process constantly reminds us, it is better for ninety-nine guilty to go free than to convict one innocent person. Though perhaps not as heavily weighted in one direction, canon law is unmistakably slanted against dissolving possibly valid marriages. It should not be easy for a tribunal to accept a petition for processing, and in most ordinary process cases it should be even more difficult to bring forth a decree of nullity. Hardhearted as this may seem, it is readily inferred from the letter and spirit of C. 1060 and other canonical procedures, such as the requirement of two conforming decisions for nullity. There is nothing inherently wrong with tribunals freely accepting and processing petitions for annulment. It becomes wrong when it is motivated by zeal to annul even cases with no juridic basis, when it produces caseloads so burdensome that individual cases must be rushed to completion, when assembly-line processing necessitates reliance on "junk science," when the right of defense is compromised, and when the benefit of doubt goes to nullity rather than validity.

Access to the Sentence

The restriction of access to the body of evidence and testimony is often compounded by further secrecy. The right of defense requires that the contentious respondent have access to an unexpurgated copy of the tribunal's decision. Acting under the aegis of confidentiality, some tribunals provide only a summary statement or the dispositive section (the portion where only the tribunal's final decision appears) of the complete sentence. Others purge the document of the identities of witnesses and portions of the acts that may be considered "sensitive." Still others provide copies to advocates with instructions not to share them with those they represent.[46] Some tribunals allow the parties to examine the sentence in the tribunal office; others simply mail notice of the tribunal's decision. Wrenn, citing C. 1598, 1, states that "It cannot be said that the right of defense has been denied if . . . the respondent is not allowed to see every document in its entirety."[47] Technically he may be correct, if the material withheld has no effect on the outcome of the tribunal's deliberations and if the shielded material does not include any portion of the sentence. But it seems unlikely that most tribunals are so scrupulous in deciding what to shield.

The restrictive practices reported in Proctor's survey of California tribunals and found in Wrenn's views on publication of the acts are plainly at odds with the John Paul II's instruction to the Rota on this aspect of the right of defense:

> It is sometimes said that the obligation to observe the canonical legislation in this regard, especially concerning the publication of the acts and the judgement, could impede the search for the truth because of the witnesses' refusal to cooperate in the trial in such circumstances. In the first place, it should be quite clear that the "publicity" of the canonical trial as far as the parties are concerned does not affect its reserved nature as regards all others. It should also be noted that canon law exempts from the obligation of replying to questions all those who are bound by the secret of their office.[48]

Thus what Wrenn believed unspeakable has been spoken, by the Holy Father himself. Either party can inspect the acts as well as the sentence. This is elementary, commonsense justice. A respondent cannot actively and intelligently participate in the right of defense without being privy to the body of evidence and the court's judgment. Nor is this aspect of the right of defense satisfied when the respondent's advocate and the defender, but not the respondent, can examine the material in question. While they act on behalf of the respondent and the marriage, their surrogacy is not absolute. Wrenn's position on publication also diverges from Signatura and Rota statements made well in advance of the Holy Father's 1989 Address to the Rota,[49] yet it still represents standard procedure in many American tribunals.

The Star Chamber secrecy practiced by tribunals, besides having the potential to limit if not irremediably deny the respondent's right of defense, might also be unnecessary. Portions of the acts which tribunals consider extremely sensitive may have been aired during preannulment divorce proceedings. This is especially likely if there was protracted conflict between the spouses, particularly with respect to child custody. But however delicate the contents of the acts, canon law does not grant confidentiality parity with the right of defense. Confidentiality protects privacy. The right of defense protects the integrity of the sacrament. We also cannot rule out the possibility that a different motive lies behind the tribunals' almost obsessive concern with confidentiality. Full disclosure might reveal material that would motivate respondents to pursue their right of defense through appeal, or material pointing to reversible error. Varvaro cites Rota decisions showing how these possibilities become realities. In one instance the Rota judges complained that English-speaking tribunals often failed to specify whether a finding of defective consent applied to the petitioner, the respondent, or both.[50] It would require an exceptionally astute respondent to identify that sort of misstep, but any advocate with a modicum of canonical competence would pick it up at a glance, much as the Rota judges did.

In most Western legal systems, an appellant and the appellate court must have copies of the transcript of trial court proceedings. Without a transcript it becomes exceedingly difficult for an appellant, his advocate, and the higher court to discern whether and how the trial court erred. Indeed, denying the appellant a transcript, or providing one which has been edited, can in itself be grounds for reversal on appeal. Shorn of the obfuscation with which it has been surrounded, the new code attempts to provide the same safeguards to respondents who exercise the right of defense. In practice, however, those safeguards are attenuated, if not crippled, by tribunal tactics. Rotal incredulity was aroused by one American case where the respondent, though notified that her marriage had been declared null, knew nothing about the sentence and the grounds for nullity. She claimed never to have been personally involved in the annulment process except for signing some documents without knowing what they contained.[51]

❖ 11 ❖

Appellate Review

Canon law affords the opportunity to appeal a tribunal's ruling to a higher Church court when "a party . . . considers him or herself to be injured by a judgement. . . ."[1] The wording of the canon, it might be noted, gives no support to the view that in an annulment proceeding only the marriage is on trial. Marriages are metaphysically incapable of considering themselves injured parties. Marriages are subject to injury sacramentally, canonically, and in terms of spousal interaction, but only petitioners, respondents, and those who might be scandalized can rightly perceive themselves as aggrieved. However that may be, let us examine the mechanics of appeal within the American tribunal system. It will be seen that appeals can take some fascinating twists and turns.

Forms of Appeal

A contentious respondent can pursue the right of defense by appealing to a higher court to overturn decrees of nullity. The same objective may be sought by recourse, a means of obtaining redress after the deadline for appeal has expired. Technically recourse is not classified as an appeal, but functionally it serves the same purpose. Canon law provides three avenues of appellate relief from First Instance decrees of nullity reached by ordinary process: mandatory appeal, adversarial appeal,[2] and recourse. All such decrees must undergo mandatory (i.e., automatic) appeal to a Second Instance tribunal for a concurring opinion before the annulment takes effect. This represents a return to procedure followed before the thirteen-year APN experiment, which allowed tribunals in the United States to finalize annulment without a conforming judgment from a higher court. Under the APN, First Instance decrees could still be appealed to Second Instance by defenders and respondents opposing nullity, or by petitioners denied annulments. In such cases, Second Instance ratification would make the First Instance declaration of nullity or denial of nullity effective.

Mandatory appeal occurs irrespective of the desires and initiatives of the parties, the defender, and advocates. In nearly all cases it entails review, rather than retrial, of First Instance judgments. If ratification is withheld, the Second Instance tribunal can remand the case or retry it under the same procedures that govern trial at First Instance. Remand is not supposed to result in First Instance retrial unless there is new evidence and different grounds. Mandatory appeal does not occur if the validity of the marriage is upheld at First Instance. Its intended benefits, therefore, do not extend to petitioners. That nullity but not its denial triggers mandatory appeal is consistent with the principle of giving validity the benefit of doubt and with the Church's intention of building into annulment proceedings safeguards against the nullification of bona fide marriages. Petitioners aggrieved by a ruling against nullity can, however, take an appeal to Second Instance. Under the terminology used here, this would be an adversarial appeal. The appeal may be based on the original ground for nullity or on new grounds, admissible at the discretion of a competent Second Instance judge. Whether the grounds are old or new, the case will be retried by the Second Instance court. If the latter rejects the First Instance denial and rules for nullity, the defender is supposed to appeal to the Rota, because two conforming sentences are necessary for ordinary process annulments. This, too, is a form of mandatory appeal.

As will become more evident below, in nearly all cases mandatory appeal is pro forma, a kind of judicial play-acting to provide the required second conforming judgment. Rather than rely on mandatory review the respondent, the respondent's advocate, the defender, or even a member of the Second Instance tribunal can initiate an appeal. No longer, therefore, are they merely passive agents in the appellate process. The appeal, in other words, becomes adversarial. Petitioners who appeal are seeking to have the denial of annulment reversed; respondents who appeal seek to have a decree of nullity overturned. In either situation, the case will be retried at Second Instance. Presumably, adversarial appeals are dealt with much less summarily than mandatory appeals, especially when the court of final jurisdiction is the Rota. Appellate courts do not ordinarily relish the prospect of overruling trial courts. Typically, they assume the best possible case for lower court decisions. But as we have seen, the Rota apparently has few compunctions about overturning American decrees of nullity.

Getting Help

Within twenty days from their date of publication, First Instance judgments for nullity and any adversarial appeals are to be sent to a Second Instance tribunal.[3] When annulment is granted at First Instance, the Second Instance tribunal, after weighing any comments by the defender, the advocates, and respondent, is to ratify the sentence immediately or reopen hearings on the case.[4] Initiating an adversarial appeal is simple—if the prospective appellant knows how to do it. All it takes is a certified return-receipt letter sent to the tribunal within twenty days after the party is able to inspect a copy of the First Instance sentence. This right of inspection is not always honored, however.

Considerably more is required to master the intricacies of what then follows.[5] Probably in anticipation of a prospective appellant's predicament, C. 1614 requires that "A judgement is to be published as soon as possible, with an indication of the ways in which it can be challenged." The language of the statute, unfortunately, invites confusion and minimalism. "Indication" in the singular seems at odds with "ways" in the plural. It might be construed as demanding little more than an announcement of the right to appeal, informing respondents that they can actively engage in the process instead of waiting on the sidelines for mandatory appeal to run its course, or telling them there is a filing deadline. None of my informants reported being given even a semblance of detailed instruction on strategy and tactics (i.e., "ways") for challenging a judgment in favor of nullity. None had any recollection of being told they could be represented by an advocate who was not a member of the tribunal staff. None ever heard of the option of appealing to the Rota at Second Instance. When tribunals deny respondents the opportunity to inspect sentences (i.e., judgments) as well as the acts, it is virtually impossible for a respondent to participate in mounting an effective challenge. What sort of useful "indication" can possibly be conveyed to contentious respondents who are kept from examining the tribunal's decision and the material on which it is based?

Even when allowance is made for the ambiguity of C. 1614, to give notice of the right of appeal and nothing more is tantamount to denial of that right. Americans in general are not very knowledgeable about civil law and procedure, but American Catholics are almost invincibly ignorant about canon law and procedure. Indeed, rarely have I found that parties to a decree of nullity could even state the ground(s) on which it was granted. That matter aside, the available data and anecdotal material on appeals suggest that adversarial respondents receive little encouragement or meaningful assistance. Many potential appellants are led down a primrose path of mandatory appeal. Told that every annulment granted after a trial is automatically appealed, they never realize that, compared to adversarial appeal, mandatory appeal is peremptory.

Some respondents, stunned and irate over nullification of what they know to be a valid marriage, report being coaxed out of their intention to lodge appeals by tribunal staff persons. Such dissuasion might be thought to resemble what is known in criminology as "cooling the mark," a practice whereby swindlers persuade victims (i.e., "marks") of the folly of reporting their victimization to the police. In one case that came to my attention, a more subtle method was employed. The respondent's sense of victimization and injustice was to be dissipated through prayer and reflection. He was asked to meditate on appealing until the end of Lent. The respondent agreed to go along with what seemed to be an utterly harmless request. He thus unknowingly waived his right to appeal, since the deadline for filing occurred before Easter. Finessing the respondent's right to appeal was apparently considered the pastoral thing to do, inasmuch as the petitioner in the case had embarked on a relationship she wanted to culminate as soon as possible with remarriage in the Church. Persuading a respondent not to take steps beyond routine mandatory appeal also relieves the tribunal of involvement in a cumbersome proceeding. It keeps the annulment machinery from being slowed, and also spares the tribunal whatever embarrassment is associated with having a decree of nullity countermanded—the probable result if the respondent has sufficient knowledge, resolve, and financial wherewithal to seek Second or Third Instance redress from the Rota.

Bare-bones assistance to respondents who wish to engage actively in an appeal to an American tribunal of Second Instance makes the prospect of redress no better than a roll of the dice. A common but seldom effective remedy for respondents in these straits, of course, is to entrust their challenge to the defender or to an advocate. If, as is likely, the defender and advocate share the prevailing American perspective on the nature of marriage, the state of Rotal jurisprudence, and matrimonial consent, contentious appeal to any court other than the Rota or to the Signatura is nearly always doomed from the outset. Probably nothing less than the most transparent miscarriages of justice would evoke vigorous representation by these members of the tribunal cast. Moreover, if the First Instance tribunal is chargeable with reversible error, the chances are that it would be perceived as procedural rather than substantive by the defender and advocate. If a respondent is prevented from examining the sentence, a defender or advocate might be moved to argue denial of the right of defense. But it is hard to imagine, in the context of the American tribunal system, any of these functionaries pressing an appeal based on the belief—their own or the respondent's—that a tribunal committed an error of substance, such as misconstruing the meaning of defective consent or the proper application of C. 1095.

Revival of mandatory appeal appeared to be the most significant blow dealt by the new code to the APN. Despite the Signatura's documentation of abuses associated with the APN, most American bishops and canonists were solidly behind the special rules for tribunals in the United States. Archbishop Quinn's 1978 response to Signatura complaints was an exercise in damage control. Errant behavior by a "small number" of tribunals in a "minute percentage of their cases," he assured, "should be viewed in the context of the truly commendable work being done by tribunals in the United States" and should not "overshadow the tremendous contribution of the American Procedural Norms to the Church." Quinn's letter closed with a plea for continuation of the norms, noting that "various votes taken over the years have reflected the strong hope of the bishops to see retention of the key elements of the Procedural Norms in any future legislation, at least for the United States."[6] Although the then-president of the NCCB voiced regret for the untoward tribunal behavior cited by the Signatura, no apologies were offered for the unremitting flow of American annulments. Neither were expressions of remorse or commiseration extended to respondents whose marriages were illicitly terminated. In reality, the "tremendous contribution" the APN gave to the Church was a tremendous number of decrees of nullity.

The resurrection of the two-tribunal norm for nullity by ordinary process evoked distress among proponents of more generous standards for annulment. Brunsman, for example, was troubled by the estimated $2 million it would add to the tribunal system's costs. He also observed, in shocked understatement, that restoration of mandatory review "does not seem to be a vote of confidence for the tribunal system at least in America. People who are conscious of social justice issues find it hard to understand why the institution would make the annulment process more onerous. . . ."[7] Brunsman does not specify what the system had done, other than expedite nullity, to merit a vote of confidence. But he asserts that even during the halcyon years of the APN tribunals were unable to meet the pent-up demand for annulments. In short, repeal of the single-judge arrangement and other facets of the APN experiment would hamper the system's demonstrable potential for linear increases in the size of its matrimonial graveyard.

Outcome of Appeals

The restoration of mandatory appeal via C. 1682 doubtless embodied the hope of decreasing the volume of annulments produced by tribunals in America and other English-speaking countries. Two tribunals should provide more reliability than one. Second Instance review and possible retrial would act as a safety net, catching First Instance errors before they hardened into injustice and specious decrees of nullity. It would help ensure that the nullification of a valid marriage would be as difficult and rare as the passage of the proverbial camel through the eye of a needle. Within the American tribunal system, this objective proved chimerical. Apart from adding to expenditure of money and time in the processing of petitions, restoration of mandatory review has not functioned as anticipated. Neither Rome's hopes nor American fears materialized. Even in combination with the Signatura's dissatisfaction, papal instructions and exhortations, and frequent Rota reversals of nullity decrees, mandatory review had a negligible effect on the volume of American defective consent annulments. As shown earlier (Table 1-1, p. 5) the number of ordinary process annulments granted annually by First and Second Instance tribunals after introduction of the new code remained high. Slight decreases in 1988 and 1989 were followed by upward swings. A larger downturn of almost 2,500 occurred between 1991 and 1992. Despite these small fluctuations, 1,907 more annulments were granted in 1994 than in 1984, even though the system had fewer tribunalists to process cases.

Vatican statistics show conclusively how trifling the effect of mandatory review and adversarial appeal has been on the volume of American annulments (Table 11-1). Second Instance failures to concur with (i.e., ratify) First Instance decisions are so rare as to be canonical and statistical flukes. "Sentence for

Table 11–1. Outcome of Ordinary-Process Cases Adjudicated by Second Instance Tribunals in the United States and the Rest of World, 1984–1994.

Year	Ratification U.S.	Ratification World	Sentence for nullity U.S.	Sentence for nullity World	Contrary to nullity U.S.	Contrary to nullity World	Percent of total contrary U.S.	Percent of total contrary World
1984	17,903	3,457	989	1,037	147	420	.008	.085
1985	NA	NA	NA	NA	NA	NA	NA	NA
1986	33,733	7,467	942	2,263	141	740	.004	.071
1987	35,458	8,056	2,338	2,901	140	659	.004	.057
1988	35,420	8,491	1,654	2,457	180	573	.005	.057
1989	35,967	10,058	840	1,469	156	634	.004	.052
1990	36,888	10,220	832	1,741	138	675	.004	.053
1991	38,391	7,691	1,983	1,488	67	463	.002	.050
1992	38,577	11,248	160	2,179	85	589	.002	.042
1993	37,470	12,370	1,157	1,449	146	573	.004	.040
1994	32,569	11,441	2,408	1,866	412	564	.006	.056
TOTALS	342,218	80,500	13,303	18,850	1,412	5,890	.004	.056

Source: Adapted from *Statistical Yearbooks of the Church,* 1984–1994.

Nullity" refers to cases appealed and retried, as opposed to cases mandatorily appealed to Second Instance and summarily ratified. Were that not so, they would represent petitions for nullity that were denied at First Instance but granted at Second Instance. That sequence, as noted, requires a second conforming decision at Third Instance (i.e., by the Rota) before the marriage is considered annulled. But the Rota's typical annual caseload seldom includes more than fifteen to twenty cases originating in the United States, an infinitesimally small fraction of the sentences for nullity decreed by American tribunals.

The Vatican has published data on the trials of ordinary process cases at Second Instance since 1984.[8] The number of Second Instance trials in the United States varied from year to year, ranging from 160 cases in 1992 to 2,408 in 1994, the most recent year for which data are available. Of 14,715 cases adjudicated by America's Second Instance tribunals during those years, 13,303 (90 percent) resulted in sentences for nullity. In 1994, sentences for nullity resulted in 2,408 (92 percent) of the 2,620 cases retried at Second Instance in the United States. Since 1984 America's Second Instance tribunals, either by ratification or retrial, approved at least 355,521 ordinary process annulments. That figure is more than 3.5 times the 99,350 ordinary process annulments either ratified or granted after retrial by all Second Instance tribunals outside the United States. America's Second Instance tribunals saw fit to rule against nullity in 1,412 (.004) of the 356,933 cases ratified or retried. Assuming, somewhat improbably, that *all* 1,412 negative rulings involved appeals against annulment,[9] a randomly chosen respondent's marriage would have had four chances in one thousand of being declared valid by a Second Instance tribunal. In comparison, Second Instance tribunals in the rest of the Catholic world ruled against nullity in 5,890 (.056) of 105,240 cases, giving a randomly chosen respondent fifty-six chances in one thousand of seeing his or her marriage declared valid. It does not take a professional statistician to realize that four chances in a thousand is a long shot, presenting considerably more formidable odds than fifty-six chances in a thousand. The odds against an annulment being overturned by an American Second Instance tribunal in 1994 were almost identical to those that existed ten years earlier. If nothing else, Second Instance tribunals in the United States had shown remarkable consistency since the revival of mandatory review.

In 1991 the odds were probably most prohibitive with the Interdiocesan tribunal for Ohio and Washington, D.C. Just two of 2,652 cases submitted for ratification were reversed. Assuming the appellants in both cases were respondents, a marriage annulled at First Instance had one chance in 1,326 of being subsequently found valid. While this particular tribunal may be considered an extreme example, its record does little to distort the larger systemic picture. What that picture reveals is that mandatory review and appeals leading to retrials at Second Instance have done very little to tarnish America's reputation as annulment capital of the universe.

At least one additional comment on the data is called for. The sharp drop in ratifications in 1994 does not signify a corresponding decrease in annulments. In most years First and Second Instance tribunals process pretty much the same number of cases. Actually, only 663 more annulments were granted in 1993 than in 1994. For whatever reason, Second Instance tribunals did not keep pace with First Instance tribunals. Increased compliance with Vatican insistence that tribunal judges serve only at one level—rather than shifting between trial and appellate levels—might have had something to do with this.

Further Redress

Since death alone renders marriage cases *res judicata,* losing an appeal at Second Instance or Third Instance does not exhaust the appellant's options. Vindication and remedy might still be gained through additional recourse to the Rota, the Signatura, or even to the Holy Father himself. C. 1417, 1 states that "Because of the primacy of the Roman Pontiff, any of the faithful may either refer their case to, or introduce it before, the Holy See, whether the case be contentious or penal. They may do so at any grade of trial or at any stage of the suit." The second part of the canon stipulates that unless there is an adversarial appeal, or unless the pope reserves the case to himself, recourse to the Holy Father does not halt the exercise of jurisdiction by a judge who has already begun to try the case.[10] No statistics on recourse are published, but it seems safe to assume that it is much less common than adversarial appeal. Recourse is not designated as such by the code, but functionally it is another form of appeal. It differs from mandatory and adversarial appeals in that the appellate court can choose whether it wishes to hear the case.

Most appeals in the United States are heard by the American Church's twenty-nine Second Instance tribunals.[11] As previously noted, the right to proceed directly to the Rota for Second Instance review is not well publicized or encouraged by American tribunals, and therefore seldom exercised by contentious parties. Petitioners denied annulments and respondents whose marriages are annulled should, however, be explicitly told they can appeal either to a Second Instance tribunal in America[12] or to the Rota.[13] As noted above, failure to provide respondents with that information is an affront to the right of defense.

Although ratification of an annulment by a Second Instance tribunal does not rule out subsequent redress, it can dissuade all but the most intrepid from carrying their cause any further. The average contentious respondent probably regards such ratification as having more finality than it really does. After two Church courts have both ruled for nullity, an understandable reaction would be "Why fight City Hall?" Reinforcing respondent resignation and reluctance to push on is the cost factor. Respondents, unlike petitioners, are spared payment of fees for involvement in annulment proceedings that do not go beyond mandatory appeal. But when either party elects to appeal to Third Instance, he or she becomes liable for fees. If the appellant is indigent, fees will be waived and a canon lawyer assigned to serve *pro bono* as advocate, but those not meeting indigency standards face a substantial outlay of money if they want to take their case to Rome.

Rubber-Stamp Ratification

The near-total agreement between First and Second Instance decisions might be explained in several ways. Conceivably, First Instance ordinary process decisions are so judiciously inerrant in assessment of the acts and in application of Church teaching and law that Second Instance tribunals can only appropriately ratify. That explanation collapses under the weight of the outcome of American cases reviewed by the Rota, which reverses over ninety percent of American defective consent decrees it adjudicates. An unspecified number of cases responsible for that percentage were decided in the early 1980s, before restoration of mandatory appeal, with the Rota functioning as the Second Instance tribunal. The difference between the 92 percent reversal rate of American defective consent cases that reach the Rota and the four-tenths of one percent reversal rate occurring in American Second Instance tribunals is staggering. It points to a huge gulf between how the Rota and American tribunals reckon defective consent and validity, and it probably motivates American tribunals to soft-pedal the right to appeal to the Rota at Second Instance. The differential in reversal rates is not merely statistically significant. It is schismatic.

A more persuasive explanation for their near-perfect conformity is that America's First and Second Instance tribunals march to the same drummer. Indeed, they are in virtual lockstep on post–Vatican II revisionism on marriage, nullity, and the "new pastoralism." One reason they walk the same line with the same cadence is that often the same judges do the walking. First Instance judges also serve on Interdiocesan of Provincial courts of appeal. There are even reports of a single person acting as judical vicar for tribunals at both levels.[14] While care is taken that Second Instance judges do not review cases they themselves previously tried, for one individual to hold simultaneous responsibilities at First and Second Instance invites conflicts of interests and loyalties. Probably the most questionable situation occurs when tribunalists who serve on both levels sit in Second Instance judgment of decisions originating with their First Instance confreres.

Negatively, canonical norms governing appeal contribute to First and Second Instance lockstep. As we have seen, First Instance ordinary process annulments must be appealed to Second Instance, where in all but a small number of cases they are ratified. But what if a petition for annulment, denied at First Instance, is appealed to Second Instance by the petitioner and granted by the appellate tribunal, or a First Instance ordinary process annulment, appealed to Second Instance by the respondent, is overturned? Each of these situations requires a second conforming opinion by the Rota before the case is considered settled.[15]

To make matters still more complicated, if the Rota overrules a decree of nullity granted at First and Second Instance, there must be a conforming sentence before the Rota's decision takes effect. If in any one year even as little as 5 percent of American ordinary process First Instance annulments were negated by appeal to Second Instance, the repercussions within the American tribunal system would be profound. Almost two thousand cases annually would have to be forwarded to the Rota for additional review. Based on the findings of the Varvaro and Hettinger surveys, about 1,850 would be overturned. That many reversals, as opposed to the ten to fifteen decrees now reversed annually, would really force American tribunalists to take serious notice. It would also severely tax the Rota, which current adjudicates about two hundred cases a year. In short, there would be a lot of weeping and gnashing of teeth on both sides of the Atlantic.

Rapid-fire Second Instance ratifications of sentences for nullity also prevent delay in the healing process. Appeals are intended to ensure justice and moral certitude. But if they do not facilitate swift ratification, they are cumbersome, time-consuming, and often expensive. Adversarial appeal taken before a second conforming sentence is handed down suspends the execution of the previous sentence pending the outcome of another trial. In other words, the marriage is not yet officially annulled. Those who have been awarded annulments by only one of two tribunals are not yet free to remarry in the Church. Those already remarried but lacking a conforming sentence are still denied access to the sacraments. Healing comes to a standstill, weddings are postponed, and the outcome of the case remains in limbo while the case is being litigated. If the appeal is being heard by the Rota, the delay could last for years. Moreover, if the grounds for nullity were defective consent, the annulment stands better than a 90 percent chance of being itself nullified by the Rota. Is it any wonder that American Second Instance tribunals are so anxious to ratify, and that tribunalists are averse to instructing contentious respondents on how to take appeals to the Rota? In one case known to me the judicial vicar, fully aware that Rota officially agreed to reexamine two conforming decisions in favor of nullity, allowed the petitioner to remarry within the Church. By failing or refusing to call the nuptials to a halt, the judicial vicar was either prejudging how the Rota would rule or perhaps simply indifferent to the possibility that the annulment he and the Second Instance tribunal granted would itself be nullified.

Although the Rota's annual caseload may seem tiny, it approximates that of the U.S. Supreme Court. Neither court can be accused of sloth or mere paper-shuffling. They do what is expected of appellate courts: examine the record, read briefs and hear oral arguments, research the law, and deliberate on the merits of the cases before them. These activities are burdensome. The Supreme Court enjoys the luxury of managing its caseload size by choosing the cases it wishes to hear. The Rota, however, is obliged to hear all appeals properly submitted, although it can refuse cases presented by means of recourse. Its docket seems to move with agonizing slowness. The Rota, in short, is not equipped by staffing and temperament to adjudicate cases on a mass scale. By special dispensation three-judge Third Instance tribunals can be empaneled outside the Rota itself, though that seldom happens. During the 1970s and '80s a small number of cases were decided by American Third Instance tribunals, but Rome, for rather obvious reasons, put an end to that practice. The dignity of marriage and canonical procedure are further trivialized when Second Instance rubber-stamping is reprised at Third Instance. Respondents desirous of appealing two conforming decisions for nullity would have to deal with yet another pronullity American tribunal. More important, the Rota's role as a check on the excesses of the tribunal system in the United States would be diminished if not eliminated. In point of fact, neither the 1917 code nor the new one was designed to allow tribunals to whisk cases through on a grand scale. Both presuppose intensive deliberation, good faith, resolve to say no, and fidelity to the Magisterium. But these are the very qualities enfeebled or absent throughout much of the American tribunal system, enabling if not forcing it into assembly-line processing of petitions for annulment.

More Credential Lag

Many tribunalists lead double judicial lives, yet another source of Signatura chagrin. Grocholewski, a member of that body, has "diligently insisted" that "the personnel of the interdiocesan tribunal of appeal be distinct from the personnel of the subordinate diocesan tribunals of first instance." Otherwise the dispensation of impartial justice is threatened. No judicial system would even contemplate that "a person concurrently serve in the offices of judge and public minister in two tribunals hierarchically subordinated one to another."[16] Appellate tribunal jurists, moreover, should have better qualifications and more experience than their First Instance counterparts. Grocholewski's statements, appearing in a book edited by Sable and published in 1987, were directed at conditions in American appellate tribunals in 1985.

Tribunal rosters in the 1993 and 1996 editions of the *Catholic Directory,* years after Grocholewski's stern lecture appeared in print, show to what extent interdiocesan appellate tribunals adhered to Signatura specifications. The Brooklyn branch of the Interdiocesan Tribunal of New York State listed twenty-seven Appellate Collegial Judges, twenty of them monsignors. Ten held degrees in canon law, while the remainder had degrees in other areas. Five with degrees in canon law were retired. Of the twenty-seven judges, fifteen had advanced training in canon law. Clearly, Brooklyn's Second Instance jurisprudents did not measure up to Signatura standards. Including its judicial vicar, the Boston Province-Regional Matrimonial Appeal Court had fifty-nine tribunalists. Ten listed as both Associate Judicial Vicars and defenders of the bond, a questionable melding of roles. Each vicar, defender, and promoter of justice had a JCD or JCL. The same was true for forty-six of the forty-seven judges who represented the archdiocese of Boston and the five dioceses in the province. The lone exception was a priest with a master's degree in an undesignated specialty. All six judicial vicars also served on the archdiocese's Metropolitan tribunal. Among the remaining forty-one appellate judges, thirty-two served on their respective First Instance tribunals as well: eight as judicial vicars or associate vice-adjutant judicial vicars; fifteen as judges; three as defenders; one as promoter of Justice; one as vice-officialis, judge, and defender; two as judge and defender; one as advocate; and one, a nun, as Director of the Tribunal and defender. Evidently, the personnel of the Regional Matrimonial Appeal Court are graced with considerable versatility. But unless the court received a wholesale dispensation, its staffing and division of labor were well outside the Signatura guidelines.

Compared to other interdiocesan tribunals, however, the Regional Matrimonial Appeal Court for Boston was an exemplar of Signatura specifications. Consider the situation with the North Central section of the Interdiocesan Court of Appeal for Ohio and Washington, D.C. The 1993 *Directory* lists five adjutant judical vicars and three presiding judges, all eight with JCDs or JCLs. These impressively credentialed tribunalists had as colleagues twenty judges and two defenders. Nineteen of the judges were priests, the twentieth a deacon. Not one of these twenty judges had a degree in canon law, and nine had no degree in any other field. One of the defenders, a priest, was a master of divinity, the other, a brother, had no degree.

It would be inconceivable for a civil appellate court in any legal system in the civilized world to operate with twenty out of twenty-eight justices lacking law degrees. Similarly inconceivable is an appellate proceeding where the only nonjudge present (the defender) who might argue for the common good (the validity of the marriage) and for what might be considered the interests of one of the litigants (the respondent) has no formal training in law. But the mechanics of mandatory appeal are conducive to inadequate staffing of the interdiocesan appellate tribunals. Mandatory appeal is rather summary by design. Each judge and the defender is expected to read the First Instance sentence, the expert's report, if there is one, and a statement by the defender. Unlike a civil appellate proceeding, rarely are briefs filed by opposing attorneys, nor do advocates present the court with oral arguments. It is possible for a First Instance tribunalist to write a dissent, but that seldom happens. Ordinarily the closest thing to a brief is the defender's statement which more often than not is prepackaged. There are no written majority opinions. First Instance decrees of nullity are affirmed or denied by voice vote, either unanimously or by a simple two-to-one majority. The procedure is analogous to a civil appellate court allowing, without comment, a trial court's decision to stand. If, as seldom happens, the panel has problems with the First Instance ruling, the case is admitted to a full hearing or retried to decide whether the ruling should be confirmed or reversed.

The data show that it is virtually delusional for contentious respondents to hope, much less expect, to have their marriages validated on appeal to an American Second Instance tribunal. The effect of obligatory and other appeals on capping the production of American annulments is barely noticeable. To the extent that the right of defense hinges on either kind of appeal to Second Instance in the United States, it is a paper right. With precious few exceptions, America's Second Instance tribunals function as ceremonial rubber stamps for First Instance decrees of nullity.

The system brings to mind Jerome Frank's concept of the "upper court myth." Frank, an American federal appellate court judge and a founder of the school of legal realism, argued that, contrary to popular belief, injustices at the trial court level are not always rectified on appeal. Instead, they are often repeated.[17] In the American tribunal system appellate affirmation of First Instance outcome is practically reflexive. Why should Interdiocesan appellate judges be expected to overrule what many of them routinely do on other days when they serve at the First Instance level? Frank, whose incisive mind never had to grapple with the idea of double-duty judges, believed that appellate failure is due mainly to factual errors at the trial level. In the tribunal system the errors common to both court levels are doctrinal, psychological, and procedural.

Inadequacies in the qualifications and assignments of American tribunalists are widespread. Although many jurisdictions have made efforts to upgrade tribunal personnel, serious deficiencies persist more than a decade after the new code's introduction. Bishops and judicial vicars may attribute those deficiencies to the lack of priests or to the time and expense associated with training personnel. The Signatura, on the other hand, can just as reasonably regard them as further evidence of the American canonical community's recalcitrance and a key factor in the glut of American annulments. Some truth may dwell in each of these interpretations. A different analysis will be offered here, however.

Keeping Things Moving

The credential gap is as much an effect as a cause of America's production of annulments. In managerial terms, it derives primarily from the virtually open-ended acceptance of petitions for nullity. The tribunals' warm hospitality for petitions creates pressure to staff tribunals with warm bodies. Untrained priests and laypersons must be pressed into service as judges, defenders, and advocates.

Elderly priest-canonists whose long service to the Church earned them some respite during their twilight years are called from retirement to try and ratify cases. Yet even with septuagenarian helpers, the American tribunal work force diminished in size since 1986 while maintaining a high level of productivity. The credential lag, and much of the attendant shoddy judicial deliberation, could disappear if tribunals accepted for trial only petitions with solid juridical foundation. But such a solution is unlikely so long as the premises that now inform tribunal operations remain unchanged. Reducing the speed of the assembly line will require sweeping reeducation—if not mass conversion—of most American canonists, or sterner measures than we have heretofore seen on the part of Rome and the American bishops.

A canonist who served on a provincial tribunal engaged in mandatory review intimates that cases were ratified at a thirteen-per-hour rate. Even if it is assumed, perhaps too generously, that each judge had read the acts before the tribunal convened, the processing of cases had to take place without thorough study. Affording an average of less than five minutes to each case leaves barely enough time to read First instance sentences, let alone opportunity to discuss the case and arrive at a reflective collegial decision.

The extent of First and Second Instance complicity within the American tribunal system, the fate of American decrees of nullity that reach Rome, and the unsuitable qualifications of many tribunalists who contribute to those decrees should be a monumental embarrassment to the American Church. But whatever embarrassment or scandal exists is almost exclusively in-house, confined to the canonical establishment. Very few lay Catholics have heard of the juridical rebukes suffered by American tribunals when the Rota gets hold of their handiwork. Few even suspect that some of the people at the diocesan tribunal are unqualified for the work they do. Indeed, one wonders how many bishops are conversant with the tribunal system's infirmities.

Paying the Piper

For a contentious respondent apprised of the Rota's existence and function, the cost of an appeal or recourse can be prohibitive. Perhaps in response to complaints about right of defense violations, the NCCB and Rota reportedly agreed to facilitate Rotal appeals by petitioners and respondents of limited means. For a fixed fee of $800 or thereabouts, waived for those who qualify, First Instance sentences can be appealed directly to the Rota. Advocates who practice before the Rota, usually excellent canon lawyers, are assigned on a rotating basis to handle such cases *pro bono*. Appellants who wish to retain a canon lawyer of their choice must pay the lawyer's fee and other costs as well. My own recourse, initiated before the NCCB-Rota agreement, cost more than $8,000, a princely sum for most professors (although a modest amount compared to the expenses incurred by a nonindigent appealing a civil or criminal case in American courts). The figure includes, in addition to the canon lawyer's fee, expenses for duplicating and shipping five copies of the voluminous acts, having them translated into Italian, and a fee for another expert opinion.

Cut-rate fees might be seen as a giant step forward in the administration of Church justice, though one wonders why it took so long to happen. Under C. 1649 the bishop governing the tribunal is supposed to establish norms dealing with payment and reimbursement of litigation costs; fees for advocates, experts, and interpreters; witness expenses; free legal aid; damage payments by those who lose at trial and by those who initiate frivolous suits; and setting bond levels for paying trial expenses and damages that might be awarded. I have never heard of an appellant in a marriage case, either petitioner or respondent, benefitting from these norms or even being told of their existence. Perhaps bishops are unaware of—or satisfied with—how their tribunals impose and collect fees. Perhaps, too, they believe that mandatory and adversarial appeals to interdiocesan tribunals provide ample redress from alleged First Instance injustices. Making it easier for appellants to gain a hearing before the Rota might be thought superfluous as well as an invitation for outside interference in diocesan affairs. Given frequent expressions of Rotal and Signatura dissatisfaction with the American tribunal system, the likelihood is strong that the Rota-NCCB agreement was initiated by Rome rather than by American bishops.

In the interest of fairness, some consideration should also be given to reimbursing fee-paying petitioners and respondents who prevail on appeal or recourse. Since the law empowers bishops to provide free legal assistance and reduce fees, thought should be given to requiring the tribunals to use some of the bishops' subsidy to compensate for their mistakes. At least three important benefits would accrue to this redemptive scheme: bishops would pay closer attention to what their tribunals do, tribunals would be more selective in accepting petitions, and fewer meritless annulments would be granted. On the other hand, it could make some tribunals even more tight-lipped about helping respondents pursue the right of defense.

In practical terms, mandatory appeal, adversarial appeal, and recourse add virtually nothing systemically to the efficacy of the right of defense. They are inconsequential speed bumps in the assembly line. Appellate review does create some delay and staffing problems. Personnel must be diverted from turning out First Instance decrees of nullity to going through the motions of quality control at Second Instance and, in rare instances, explaining and defending the system's end products before the Rota. But so few ordinary process annulments made in the United States are subjected to Rotal review that reversals in Rome have small effect not only on the assembly line's production, but also on the canonical craftsmanship of the workers.

Conclusion

What emerges from this study of defective consult annulments in the United States is an empirical portrait of a tribunal system dedicated to expediting nullity. A well-oiled canonical assembly line is in operation, geared to provide apparent ecclesial and juridical legitimacy for divorce and remarriage. "Permanence and indissolubility," "until death do us part," and Christ's own words—"let no man put asunder"—have been reduced to mere antiquated slogans. Retrospectively, they are implicitly treated as unrealistic ideals for most parties to "bad" marriages, vestigial stumbling blocks for the majority of petitioners who present themselves to tribunal offices. Thus the line, despite egregious deficiencies in the number and quality of its operatives, is able to sustain its nonstop production of annulments. There are few signs of appreciable near-term abatement, very modest decreases in 1992 and 1993 notwithstanding. Civil trial lawyers often refer to "runaway juries," impaneled citizens out of control. The American Church suffers a runaway tribunal system, bent on making annulment as easy and painless as possible.

The statistical evidence supporting this characterization is overpowering. Called upon to service but 6 percent of the world's Catholics, the system accounts for nearly three quarters of all Church annulments. Two thirds of the output is based on allegations of defective consent in one form or another. Unless one accepts the self-serving claims of the system's efficiency, the improbable implication is that American petitioners for nullity, compared to those in other societies, are more prone to serious mental problems which are supposed to be present in most defective consent annulments.

Qualitative evidence—exegetical, historical, jurisprudential, psychological, organizational, and anecdotal—fleshes out and corroborates the portrait drawn from numerical data. If anything, both forms of evidence underrepresent the magnitude of the American annulment crisis. Even running at top speed, the assembly line cannot keep up with the demand the system itself helps generate. Some slack is taken up by dissident clerics who act as one-man rump tribunals, making decisions canonically reserved to Church courts. Extra-legal, ad hoc "internal forum" and quasi–"internal forum" resolutions for those turned aside by tribunals are desperately in need of study. At all events, neither jerry-built annulments nor more discriminating "internal forum" terminations of marriage appear in the official Church statistics. In a word, the situation is even worse than the numbers show.

Social systems marred by internal corruption are often likened to the few bad apples spoiling the entire barrel. With the American tribunal system, the folklore ratio of bad to good apples is inverted. Tribunals resistant to permissive annulment—the good apples—are heavily outnumbered. Islands of orthodoxy, they offer hope for the future as canonical cadres that could lead the restoration of the system's integrity. Currently, however, they wage a lonely and difficult rearguard action. As now constituted the system is corrupt and corrupting. It represents a kind of canonical corollary to Gresham's law that "bad" money drives out "good" money. In the American tribunal system the bad apples have hegemony over the good. This corollary is most pathetically manifested in tribunalists who wish to play by Church rules and recognize the system's fraudulence yet resign themselves to going along with the crowd. Their orthodox instincts have been coopted, overwhelmed, deadened, and redirected by what goes on around them and by their own weakness of will. Tribunals standing their ground are subjected to systemic pressures to unbend, and often ostracized for hardheartedness and living in the past. Interdiocesan tribunals friendly to easy annulment have been known to treat dissident tribunals within their jurisdiction as pariahs, intransigently resistant to purported postConciliar developments in the Church's approach to marriage.

Maverick marriage courts win few friends by advising petitioners lacking truly justiciable grounds that they must bear their crosses. The antagonism grows more acute when those denied relief see or hear of tribunals in neighboring dioceses readily dispensing decrees of nullity in cases similar to their own. A veteran canonist serving on a "tough" tribunal confides that the "internal forum" solution is not the only way to circumvent the heavy hand of orthodoxy and apparent lack of compassion. Diocesan priests at loggerheads with their tribunal's restrictive policy coach petitioners on how to fabricate accounts of courtship and marriage that point to defective consent. The immediate objective is acceptance of a petition that would otherwise be rejected, while the ultimate goal is to winkle an annulment out of a difficult-to-please tribunal. In common-law terms, this approximates what is called subornation of perjury, the crime of inducing another to utter a false oath. That it is instigated by supposedly well-intentioned priests, pastoral to the core, makes it no less culpable. Subterfuge and subornation are not always required. Many priests simply and knowingly give communion to those who are supposed to be denied access to the sacrament.[1]

The American tribunal system has undergone a radical revolution. It was a relatively quiet revolution, without extensive media coverage until it was fait accompli. Although no dissident theses on marriage and nullity were nailed or taped to any church doors, it was a revolution nonetheless. Germinated out of public view in the minds of theologians and canonists, it first saw the light in the secretive recesses of tribunal offices. The process itself was shielded from outside scrutiny by the mantra of strict and frequently unwarranted confidentiality and by the complicity and ignorance of respondents. But the fruits of the process—remarriage and return to the sacraments—were there for all to see. Relatives and acquaintances suddenly and mysteriously reverted to good standing in the Church. Tribunals openly solicited petitioners. The word was out, and in due course it became common knowledge that the lid was off annulment.

Against the authentic magisterial backdrop, legal, ecclesial, and sociological analysis of the American tribunal system unavoidably leads to a sweeping multiple-count indictment. Most of the particulars that go into the true bill have generated consternation in Rome for the better part of thirty years. The American canon law establishment routinely pleads innocent to all but the lesser charges, usually procedural in nature. Invariably the denials are cloaked in professions of fidelity to Church teaching, in defensive legal and theological ruminations, and in vague references to contemporary science. Taken singly or collectively, the pleas fail to provide credible justification for thousands of defective consent annulments decreed annually by American tribunals.

A splendid example of the prevailing apologia is found in a presentation by the faculty of Catholic University's 1980 Institute on Matrimonial Practice to the NCCB:

> Tribunals in the United States are applying the Magisterium's own teaching on matrimony as expressed by recent Popes and the Second Vatican Council. They are also making use of the findings of modern science, as . . . directed by recent Popes and in keeping with the practices of the Sacred Roman Rota. This must not be mistaken for an anti-indissolubility attitude.
>
> Tribunals . . . have discerned in . . . *Gaudium et Spes* the authentic expression of the Church's understanding of matrimony, and have drawn on the further discussion of this in . . . *Humanae Vitae*.
>
> Tribunals in the United States are not inventing new jurisprudence as the memorandum of 21 March 1978 from the Signatura would seem to imply. The grounds in question have been developed by earlier decisions in the Sacred Roman Rota. They have also been the object of scholarly study in various centers, and were analyzed carefully by canon lawyers in Great Britain and Ireland in 1975.[2]

The professors' statement embodies premises still virtually dogmatized within the American tribunal system. Those premises remain salient in the scholarly canonical literature, in ostensibly authoritative references, in publications of popular genre, in public presentations by diocesan tribunalists, and, of course, in the policies and deliberations of tribunals.

The statement is generally valid insofar as it applies to documentary process annulments and those granted on nonpsychological grounds. Applied to the approximately thirty-eight thousand ordinary process defective consent annulments decreed annually by American tribunals, it falls on its face. In the language of the Recovery Movement, the professors were "in denial" when they addressed the bishops. Today, denial is systemic. What the NCCB heard is a mélange of half-truths, distortions, and outright errors which fly in the face of the evidence. Clarification gives way to obfuscation, reality is displaced by rhetoric. Tribunals in the United States are in fact applying a magisterium of their own making on the nature of marriage and marital consent. The present pope has repeatedly taken American tribunals and their ilk in other countries to task for acting out their pastoral impulses to annul "bad" marriages. Discernment as practiced by leading American tribunalists refers not to what the text of *Gaudium et Spes* actually says, but to meanings more or less forced upon it through canonical sleight of hand. When the meanings are proper, their implementation is not. The tribunal system's problem with indissolubility is not attitudinal; it is conceptual and behavioral. The venerable phrase *permanence and indissolubility* has been stripped of its literal and true magisterial meaning. A hybrid meaning without hybrid truth has been ascribed to it, making it a mutant cross between a remote ideal and an empty slogan. Several tribunalists tacitly concede this when they state, quite offhandedly, that any marriage can be made susceptible to nullity.

Citation of *Humanae Vitae*'s authenticity in connection with the "Church's understanding of matrimony" is palpably suspect. Catholic University, its Pontifical status notwithstanding, enjoyed no special renown as a hotbed for defenders of *Humanae Vitae*'s principal message: affirmation of the Church's prohibition against artificial contraception. American canonists and theologians, including some at Catholic University, were in the vanguard of efforts to repudiate the encyclical and dismiss its significance. Perhaps the professors who spoke to the NCCB were not among them, however, for they managed to glean from a document held in considerable disrepute by many Catholic academicians apparent support for the revisionist conception of marriage.

In the encyclical Paul VI's main concerns were conjugal love and the conjugal act. When the nature of marriage is addressed, it is almost tangentially. Toward the beginning he states that "the Church has always provided—and even more amply in recent times—a coherent teaching concerning both the nature of marriage and the correct use of conjugal rights and the duties of husband and wife." Instead of developing that passage at greater length, he relied on a bibliographical footnote which cites the Council of Trent catechism; Leo XIII's encyclical *Arcanum*, Pius XI's encyclicals *Divini Illius Magistri* and *Casti Connubii*; Pius XII's allocutions to the Italian Medical-Biological Union of St. Luke, the Italian Midwives, and the International Society of Haematology; John XXIII's encyclical *Mater et Magistri*; the 1917 code of canon law; and *Gaudium et Spes*,

Nos. 47–52. This is hardly an avant garde list of references from which it could be inferred that Paul VI shared the American canonists' interpretation of the last-named source, whereby the Church's "understanding of matrimony" had taken a new fork in the road.

A subsequent passage touches on the nature of marriage more directly. "Marriage . . . is the wise institution of the Creator to realize in mankind His design of love. By means of the reciprocal personal gift of self, proper and exclusive to them, husband and wife *tend* towards the *communion of their beings* in view of mutual personal perfection, to collaborate with God in the generation and education of new lives."[3] Paul VI's words do not depart from traditional Church teaching, and provide no support for the contention that the "communion of life"—or a right to same—is essential to valid marriage. A substantial difference exists between saying that marriage *tends* toward a communion of beings[4] and holding, with American canonists, that it *is* or *must be* that kind of relationship. Similarly, "mutual personal perfection" is teleological, referring to an ideal that couples strive to attain, not a necessary condition for the exchange of valid marital consent.

American tribunals have not invented new jurisprudence, in the sense that Edison devised the incandescent light bulb, but they have been extraordinarily creative with existing jurisprudence. As shown in an earlier chapter, American canonists dwell obsessively on a handful of Rotal decisions, disregard rulings at variance with the chosen ones, and then claim pedigree status for their selectively concocted jurisprudence. That the grounds in question have undergone scholarly study in various unnamed centers and careful analysis by British and Irish canonists is irrelevant if not dissembling. Authentic marriage jurisprudence emanates from the Rota itself, seated in Rome, not from canonical centers elsewhere. The musings of canon lawyers not on the Rota may be provocative and insightful, but they carry no force of law. Moreover, their authoritativeness is trifling compared to Rota decisions, Signatura commentaries and directives, and papal allocutions.

Discernment of the meaning, purpose, and spirit of the second and third sections of C. 1095 has been no less innovative. As imaginative jurisprudence, it ranks with the historic U.S. Supreme Court opinion holding that a Negro is three fifths of a person. Marriage becomes five fifths of a nonmarriage. The canon has been artfully tooled into a loophole of gargantuan proportions, a convenient, multipurpose basis for conferring apparent legality on thousands of defective consent annulments. Neither papal allocutions nor Signatura corrective measures nor Rota decisions to the contrary have stayed American canonists' use of the canon for leverage to annul.

The Signatura's 1978 memorandum is but one of many expressions of Rome's discontent with annulment in America. The faculty members' reply reflects audacity as well as defensiveness, denial, and sophistry. Their statement before the NCCB carries the insolent implication that the Signatura is out of touch with canonical developments in the English-speaking world and not fully conversant with the Magisterium, Rotal jurisprudence, scientific advances, and pronouncements by "recent Popes." It could be more plausibly alleged that the persistently high volume of American decrees of nullity raises questions about how well informed American canonists are concerning affairs in Rome.

Those who addressed the NCCB in 1980 could not have been expected to claim fealty to the "Magisterium's own teaching on matrimony as expressed by" John Paul II, whose papacy had barely begun. But what can be said about more contemporary failures to heed his instructions on matrimony? Commenting on the proper role of tribunal judge, John Paul II characterized it as "a ministry of *charity* towards the ecclesial community which is preserved from the scandal of seeing the value of Christian marriage being practically destroyed by the exaggerated and almost automatic multiplication of declarations of nullity of marriage in cases of the failure of marriage on the pretext of some immaturity or psychic weakness on the part of the contracting parties."[5] Presumably the Holy Father's comments apply to the entire gamut of canonists—professors of canon law, procurators, advocates, promoters of justice, and defenders of the bond, as well as tribunal judges. Moreover, he has expressed on other occasions sentiments similar to those quoted.[6] Despite obvious and frequent clashes between the pope's views on defective consent annulment and the sugar-coated palliatives given to the NCCB in 1980, what the bishops heard then is substantially the same as explanations produced today when America's annulment practices are questioned.

The minutes of the June 22, 1996 executive session of the General Meeting of the NCCB show that the Committee on Canonical Affairs was reminded anew of the Holy See's perennial concerns about the volume of annulments granted by American tribunals, the number of C. 1095 annulments, the need for bringing tribunalists' credentials up to code, tribunalists serving on both First and Second Instance tribunals, and restrictions on the publication of sentences in violation of the right of defense. The minutes do not reveal whether the Vatican's concerns generated any sense of urgency among committee members. If so, it was tempered by a summary of a survey of American diocesan tribunals, evidently conducted under CLSA auspices, that was distributed to those present. The survey found some basis for Rome's edginess about annulments granted via C. 1095, and noted that the tribunals are "becoming more aware of the relevance of other, more traditional grounds." The grounds are not identified in the minutes, but a reasonable guess would be that they also relate to defective consent. The minutes are ominously silent on what effect, if any, reliance on other grounds will have on the volume of decrees of nullity.

The survey purports to show that "the bishops and tribunals of the United States continue to be responsive to the Holy See." Since 1991, it is claimed, there has been a "great increase" in the number of properly degreed tribunalists. The claim is only mildly supported by the exploratory survey of credentials shown in the 1993 and 1996 editions of the *Catholic Directory*. Undeniably, some tribunals in the sample and others not included have upgraded the qualifications of their personnel. Although not all the tribunal rosters in the directories were examined, it is my impression that most of the staffing improvement has occurred in archdiocesan tribunals. But even among them the improvement is spotty. Three of Portland's (Oregon) judges and ten of Pittsburgh's fifteen lack degrees in canon law, as is the case with six of Philadelphia's seven defenders. New York's metropolitan tribunal is rather solidly degreed, but the state's interdiocesan tribunal consists mainly of the its eight diocesan judicial vicars, an arrangement frowned upon by the Signatura. Ultimately, of course, staffing throughout the U.S. tribunal system will likely be chronically in arrears as long as caseloads remain inordinately high, and as long as current views on defective consent annulment persist.

The minutes suggest befuddlement over why the "Rota and Signatura insist on publication of the sentence," and assure committee members that "tribunal staffs have found a way to accommodate" the inherent conflict between confidentiality and discovery. No indication is given how the accommodation might affect the right of defense, however. As for the annulment rate in the United States, the survey statistics supposedly demonstrate that it is comparable to rates in other countries.

Ever since the annulment genie was let out of the bottle, the Vatican and the American tribunal system have been at odds over the volume of ordinary process declarations of nullity in the United States. The tensions, fairly benign during the papacy of Paul VI, became more acute when John Paul II ascended to the Chair of Peter. In general, the more responsive to Rome American tribunals claim to be, the more things remain much the same. Only time and future annulment output will tell whether conceding that C. 1095 annulments are overdone signals a systemic change. Providing the committee with a statistical rather than rhetorical defense of American tribunals is another new development. On the other hand, the assertion that statistics gathered in the survey of diocesan tribunals show America's annulment rates are comparable to those of other countries can be construed as a defense of the status quo. Although the summary report of the survey distributed to members of the Committee on Canonical Affairs has not been made public, presumably the statistical analysis was foreshadowed in an article by Provost.[7] That tribunals in other countries have annulment rates comparable to ours does not necessarily speak well of their tribunals or those in the United States. They could have the same deficiencies as ours, albeit to a lesser extent. The logic is analogous to the response of adolescents forbidden by their parents from seeing R-rated movies: "But all my friends are allowed to see them."

Provost's statistical analysis fraught is with conceptual, methodological, and canonical difficulties. *Comparable* is an equivocal term. It can mean that two things are capable of being held up against one another. In that sense, the multitrillion-dollar Gross National Product of the United States can be juxtaposed with the multimillion-dollar GNP of Uganda. The term can also connote that the things being compared approximate one another. In the latter sense, the two GNPs could be understood to be almost equal, a conclusion that flies in the face of immense disparity. In all likelihood, members of the NCCB's Committee on

Canonical Affairs assumed that the survey showed near equivalence between the American annulment rate and that of other countries.

Provost compares ordinary process tribunal activity in the United States in 1992 with that in Canada, Australia, Great Britain, and six European countries. His key independent variables are "potential Catholic petitioners" (a crude estimate of the number of divorces involving Catholics) and the number of "mixed marriages." The principal dependent variables are tribunal decisions and the number of affirmative decisions. Provost actually hoists himself onto his own statistical petard. The very data appearing in his tables give the lie to the justificatory claim of near parity. Tribunals in the nine other countries, with thirty-five thousand *more* potential Catholic petitioners, granted less than one fourth as many ordinary process annulments as American tribunals.[8] Similarly, the one to four ratio obtains even though the number of mixed marriages in the other countries is 85 percent of the number of mixed marriages in the United States.[9] Canada came closest to America, yet with roughly eight times as many potential Catholic petitioners, the United States grants almost twelve times as many annulments. Finally, American tribunals produce more annulments than all other nine countries combined, even though the United States has less than one fourth as many Catholics. These striking differences are not even addressed in Provost's analysis of the data.

In the language of social science, his independent variables have little explanatory power. They fail to account for the unrivaled production of annulments by American tribunals, and they fail to establish that tribunal systems elsewhere, despite showing similar tendencies, closely match the American experience. How the various systems reckon defective consent would have been a more potent explanatory variable for similarities and differences than the variables Provost employs. His treatment of the data, moreover, betrays a canonically untenable premise that is shared by most American tribunals. The premise undergirds the contention that tribunals in the United States deal with only a fraction of potential petitioners, implying that the annulment rate could properly be even higher. While it is true that divorced Catholics (potential Catholic petitioners) have the right to petition for nullity, tribunals have no corresponding duty to go to extraordinary lengths to provide them with annulments. Marriages ending in divorce and mixed marriages can be just as valid as marriages remaining intact. Putting it more bluntly, the right to petition is not an entitlement to a decree of nullity.

Provost sets up a straw man by suggesting that numbers are the basis for the Vatican's "fundamental" objection to the performance of American tribunals. The Vatican is not engaged in speculative numerology, looking for hidden, magical significance to the annulment data emanating from the American tribunal system. Documentary process annulments represent about one-third of the total granted in the United States, a considerable figure. Baptized Catholics marrying outside the Church and divorced people remarrying without previous marriages annulled are not mere minor annoyances to Rome. But they are not the primary source for the Vatican's displeasure with annulment in the United States. Nor is Rome upset by the number of people beating paths to tribunal offices for ordinary process annulments. What aggrieves Rome is the near-indiscriminate acceptance of ordinary process petitions, followed by trials that virtually guarantee decrees of nullity by purporting to divine what was in the minds of the parties when they exchanged consent. As if this were not enough, it occurs in a system with many individual tribunals still not properly staffed, one in which even those that are often run roughshod over respondents' right of defense. Assuming that the statistical rationale presented to the NCCB Committee on Canonical Affairs resembles the one developed by Provost, if the committee found it persuasive the Committee will likely learn at some future date that Rome has a different outlook on its plausibility.

"NCCB/USCC committees and their staffs help the bishops establish and implement policy on many matters intimately connected with Catholic life, such as doctrine, worship, the parish, evangelization, and canon law."[10] Thus reads part of the introduction to a recent compendium of pastoral letters, statements, and resolutions originating with the NCCB and USCC. The two bodies accounted for seventy-five documents during the six years covered by the volume. Not a single document relates to divorce, divorce and remarriage, or annulment. There were, however, publications on South Africa, MX missiles, Lithuania, the federal budget, Lebanon, homelessness, and emergency hunger policy. Earlier, from 1960 to 1983, the American Church's two leading administrative organizations were responsible for two documents germane to annulment, a 1971 article dealing with the APN and a 1977 statement on the pastoral care of divorced Catholics. In 1989 Cardinals Edouard Gagnon and Achille Silvestrini (Prefect of the Apostolic Signatura), and Archbishop John Quinn of San Francisco combined to produce a three-part, eighteen-page document titled "Pastoral Ministry to the Family, the Indissolubility of Marriage, Marriage Cases Handled in the Local Tribunal."[11] Based on this survey of official pronouncements, the NCCB and USCC have not counted annulment and the tribunal system among the more pressing problems facing the Church in the United States.

The apparent paucity of interest is difficult to reconcile with the annulment statistics and with the Vatican's many expressions of dissatisfaction with the policies of American tribunals. Despite Rome's frequent admonitions, rulings, and entreaties, and the proliferation of decrees of nullity in the ensuing years, the hierarchy seems to show almost smug satisfaction with the performance of its diocesan tribunals. Perhaps the most charitable hypothesis is that many bishops are simply unaware of what goes on within the confines of their tribunal offices as well as what comes out of them.

Since diocesan tribunal activities occur backstage, not only are they out of public view but also somewhat removed from the bishop's direct field of vision. This tends to put them out of mind as well as sight. Complaints about tribunal affairs are less likely to come to his attention than dissatisfaction with other diocesan matters, such as sex education in parish schools, dwindling contributions, or an empty seminary. Obviously, there are no complaints when a decree of nullity brings satisfaction to both parties. Furthermore, as we have seen, most respondents are not contentious. Those who are typically have slender knowledge of canon law and seldom are helped to be contentious in any effective way. In short, parties to an annulment, especially respondents, ordinarily do not really know what to complain about.

Bishops, to be sure, have difficulty keeping on top of everything that goes on within their diocesan boundaries and bureaucracies. For that very reason some authority and responsibility must be delegated to subordinates, including the judicial vicar and his tribunal staff. Yet each bishop, acting in concert with the Holy Father, remains the diocese's ultimate decision-maker. Legally the bishop is chief judge of the diocesan tribunal. It is not unreasonable to expect bishops to monitor the vital work of their tribunals. Evidently, however, most tribunals are given fairly free rein. In dioceses where tribunals play fast and loose with official standards governing Christian marriage, the bishops either overtly or tacitly approve the spate of annulments, give low priority to marital dissolution, or simply do not care. The hands-off policy becomes all the more difficult to comprehend when it is realized that an estimated third or more bishops are canon lawyers.

The U.S. bishops and their bureaucracy have no control over events in Central America, Africa, and the Baltic states. In the realm of world and national politics theirs is a faint voice.[12] Extensive poll data shows that the hierarchy has trouble enough convincing the laity of the rectitude of many of Catholicism's core beliefs. But within the parameters of the Church power structure and canon law, they have nearly absolute control over their tribunals. They select judicial vicars and have veto authority over the appointments of lesser tribunal personnel. Every tribunal member is answerable to the bishop, and it is his responsibility to ensure that the tribunal adheres to Church teaching and law. Yet under their very miters the integrity of the sacrament of marriage is undergoing mortal damage on a daily basis.

A certain morbid fascination attends observing dissent within the Church when it takes on a bilateral hue. American dissenters often claim to be exercising a fundamental right purportedly rooted in Vatican II. Ivory-tower dissidents seek refuge in academic freedom as well as in the amorphous Conciliar "spirit." But if Rome dares to confront dissenters head on, the air fills with charges of rigidity, authoritarianism, legalism, medievalism, and efforts to turn back the clock purportedly so wisely wound and set by the Council Fathers. Often, too, if Rome finds fault with some policy or practice indubitably associated with the American Church, it is countered by assurances that while things may occasionally go awry in this sector of the Catholic world, overall American Catholicism is ship-shape and vibrant. Frequently the disclaimers are coupled with the theme that Rome does not really understand the sociocultural complexities of the United States and the milieu in which the American Church must function. Does it not strain credulity, however, to suppose that the Vatican, so well informed of developments in the Soviet Union when it was a closed society, should be blissfully ignorant about conditions in an open society such as ours? Nonetheless,

Vatican bills of particulars addressed to American tribunals often evoke a "Who me?" reaction similar to the feigned innocence of a child caught in the act.

The Vatican might not fathom why baseball rather than soccer is America's national pastime or how the Electoral College fits into our political system. But members of the Curia are quite capable of grasping the significance of numbers—Arabic as well as Roman—whether they relate to Church finances, ordinations, or the incidence of annulment. There is every indication that Rota judges, the Signatura, and the Holy Father himself, among others, are fully aware of the mindset of America's canonists, the modus operandi of the majority of its tribunals, and the strengths and limitations of modern psychology. Moreover, the Vatican is quite cognizant of how these variables relate to national annulment data.

America's secular legal system gave up the ghost on conserving marriage with the introduction of no-fault divorce. The new mode of marital dissolution, unlike permissive annulment, occurred without assistance from theologians. It was engineered primarily by lawyers driven by impulses resembling those which gave direction to the ascendant pastoralism of American tribunals. While not interested in returning clients to the sacraments or ensuring guilt-free remarriages, the civil bar believed the change would be beneficial. It would eliminate much of the dishonesty and rancor so often part and parcel of traditional divorce proceedings. Marital dissolution would become an amicable, civilized, almost pastoral parting of the ways, a legal remediation for "irreconcilable differences."

In recent years even once ardent proponents of no-fault divorce have begun to realize the depth and breadth of its unintended consequences. Mendacity and bitterness persist in divorce proceedings, particularly with respect to the distribution of marital assets, attorneys' fees, custody of children, and visitation privileges.[13] There has been an upsurge in concern with single-parent families, the feminization of poverty, laggard child-support payments (often withheld by fathers unable to see their children), and the violent mayhem committed by young males growing up without the presence of a father.[14] A host of programs, proposals, and laws have aimed at amelioration of the effects of marital breakup. A few states have considered longer waiting periods before granting divorce in the somewhat forlorn hope that spouses might reconcile before a court declares their marriage "irretrievably broken." But by and large these measures deal with symptoms rather than causes. There is little agitation on a national scale to reform what is clearly at the root of these problems: divorce itself. While the Constitution says nothing whatever about divorce, in the courts and body politic it is now considered an inalienable right. As long as that state of affairs persists, society will have to keep applying bandaids to the consequences of broken marriages. A recent book by Gallagher probes in distressing if not tragic detail the ruinous consequences of the "culture of divorce."[15]

As if cued by that culture, the American tribunal system further loosened the bonds of Christian marriage. It was not as though canonists welcomed or advocated easy divorce.[16] Their reaction to the trend might be characterized as reluctant passivity, the divorce rate being something beyond their control. Thus the rising incidence of divorce among Catholics is often cited as an almost irresistible force behind the necessity for more annulments. Put more sociologically, canonists implied a linear relationship between divorces and invalid marriages. As one increases, the other follows suit. No tribunalist cares to hear that annulment can be a cause as well as an effect of divorce. The laity, however, is tuned to a different frequency. Potential petitioners in troubled marriages learn that tribunals consider civil divorce a prerequisite for annulment. The divorce requirement, together with virtual assurance of an annulment, is a powerful inducement to end troubled or "bad" marriages in civil actions. Whether a person is still in a marriage, already divorced, or divorced and remarried, annulment has significant exculpatory functions. It helps eradicate whatever remaining stigma divorce entails and neutralizes Church sanctions against divorce and remarriage. Church courts provide a legitimizing flourish to earlier action by their state counterparts. "You see," a father can tell his angry and disbelieving children, "even the Church says it was okay for Daddy to divorce Mommy and marry your stepmother. I can go up and receive communion just like anyone else."

Assembly-line annulment has cost the American Church dearly. Fiscally, the cost is seen in tribunal subsidies, sizable line items in all diocesan budgets. Canon law mandates a tribunal in each diocese and details the tribunal's makeup and responsibilities. But nothing in the law ordains tribunals to act as expensive engines of nullity. Hardly a diocese could not put the money to other needs, such as the care of retired religious or competitive salaries for parochial school teachers. There is no diocese that could not allocate the man-hours priests expend on tribunal operations to other important ministries. Reducing the flow of annulments could release some tribunalists to parishes short of priests. If outright transfers are not feasible, some would have more time to devote to such non-judicial activities as celebrating Mass, hearing confessions, and visiting the sick. It seems safe to assume many of the faithful have pastoral and spiritual needs requiring as much if not more attention than processing petitions for annulment.

The price exacted by the tribunal system as now constituted cannot be reckoned simply in terms of balance sheets and man-hours. By relaxing standards for nullity, the American Church has ceded an expanse of the moral high ground it held since the first Catholic colonists set foot on the shores of Chesapeake Bay. Long society's principal institutional guardian of the sanctity and permanence of marriage, the American Church now seems bent on relinquishing that honorable facet of its historic identity. Instead of being Christian marriage's last line of defense, this once-formidable redoubt has grown porous, made irresolute by actions of its own tribunals and the silence of its bishops. Devout old-line Catholics refer to easy annulment as an incomprehensible abomination, contrary to practically everything they were taught. Younger Catholics and non-Catholics think of it either as the end of past sanctimoniousness or as a joke.

Adding to the hidden cost of annulment is the contagion factor. This phenomenon is nurtured by the tribunals themselves, but especially by word-of-mouth testimonials. Recipients of decrees of nullity share the experience with others, often providing advice and encouragement to give annulment a try. What little is written on the diffusion of annulment mentality focuses mainly on its potential for stimulating petitions for nullity.[17] One searches the canonical literature in vain for discussion of the impact annulment has on children. Canon law affirms their legitimacy and urges that they be properly supported and cared for, but what is said of annulment's other effects on children? What law cannot stipulate or anticipate is how children react to seeing their parents' marriage voided by the Church as well as by the state. What are the catechetical consequences? What does the experience teach them about the sanctity and permanence of marriage? And what turmoil is visited upon them if the respondent-parent insists that the marriage was valid? Why did Daddy but not Mommy remarry? Commentaries on the "internal forum" routinely refer to the avoidance of scandal when the divorced and remarried are allowed to return to the sacraments without benefit of a decree of nullity. Normally the frame of reference is public scandal, the principal concern being the reactions of other parishioners and neighbors. But children in the household of either ex-spouse are an intra-family "public" whose scandalization is inevitable.[18] In the end, the scandal generated by any given inexplicable annulment is infinitesimal compared to the scandal generated by the tribunal system. The system as a whole is scandalous.

The damage inflicted on Christian marriage by the American tribunal system's gamesmanship with marital consent is incalculable. Many marriages, to be sure, have been properly declared null on psychological grounds. But they are a small minority of those wiped out on grounds of defective consent. When John Paul II refers to Christian marriage being threatened with destruction, he is not indulging in papal hyperbole. The enormity of the threat is altogether real and systemic in nature. Notwithstanding the good intentions of individual tribunalists, the tribunal system itself is the prime mover in the evisceration of Christian marriage. Reforming the system will be a monumental undertaking. It has proven resistant to countless remedial initiatives. They have come from the Holy Father, the Apostolic Signatura, the Rota, and, in rare instances, from the system's own members.

The blunt truth of the matter is that an entire generation of tribunalists has been indoctrinated in the rectitude of what they do. By now, permissive annulment is second nature to them. Massive and intensive resocialization of the canonical community must occur before the tribunal system will get even close to being in harmony with Christ's teaching on the permanence and indissolubility of marriage. But the question that immediately presents itself is Who would conduct the necessary reeducation program? The leading professors of canon law are precisely those largely responsible for making the system what it is. The bishops may be in a better position to reshape the system, though many appear comfortable with what they have. Until the needed changes occur, *de facto* the American tribunal system will continue to be in virtual schism with Rome with respect to defective consent annulment.

References to annulment as "Catholic divorce" are now part of everyday speech. In the public mind, divorce subsumes all marital breakups accorded legal recognition. Strictly speaking, however, applied to annulment the phrase is oxymoronic. Divorce denotes that there was a marriage; annulment proclaims that a marriage never existed. Canonically, wiping the slate clean in the fullest sense is defensible when the union is demonstrably invalid, when impediments or defective consent can be established firmly enough to sustain the moral certitude tribunals often generously confer on themselves. It is indefensible, however, when valid marriages are nullified by tribunal fiat based on imaginary changes in the nature of marriage, contorted use of canon law and Rotal jurisprudence, pseudo-psychology, and misguided pastoral zeal. But that is precisely what happens in most defective consent cases. In such cases divorce is in fact a more honest term than annulment, because it recognizes that there was a marriage.

Nullity has become the American Church's oblique way of acquiescing to the plague of divorce, even as its imperial tribunal system contributes to its spread. American canonists, as we have seen, constantly pay tribute to anonymous scientific advances that allegedly enable tribunals to establish defective consent when marriages are contracted. They seem oblivious to their own scientific prowess, however. Whenever an objectively valid marriage is nullified it is an astonishing scientific and theological feat. Resourceful and inventive tribunalists are accomplishing something without precedent in the annals of science: they are making nothing out of something. But besides suspending the laws of nature and logic, they are making mockery of Christ's solemn enjoinder that no mere mortals, including well-intentioned tribunalists, can tear asunder what God Himself has put together.

Notes

Chapter 1

1. The pacesetters included tribunals in Boston, Brooklyn, Chicago, Cleveland, Detroit, and San Antonio. The list might be longer but for the fact that two archdiocesan tribunals—Philadelphia and St. Louis—did not submit any data. Statistics for the tribunals listed here were published in *Canon Law Society of America Proceedings 1979* (1980): 112–7. The Canon Law Society of America's (CLSA) annual statistical summaries do not specify the number of annulments granted. But until 1986 a rough approximation could be gotten by subtracting the number of "Informal 'Negative' Decisions" from the number of cases "Decided by Sentence." *The Statistical Yearbook of the Church*, published by the Vatican, is the sole source of reliable annulment data.

2. *CLSA Proceedings* 1980 (1981): 223.

3. *Statistical Yearbook of the Church*, 1980.

4. Throughout this study references to the new code are based on the *Code of Canon Law (In English Translation)* (London: Collins Liturgical Publications, 1983). Another reporting change of note occurred in 1985, when the CLSA, in its annual statistical summaries of American tribunal activities, ceased providing data on "Informal Negative Decisions." As a result it was no longer possible to use the summaries to obtain an estimate of the total number of annulments granted by American tribunals in any given year. I have not seen an explanation for the change, though for the purpose at hand that is of minor moment. Reporting to the *Statistical Yearbook of the Church* is mandatory, but voluntary with respect to CLSA. Some diocesan tribunals do not submit data to CLSA. Accordingly, its data are not as reliable or as complete as those published in the *Statistical Yearbook of the Church*. But even Vatican data are not totally comprehensive. For obvious reasons, there are no figures for mainland China and North Korea.

5. For evidence on how common they are, see Bowman, Bending the Rules.

6. "American Church" is used primarily for stylistic reasons. Though there are serious differences between the Church in the United States and Rome, there is no intention here to suggest that overall the American Church is in schism. But when it comes to defective consent annulment, de facto that is pretty much the case.

7. Catholic News Service, 3 June 1993.

8. For recent examples see Provost, "The Volume of Cases," and Peters, "Annulments in America."

9. Quoted in Zwack, *Annulment*, 6–7.

10. Verbrugghe, "The Work of Marriage Tribunals," 24.

11. A worthwhile exception is found in Peter, "Divorce, Remarriage, and the Sacraments" *Quod Potest Debet?* Peter's contribution is more qualitative than quantitative.

12. There are frequent references to anthopology in the annulment literature. Especially when used by the pope and members of the Rota, it usually signifies the study of humanity or human nature. But among behavioral scientists who call themselves anthropologists the formal object of the discipline is the study or societies and groups from a cultural perspective.

13. Moynihan, *The Negro Family*.

14. For an excellent account of the controversy see Rainwater and Yancey, *The Moynihan Report and the Politics of Controversy*.

15. For longitudinal study of the effects of divorce on children see Wallerstein and Blakeslee, *Second Chances*.

16. *Lumen Gentium*, Ch.II, 11 (The Dogmatic Constitution of the Church).

17. Pius XII, Address to the Roman Rota, 3 Oct. 1941, in *Acta Apostolicae Sedis*, 423–24.

18. John Paul II. Address to the Roman Rota, 24 Jan. 1981. *L'Osservatore Romano*, 2 Feb. 1981. All citations herein from this source are taken from the English edition.

Chapter 2

1. Popishil, *Divorce and Remarriage*, 141–73.

2. Ibid., 161.

3. Ibid., 176.

4. Mackin, *Divorce and Remarriage*.

5. The passage preceding those quoted is worth noting: "To the married, however, I give this instruction (not I, but the Lord): a wife should not separate from her husband—and if she does separate she must either remain single or become reconciled to her husband—and a husband should not divorce his wife."

6. *CLSA Proceedings 1990* (1991) 305–17.

7. Ibid., 484.

8. Similar reasoning occurred with those who argued that the ordination of women is not a closed issue because John Paul II did not speak *ex cathedra* when ruling it prohibited in his May 30, 1994 apostolic letter *Ordinatio Sacerdotalis*. In an October 28, 1995 statement released on November 18, 1995 the Vatican Congregation for the Doctrine of the Faith announced that the pope's teaching is indeed "set forth infallibly" and must be held as "belonging to the deposit of the faith."

9. Speaking as one whose church attendance lies somewhere between daily and weekly, communicant, the following are among other post–Vatican II changes I have never heard explained from the pulpit: communion in the hand, priests facing the congregation, referring to celebrants as presiders, relocation of the tabernacle, reception of communion while standing, face-to-face confession, and the peace greeting. Homilies are supposed to relate to the Scripture readings of the day, but as any frequent churchgoer knows, they often have little to do with biblical matters. Reasons for the changes could be found in Catholic publications, which many Catholics never bother to read. The listing above, it should be noted, carries no implications about my personal preferences. It is simply a statement on the empirical reality.

10. This situation is chronicled in depth in Kelly, *The Battle for the American Church.*

11. *L'Osservatore Romano,* 2 Feb. 1994.

12. See, for example, Gallup, Jr. and Castelli, *The American Catholic People,* and D'Antonio, et al *American Catholic Laity.*

13. Menninger, *Whatever Became of Sin?*

14. For an account of how the notion of social sin gained hold within the highest reaches of the American Church's hierarchy and bureaucracy, see Warner, *Changing Witness,* 97–121.

15. Provost, "The Volume of Cases," 394.

16. Address to the Roman Rota, 19 Jan. 1990.

17. X Grocholewski, "Theological Aspects of the Judicial Activity of the Church," 20–21.

18. Kelleher, *Divorce and Remarriage,* 157.

19. Quoted in Murphy, "Bishop Details Church of Future,"

20. For a history of annulment prior to Vatican Council II see Noonan, Jr. *Power to Dissolve.*

21. C(anon) 1073. The old code distinguished between *diriment* and *prohibitive* impediments. The former made a person incapable of valid marriage, the latter prohibited a person from marrying. Those who married despite the prohibition would marry illicitly but not necessarily invalidly. The distinction was not carried over into the new code.

22. Canonically, impotence and frigidity must be absolute to qualify as impediments. The spouse must be totally incapable of performing the conjugal act. In contemporary parlance, the terms often refer to temporary inability to engage in intercourse. A marriage consummated but later marred by the onset of impotence or frigidity is not covered by this ground.

23. Consult chs. I–III in *The Code of Canon Law,* 190–94. For a lucid discussion of impediments, see Robinson. *Marriage, Divorce and Nullity,* 80–85. A useful annotated listing of general and specific impediments is found in Gramunt et al., *Canons and Commentaries,* 17–35.

24. For a brief treatment of the distinction see Gramunt *Canons and Commentaries,* 25. Technically, a person with an impediment would not be eligible to participate in the exchange of consent.

25. *Catechism of the Catholic Church,* No. 1626, 406.

26. Especially in the United States, the Church even sanctions divorce as a lesser

and necessary evil if the sustenance and material well-being of the spouse and children depend on a court order obtainable only through a divorce action.

27. For more recent examples of efforts to expand upon existing grounds for nullity see Garrity, "Shame," Sanson, "Implied Simulation," Vann, "*Dolus*: Canon 1098." and Provost "Error as a Ground in Marriage Nullity Cases."

28. This brief account of the transatlantic politicking that occurred is taken from Reese, *A Flock of Shepherds*, 253.

Chapter 3

1. Flannery, *Vatican Council II*, 950–52. Most of my references to the Council documents will rely on the Flannery translation. There are several translations of the documents, but the most widely used English versions are those edited by Flannery and Abbott, *The Documents of Vatican II*.

2. Ibid., 949.

3. Ibid., 950; italics added.

4. Under the terms of deconstruction the meaning of any text is entirely subjective. A law, poem, novel, and so on mean whatever the reader believes they mean.

5. Abbott, *Documents*, 250; italics added.

6. D. R. Campion in ibid., 189.

7. Cardinal John Wright in Flannery, *Vatican Council II*, xxiii–xxiv.

8. *Coram* Doran, 21 May 1992. This is the format for citing Rota "definitive sentences," that is, decisions. *Coram* simply means "before." The name following is that of the *ponens*, the presiding member of the three-judge panel that heard the case. Although the wording might suggest that the *ponens* authors the opinion, the sentence is really a collective enterprise.

9. *Catechism of the Catholic Church*, No. 1640, p. 409.

10. Häring, *No Way Out?* This is the English translation of a work first published in German in 1989.

11. Ibid., p. 21.

12. Ibid., p. 59. It will be interesting to see whether efforts are made to polarize John Paul II's effort, in *Veritatis Splendor*, to wed truth and freedom.

13. Burke, *Freedom and Authority in the Church*, 11.

14. Quoted in Devlin, *The Enforcement of Morals*, 101.

15. John Paul II, "Apostolic Constitution," 25 Jan. 1983, in *The Code of Canon Law*, p. xiii.

16. Ibid., xiv.

17. Palmer, "Christian Marriage," 617.

18. Orsy, "Christian Marriage," 291–93.

19. See Wright in Flannery, *Vatican Council II*, xxiii–xxiv n. 7.

20. Flannery, *Vatican Council II*, 950; italics added. The *Catechism of the Catholic Church*'s section "The Sacrament of Matrimony" draws heavily but not exclusively on *Gaudium et Spes*, Nos. 47–52. While it relies on the Flannery translation of Vatican II documents, it shows preference for *covenant*. Still, it refers to "contracting parties" (p. 406) and those who "contract marriage" (p. 407). At all events, none of the material on marriage refutes the lines of thought advanced here.

21. Ibid.; italics added.

22. All italics in this and ensuing paragraphs are added.

23. Wrenn also authored the material on annulment in McBrien, *The Harper-Collins Encyclopedia of Catholicism*, 53–56.

24. Becker, "Cases," 274. From this perspective it appears that the content of No. 48 and how it is incorporated into the new code is no longer debatable. Perhaps the last thing in the world one expects of a canon lawyer—or, for that matter, any lawyer—is foreclosure of debate. The paragraphs to which Becker refers are found in Canons 1055 and 1057. There is abundant evidence that Rome does not accept with complete equanimity the "distinctly new approach" to marital consent or the degree of faithfulness associated with the incorporation of Vatican II "insights."

25. An updating of Wrenn's views appear in his "Refining the Essence of Marriage." The very title of the article suggests the malleability of the essence of marriage. In this particular piece, Wrenn, working from a hypothetical case, deals with motivation and the invalidity of marriage. Also, it is rather plainly suggested that "mainstream jurisprudence" rather than the Magisterium is the proper arbiter of change. A concise critique of the particular refinement posited by Wrenn is found in Burke, "The *Bonum Coniugum* and the *Bonum Prolis*: Ends or Properties of Marriage."

26. Wrenn, *Annulments*, 3d ed. rev., 22–23. Cf. his *Annulments*, 4th ed. rev., 81–82. Aside from the references to *Humanae Vitae*, to two allocutions given by Pius XII, and to Paul VI's apostolic letter allowing selected procedural norms in tribunal affairs, no papal documents are listed in the bibliographical section of either edition. But the bibliographies do list works by such recognized dissenters as Bernard Häring, Edward Schillebeeckx, Charles Curran, Stephen Kelleher, Eugene Kennedy, and Rosemary Reuther. The *Humanae Vitae* quotation is dropped from Wrenn's fourth edition. In the fifth edition it is paraphrased. The translation of Paul VI's statement, as it appears in the undated edition of *Humanae Vitae* published by the U. S. Catholic Conference, reads as follows: "By means of the reciprocal personal gift of self, proper and exclusive to them, husband and wife *tend* towards the communion of their beings in view of mutual personal perfection, to collaborate with God in the generation and education of new lives" (italics added).

27. Pius XI, *Casti Connubii*, 79; italics added.

28. Ibid., 84.

29. Wrenn, *Annulments*, 5th ed. rev., 83.

30. Doyle, "Matrimonial Consent," 774. For additional examples see Campion, in Abbott, *Documents*, 84; see also Dolciamore, "Interpersonal Relationships," 86.

31. Leo XIII, *Arcanum Divinae Sapientiae*, italics added.

32. Wrenn, *Annulments*, 4th ed. rev., 75.

33. See n. 26 (italics added).

34. Doyle, "Matrimonial Consent," 777.

35. Ibid., 778.

36. Ibid., 777.

37. Ibid.

38. Egan, "The Nullity of Marriage" (1984), 22–23.

39. Ibid, 23.

40. Reported in *L'Osservatore Romano*, 5 Feb. 1997.

41. Ibid.

42. Mendonça, "Consensual Incapacity for Marriage," *The Jurist* 54 (1994) 480–81.

43. For reasons not fully understood, the age at which the onset of puberty occurs in America and other societies has been dropping. This development adds to the already considerable problem of teenage sex and pregnancy. But the American Church rarely allows those who recently entered their teens to marry, hence the reach of nullity does not ordinarily extend to youths in their early teens.

44. The formula and its potential for lengthening what is already an almost open season on marriage is illustrated in Schmidt, *"Educatio Prolis."*

Chapter 4

1. C. 1419.

2. Cs. 1419 and 1420. In most dioceses the bishop, *de facto,* delagates the power to the judicial vicar.

3. John Paul II, Address to the Roman Rota, 29 Jan. 1993.

4. John Paul II, Address to the Roman Rota, 26 Jan. 1984.

5. C. 19. Such situations are likely to be quite rare, but the means for handling them comes close to case law.

6. Wrenn, *Annulments*, 4th ed. rev., 82.

7. Thomas Aquinas. Quoted in the *Catechism of the Catholic Church*, No. 1955, p. 475.

8. Ibid., 474.

9. This approach is found in a Rota decision stating that the "communion of life" is not "independent of the right to the conjugal act with its essential properties but more correctly it signifies . . . all those things, account being taken of those things which compose it, viz., ordination to offspring, perpetuity, and exclusivity." *Coram* Lefebvre, 31 Jan. 1976. What is now called permanence (or perpetuity) was termed *sacramentum* by Augustine.

10. *Coram* Stankiewicz, 22 May 1986.

11. *Coram* Pompedda, 11 Apr. 1988.

12. *Coram* Burke, 20 Oct. 1994. This is an unofficial English translation.

13. *Coram* Lefebvre, 31 Jan. 1976.

14. Egan. "The Nullity of Marriage" (1984), 17. Throughout this discussion my indebtedness to Egan, now Bishop of Bridgeport, is extensive. The article cited here and a 1983 companion piece in the same journal are the most cogent, eloquent, and orthodox commentaries on C. 1095 and defective consent I have come upon.

15. Egan, it seems to me, implicitly denies the right to a "communion of life" when he states that *"One consents to marriage by giving to and receiving from another of the opposite sex not the right to marriage nor even the right to a marriage relationship, but rather the exclusive right to conjugal acts as long as both parties are alive* (ibid., 11). Unless the right to a "communion of life" and the right to conjugal acts are one and the same, as some Rotalists have suggested, Egan appears to be arguing that the right to conjugal acts is the only right exchanged when marriage is entered.

16. *Catechism of the Catholic Church*, No. 1650, italics added.

17. M. Thomas, "The Consortium Vitae Coniugalis," 176. The inventory is taken from Lesage, "The *Consortium Vitae Conjugalis*."

18. See *Coram* Serrano, 5 Apr. 1973, *Coram* Raad, 14 Apr. 1975, and *Coram* Lefebvre, 31 Jan. 1976.

19. Egan, "The Nullity of Marriage" (1984), 9.

20. Ibid., 10.

21. LaDue, "Conjugal Love," 43–44.

22. Translation of this passage from *Coram* Anné, 25 Feb. 1969 was graciously provided by Msgr. Clarence J. Hettinger, JCL (italics added).

23. Egan, "The Nullity of Marriage" (1984), 28–29; italics added.

24. Ibid., 11.

25. For a concise yet superb treatment of how case law works, see Levi. *Introduction to Legal Reasoning*.

26. *Compassion in Dying v. State of Washington*, 850 Federal Supplement at 1454 (1994).

27. *Compassion in Dying v. State of Washington*, 49 Federal Reporter 3rd at 586 (1995).

28. *Compassion in Dying v. State of Washington*, 79 Federal Reporter 3rd at 790 (1996).

29. Brundage, "The Creative Canonist," 315–16. Prior to the appearance of the new code, there was among American canonists a spate of wishful thinking on what it should contain and how it would depart from the old code.

30. C. 26 might be interpreted so as to hint at compatibility with case law. Customs contrary to canon law can acquire the force of law, but only after they have been lawfully observed continuously over a thirty-year period. Speaking as one self-taught in canon-law basics, it is difficult to understand how something contrary to canon law can be "lawfully observed." Much, of course, depends on the type of customs involved. Decrees of nullity can hardly be relegated to the category of customs. Canon 16-3 also hints at compatibility with case law, though on a very narrow basis.

31. LaDue, "Conjugal Love," 41. Discussion of another landmark ruling, this one by Serrano and dealing with incapacity due to lack of interpersonal conjugal consent, is found in Lavin, "The Rotal Decision."

32. See for example Orsy, "Quantity and Quality," Morrisey, "Preparing Ourselves," Coriden, *We, the People of God*, Coriden, *The Once and Future Church*, Coriden, "The Future of the Law," Alesandro, "The Revision of Church Law," Green, "Marriage Nullity Procedures," and Green, "The Revised Schema *De Matrimonio*."

33. Address to the Roman Rota, 29 Jan. 1993.

34. Varvaro, "Trends in Rotal Jurisprudence," 19–62.

35. Ibid., 28–29.

36. Quoted in ibid., 33. The other three cases are briefly discussed on p. 32. Varvaro, to be fair, concedes that long-term marriages require special treatment, but does not indicate whether the odds against annulment increase.

37. Varvaro, "Rotal Jurisprudence 1985–1990," 157. There was a time lag of about four years between when Rota decisions were dated and their official com-

pilation in *Decisiones seu Sententiae*. At the time Varvaro wrote the article the volume for cases decided in 1988, only recently published, was not available to him. I am given to understand that Rome has reduced the time lag to two years.

38. Hettinger, "Too Many Invalid Annulments," 17. In a personal communication Hettinger asserts that all the cases involved defective consent.

39. C. J. Hettinger, personal communication, 15 May 1994 and 10 Feb. 1995. All thirty-seven cases involved C. 1095.

40. Prior to 1984 the *Statistical Yearbook of the Church* did not give exact figures for Ordinary Process and Documentary Process annulments; hence the use of an estimate here.

41. Most national polling organizations use a sample of approximately one thousand respondents, which means a predicted margin of error of about plus or minus 3.5 percent. Doubling the sample size adds to reliability, and reduces but does not halve the margin of error.

42. An English translation of the letter appears in *The Jurist* 33 (1973): 296–300.

43. Ibid., 299–300.

44. Varvaro, "Rotal Jurisprudence," 157; italics added.

Chapter 5

1. For an account of how psychology became as American as apple pie, see Herman, *The Romance of American Psychology*.

2. Andrews. "Religion's Challenge to Psychiatry."

3. Ibid., 83–8.

4. A randomly chosen Sunday edition of a small city newspaper listed support groups dealing with vegetarianism, those who lost a friend or relative to suicide, widowhood and widowerhood, cancer patients, bereaved parents, head injury, dystrophy, respiratory problems, men in or recently out of emotionally abusive marriages or relationships, women survivors of domestic violence, chronic fatigue, eating disorders, dysfunctional family victims, addictions, people suffering from such emotional problems as fear and nervousness, relatives of those with substance abuse or alcohol problems, self-worth, a twelve-step Christian approach to problems, parenting, divorce, rape survivors, overweight, codependency, depression, manic depression, smoking, parents without partners, and those who had colostomies (*South Bend Tribune*, 9 Oct. 1994).

5. See, for example, Vitz, *Psychology as Religion*, and Rieff, *The Triumph of the Therapeutic*.

6. An acquaintance who is priest asked his bishop whether he ever got into psychology while hearing confessions. The bishop, known for his acerbic wit, replied, "No, I only deal with the ordinary sins."

7. The trend is documented in Dawes, *House of Cards*, 3–5, 38–74. Dawes himself is a clinical psychologist.

8. Quoted in ibid., 16–7.

9. Ibid., 12.

10. Llewellyn's jibe, it must be confessed, was directed at sociologists who maintained that the primary function of law is "social control." V. J. Peter, a canonist well read in behavioral science, urges tribunals to examine more carefully how the

social, cultural, and economic features of our society relate to their work. But I am not persuaded that he identifies any specific development of breakthrough caliber that provides an acid test for the validity of marital consent. See his "Divorce, Remarriage, and the Sacraments."

11. Wrenn, *Annulments*, 5th ed. rev., 147–8. Once more he cites *Coram* Anné, 25, Feb. 1969 in support of his views.

12. Ibid., 152–53.

13. A seminal work on this topic is Lasch, *The Culture of Narcissism*. The author, it should be noted, was a social historian, not a psychologist.

14. The havoc wrought on Immaculate Heart of Mary nuns in Los Angeles by more than two years' exposure to Carl Rogers and encounter-group therapy is documented in Coulson, *Groups, Gimmicks, and Instant Gurus*. The author was one of Rogers's associates in a project originally designed as an experiment in educational innovation. When the experiment began, six hundred IHM nuns ran a college, eight high schools, and fifty elementary schools. Within a year after its completion, only two schools remained, and within three years the number of nuns in the order was more than halved. For an account of the untoward effects of group dynamics and Rogerian psychology on Jesuit communities, see Becker, *The Re-Formed Jesuits*, 84–90.

15. C. 1097.

16. C. 1098.

17. C. 1099.

18. C. 1100.

19. C. 1101.

20. C. 1102.

21. C 1103.

22. Cs. 1104 and 1105.

23. C. 1106.

24. C. 1107.

25. *Catechism of the Catholic Church*, No. 1626, 406.

26. Emphasis added. Again, this is but one of many canons in which a variant of *contract* appears.

27. John Paul II, Address to the Roman Rota 26 Jan. 1984.

28. John Paul II, Address to the Roman Rota, 26 Jan. 1988.

29. Wrenn, *Annulments*, 5th ed. rev., 41–42.

30. Ibid., 143.

31. Ibid., 40.

32. Ibid., 42.

33. Ibid.

34. Coram Serrano, 5, Apr. 1973. This case ranks with Coram Anné, 25 Feb. 1969 with respect to the significance attached to it by American canonists. Its application contributed to the Signatura's dispute with Dutch tribunals. See Lavin, "The Rotal Decision."

35. A priest who is also a clinical psychologist who served as consultant for the Diocese of Syracuse's tribunal provides a laundry list of conditions that can be symptomatic of incapacity for proper consent. Working within the "communion-of-life" framework, he mentions the following: a sense of alienation or inadequacy,

self-depreciation, hostility, sexual problems (presumably other than impotence), chronic impulsiveness or selfishness, alcoholism, temper outbursts, demanding and depreciating attacks on the spouse and children, physical abuse, a sense of insecurity, lack of trust, hypersensitivity, workaholism, and fear of dependency. Obviously, some conditions listed fall in what the author calls a "sampling" overlap. Reference is made to "advances in psychology," "psychology's study of decision-making," and. "further psychological insights." No "advance," "study," or "insight" is named or identified (Keefe, "Why the Church is Granting More Annulments").

36. Wrenn, *Annulments*, 5th. ed. rev., 142.

37. Olson, *The Litigation Explosion*, 203.

38. There have been commitment proceedings where the person fighting commitment was considered all the more in need of it for refusing to submit to psychiatric examination or for insisting on being represented by counsel.

39. I have borrowed here from Scheff, *Being Mentally Ill*, 110–11.

40. Quoted in Halleck, *Psychiatry and the Dilemmas of Crime*, 40. By no means do all students of human deviance regard mental problems as forms of illness. The issue is treated in some depth in chapter 6.

41. John Paul II, Address to the Roman Rota, 26 Jan. 1988.

42. In the trial of John W. Hinckley, Jr., President Reagan's would-be assassin, the prosecution had to prove he was "normal." The government's lawyers and psychiatrists found the requirement impossible. For a brief but fascinating account of their futile efforts see Low, *The Trial of John W. Hinckley, Jr.* The federal law imposing that requirement has since been changed.

43. Garrity, "Shame," 364–89. The passage quoted appears on p. 364.

44. John Paul II, Address to the Roman Rota, 5 Feb. 1987.

45. John Paul II, Address to the Roman Rota, 26 Jan. 1988.

46. These issues are treated in depth and in a manner faithful to the Holy Father's teaching in Egan's two superb articles, "The Nullity of Marriage" (1983), and "The Nullity of Marriage" (1984).

47. Garrity, "Shame," 364; italics added.

48. Robinson, *Marriage, Divorce, and Nullity*, 84–85.

49. *Coram* Bruno, 17, Dec. 1982, as quoted in Varvaro, "Trends in Rotal Jurisprudence," 40.

50. *Coram* Egan, 10, Nov. 1983, as quoted in ibid., 41.

51. Ibid 40.

52. Ibid., 42.

53. Ibid., 28. See *coram* Doran, 1 July 1988, for yet another expression of Rotal unhappiness. An American annulment granted for inability to build the interpersonality required for the communion of life was overturned.

54. Egan, "The Nullity of Marriage" (1983), 37.

Chapter 6

1. Until razed in the early 1980s one building at the Michigan Reformatory, opened in 1890, bore signs of early "treatment" accorded inmates considered deranged. In a long, dank, rectangular chamber one could see the marks where shackles that tethered them to a long concrete wall had once been fastened.

2. 1912, p. 466.

3. The rule states: "If the accused was possessed of sufficient understanding when he committed the criminal act to know what he was doing and to know that it was wrong, he is responsible therefor, but if he did not know the nature and quality of the act or did know what he was doing but did not know that it was wrong, he is not responsible."

4. The Church's lexicon often has "anthropology" as the study of human nature. As a behavioral science, anthropology traditionally referred to the study of primitive societies. More recently, with such societies in short supply, the discipline specializes in examining all societies largely in terms of culture.

5. Peter, "Judges Must Judge Justly," 177–78.

6. Rieff, *The Triumph of the Therapeutic*, 33–34. For a succinct account of Freud's ideas on religion see his *The Future of an Illusion*. For a Catholic perspective on this matter see Zilboorg. *Freud and Religion*.

7. Rieff, 108–40.

8. An older but not yet altogether untypical example is found in Catoir, "An Analysis of the Evolution of Tribunal Practice. Catoir speaks of the "knowledge explosion" in psychiatry as one of the main reasons behind reforms sought by the CLSA. Many psychiatrists, I suspect, would like to know more about the nature of the "explosion." There have been significant advances in pharmacology and brain research, but it is unclear how they might relate to the annulment process.

9. Garrity, "Shame."

10. For a lucid and incisive critique of this approach to mental health and morbidity see Kaminer. *I'm Dysfunctional, You're Dysfunctional*. Brief but pungent treatment of the claims of codependence evangelists is found in Kristol, "Declarations of Codependence."

11. Influential publications in this area include Beattie, *Codependent No More*; Bradshaw, *Bradshaw On: The Family*; Kasl, *Women, Sex and Addiction*; Schaef, *Co-Dependence* and *When Society Becomes an Addict*.

12. The project results are reported in Mecca et al., *The Social Importance of Self-Esteem*.

13. Felsen, "The Effects of Self-Appraisal."

14. See, for example, Wrenn, *Annulments*, 4th ed. rev., *passim*.

15. American Psychiatric Association, *Quick Reference to the Diagnostic Criteria from DSM-III-R*, iii–iv. The quotation is taken from p. iv.

16. For a sympathetic and revealing account of the change see Bayer, *Homosexuality and American Psychiatry*. The change was opposed by the American Psychoanalytic Association.

17. Significant benefits accrue to those afflicted and their treaters when a behavior is officially proclaimed to be an illness or disease. In many jurisdictions it means that the "victim" qualifies for health-insurance payments, workmen's compensation, and other government benefits. Therapists can count on fees from a larger pool of "victims." But not least, victims are not held responsible for their behavior. If indeed compulsive gambling is an illness, a person with the disorder can be no more accountable for the condition than someone suffering from rheumatoid arthritis.

18. See for example Rutter and Shaffer, "DSM III," and Michels, "First Rebuttal."

19. American Psychiatric Association, *Quick Reference*, vii; italics added. The same prefatory caution appears in the main edition of the work.

20. Barlow, "Special Issue on Diagnoses."

21. Carson, "Dilemmas in the Pathway of *DSM-IV*," 304.

22. See Million, "Classification in Psychopathology," and Widiger et al., "Toward an Empirical Classification."

23. See his *The Myth of Mental Illness, The Manufacture of Madness*, and *A Lexicon of Lunacy*. More moderate labelist views on the same topic are found in Scheff, *Being Mentally Ill*.

24. An isolated but candid discussion of these issues appears in Hannon, "The Role of Diagnosis." Hannon, a clinician who worked with the Diocese of Brooklyn's tribunal, focuses mainly on "personality disorders," analyzing a specific case where the petitioner was diagnosed as having that malaise. Based on his analysis, he suggests that "no direct cause and effect relationship can be adduced between diagnostic category and a person's ability to make valid judgments and adequately relate" (p. 188). No indication is given on how the tribunal ruled on the case.

25. Wrenn, *Annulments*, 4th ed. rev., *passim*.

26. The studies are reviewed in Rosenhan, "On Being Sane in Insane Places."

27. No one can calculate with complete confidence the precise percentage of Americans with mental disorders at a given point in time or the percentage experiencing mental disorder(s) during their lifetimes. The University of Michigan's Survey Research Center recently conducted a massive study of national comorbidity among noninstitutionalized Americans aged fifteen to fifty-four. It was the first survey of its kind to conduct structured psychiatric interviews with a national probability sample of the civilian population. But the research was restricted to fourteen of the nearly three hundred mental conditions listed in *DSM-III-R*. Some of the fourteen (e.g., "simple phobia," "any anxiety disorder," and "alcohol abuse without dependence") would not qualify as severe, while others would be marginal in that respect. The survey produced a higher-than-expected prevalence of psychiatric disorders, but the data were not amenable to showing how all disorders are distributed through the population. It is important to note that the subjects were canvassed by well-trained interviewers, not by clinicians. Kessler et al., "Lifetime and 12-Month Prevalence."

28. The multiplier would appear to be closer to four than three. Ordinarily the petitioner's consent is found lacking. But in some cases the condition is ascribed to the respondent as well. Thus, one annulment can involve two individuals with mental disorders. To avoid unduly inflating the figures the lower multiplier is used here. The result is quite probably a very conservative estimate.

29. Varvaro, "Trends in Rotal Jurisprudence," 45.

30. See ibid., 44.

31. Wrenn, "Marriage Tribunals and the Expert," 53–54.

32. *Statistical Yearbook of the Church*, 1991, Table 55, p. 417.

33. C. 1578, 2.

34. Cuneo, "Lack of Due Discretion." Cuneo, writing before the new code became operative, wrestles with some of the ramifications of tribunal judges' taking on the role of expert. Depending heavily on Rotal jurisprudence seen through the eyes of Lawrence G. Wrenn and English canonist Ralph Brown, Cuneo suggests

that judges can be as expert as psychiatrists. Perhaps inadvertently, he places the validity of marriage in a no-win situation. If the outside expert finds no psychological basis for lack of due discretion, the judge, drawing upon his experience and *rational psychology* (as opposed to clinical psychology or psychiatry), can still find for lack of due discretion and nullity. Little guesswork is required to foretell how the judge would decide if the outside expert found evidence for lack of due discretion. While I yield to no one in my respect for rational or Thomistic psychology, relying on it to annul is difficult to reconcile with the modern canonical community's fascination with wondrous advances in the behavioral sciences. Practically all of Cuneo's suggestions are countermanded by more recent Rotal jurisprudence and by John Paul II's 1987 and 1988 allocutions to the Rota. Nevertheless, many of his suggestions are alive and well today in the confines of American tribunals.

35. Interestingly, when the Dutch tribunals were taken to task in 1971 for their annulment frame of mind, one of the Signatura's complaints concerned the tribunals' view that marital consent is processual.

36. Gaylin, *The Killing of Bonnie Garland.* This is a gripping tale of the grisly murder of one Yale student by another and the ensuing trial of the perpetrator, who pleaded insanity. Of particular interest to Catholics is the role of Yale's Thomas More Society in the drama.

37. *Coram* Serrano Ruiz, 16 Dec. 1983, quoted in Varvaro, "Trends in Rotal Jurisprudence," 42.

38. A classic example along these lines occurred with Korean War hero Major General Edwin Walker, who considered it his manifest destiny to prevent James Meredith from being the first black to enroll at the University of Mississippi. Walker commanded segregationists in pitched battles against federal law-enforcement personnel. After his arrest, Walker, without a trial, was committed to the Federal Medical Center in Springfield, Missouri, a prison for mentally and physically ill federal offenders. The commitment was based on a diagnosis by a New York psychiatrist who never examined Walker and later admitted that he relied on newspaper accounts of the events in Mississippi to recommend incarceration. Walker's petition for *habeas corpus* was heard by a federal district court, which ordered his release. Even a diehard racist is entitled to due process and a valid psychiatric examination before being denied his freedom. Similar fairness requisites apply to marriages before they are denied their validity.

39. *Coram* Serrano Ruiz, 28 July 1981, quoted in Varvaro, "Trends in Rotal Jurisprudence," 47.

40. Reported in Kelly, *Keeping the Church Catholic*, 104–5.

41. The example is not all that hypothetical. It is widely believed that alcoholism is a disease, whether physical or psychological. Arguing to the contrary is regarded as heretical, even though the disease conception of excessive drinking is open to serious question. See Fingarette, "Alcoholism."

42. Huber, *Galileo's Revenge.*

43. Ibid., p. 3.

44. Ibid., p. 2.

45. *Daubert v. Merrell Dow Pharmaceuticals, Inc.* 113 Supreme Court (1993): 2795–97.

46. *Daubert v. Merrill Dow Pharmaceuticals, Inc.* 43 Federal Reporter 3d (1995): 1311.

47. *Coram* Giannecchini, 13 Apr. 1984, quoted in Varvaro, 42–43.

48. A recent example is provided by Peters, "Annulments in America."

49. See Johnson, "Another Look at Ligamen." With multiple marriages, many canonists favor a procedure whereby annulment of the first marriage automatically nullifies subsequent marriages. Appended to Johnson's article is a document from the Apostolic Signatura prohibiting that procedure. Thus a person married four times must have all the marriages investigated for nullity before being eligible to marry in the Church. See Appendix A, 369–70. Adhering to the Apostolic Signatura's mandate would likely have some effect on the growth rate for annulment in the United States.

50. For historical treatment of *vetitum* and how it has been used by various tribunals see Hopka, "The *Vetitum*," and Lucas, "The Prohibition Imposed by a Tribunal."

51. Guarino and Varvaro, "Survey of the Use of the 'Vetitum.' " 285–89.

52. A superb analyis of these developments is found in Rieff, The Triumph of the Therapeutic," esp. 87–90. Rieff's book should be required reading for anyone trying to synthesize religion and psychology.

53. For a comprehensive survey of rehabilitation efforts see Lifton et al., *The Effectiveness of Correctional Treatment.* Nothing as encompassing as this survey has been done since, and its very thoroughness is a chief reason why. For a shorter treatment see Martinson, "What Works?" 22–54.

54. Guarino and Varvaro., "Survey of the Use of the 'Vetitum,' " 287–88.

55. Guiry, "Canonical and Psychological Reflections."

56. *The Catholic Standard and Times*, 24 Sept. 1992.

Chapter 7

1. For an example see Peters, "Annulments in America."

2. See, for example, the discussion above on Garrity and toxic shame, chap. 6.

3. A exception would be Peter, "Divorce Remarriage and the Sacraments, 1982."

4. Peters. "Annulments in America," 63.

5. Wrenn. *Procedures.* Appendixes Three and Four deal with Pauline and Petrine privileges, which are handled by documentary Process.

6. Quoted in Varvaro, "Trends in Rotal Jurisprudence," 36.

7. See for example Brunsman, *New Hope*, Castelli, *What the Church is Doing*, Coleman, *Divorce and Remarriage* Kelleher, *Divorce and Remarriage*, Poposhil, *Divorce and Remarriage*, Robinson, *Marriage, Divorce and Nullity*, Smith, *Annulment*, Tierney, *Annulment* (both its original 1978 version and its revised and updated 1993 version by Tierney and Campo), Wrenn, *Divorce and Remarriage*, Young, *Divorce Ministry*, and Zwack, *Annulment.*

8. Vatican statistics show that English-speaking countries contribute disproportionately to the world annulment total. Canadian tribunals, for example, rival those in the United States for permissiveness. American tribunals, however, grant more annulments than all the other tribunals in English-speaking countries combined.

9. Material cited here is from F. A. Foy. (ed.) *1994 Catholic Almanac*, 236. Evidently the reference is to John Paul II's January 26, 1984 allocution to the Rota in which the pope refers to matrimonial canons in the new code, formulated in a generic way, which "await further determination." Rotal jurisprudence can contribute to such determination if conducted in the "light of the perennial principles of Catholic theology" and "the new canonical legislation inspired" by Vatican II.

10. *Chicago Tribune*, 18 Oct. 1993, The quotations used here are attributed to the reporter, not the archbishop. Similar coverage appeared in the *Detroit Free Press*, 28 Mar. 1992, the *South Bend Tribune*, 25 Apr. 1993, and the *Los Angeles Times*, 25 Aug. 1993.

11. The reporter, not the adjutant vicar, is quoted here.

12. An ex-priest, now a Michigan judge, who served on the Detroit tribunal in the late 1970s, used that very term to express his disillusionment with the speedy dispensation of annulments. He contends that annulments are "a hypocritical way for church leaders to wink at divorce while claiming to defend Pope John Paul II's teaching that a properly conducted marriage sacrament should last forever" *Detroit Free Press*, 28 Mar. 1992. The reporter is quoted here.

13. *South Bend Tribune*, 25 Apr. 1993.

14. Prohibition against advertising was based on other reasons as well. Perhaps as a sop to those just entering practice, the public is supposed to assume that everyone admitted to the bar is ipso facto a competent attorney. Most of the public, of course, knows better. Also, advertising implies that consumers are able to make informed decisions on attorneys they retain. But professionals like to believe that their worth can be gauged only by fellow professionals.

15. *Bates v. State Bar of Arizona* 97 Supreme Court (1977): 2691.

16. J. Crum and R. Bessendorfer, "Questions and Answers about Annulments."

17. Ibid.

18. John Paul II, address to the Roman Rota, 5 Feb. 1987, *L'Osservatore Romano*, 23 Feb. 1987. See also *Coram Burke*, 10 Oct. 1991.

19. Figures are taken from the statistical summaries in *CLSA Proceedings* (1990–1992). The 575 cases decided included some carried over from 1988, a year for which the diocese submitted no data to the CLSA.

20. Examples would include Burke, "Matrimonial Indissolubility and the Rights of Persons," Dunphy, "Church Justice—the Hard Way," Hettinger, "Too Many Invalid Annulments," Wenske. "Validity and the Use of Reason," Polonaise, "Annulment. Polonaise, a pastor with graduate training in systematic theology and marriage and the family, aims much of his gravamen at Cormac Burke, often considered one of the Rota's hard-liners in the defense of marital validity. See Burke's rejoinder, "Marriage, Annulment, and the Quest for Lasting Commitment."

21. *Divorce and Remarriage for Catholics.*

22. *New Hope for Divorced Catholics.*

23. Quoted in Poust. " 'We're Reaching Out'." *Catholic New York*, 22 May 1977. No anathema is pronounced on Catholics who divorce and remarry without benefit of annulments. Although denied access to the sacraments, they are still welcome at Mass and other Church activities.

24. Goodstein. "Considering Annulment." *Newsday*, 1 May 1997.

Chapter 8

1. Cs. 1504 and 1505.

2. C. 1505.

3. *CLSA Proceedings 1990* (1991); 277–89. For whatever reasons, this was a one-year downturn for Denver. The percentage of acceptances was close to the national average in 1990.

4. The canonical term is *renunciation,* which is treated in Cs. 1524 and 1525. Cases dropped by tribunal judges, usually at least six months after requesting an action by the petitioner, are covered by the term *abatement,* canonically known as *peremption,* and covered by Cs. 1520–1523.

5. *Chicago Tribune,* 18 Oct. 1993. The reporter, not Lagges, is quoted.

6. *CLSA Procedings,* 1988–1992.

7. The rules appear in C. 1673.

8. One wag suggested that it was the only diocese in the United States where preparation for marriage ended with the couple being presented with a certificate showing they took the course and with forms for petitioning for an annulment. A new bishop is expected to normalize the tribunal's annulment output.

9. Varvaro, 31–32. The Rota quote appears on p. 32.

10. Cited in Friedman, *American Law,* 60.

11. *Annual Report of the Director of the Administrative Office of the United States, 1990: Courts,* Table C 4A, p. 155.

12. *CLSA Proceedings, 1987* (1988): 311, 312, 316.

13. *CLSA Proceedings, 1989* (1990): 277–89.

14. For the better part of twenty years I monitored undergraduate interns working in a legal services office for the poor. Their chief responsibility was to screen applicants for overworked staff attorneys. Few applicants who survived the intake process had cases the attorneys would take to trial. The overwhelming majority of cases accepted were settled out of court, often through diversion to social agencies.

15. Palimony suits might somewhat loosely be considered an exception. They involve relatively long-term live-in relationships, much like common-law marriages, terminated by either partner. They often involve such issues as alimony and the distribution of assets.

16. Wrenn, *Procedures,* 131–32; italics added.

17. Figures for 1987 are taken from *CLSA Proceedings 198,* (1988): 313; those for 1988 from *CLSA Proceedings, 1988* (1989): 248.

18. *Coram* Egan, 29 Mar. 1984, quoted in Varvaro, "Trends in Rotal Jurisprudence," 52. The Latin phrase at the end of the quote translates literally as "smoke of good right." Idiomatically, in this context it refers to "case of some merit." In an American legal context, it could be "smoking gun."

19. *Today's Catholic,* 27 Mar. 1988. The advocate's remarks indicate that she also serves as an auditor. An experienced canon lawyer informs me that this is permissible only when the tribunalist does not perform both roles in the same case. The tribunal on which this advocate serves apparently routinely ignored this rule.

20. C. 1425, 1–1.

21. Per Cs. 1686–1688 the defender is to monitor even documentary process cases.

22. Lagges, quoted in *Chicago Tribune*, 18 Oct. 1993, italics added. While only the hard of heart can fault motivation to heal, there remains the nagging question whether the primary mission of tribunals is juridical or pastoral. Before accepting petitions for nullity, tribunals are supposed to explore the possibilities for reconciliation. But once conciliatory intervention yields no results and cases go to trial, the tribunals' proper task is to judge the validity of marriages.

23. Canon 1425, 1–1.

24. If the defender disputes the documentary basis for nullity, he is to appeal to Second Instance. The Second Instance judge can ratify without going through the formalities of ordinary process or remand the case to First Instance. See Cs. 1686–1688,

25. C. 1425, 1, 4.

26. Just as some tribunals do not supply the CLSA with data on petitions presented and petitions accepted, not all tribunals submit staffing data to the CLSA.

27. The decrease remains substantial even after discounting the unusually high number of Military Ordinariate part-time professionals

28. See Provost, "Clarifications Concerning Certain Questions," 193–94. This is a revised version of a memorandum prepared by Catholic University faculty of the 1980 Institute on Matrimonial Tribunal Practice and submitted to the NCCB at the 1980 Synod of Bishops.

29. The statement allows for the fact that while the annual number of "ordinary process" cases remained stable, tribunal personnel were required to deal with mandatory review at Second Instance. Revival of this theme is found in Provost, "The Volume of Cases."

30. All figures used in this discussion are derived from *CLSA Proceedings 1992* (1993): 254–68.

31. The roster is taken from *The Official Catholic Directory* for 1993, p. 869. As previously noted, the bishop is reportedly in favor of abandoning tribunals and simply praying for those who divorce.

32. Two tribunals sent no statistics for cases decided by sentence.

33. As if to underscore that preference, C. 1441 specifies that if a single-judge trial occurs at First Instance, Second Instance review must be collegiate.

34. In one of the tribunal's cases that came to my attention, the petitioner had not paid a $65 fee to cover the cost of sending his case to the Provincial Tribunal. Although the need for a conforming opinion was the only apparent reason for sending the case to Second Instance, the assistant judicial vicar strenuously denied that the First Instance tribunal had ruled for nullity.

35. C. 1686.

Chapter 9

1. Cs. 1420, 4; 1421, 3; and 1435.

2. Evidently those who translated the new code into English relied on transliteration of the Latin to spell "promoter" as "promotor." The more familiar spelling will be used herein.

3. The title is used generically here, so as to include adjutant, assistant, and associate judicial vicars.

4. C. 1483.

5. C. 1481. The advocate, unlike attorneys in the American legal system, is not an "officer of the court."

6. C. 1487.

7. C. 1428–1, 2. The auditor can be a cleric or lay person, so long as the individual has a reputation for "good conduct, prudence and learning."

8. C. 1428–3.

9. This charge is reiterated in C. 1432 of the new code. "The defender of the bond is bound by office to present and expound all that can reasonably be argued against the nullity or dissolution."

10. C. 1435. Per C. 1436 the same person can serve as defender and promoter, but not in the same case.

11. John Paul II, Address to the Roman Rota, 26 Jan. 1988.

12. Ibid.

13. Material on the byplay between the Signatura and American canonists appears in "Report on Roman Letter."

14. Ibid., 5. For a lengthier discussion see Provost. "The Requirements of Canon Law Degrees." Provost argues that the judicial appointments challenged by the Signatura are valid and, if bishops exercise their dispensing powers, licit as well.

15. A more cautious response to the Signatura's wishes is found in Proctor, "Procedural Change in the 1983 Code," 471–3.

16. C. 1445–3, 1.

17. Varvaro, 35–36. All but one of the cases noted here are drawn from this article.

18. The significance of the role they play is further underscored by the fact that defenders are supposed to have a JCD, not a JCL.

19. John Paul II, Address to the Roman Rota, 26 Jan. 1988.

20. The Catholic University of America and St. Paul's University in Canada. Duquesne University now offers a JCL, but the courses are taken abroad.

21. C. 1420–4 reads: "The judicial vicar and the associate judicial vicars must be *priests* of good repute, with a doctorate or at least licentiate in canon law, and not less than thirty years of age." (italics added). Women with proper degrees can (and do) serve as judges, advocates, defenders, and promoters of justice. According to the 1996 *Catholic Directory*, the nun has been replaced by a laywoman with a PhD in a field not specified.

22. Grocholewski, "Current Questions," 228–29. Much of what follows is based on his critique of American tribunals appearing on pp. 227–50.

23. They bear some resemblance to *pro tem (pro tempore)* judges in our secular legal system. But *pro tem* judges are certified lawyers who sit "for the time being" for very limited periods of duty.

24. John Paul II, Address to the Roman Rota, 28 Jan. 1982.

25. Grocholewski, "Current Questions," 237.

26. C. 1483

27. Ibid., 238.

28. Provost, "Intolerable Marriage Situations: A Second Decade," 597.

29. Ibid.
30. Grocholewski, "Current Questions," 228n. 24.
31. Gagnon, "The Family," 704.
32. Leveritt, "The Marriage Game."
33. The report and quotations appear in *The Wanderer*, 13 Aug. 1987.
34. *Detroit Free Press*, 28 Mar. 1992. Presumably, if the portrayal is accurate, the archbishop seeks liberalizaton on an international scale. It is difficult to imagine what might be done to liberalize further the American system, short of granting annulment on demand.
35. Ibid.

Chapter 10

1. Cadigan, "On Being Annulled." The particular overture was after a twenty-three-year marriage that produced four children, followed by a year of separation and fifteen years of divorce. Apart from relating that the proposal made her retch, Cadigan gives no details on whether the marriage was annulled.

2. Respondent reactions like those described here are found in the case histories appearing in Kennedy, *Shattered Faith*.

3. Bowman, *Bending the Rules*. The book could be more aptly titled "Bending, Breaking, and Making Rules." In scholarly circles, referring to an article or book as "journalistic" is worse than damning it with faint praise. But Bowman, an ex-priest who served as religion editor for the *Chicago Daily News*, does not claim that his sample is representative of all pastors.

4. For additional material, pro and con, on the "internal forum," see Brunsman, *New Hope for Divorced Catholics*; Provost, "Intolerable Marriage Situations Revisited," Urrutia, "The 'Internal Forum Solution,' " Seper, "Letter on 'Internal Forum' Solutions," translation of the July 10, 1993 Pastoral Letter of German Bishops in *Origins*, 10 Mar. 1994, pp. 670–76 and Grizez et al., "Open Letter to the German Bishops."

5. Bowman, p. 140.

6. Reported in *The Wanderer*, 1 Dec. 1988, p. The decree was overturned by the Rota.

7. Felici, "Memorandum."

8. Ibid., 224.

9. "Letter of Archbishop Quinn." A lengthier response is found in a memorandum drafted by the faculty of the 1980 Institute on Matrimonial Tribunal Practice at Catholic University and submitted to the NCCB Provost, "Clarifications Concerning Certain Questions," 189–207. Germane to the discussion here is the appendix titled "Memorandum for the Episcopal Conference of Spain on Foreign Treatment of Marriage Cases," excerpted on pp. 202–7.

10. C. 1676.

11. Substantive due process requires that law be related to proper objectives, while procedural due process refers to rules to ensure that the law is applied with fairness. Most discussions of due process deal with its procedural side.

12. C. 1101, 2.

13. For a discussion of simulation or "implied exclusion," see Sanson, "Implied

Simulation." Sanson reports that some tribunals have used this ground since the mid-1970s, even though they do not necessarily refer to it by that name. In what is a clearcut example of efforts to expand the nullity frontier, he proposes adding "defective intention" to defective consent as ground for annulment.

14. John Paul II, Address to the Roman Rota, 29 Jan. 1993.

15. Letters exchanged during the courtship period, especially shortly before the wedding date, can provide solid documentation on the character of marital consent subsequently given.

16. *Coram* Burke, 18 July 1991.

17. Johnson, "Publish and Be Damned," 230.

18. Burke, "Marital Indissolubility," 28.

19. Ibid., 28–29. Burke's views encompass the once-prevalent American sociolegal expectation that spouses in a troubled marriage should remain together for the sake of the children. That notion is now regarded as quaintly archaic. Sustaining a marriage laden with conflict came to be regarded as harder on children than divorce. More recently, the pathologies associated with single-parent families have led many family therapists to rethink the question of family dissolution. A two-parent family where the spouses do not get along may be a lesser evil for children than a family broken by divorce.

20. Ibid.

21. Dillon, "The Rights of the Respondent." See also McGuckin, "The Respondent's Rights," also published without bibliography in Doogan, *Catholic Tribunals.* Canons pertaining to appealing a decree of nullity are listed and briefly explained in Wrenn, *Procedures,* 74–82. Four Rotal decisions involving the right of defense are discussed in Plewka, "The Right of Defense."

22. Felici, "Memordum," 221.

23. Ibid., 222.

24. Quinn, "Letter," 219.

25. C. 1673.

26. John Paul II, Address to the Roman Rota, 26 Jan. 1989. The phrase *irremediable nullity of the sentence* can easily confuse anyone reading about annulment who is not familiar with the jargon of canon law. Nullity here refers to the reversal of a tribunal ruling (i.e., sentence) because the right of defense was not honored. Putting it differently, the decree of nullity was itself nullified for that reason.

27. *Coram* Boccafola, 25 July 1989.

28. Wrenn, *Procedures,* 72.

29. John Paul II, Address to the Roman Rota, 26 Jan. 1989.

30. Ibid.

31. Proctor, "Procedural Change in the 1983 Code," 474.

32. *Statistical Yearbook of the Church,* 1983, p. 355. Several thousand cases were carried over from the preceding year.

33. *CLSA Proceedings,* 1980–1983.

34. *CLSA Proceedings, 1983* (1984): pp. 264–273.

35. *Statistical Yearbook of the Church,* 1984, p. 363. It is important to note that cases concluded include those abandoned by petitioners and tribunals, as well as decrees and denials of nullity. Data on annulments and denials are presented in Table 9-1.

36. *Statistical Yearbook of the Church*, 1990, p. 399.

37. See Dillon, "Confidentiality in Tribunals," also his "Confidentiality of Testimony," 289–91. See also J. G. Johnson, "Publish and Be Damned," 233.

38. Johnson, "Publish and Be Damned," 234–35.

39. Dillon, "Confidentiality in Tribunals," 295.

40. *Coram* Boccafola, 25 July 1989.

41. Proctor, "Procedural Change in the 1983 Code," 474.

42. Dillon, "Confidentiality of Testimony," 289–90.

43. Quoted in Proctor, "Procedural Change in the 1983 Code," 475.

44. Wrenn, Unpublished ms., quoted and cited in Ibid. 475–76.

45. Lochiano, "Answers about Annulments."

46. Johnson, "Published and Be Damned," 238. Johnson grudgingly concedes that such policies flout the letter of the law. I believe they also do violence to its spirit. He repeats the argument that in an annulment proceeding the marriage, not the respondent, is under attack. Evidently it does not occur to him that the tribunals themselves are attacking the Church's teaching on marriage and that the respondent might in conscience wish to defend that teaching. See p. 217.

47. Wrenn, *Procedures*, 72.

48. John Paul II, Address to the Roman Rota, 26 Jan. 1989.

49. See Varvaro, "Trends in Rotal Jurisprudence," 38.

50. Ibid., 37.

51. Ibid., 38.

Chapter 11

1. C. 1628.

2. The title is not part of the code's nomenclature. It is coined here to distinguish between mandatory appeal and another appeal option that really has no official name.

3. C. 1682, 1.

4. C. 1682, 2. The procedure is the same when petitioners appeal a ruling upholding the validity of the marriage.

5. In this vein, many experienced civil lawyers will not handle appeals. Would-be appellants are referred to attorneys who specialize in appellate cases.

6. Quinn, "Letter," 219. Additional documentation on the American hierarchy's resistance to mandatory Second Instance review is found in Schumacher. "Regional Tribunals in the U.S.A."

7. Brunsman, *New Hope for Divorced Catholics*, 70.

8. For reasons unknown to me, there are no statistics for 1985.

9. Some of the 1,412 were doubtlessy formal appeals taken by petitioners denied annulments at First Instance.

10. The Signatura has interpreted this canon so as to lend additional support to the right of defense. In an exchange with the judicial vicar of Athens the Signatura stated that not even extraordinary recourse to the pope implies a waiver of the right to appeal to the Rota in Second Instance. Unofficial translations of the letters appear in *Roman Replies*, 64–69.

11. No more than ten cases were tried at Third Instance in the United States since the new code took effect.

12. Cs. 1438–1439.

13. C 1444, 1–1.

14. Grocholewski, "Current Questions," 233.

15. C. 1641–1.

16. Both quotations are from Grochelewski, "Current Questions," 233–34.

17. Frank. *Courts on Trial.*

Conclusion

1. See Steinfels, "Kennedy Blessing Raises Questions," on the furor created when Senator Edward M. Kennedy, divorced after twenty-three years of marriage and remarried in a civil ceremony, was given communion at his mother's funeral Mass.

2. Provost, "Clarifications Concerning Certain Questions," 200–201.

3. Italics supplied.

4. A Latinist familiar with this passage advises that it should read "communion of persons."

5. John Paul II, Address to the Roman Rota, 5 Feb. 1987.

6. See his 26 Jan. 1984, 28 Jan. 1988, and 4 Feb. 1991. Addresses to the Roman Rota.

7. Provost, "The Volume of Cases."

8. Tables 1 and 4.

9. Tables 3 and 4.

10. Nolan, *Pastoral Letters of the United States Catholic Bishops.*

11. Reported in Talmage, *Marquette University Index.* The index covers documents issued by the National Catholic Welfare Conference, before it was reorganized into the NCCB and the United States Catholic Conference (USCC).

12. An excellent concise history of the bishops' role in public affairs is found in Warner, *Changing Witness.*

13. A striking example is found in the recent contention that a divorce lawyer could be sued for malpractice if during a custody dispute allegations of child abuse by the opposing party are not raised. The truth or falsity of the allegation is irrelevant.

14. A timely book raising the public consciousness and conscience on many of these issues is Blankenhorn, *Fatherless America.*

15. Gallagher, *The Abolition of Marriage.* See also Whitehead, *The Divorce Culture.*

16. Hettinger, "The Annulment Mentality." Hettinger argues that changes in the "divorce mentality" are necessary before the "annulment mentality" will weaken. As regular churchgoers can attest, there seems to be a powerful taboo against homilists discussing Church views on divorce.

17. For some interesting observations on this phenomenon see Van Der Poel, "Influences of an 'Annulment Mentality.' " In keeping with what is still the conventional canonical wisdom, Van Der Poel holds that "an annulment mentality accepts the theory of indissolubility but when the relationship fails it tries to search

for defects in the personality or in matrimonial consent" (p. 387). That, in a nutshell, captures the leitmotif of the American tribunal system, ever at the ready to find ways to annul.

18. Kennedy, an Episcopalian, touches on some of these matters in *Shattered faith*.

Bibliography

Abbott, W. M. (ed.). *The Documents of Vatican II.* Chicago: Association Press–Follett Publishing Co., 1966.

Alesandro, J. A. "The Revision of Church Law: Conflict and Reconciliation." *The Jurist* 40: (1980): 1–26.

American Psychiatric Association. *Quick Reference to the Diagnostic Criteria from DSM-III-R.* Washington, D.C.: American Psychiatric Association, 1987.

Andrews, L. M. "Religion's Challenge to Psychiatry." *The Public Interest.* No. 120 (Summer 1995): 79–88.

Annual Report of the Director of the Administrative Office of the United States, 1990: Courts. Washington, D.C.: Government Printing Office, 1991.

Barlow, D. H. (ed.). "Special Issue on Diagnoses, Dimensions, and *DSM-IV*: The Science of Classification." *Journal of Abnormal Psychology.* 100/3 (1991).

Bates v. State Bar of Arizona 97 Supreme Court (1977): 2691.

Bayer, R. *Homosexuality and American Psychiatry: The Politics of Diagnosis.* Princeton, N.J.: Princeton University Press, 1987.

Beattie, M. *Codependent No More* New York: Harper & Row, 1989.

Becker, J. M. *The Re-Formed Jesuits.* Volume 1. San Francisco: Ignatius Press, 1992.

Becker, R. C. "Cases." *The Jurist* 49 (1989): 273–79.

Blankenhorn, D. *Fatherless America: Confronting Our Most Urgent Social Problem.* New York: Basic Books, 1995.

Bowman, J. *Bending the Rules: What American Priests Tell American Catholics.* New York: The Crossroad Publishing Company, 1994.

Bradshaw, J. *Bradshaw On: The Family.* Deerfield Beach, Fla.: Health Communications, Inc. 1988.

Brundage, J. A. "Canon Law as an Instrument for Ecclesial Reform: An Historic Perspective." *CLSA Proceedings 1983* (1984): 1–17.

———. "The Creative Canonist: His Role in Church Reform." *The Jurist* 31 (1971): 301–18.

Brunsman, B. *New Hope for Divorced Catholics: A Concerned Pastor Offers Alternatives to Annulment* San Francisco: Harper & Row, 1985.

Burke, C. "The *Bonum Coniugum* and the *Bonum Prolis*: Ends or Properties of Marriage." *The Jurist* 49 (1989): 704–13.

———. *Freedom and Authority in the Church*. San Francisco: Ignatius Press, 1988.

———. "Marriage, Annulment, and the Quest for Lasting Commitment." *Catholic World Report* 6 (Jan. 1996): 54–61.

———. "Matrimonial Indissolubility and the Rights of Persons." *Homiletic & Pastoral Review* 89 (Apr. 1989–90): 27–32.

Cadigan, P. B. "On Being Annulled." *America* 165 (Aug. 10, 1991): 71–72.

Carson, R. C. "Dilemmas in the Pathway of *DSM-IV.*" *Journal of Abnormal Psychology* 100 (1991): 302–7.

Castelli, J. *What the Church is Doing for Divorced and Remarried Catholics*. Chicago: Claretian Publications, 1978.

Catechism of the Catholic Church. Liguori, Mo.: Liguori Publications, 1994.

Catholic News Service, 3 June, 1993.

Catholic Standard and Times, 24 Sept. 1992.

Catoir, J. "An Analysis of the Evolution of Tribunal Practice." *CLSA Proceedings 1973* (1974): 17–21.

Chicago Tribune, 18 Oct. 1993.

The Code of Canon Law (In English Translation). London: Collins Liturgical Publications, 1983.

The Code of Canon Law: A Text and Commentary. Mahwah, N.J.: Paulist Press, 1985.

Coleman, G. D. *Divorce and Remarriage in the Catholic Church*. New York: Paulist Press, 1988.

Coram Boccafola, 25 July 1989.

Coram Bruno, 17 Dec. 1982.

Coram Burke, 18 July 1991.

Coram Burke, 10 Oct. 1991.

Coram Burke, 20 Oct. 1994.

Coram Doran, 1 July 1988.

Coram Doran, 21 May 1992.

Coram Egan, 10 Nov. 1983.

Coram Giannecchini, 13 Apr. 1984.

Coram Lefebvre, 31 Jan. 1976.

Coram Pompedda, 11 Apr. 1988.

Coram Raad, 14 Apr. 1975.

Coram Serrano, 5 Apr. 1972.

Coram Serrano, 5 Apr. 1976.

Coram Serrano Ruiz, 28 July 1981.

Coram Serrano Ruiz, 16 Dec. 1983.

Coram Stankiewicz, 22 May 1986.

Coriden, J. A. (ed.). "The Future of the Law." *The Jurist* 34 (1974): 154–60, 1974.

Coriden, J. A. (ed.). *The Once and Future Church: A Communion of Freedom*. New York: Alba House, 1971.

Coriden, J. A. (ed.). *We, the People of God: A Study of Constitutional Government for the Church*. Huntington, Ind.: Our Sunday Visitor Press, 1968.

Coulson, W. R. *Groups, Gimmicks, and Instant Gurus*. New York: Harper & Row, 1972.

Crum, J., and R. Bessendorfer. "Questions and Answers about Annulments." *Florida Times-Union*, 18 Oct. 1992.

Cuneo, J. J. "Lack of Due Discretion: The Judge as Expert." *The Jurist* 42 (1982): 141–63.

D'Antonio, W. V., J. D. Davidson, D. R. Hoge, and R. A. Wallace. *American Catholic Laity in a Changing Church*. Kansas City, Mo.: Sheed & Ward, 1989.

Daubert v. Merrill Dow Pharmaceuticals, Inc. 43 Federal Reporter 3rd (1995): 1311.

Dawes, R. M. *House of Cards: Psychology and Psychotherapy Built on Myth*. New York: The Free Press, 1994.

Detroit Free Press, 28 Mar. 1992,

Devlin, P. *The Enforcement of Morals*. New York: Oxford University Press, 1968.

Dillon, E. J. "Confidentiality in Tribunals." *CLSA Proceedings 1983* (1984): 171–81.

———. "Confidentiality of Testimony—An Implementation of Canon 1598." *The Jurist* 45 (1985): 289–96.

———. "The Rights of the Respondent in Matrimonial Trials." *CLSA Proceedings 1990* 52 (1991): 80–106.

Dolciamore, J. V. "Interpersonal Relationships and Their Effect on the Validity of Marriage." *CLSA Proceedings 1972* (1973): 84–100.

Doogan, H. F. (ed). *Catholic Tribunals, Marriage Annulment and Dissolution*. Marrickville, Australia: Southwood Press, 1990.

Doyle, T. P. "Matrimonial Consent." In *The Code of Canon Law*, 774–79.

Dunphy, P. "Church Justice—the Hard Way." *Homiletic & Pastoral Review* 90 (Oct. 1991–92): 56–58.

Egan, E. M. "The Nullity of Marriage for Reason of Incapacity to Fulfill the Essential Obligation of Marriage." *Ephemerides Iuris Canonici* 40 (1984): 9–34.

———. "The Nullity of Marriage for Reason of Insanity or Lack of Due Discretion of Judgement." *Ephemerides Iuris Canonici* 39 (1983): 9–54.

Felici, P. "Memorandum," *The Jurist* 38 (1978): 221–4.

Felsen R., "The Effects of Self-Appraisal of Ability on Academic Performance." *Journal of Personality and Social Psychology*. 47 (1984): 944–52.

Fingarette, H. "Alcoholism: The Mythical Disease." *The Public Interest* (Spring 1988): 3–22.

Flannery, A. (ed.). *Vatican Council II: The Conciliar and Post-Conciliar Documents*. Collegeville, Minn.: The Liturgical Press, 1975.

Foy, F. A. (ed.). *1994 Catholic Almanac*. Huntington, Ind.: Our Sunday Visitor Publishing Division, 1994.

Frances, A. J., M. B. First, T. A. Widiger, G. M. Miele, S. M. Tilly, W. W. Davis, and H. A. Pincus. "The A to Z Guide to DSM-IV Conundrums." *Journal of Abnormal Psychology* 100 (1991): 407–12.

Frank, J. *Courts on Trial*. Princeton, N.J.: Princeton University Press, 1949.

Friedman, L. M. *American Law*. New York: W. W. Norton & Co., 1984.

Freud, S. *The Future of an Illusion*. Garden City, N.Y.: Doubleday Anchor Books, n.d.

Gagnon, E. "The Family." *Origins*. 18 (1989): 703–5.

Gallagher, M. *The Abolition of Marriage: How We Destroy Lasting Love*. Washington, D.C.: Regnery Publishing, Inc., 1996

Gallup, Jr., G., and J. Castelli. *The American Catholic People*. Garden City, N.Y.: Doubleday & Co., 1987.

Garrity, R. M. "Shame, Dysfunctional Families, and the Lack of Due Discretion for Marriage." *The Jurist* 48 (1991): 364–89.

Gaylin, W. *The Killing of Bonnie Garland*. New York:Simon & Schuster, 1982.

German Bishops' Pastoral Letter. *Origins*, 10 Mar. 1994, pp. 670–76.

Goodstein, L. "Considering Annulment." *Newsday*, 1 May 1997.

Gramunt, I., J. Hervada, and L. A. Wauck. *Canons and Commentaries on Marriage*. Collegeville, Minn.: The Liturgical Press, 1987.

Green, T. J. "Marriage Nullity Procedures in the Schema *De Processibus*." *The Jurist* 38 (1978): 311–411.

———. "The Revised Schema *De Matrimonio*. Text and Reflections." *The Jurist* 40 (1980): 57–127.

Grisez, G., J. M. Finnis, and W. E. May. "Indissolubility, Divorce, and Holy Communion. Open Letter to the German Bishops." *Catholic World Report* 4 (Nov. 1994): 54–58.

Grocholewski, X. "Current Questions Concerning the State and Activity of Tribunals with Particular Reference to the United States of America." In Sable (ed.), *Incapacity for Marriage*, 221–53.

———. "Theological Aspects of the Judicial Activity of the Church." In Sable (ed.), *Incapacity for Marriage*, 552–67.

Guarino, C. A., and W. A. Varvaro. "Survey of the Use of the 'Vetitum'." *CLSA Proceedings 1983* (1984): 285–99.

Guiry, R. W. "Canonical and Psychological Reflections on the *Vetitum* in Today's Tribunal." *The Jurist* 49 (1989): 191–209.

Halleck, S. L. *Psychiatry and the Dilemmas of Crime*. Berkeley: University of California Press, 1971.

Hannon, J. L. "The Role of Diagnosis in the Annulment Evaluation Process." *The Jurist* 49 (1989): 182–90.

Häring, B. *No Way Out?* Middlegreen, Eng.: St. Paul Publications, 1990.

Herman, E. *The Romance of American Psychology: Political Culture in the Age of Experts*. Berkeley: University of California Press, 1995.

Hettinger, C. J. "The Annulment Mentality: What Can You Do About It?" *Homiletic & Pastoral Review* 95 (1995): 22–31.

———. "Too Many Invalid Annulments." *Homiletic & Pastoral Review* 93 (Dec. 1993): 15–22.

Hopka, J. "The *Vetitum* and *Monitum* in Matrimonial Nullity Proceedings." *Studia Canonica* 19 (1985): 357–99.

Huber, P. W. *Galileo's Revenge*. New York: Basic Books, 1991.

John Paul II. Address to the Roman Rota, 24 Jan. 1981, *L'Osservatore Romano*, 2 Feb. 1981.

———. Address to the Roman Rota, 28 Jan. 1982, *L'Osservatore Romano*, 8, Feb. 1982.

———. Address to the Roman Rota, 26 Jan. 1984, *L'Osservatore Romano*, 13 Feb. 1984.

———. Address to the Roman Rota, 5 Feb. 1987, *L'Osservatore Romano*, 23 Feb. 1987.

———. Address to the Roman Rota, 26 Jan. 1988, *L'Osservatore Romano*, 15 Feb. 1988.

———. Address to the Roman Rota, 26 Jan. 1989, *L'Osservatore Romano*, 20 Feb. 1989.

———. Address to the Roman Rota, 19 Jan. 1990, *L'Osservatore Romano*, 29, Jan. 1990.

———. Address to the Roman Rota, 28 Jan. 1991, *L'Osservatore Romano*, 4 Feb. 1991.

———. Address to the Roman Rota, 29 Jan. 1993, *L'Osservatore Romano*, 3 Feb. 1993.

———. Address to the Roman Rota, 28 Jan. 1994, *L'Osservatore Romano*, 2 Feb. 1994.

———. Address to the Roman Rota, 27 Jan. 1997, *L'Osservatore Romano*, 5 Feb. 1997.

———. *Ordinatio Sacerdotalis.* 30 May 1994.

———. *Veritatis Splendor.* Washington, D.C.: USCC, 1993.

Johnson, J. G. "Another Look at Ligamen." *The Jurist* 47 (1987): 341–70.

———. "Publish and Be Damned: The Dilemma of Implementing the Canons on Publishing the Acts and Sentence." *The Jurist* 49 (1989): 210–40.

Kaminer, W. *I'm Dysfunctional, You're Dysfunctional: The Recovery Movement and Other Self-Help Fashions.* New York: Vintage Books, 1993.

Kasl, C. D. *Women, Sex and Addiction.* New York: Ticknor & Fields, 1989.

Keefe, J. "Why the Church is Granting More Annulments." *Catholic Update.* Cincinnati: St Anthony Messenger Press, n.d.

Kelleher, S. J. *Divorce and Remarriage for Catholics?* Garden City, N.Y.: Image Books, 1976.

Kelly, G. A. *The Battle for the American Church.* New York: Doubleday & Co., 1979.

———. *Keeping the Church Catholic Under John Paul II.* New York: Doubleday, 1990.

Kennedy, S. *Shattered Faith.* New York: Pantheon, 1997.

Kessler, R. C., K. A. McGonagle, S. Zhao, C. B. Nelson, M. Hughes, S. Eshleman, H. Wittchen, and K. S. Kendler. "Lifetime and 12-Month Prevalence of *DSM-III-R* Psychiatric Disorders in the United States." *Archives of General Psychiatry* 5 (1994): 8–19.

Kristol, E. "Declarations of Codependence." *The American Spectator* 23 (June 1990): 21–23

LaDue, W. J. "Conjugal Love and the Juridical Structure of Christian Marriage." *The Jurist* 34 (1974): 36–65.

Lasch, C. *The Culture of Narcissism.* New York: W. W. Norton, 1979.

Lavin, M. E. "The Rotal Decision Before Serrano, April 5, 1973: Some Observations

Concerning Jurisprudence, Procedure, and Risk." *The Jurist* 36 (1976): 302–16.

Levi, E. H. *Introduction to Legal Reasoning*. Chicago: University of Chicago Press, 1949.

Leveritt, M. "The Marriage Game." *Arkansas Times* 18 (Jan. 1992): 31–32.

Lifton, D., R. Martinson, and J. Wilks. *The Effectiveness of Correctional Treatment: A Survey of Treatment Evaluation Studies*. New York: Praeger Publishers, 1975.

Lochiano, C. "Answers About Annulments: Interview with the Marriage Tribunal." *The Good News From Our Lady of Mount Carmel* 1 (Dec. 1986): 2–3.

Los Angeles Times, 25 Aug. 1993.

Low, P., J. C. Jeffries, Jr., and R. J. Bonnie. *The Trial of John W. Hinckley, Jr.: A Case Study of the Insanity Defense*. Mineola, N.Y.: The Foundation Press, 1986.

Lucas, J. "The Prohibition Imposed by a Tribunal: Law, Practice, Future Development." *The Jurist* 45 (1985): 588–617.

Mackin, T. *Divorce and Remarriage*. Ramsey, N.J.: The Paulist Press, 1984.

Marshner, W. H. *Annulment or Divorce?* Front Royal, Va.: Crossroad Books, 1978.

Martinson, R. "What Works?—Questions and Answers About Prison Reform." *The Public Interest* (Spring 1974): 22–54.

McGuckin, R. "The Respondent's Rights in a Matrimonial Nullity Case." *Studia Canonica* 18 (1984): 457–81.

Mecca, A. M, N. J. Smelser, and J. Vasconcellos. *The Social Importance of Self-Esteem*. Berkeley: University of California Press, 1989.

Mendonça, A. "Consensual Incapacity for Marriage." *The Jurist* 54 (1994): 477–559.

Menninger, K. *Whatever Became of Sin?* New York: Hawthorn Books, 1973.

Michels, R. "First Rebuttal." *American Journal of Psychiatry* 141 (1984): 548–51.

Million, T. "Classification in Psychopathology: Rationale, Alternatives, and Standards." *Journal of Abnormal Psychology* 100 (1991): 245–61.

Morrisey, F. "Preparing Ourselves for the New Law: Law Alone Will Not Hold the Church Together." *Studia Canonica* 7 (1973): 113–28.

Moynihan, D. P. *The Negro Family: The Case for National Action*. Washington, D.C.: U.S. Dept. of Labor, 1965.

Murphy, M. B. "Bishop Details Church of Future." *Milwaukee Sentinel*, 10 Apr. 1993.

National Conference of Catholic Bishops, 51st General Meeting, Executive Session Minutes, 22 June 1996.

Nolan, H. J. (ed.). *Pastoral Letters of the United States Catholic Bishops*. Vol. 5: 1983–1988. Washington, D.C.: NCCB-USCC, Inc., 1989.

Noonan, Jr. J. T. *The Power to Dissolve: Lawyers and Marriages in the Courts of the Roman Curia*. Cambridge, Mass.: Harvard University Press, 1972.

Olson, W. K. *The Litigation Explosion: What Happened When America Unleashed the Lawsuit*. New York: Truman Talley Books/Plume, 1992.

Orsy, L. "Christian Marriage: Doctrine and Glossae in Canons 1012–15." *The Jurist* 40 (1980): 282–348.

————. "Quantity and Quality of Laws after Vatican II." *The Jurist* 36 (1967): 385–412.

Palmer, P. E. "Christian Marriage: Contract or Covenant." *Theological Studies* 33 (1972): 617–65.

Peter, V. J. "Divorce, Remarriage, and the Sacraments: *Quod Potest Debet?*" *The Jurist* 42 (1982): 122–40.

————. "Judges Must Judge Justly." *The Jurist* 43 (1983): 164–78.

Peters, E. "Annulments in America." *Homiletic & Pastoral Review* 96 (November): 58–66.

Pius XI. *Casti Connubii.* In *Five Great Encyclicals.* New York: Paulist Press, 1939.

Pius XII. Address to Roman Rota, 3, Oct. 1941, *Acta Apostolicae Sedis,* 33 (1941): 421–6.

Plewka, M. A. "The Right of Defense in Certain Stages of the Matrimonial Process as Found in the Decisions of the Roman Rota." *CLSA Proceedings 1990* (1991): 249–62.

Polonaise. "Annulment: Roots of a Growing Problem." *Catholic World Report* 5 (June 1995): 37–45.

Popishil, V. J. *Divorce and Remarriage: Towards a New Catholic Teaching.* New York: Herder and Herder, 1967.

Poust, M. " 'We're Reaching Out.' " *Catholic New York,* 22 May 1997.

Proctor, J. G. "Procedural Change in the 1983 Code: The Experience of the Ecclesiastical Provinces of California." *The Jurist* 44 (1984): 468–85.

Provost, J. H. "Canon 1095: Past, Present, Future." *The Jurist* 54 (1994): 81–112.

Provost, J. H. "Error as a Ground in Marriage Nullity Cases." *CLSA Proceedings 1995* (1996): 306–24.

————. "Intolerable Marriage Situations: A Second Decade." *The Jurist* 50 (1990): 573–612.

————. "Intolerable Marriage Situations Revisited." *Catholic Lawyer* 26 (Winter 1980): 1–51.

————. "The Requirements of Canon Law Degrees for Court Officials." *The Jurist* 43 (1983): 422–29.

————. "The Volume of Cases in United States Tribunals: A Canonical Reflection." *The Jurist* 5 (1995): 381–94.

Provost, J. H. (ed.). "Clarifications Concerning Certain Questions About Tribunals in the United States of America." *The Jurist* 41 (1981): 189–207.

Quinn, J. R. "Letter of Archbishop Quinn." *The Jurist* 38 (1978): 218–19.

Rainwater, L., and W. L. Yancey. *The Moynihan Report and the Politics of Controversy.* Cambridge, Mass.: M.I.T. Press, 1967.

Reese, T. J. *A Flock of Shepherds: The National Conference of Catholic Bishops.* Kansas City, Mo.: Sheed & Ward, 1992.

"Report on Roman Letter." *CLSA Newsletter* (Summer 1985): 3–6.

Rieff, P. *The Triumph of the Therapeutic: Uses of Faith After Freud.* New York: Harper & Row Torchbook Edition, 1968.

Robinson. G. *Marriage Divorce and Nullity: A Guide to the Annulment Process in the Catholic Church.* Collegeville, Minn.: The Liturgical Press, 1987.

Roman Replies and CLSA Advisory Opinions. Washington, D.C.: CLSA, 1987.

Rosenhan, D. L. "On Being Sane in Insane Places." *Science* 179 (1973): 250–58.

Rutter, M., and D. Shaffer. "DSM III: A Step Forward or Back in Terms of the Classification of Child Psychiatric Disorders?" *Journal of the American Academy of Child Psychiatry* 19 (1980): 371–94.

Sable, R. M. (ed.). *Incapacity for Marriage: Jurisprudence and Interpretation.* Rome: Pontificia Universities Gregorium, 1987.

Sanson, R. J. "Implied Simulation: Grounds for Annulment?" *The Jurist* 48 (1988): 747–70.

Schaef, A. W. *Co-Dependence: Misunderstood-Mistreated.* New York: Harper & Row, 1986.

———. *When Society Becomes an Addict.* New York: Harper & Row, 1988.

Scheff, T. J. *Being Mentally Ill.* Chicago: Aldine-Atherton, 1971.

Schmidt, K. W. "*Educatio Prolis* and the Validity of Marriage." *The Jurist* 55 (1995): 243–80.

Schumacher, W. A. "Regional Tribunals in the U.S.A.: History, Structure and Functioning." *CLSA Proceedings 1989* (1990): 137–72.

Seper, F. "Letter on Internal Forum Solutions." *The Jurist* 33 (1973): 304.

Smith, R. T. *Annulment: A Step-by-Step Guide for Divorced Catholics.* Chicago: ACTA Publications, 1995.

South Bend Tribune, 25 Apr. 1993.

South Bend Tribune, 9 Oct. 1994.

Statistical Yearbook of the Church. Rome: Vatican Press.

Szasz, T. *The Myth of Mental Illness.* New York: Delta Books, 1967.

———. *The Manufacture of Madness.* New York: Harper & Row, 1970.

———. *A Lexicon of Lunacy: Metaphoric Malady, Moral Responsibility, and Psychiatry.* New Brunswick, N.J.: Transaction Publishers, 1993.

Talmage, J. P. (ed.). *Marquette University Index: Three Decades of Documents.* Milwaukee: Marquette University, 1991.

Thomas, M. "The Consortium Vitae Coniugalis." *The Jurist* 38: (1978): 171–9

Tierney, T. E., and J. J. Campo. *Annulment: Do You Have a Case?* New York: Alba House, 1993.

Today's Catholic, 27 Mar. 1988.

Urretia, F. J. "The 'Internal Forum Solution' Some Comments." *The Jurist* 40 (1980): 128–40.

Van Der Poel, "Influences of an 'Annulment Mentality.' " *The Jurist* 40 (1980): 384–99.

Vann, K. W. "*Dolus* Canon 1098 of the Revised Code of Canon Law." *The Jurist* 47 (1987): 371–93.

Varvaro, W. A. "Rotal Jurisprudence 1985–1990." *CLSA Proceedings 1992* (1993): 156–66.

———. "Trends in Rotal Jurisprudence: Surveying U.S.A. Cases (1980–1985)." *CLSA Proceedings 1990* (1991): 19–62.

Verbrugghe, A. E. "The Work of Marriage Tribunals: The Search for the Truth." *Homiletic & Pastoral Review* 86 (1985): 22–9.

Vitz, P. C. *Psychology as Religion: The Cult of Self-Worship.* (2d ed.). Grand Rapids, Mich.: William B. Eerdmans Publishing Co., 1994.

Wallerstein, J., and S. Blakeslee. *Second Chances: Men, Women, and Children a Decade after Divorce.* New York: Ticknor & Fields, 1989.

The Wanderer, 13 Aug. 1987.

The Wanderer, 1 Dec. 1988.

Warner, M. *Changing Witness: Catholic Bishops and Public Policy, 1917–1994.* Grand Rapids, Mich.: William B. Eerdmans Publishing Company, 1995.

Wenske, F. E. "Validity and the Use of Reason." *Homiletic & Pastoral Review* 88 (1987–88): 57–61.

Whitehead, B. D. *The Divorce Culture.* New York: Alfred A. Knopf, 1997.

Widiger, T. A., A. J. Frances, H. A. Pincus, W. W. Davis, and M. B. First. "Toward an Empirical Classification of *DSM-IV." Journal of Abnormal Psychology* 100 (1991): 280–88.

Woestman, W. H. "Respecting the Petitioner's Rights to Dissolution Procedure." *The Jurist* 50 (1990): 342–49.

Wrenn, L. G. "Annulment." In R. P. McBrien (general ed.), *The HarperCollins Encyclopedia of Catholicism,* 53–56. San Francisco: Harper San Francisco, 1995

———. *Annulments.* Toledo, Ohio: CLSA, 1970. Rev. eds. in 1972 and 1978.

———. *Decisions.* (2d ed. rev.). Washington, D.C.: CLSA, 1983.

———. *Annulments.* (4th ed. rev.). Washington, D.C.: CLSA, 1983.

———. *Annulments.* (5th ed. rev.). Washington, D.C.: CLSA, 1988.

———. *Divorce and Remarriage in the Catholic Church.* New York: Newman Press, 1973.

———. "Marriage Tribunals and the Expert." *The Bulletin of the National Guild of Catholic Psychiatrists* 25 (1979): 53–68.

———. *Procedures.* Washington, D.C.: CLSA, 1987.

———. "Refining the Essence of Marriage." *The Jurist* 44 (1986): 532–51.

Young, J. J. (ed.). *Divorce Ministry and the Marriage Tribunal.* New York: Paulist Press, 1982.

Zilboorg, G. *Freud and Religion: A Restatement of an Old Controversy.* Westminster, Md.: The Newman Press, 1958.

Zwack, J. P. *Annulment: Your Chance to Remarry Within the Catholic Church.* San Francisco: Harper Collins San Francisco, 1983.

Index

CPSIA information can be obtained at www.ICGtesting.com
Printed in the USA
BVOW02*0847040615

402932BV00002B/8/P